BEAUTY
IS THE
BEAST

Shojo Beat

Beauty is the Beast™

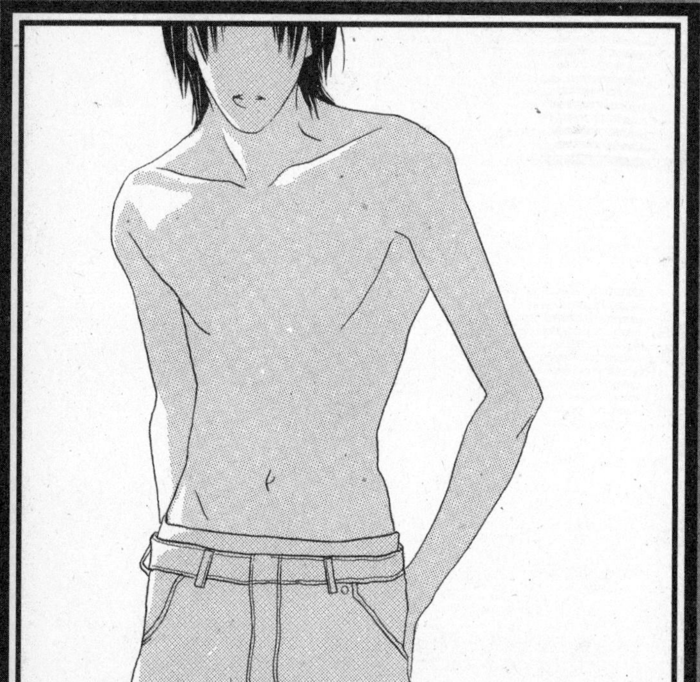

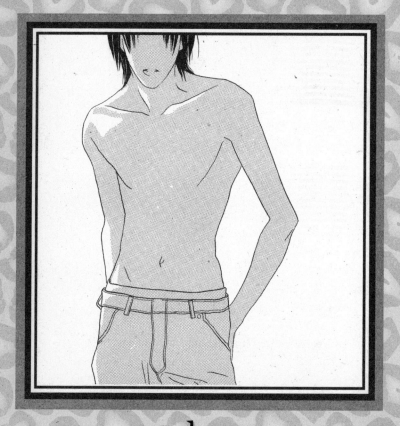

1

Story & Art by Tomo Matsumoto

Table of Contents

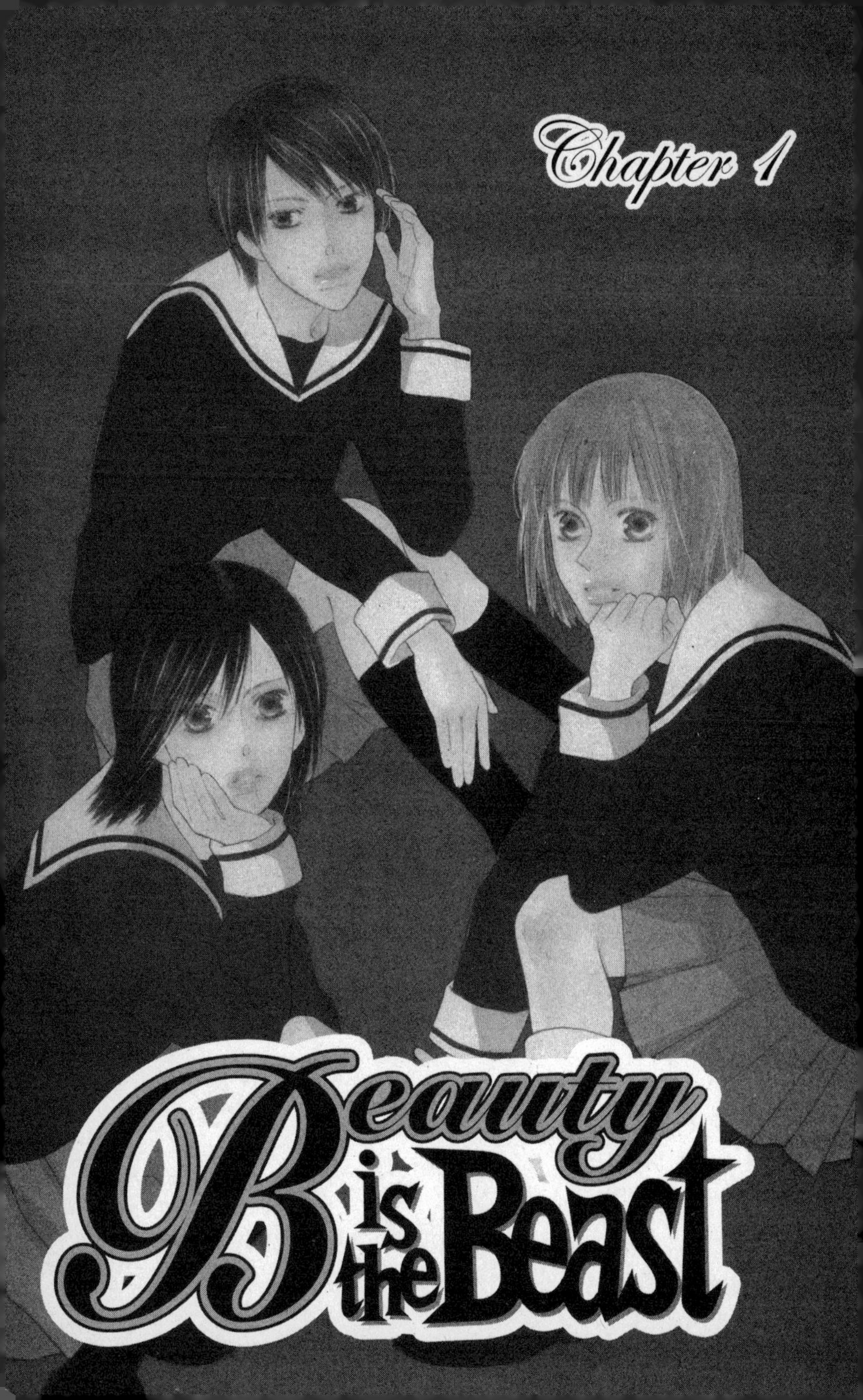
Chapter 1
Beauty is the Beast

BEAUTY
IS THE
BEAST

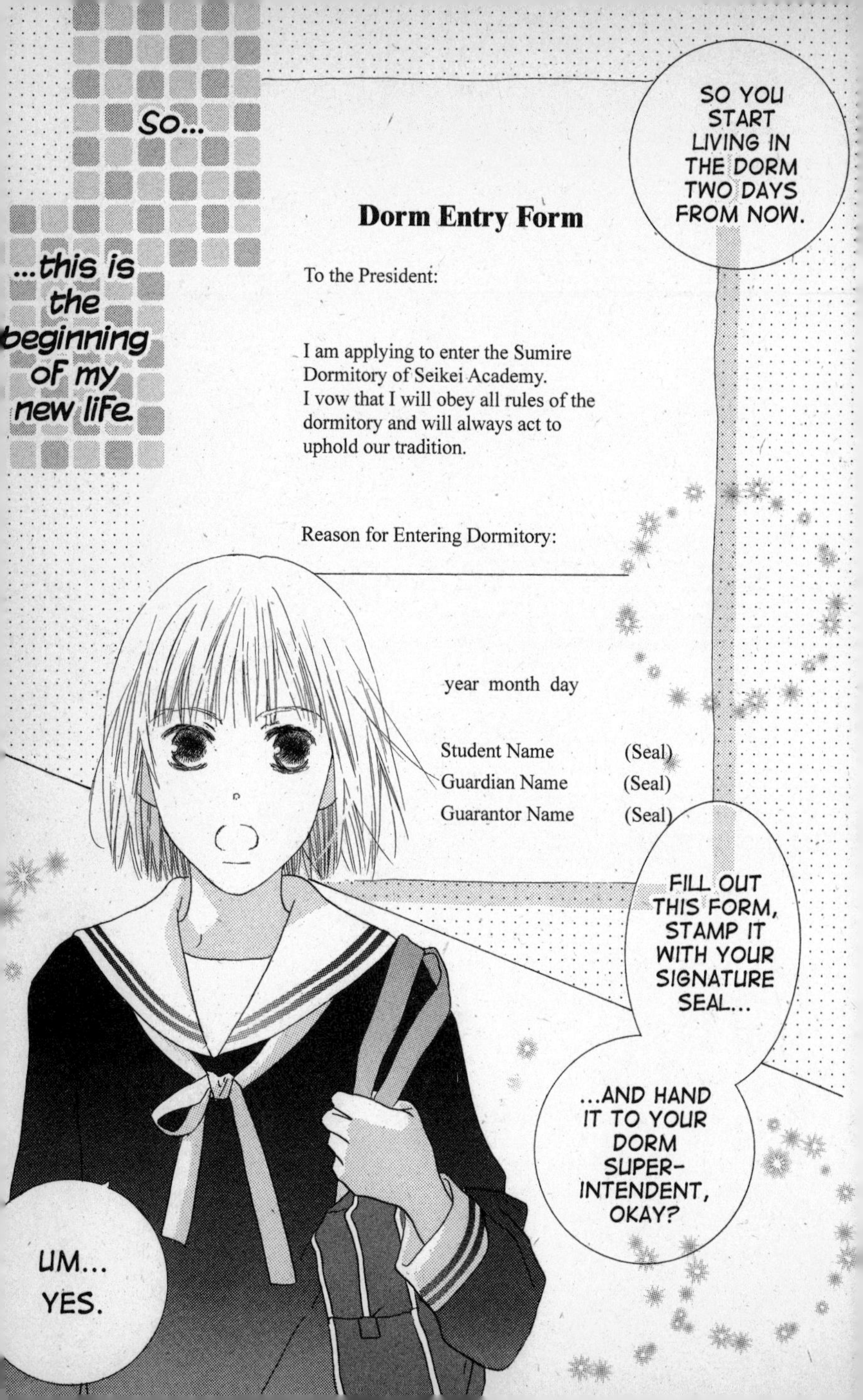

SO YOU START LIVING IN THE DORM TWO DAYS FROM NOW.
So...
...this is the beginning of my new life.
Dorm Entry Form
To the President:
I am applying to enter the Sumire Dormitory of Seikei Academy.
I vow that I will obey all rules of the dormitory and will always act to uphold our tradition.
Reason for Entering Dormitory:
year month day
Student Name (Seal)
Guardian Name (Seal)
Guarantor Name (Seal)
FILL OUT THIS FORM, STAMP IT WITH YOUR SIGNATURE SEAL...
...AND HAND IT TO YOUR DORM SUPER-INTENDENT, OKAY?
UM... YES.

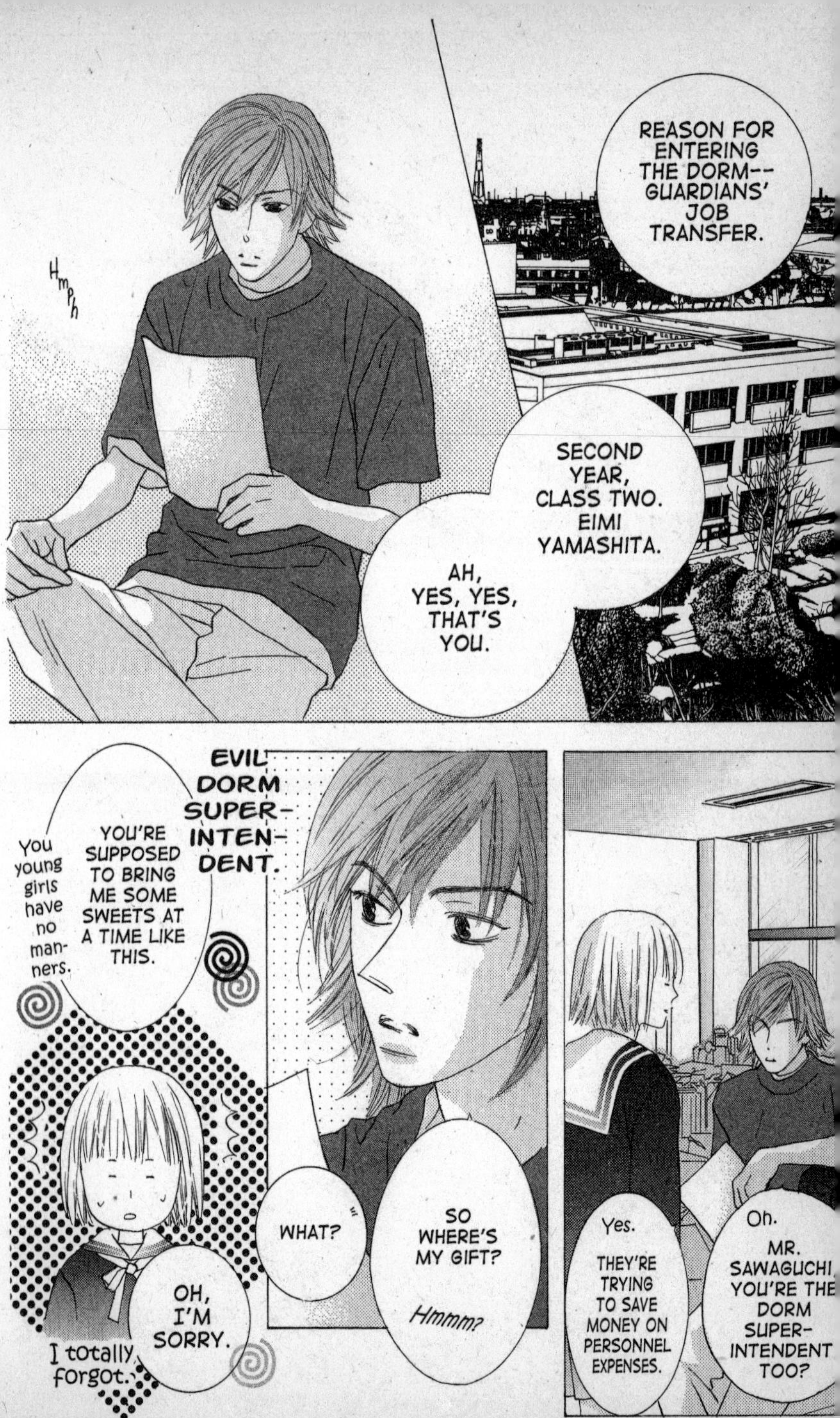
REASON FOR ENTERING THE DORM-- GUARDIANS' JOB TRANSFER.
SECOND YEAR, CLASS TWO. EIMI YAMASHITA.
AH, YES, YES, THAT'S YOU.
Hmph
Oh.
MR. SAWAGUCHI, YOU'RE THE DORM SUPER-INTENDENT TOO?
Yes.
THEY'RE TRYING TO SAVE MONEY ON PERSONNEL EXPENSES.
SO WHERE'S MY GIFT?
Hmmm?
WHAT?
EVIL DORM SUPER-INTEN-DENT.
YOU'RE SUPPOSED TO BRING ME SOME SWEETS AT A TIME LIKE THIS.
You young girls have no man-ners.
OH, I'M SORRY.
I totally forgot.

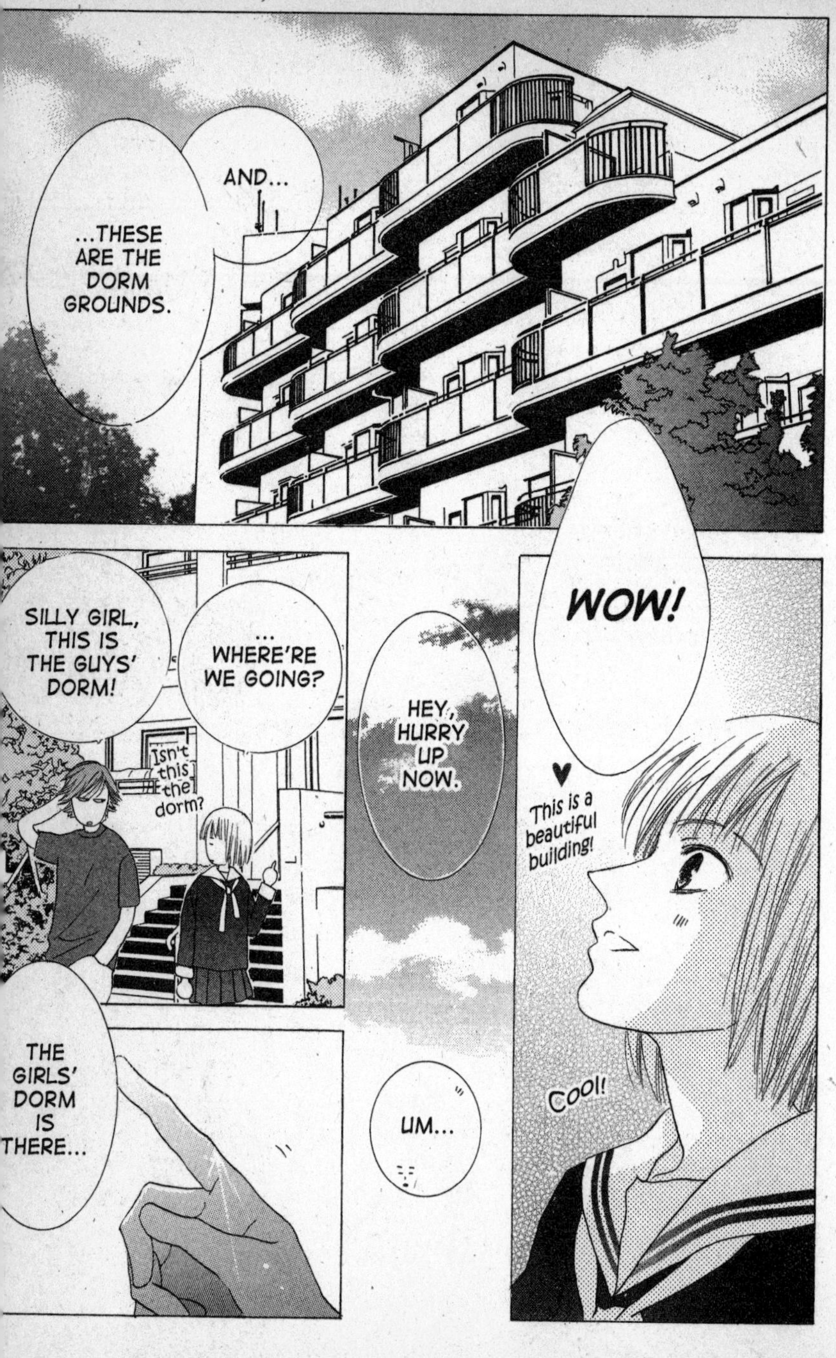
AND...
...THESE ARE THE DORM GROUNDS.
WOW!
This is a beautiful building!
Cool!
HEY, HURRY UP NOW.
...WHERE'RE WE GOING?
Isn't this the dorm?
SILLY GIRL, THIS IS THE GUYS' DORM!
UM...
THE GIRLS' DORM IS THERE...

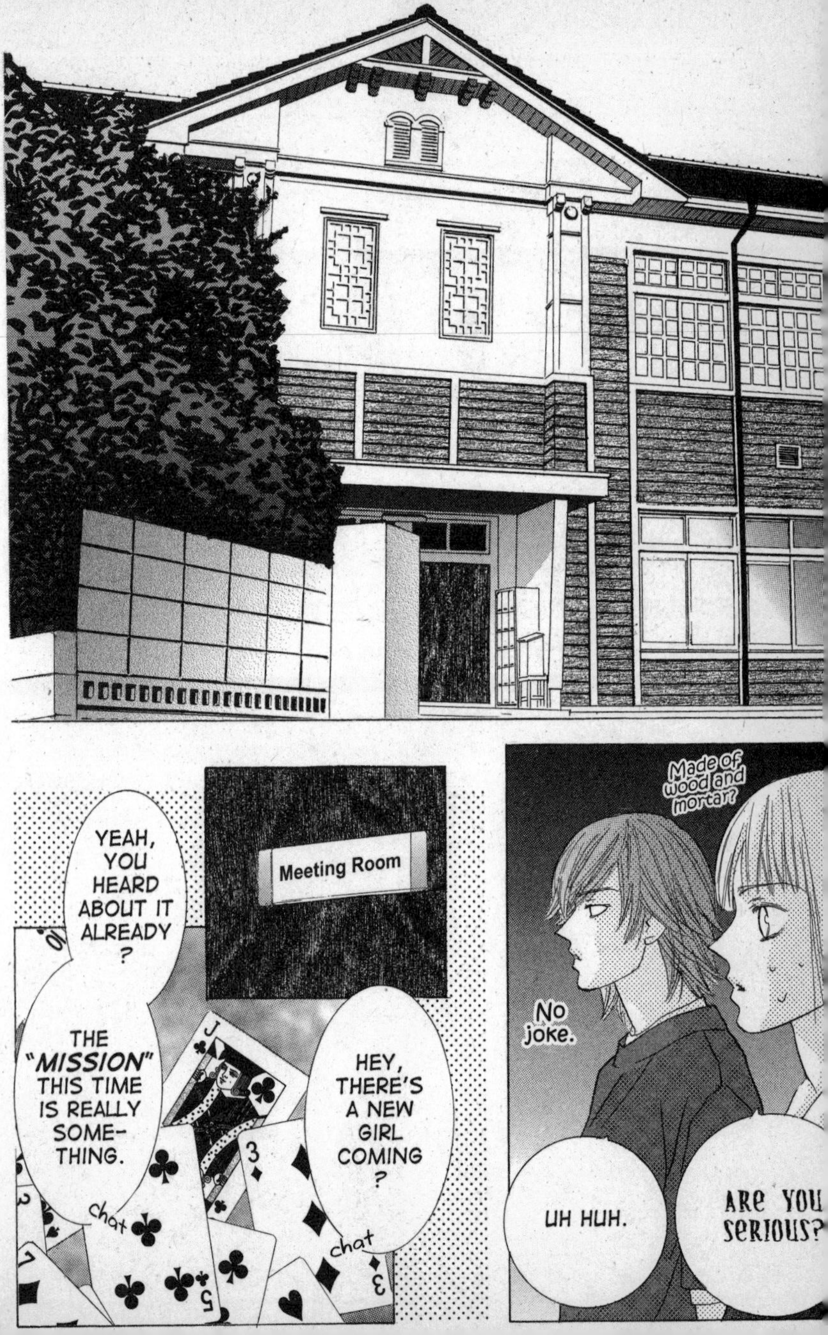

Made of wood and mortar?
No joke.
ARE YOU SERIOUS?
UH HUH.
Meeting Room
HEY, THERE'S A NEW GIRL COMING?
YEAH, YOU HEARD ABOUT IT ALREADY?
THE "MISSION" THIS TIME IS REALLY SOME-THING.
chat
chat

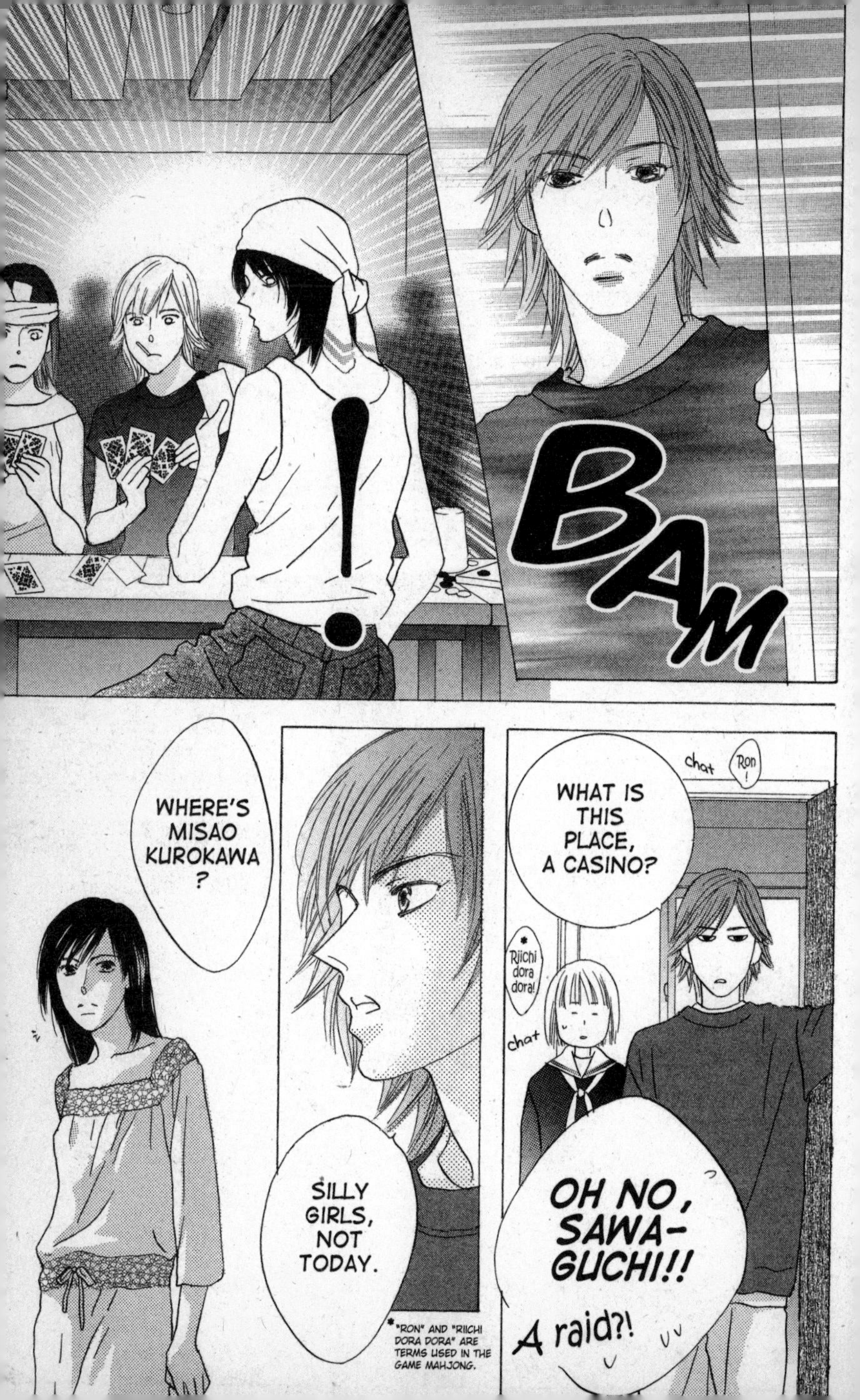
BAM
!
Ron!
chat
WHAT IS THIS PLACE, A CASINO?
*Riichi dora dora!
chat
OH NO, SAWA-GUCHI!!
A raid?!
SILLY GIRLS, NOT TODAY.
WHERE'S MISAO KUROKAWA?

*"RON" AND "RIICHI DORA DORA" ARE TERMS USED IN THE GAME MAHJONG.

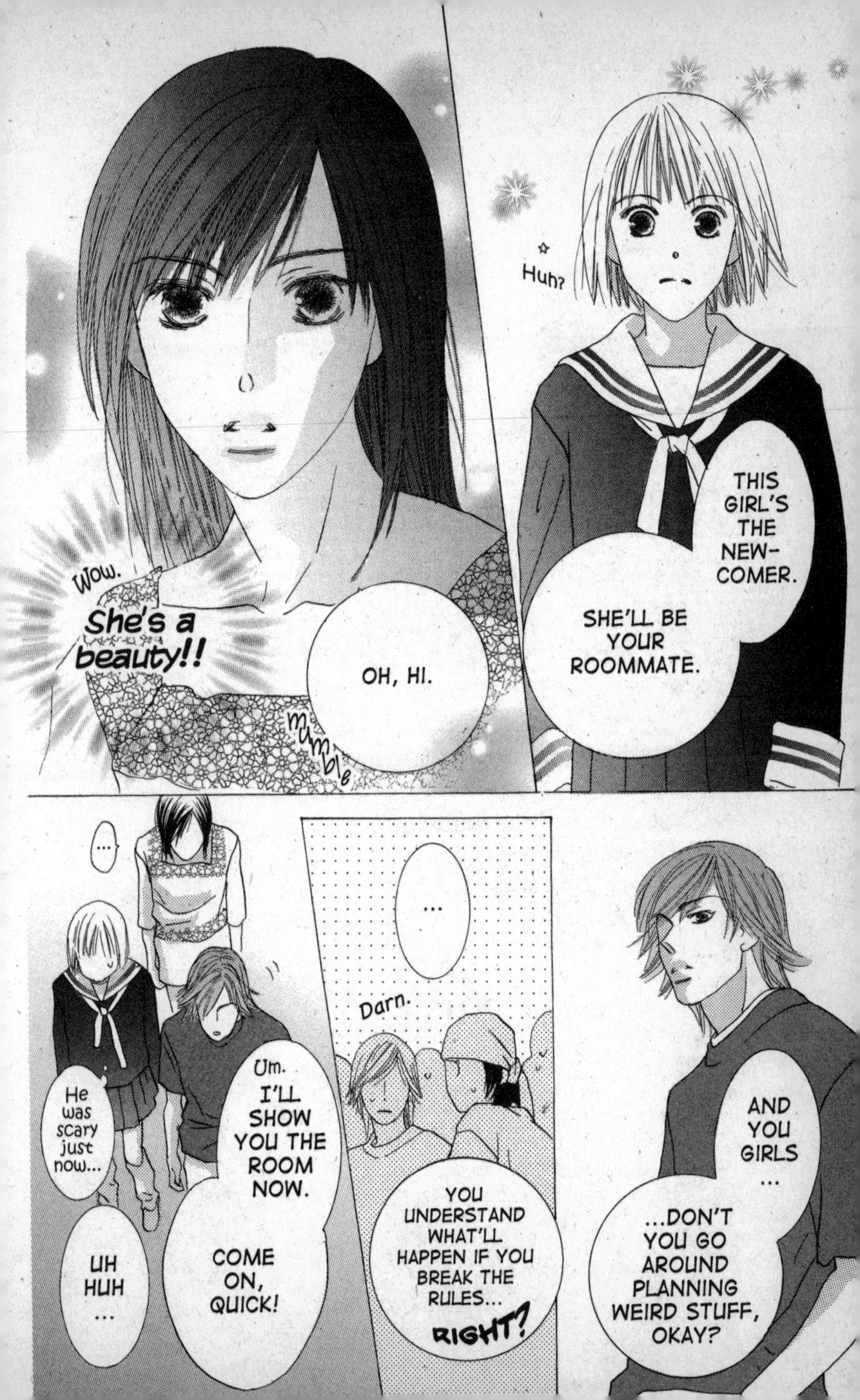

Huh?
THIS GIRL'S THE NEW-COMER.
SHE'LL BE YOUR ROOMMATE.
Wow.
She's a beauty!!
OH, HI.
mumble
AND YOU GIRLS ...
...DON'T YOU GO AROUND PLANNING WEIRD STUFF, OKAY?
...
Darn.
YOU UNDERSTAND WHAT'LL HAPPEN IF YOU BREAK THE RULES...
RIGHT?
...
Um.
I'LL SHOW YOU THE ROOM NOW.
COME ON, QUICK!
He was scary just now...
UH HUH ...

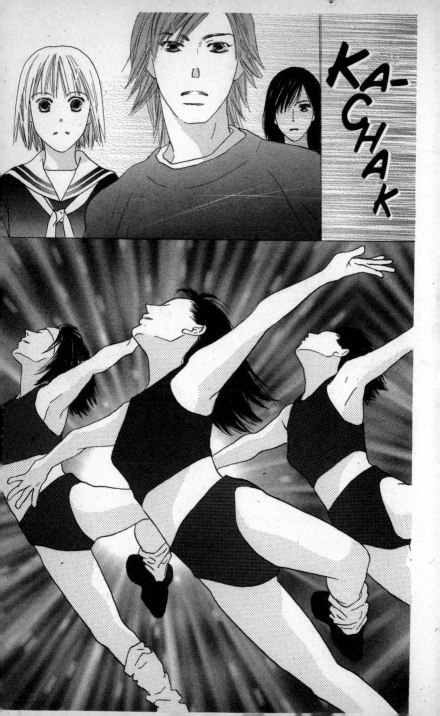

KA-
CHAK

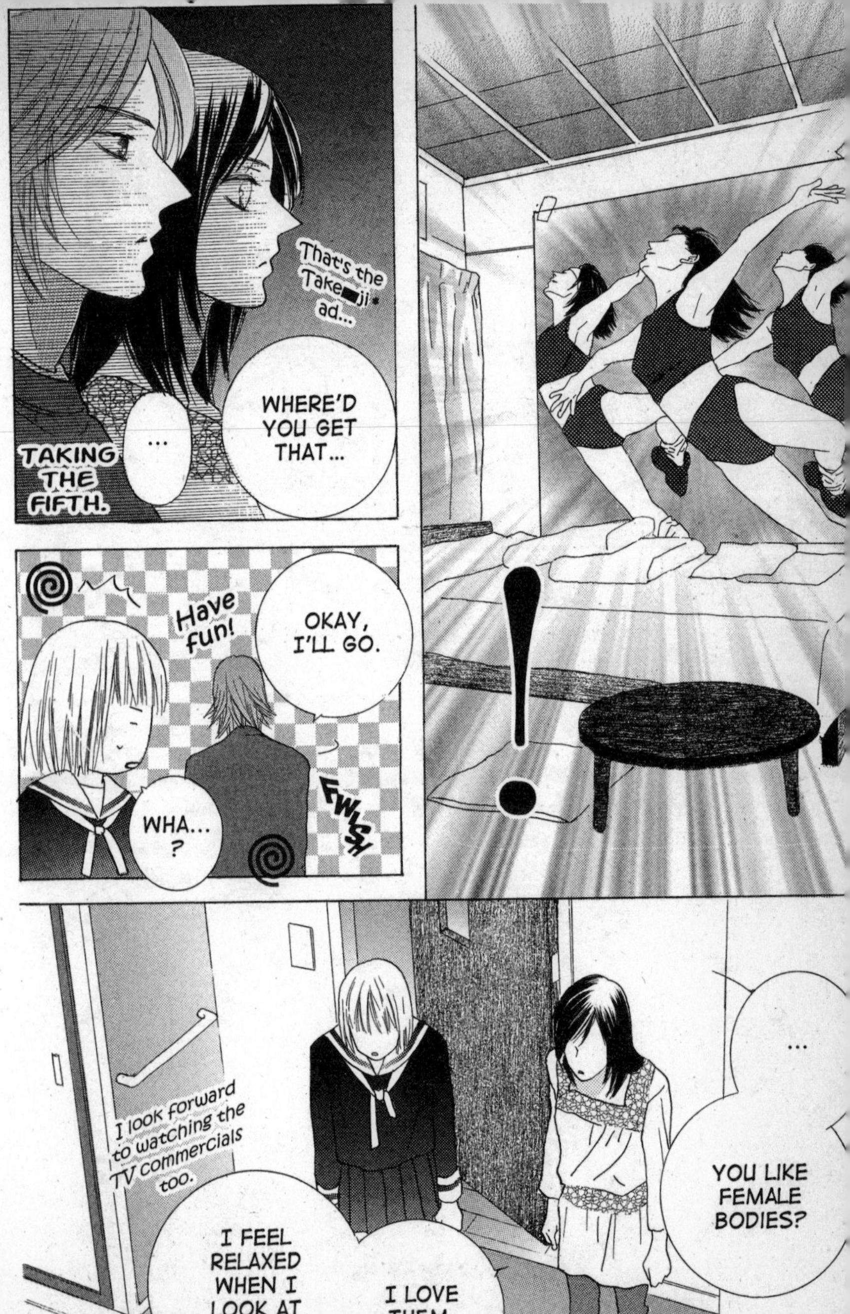
!
That's the Take[redacted]ji* ad...
WHERE'D YOU GET THAT...
...
TAKING THE FIFTH.
OKAY, I'LL GO.
Have fun!
WHA...?
FWISH
...
YOU LIKE FEMALE BODIES?
I LOVE THEM.
I FEEL RELAXED WHEN I LOOK AT THEM.
I look forward to watching the TV commercials too.

*TAKEFUJI IS A FAMOUS JAPANESE CONSUMER FINANCE COMPANY, KNOWN FOR THEIR RISQUÉ ♥ TV COMMERCIALS.

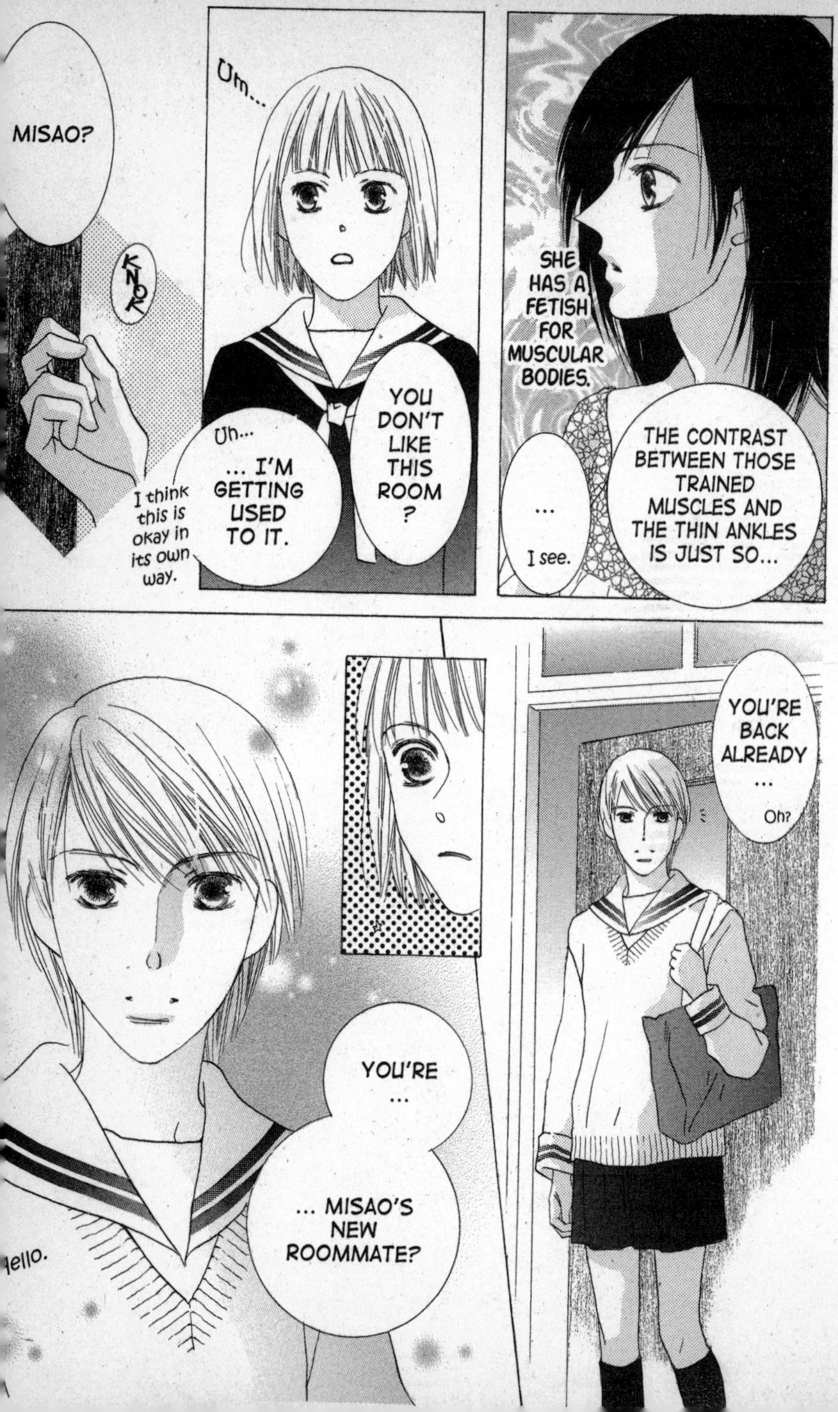
SHE HAS A FETISH FOR MUSCULAR BODIES.
THE CONTRAST BETWEEN THOSE TRAINED MUSCLES AND THE THIN ANKLES IS JUST SO...
... I see.
Um...
YOU DON'T LIKE THIS ROOM?
Uh... ... I'M GETTING USED TO IT.
I think this is okay in its own way.
MISAO?
KNOK
YOU'RE BACK ALREADY ... Oh?
YOU'RE ...
... MISAO'S NEW ROOMMATE?
Hello.

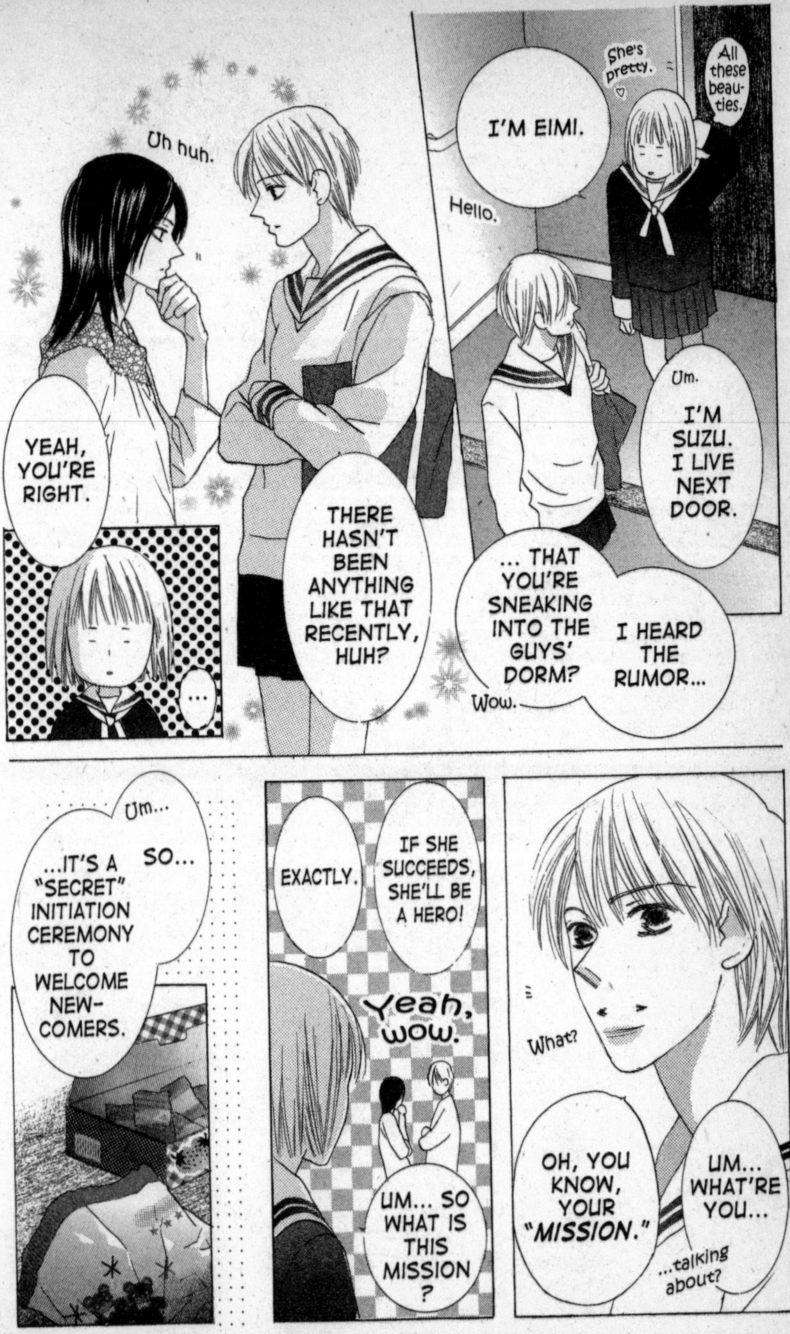
All these beau-ties.
She's pretty.
I'M EIMI.
Hello.
Um.
I'M SUZU. I LIVE NEXT DOOR.
I HEARD THE RUMOR...
... THAT YOU'RE SNEAKING INTO THE GUYS' DORM?
Wow.
Uh huh.
THERE HASN'T BEEN ANYTHING LIKE THAT RECENTLY, HUH?
YEAH, YOU'RE RIGHT.
...
UM... WHAT'RE YOU...
...talking about?
What?
OH, YOU KNOW, YOUR "MISSION."
UM... SO WHAT IS THIS MISSION?
Yeah, wow.
IF SHE SUCCEEDS, SHE'LL BE A HERO!
EXACTLY.
Um...
SO...
...IT'S A "SECRET" INITIATION CEREMONY TO WELCOME NEW-COMERS.

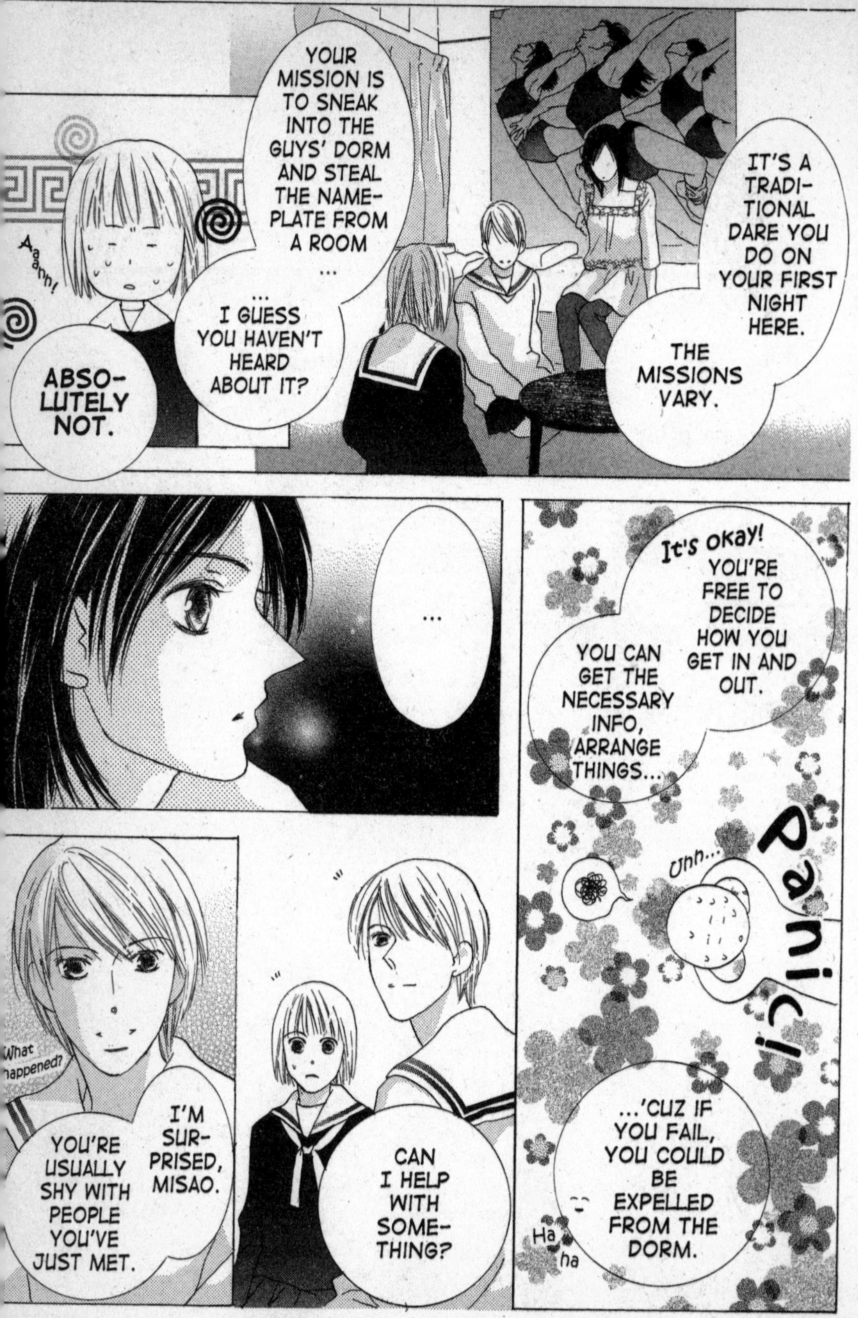
IT'S A TRADITIONAL DARE YOU DO ON YOUR FIRST NIGHT HERE.
THE MISSIONS VARY.
YOUR MISSION IS TO SNEAK INTO THE GUYS' DORM AND STEAL THE NAMEPLATE FROM A ROOM ...
... I GUESS YOU HAVEN'T HEARD ABOUT IT?
Aaanh!
ABSOLUTELY NOT.
It's okay! YOU'RE FREE TO DECIDE HOW YOU GET IN AND OUT.
YOU CAN GET THE NECESSARY INFO, ARRANGE THINGS...
Unh...
Panic!!
...'CUZ IF YOU FAIL, YOU COULD BE EXPELLED FROM THE DORM.
Ha ha
...
CAN I HELP WITH SOMETHING?
I'M SURPRISED, MISAO.
YOU'RE USUALLY SHY WITH PEOPLE YOU'VE JUST MET.
What happened?

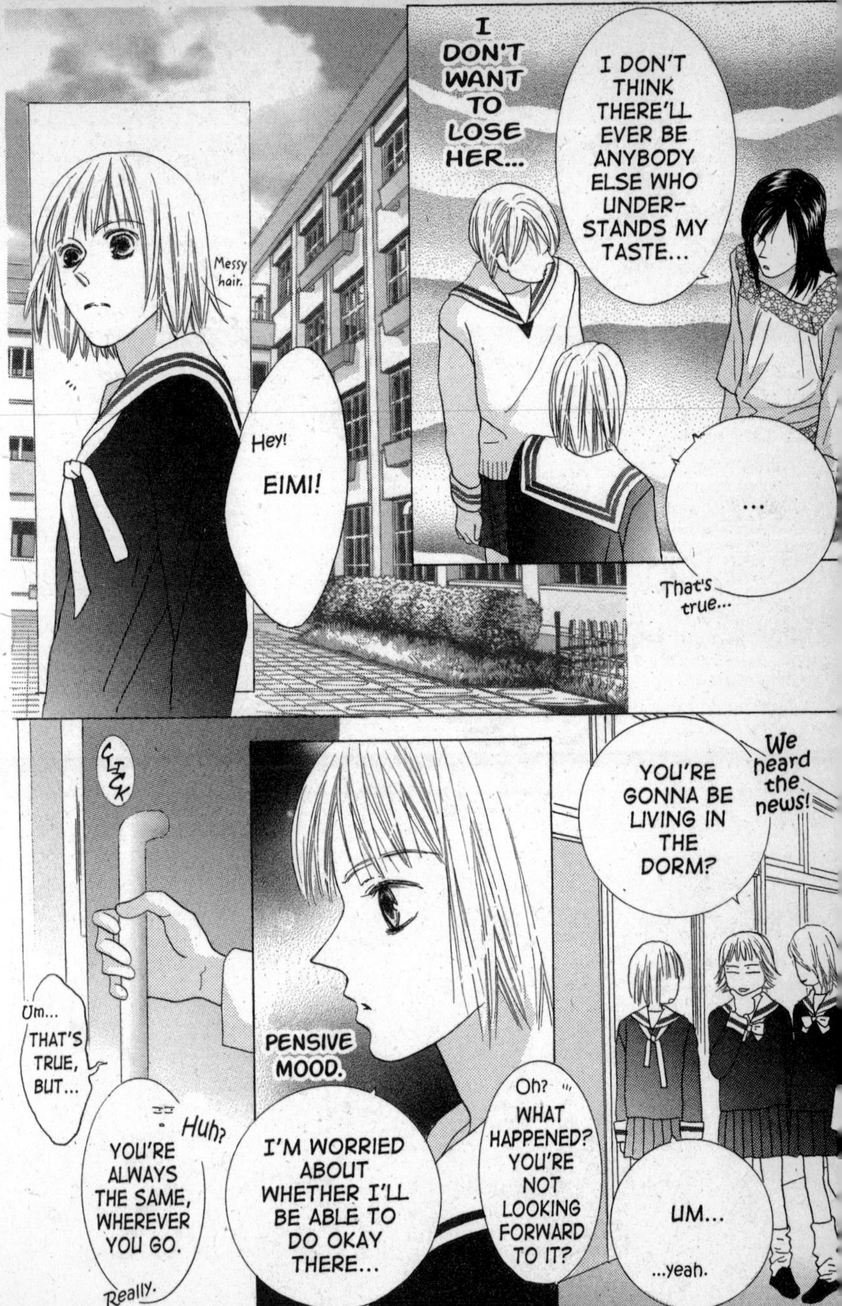
I DON'T THINK THERE'LL EVER BE ANYBODY ELSE WHO UNDER-STANDS MY TASTE...
I DON'T WANT TO LOSE HER...
...
That's true...
Hey!
EIMI!
Messy hair.
We heard the news!
YOU'RE GONNA BE LIVING IN THE DORM?
UM...
...yeah.
Oh?
WHAT HAPPENED? YOU'RE NOT LOOKING FORWARD TO IT?
PENSIVE MOOD.
I'M WORRIED ABOUT WHETHER I'LL BE ABLE TO DO OKAY THERE...
CLICK
Um... THAT'S TRUE, BUT...
Huh?
YOU'RE ALWAYS THE SAME, WHEREVER YOU GO.
Really.

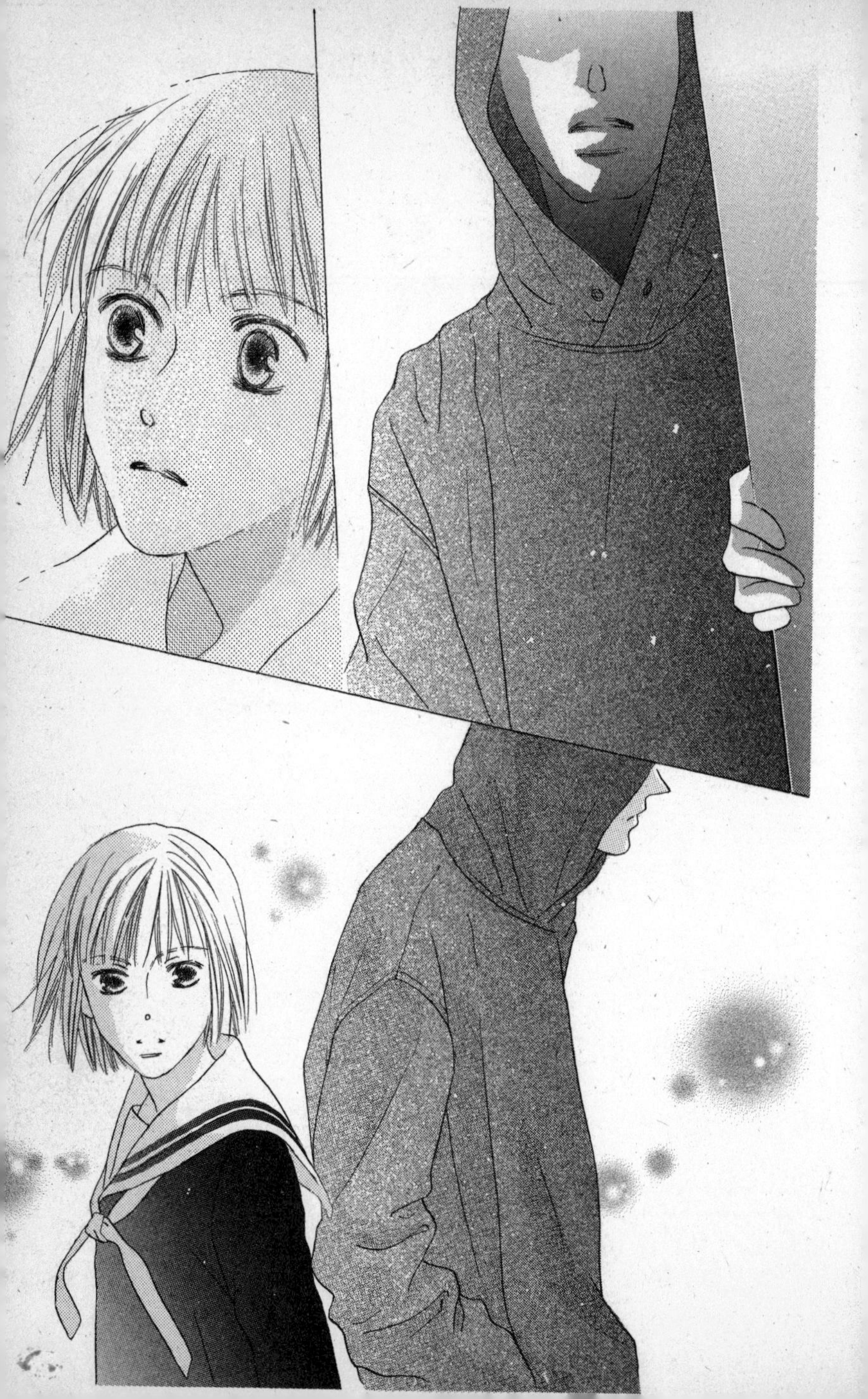

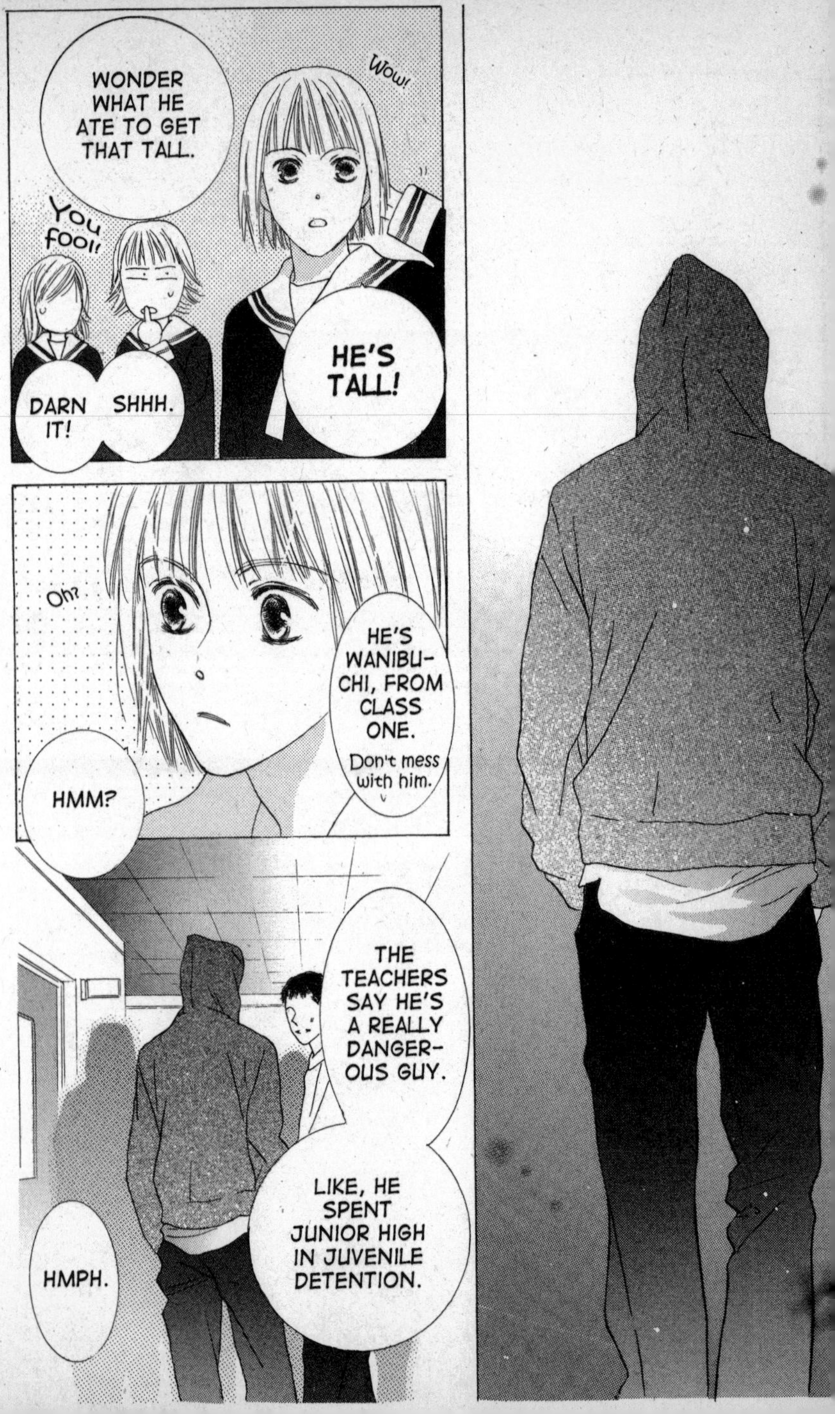
Wow!
HE'S TALL!
WONDER WHAT HE ATE TO GET THAT TALL.
You fool!
SHHH.
DARN IT!
HE'S WANIBU-CHI, FROM CLASS ONE.
Don't mess with him.
Oh?
HMM?
THE TEACHERS SAY HE'S A REALLY DANGER-OUS GUY.
LIKE, HE SPENT JUNIOR HIGH IN JUVENILE DETENTION.
HMPH.

1

Hello.

I'm Tomo Matsumoto.

To first-time readers, those who've read my previous works, thank you for reading!

Um, readers have told me they want to see this space handwritten, but I've had them printed because...my handwriting is messy. (Simple!)

I don't want to think it's my personality showing in my handwriting (bitter smile), but since it's really curvy and really hard to read, I've been firm in using this format. I'm happy if you keep with me this time around, too.

Thanks!

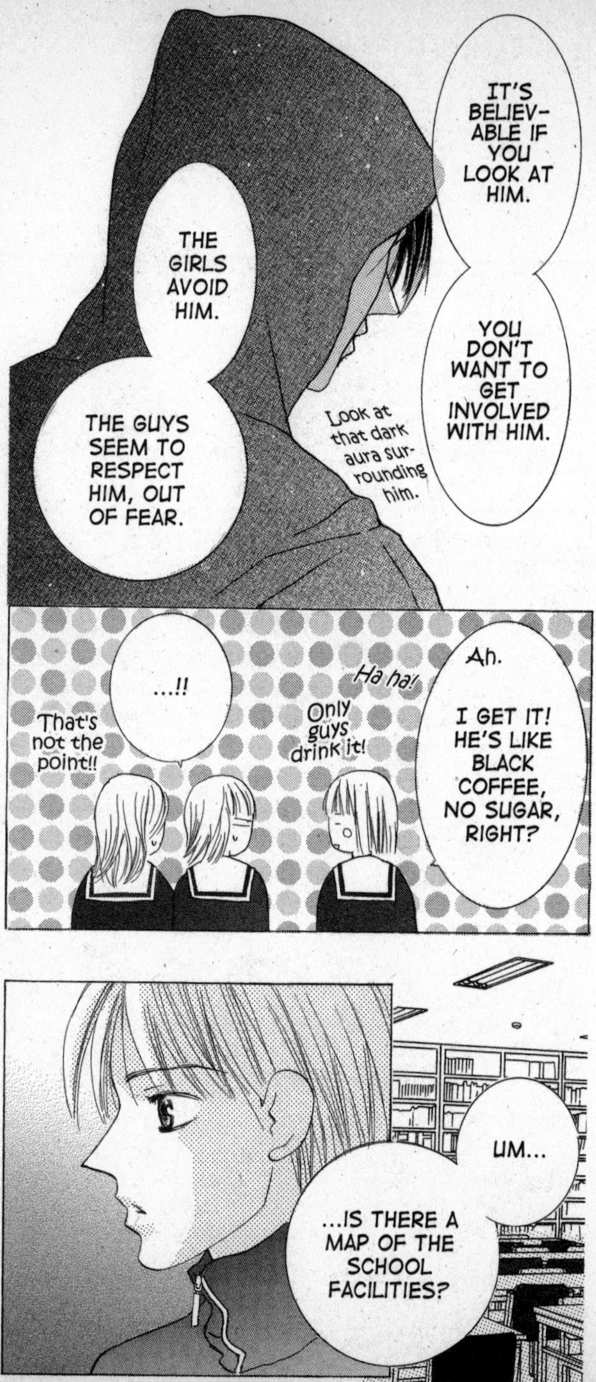
IT'S BELIEVABLE IF YOU LOOK AT HIM.
YOU DON'T WANT TO GET INVOLVED WITH HIM.
Look at that dark aura surrounding him.
THE GIRLS AVOID HIM.
THE GUYS SEEM TO RESPECT HIM, OUT OF FEAR.
Ah.
I GET IT! HE'S LIKE BLACK COFFEE, NO SUGAR, RIGHT?
Ha ha!
Only guys drink it!
...!!
That's not the point!!
UM...
...IS THERE A MAP OF THE SCHOOL FACILITIES?

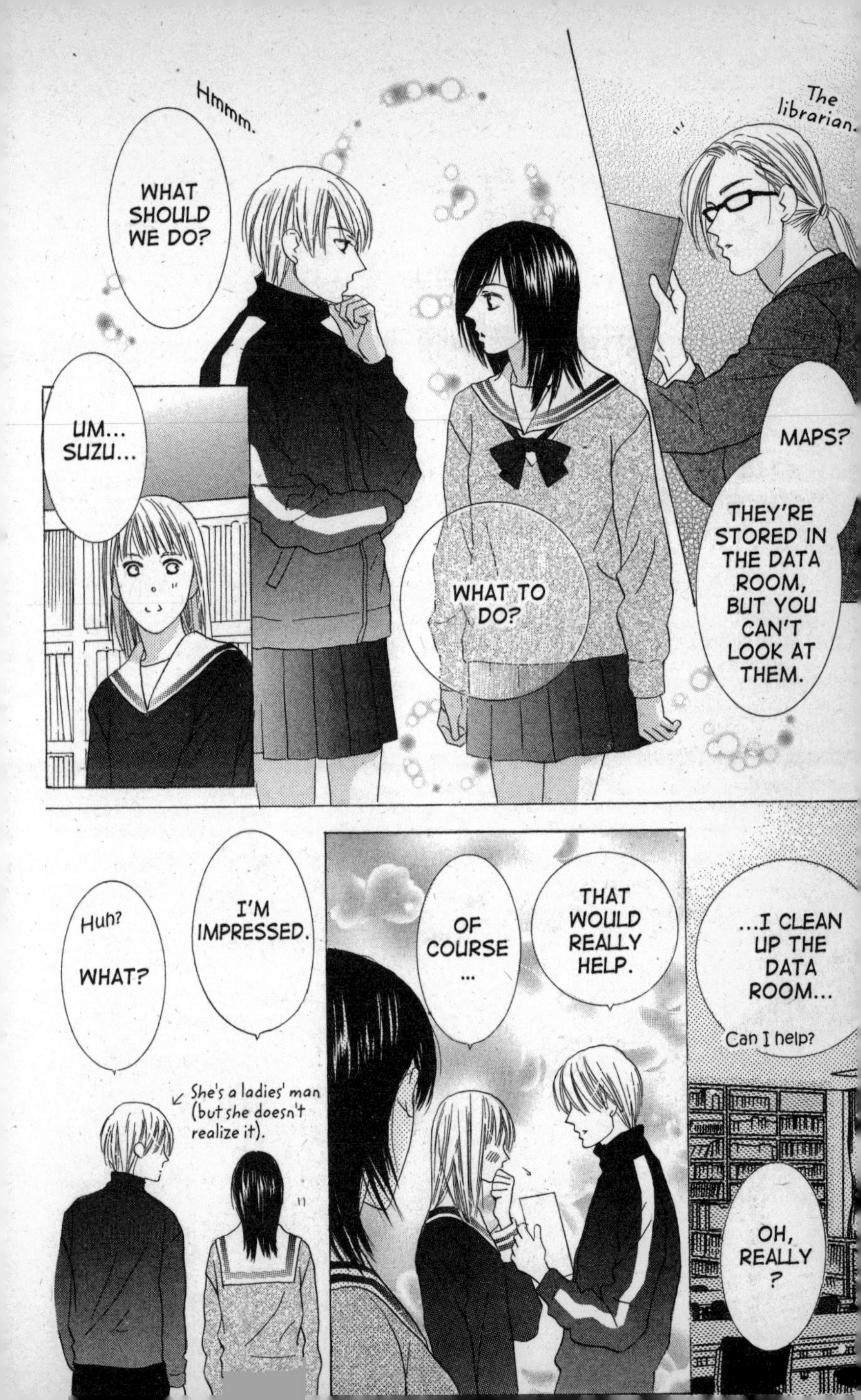
The librarian.
MAPS?
THEY'RE STORED IN THE DATA ROOM, BUT YOU CAN'T LOOK AT THEM.
Hmmm.
WHAT SHOULD WE DO?
WHAT TO DO?
UM... SUZU...
...I CLEAN UP THE DATA ROOM...
Can I help?
OH, REALLY?
THAT WOULD REALLY HELP.
OF COURSE ...
I'M IMPRESSED.
Huh?
WHAT?
She's a ladies' man (but she doesn't realize it).

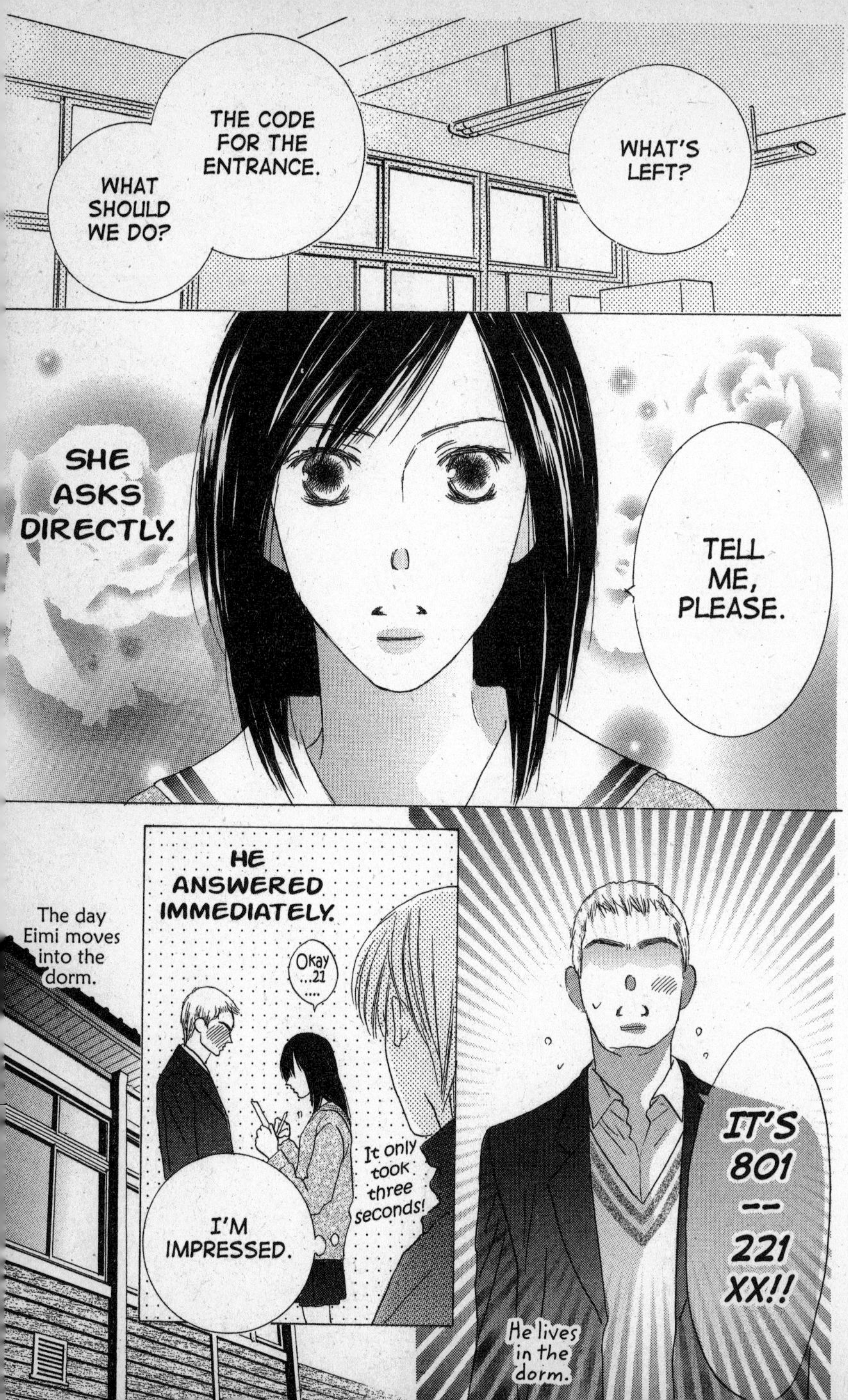
WHAT'S LEFT?
THE CODE FOR THE ENTRANCE.
WHAT SHOULD WE DO?
TELL ME, PLEASE.
SHE ASKS DIRECTLY.
IT'S 801 -- 221 XX!!
He lives in the dorm.
HE ANSWERED IMMEDIATELY.
Okay ...21 ....
It only took three seconds!
I'M IMPRESSED.
The day Eimi moves into the dorm.

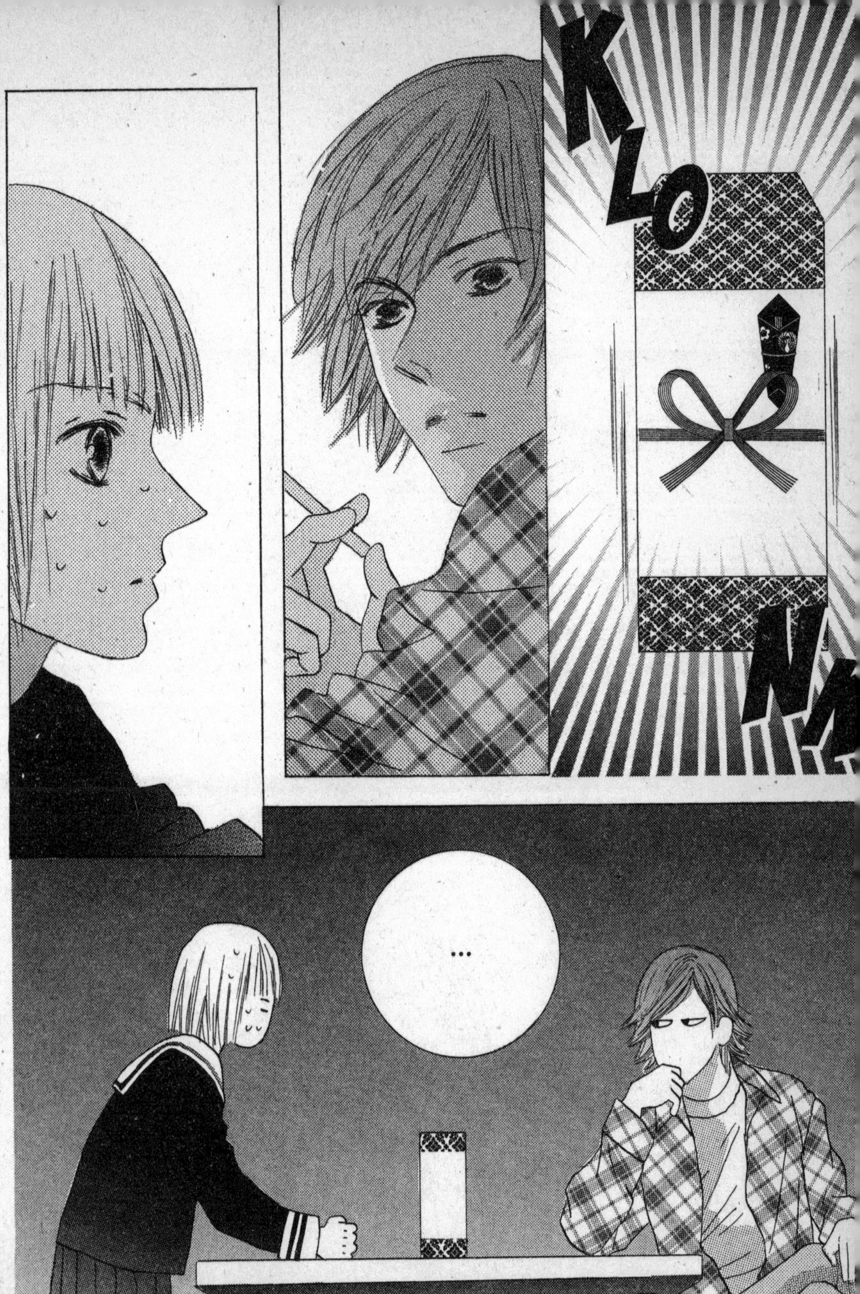
KLON
...

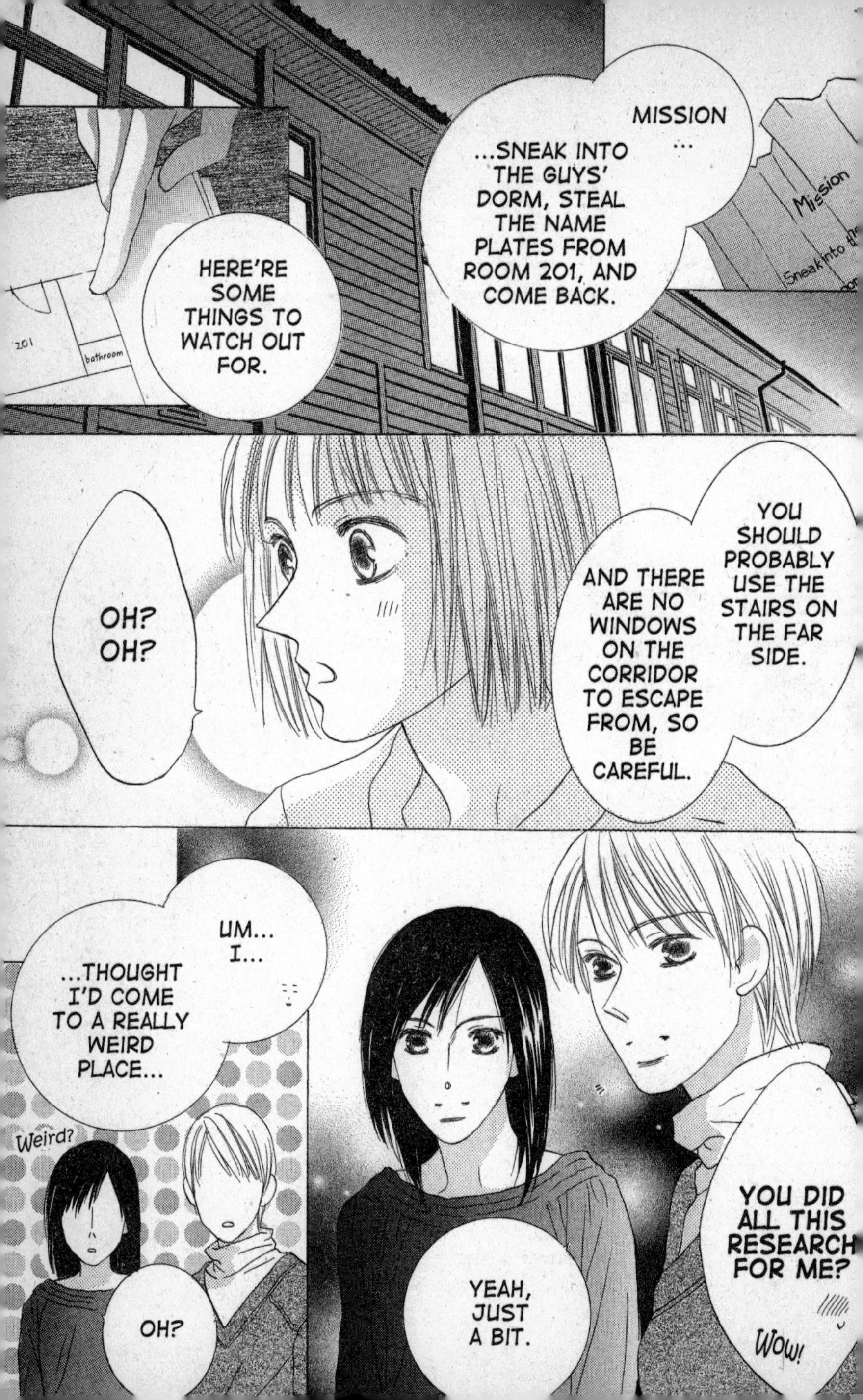
MISSION
...
...SNEAK INTO THE GUYS' DORM, STEAL THE NAME PLATES FROM ROOM 201, AND COME BACK.
Mission
HERE'RE SOME THINGS TO WATCH OUT FOR.
201
bathroom
YOU SHOULD PROBABLY USE THE STAIRS ON THE FAR SIDE.
AND THERE ARE NO WINDOWS ON THE CORRIDOR TO ESCAPE FROM, SO BE CAREFUL.
OH? OH?
YOU DID ALL THIS RESEARCH FOR ME?
WOW!
YEAH, JUST A BIT.
UM... I...
...THOUGHT I'D COME TO A REALLY WEIRD PLACE...
Weird?
OH?

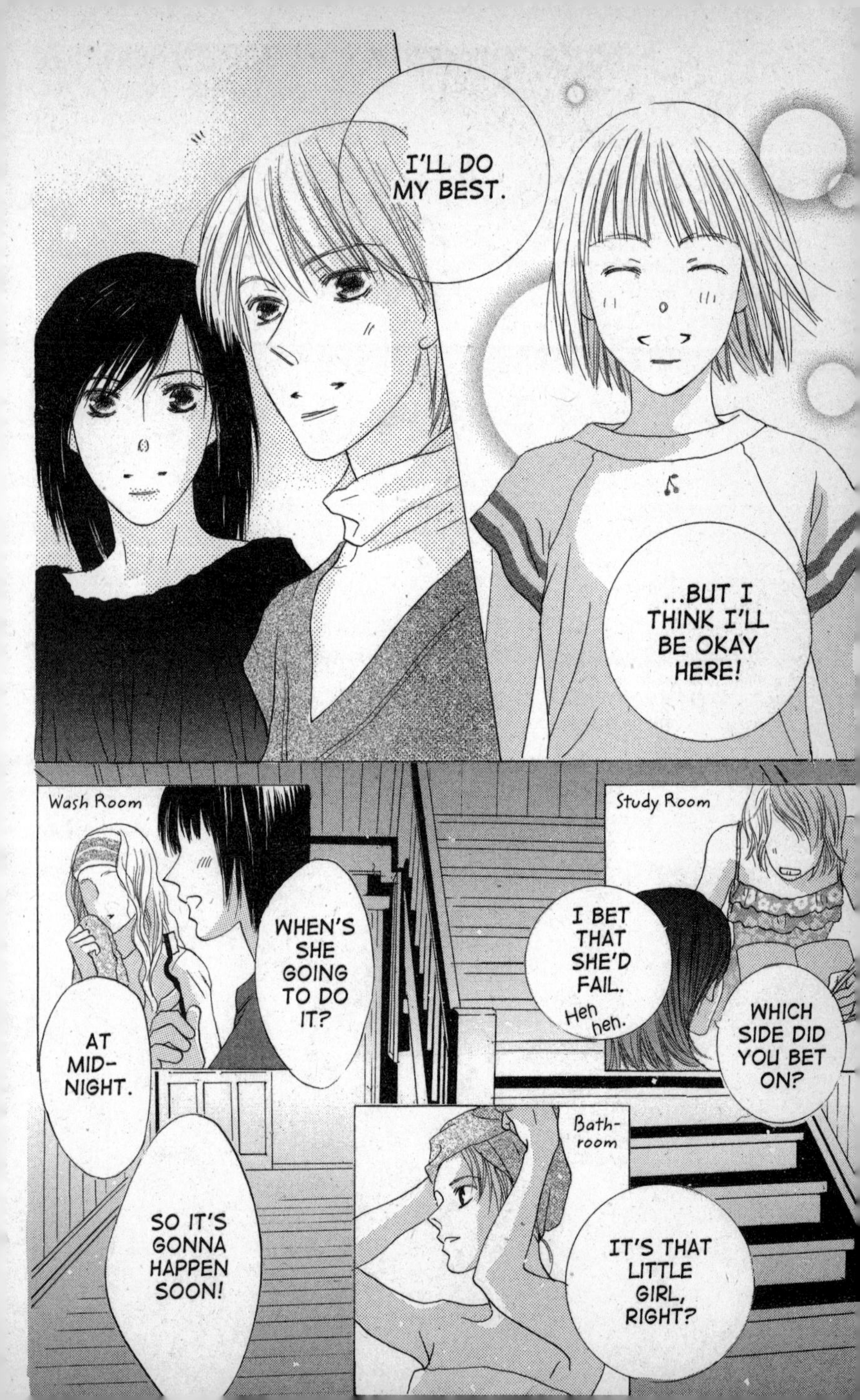
I'LL DO MY BEST.
...BUT I THINK I'LL BE OKAY HERE!
Study Room
WHICH SIDE DID YOU BET ON?
I BET THAT SHE'D FAIL.
Heh heh.
Wash Room
WHEN'S SHE GOING TO DO IT?
AT MID-NIGHT.
SO IT'S GONNA HAPPEN SOON!
Bath-room
IT'S THAT LITTLE GIRL, RIGHT?

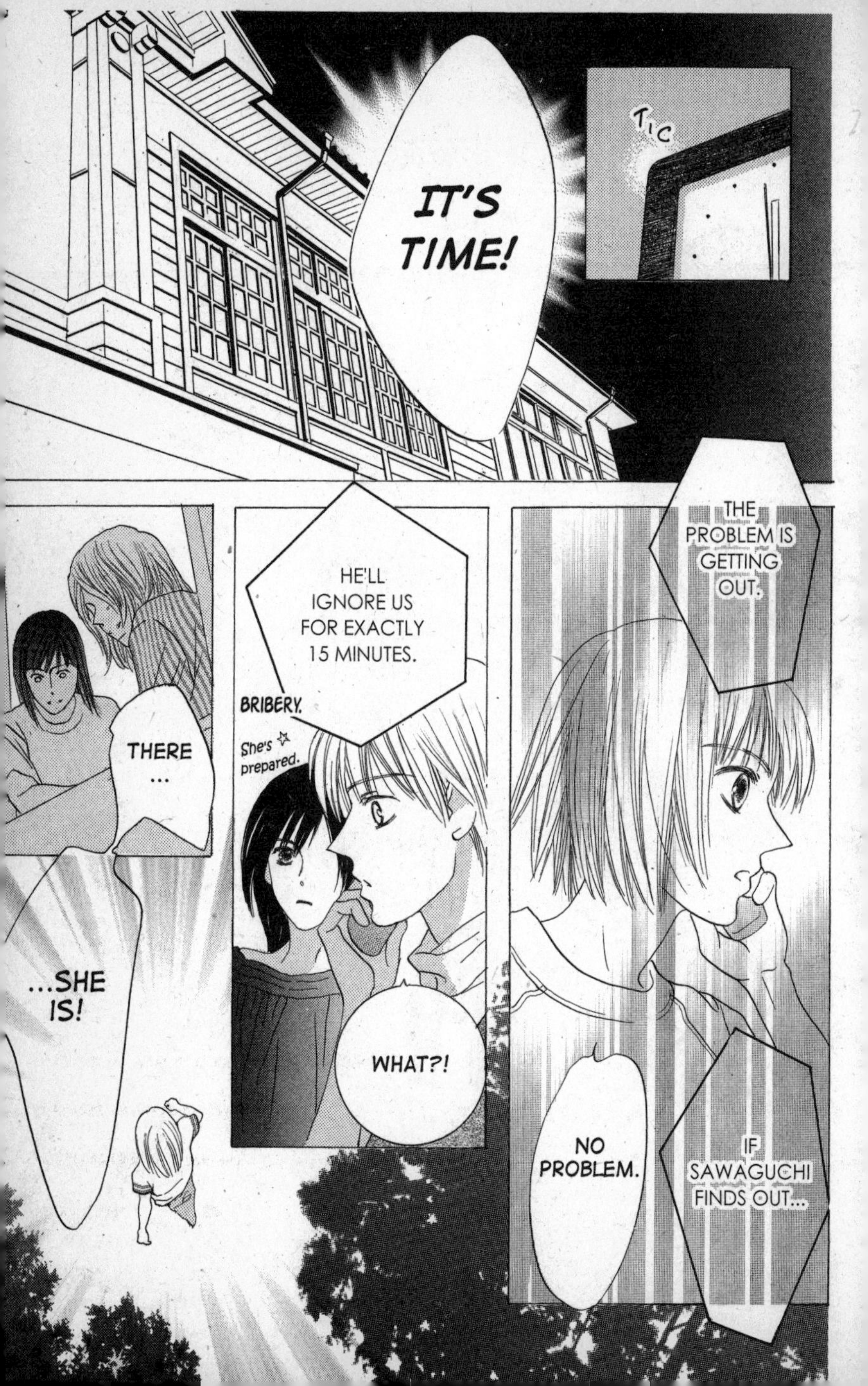
TIC
IT'S TIME!
THE PROBLEM IS GETTING OUT.
IF SAWAGUCHI FINDS OUT...
NO PROBLEM.
HE'LL IGNORE US FOR EXACTLY 15 MINUTES.
BRIBERY.
She's prepared.
WHAT?!
THERE...
...SHE IS!

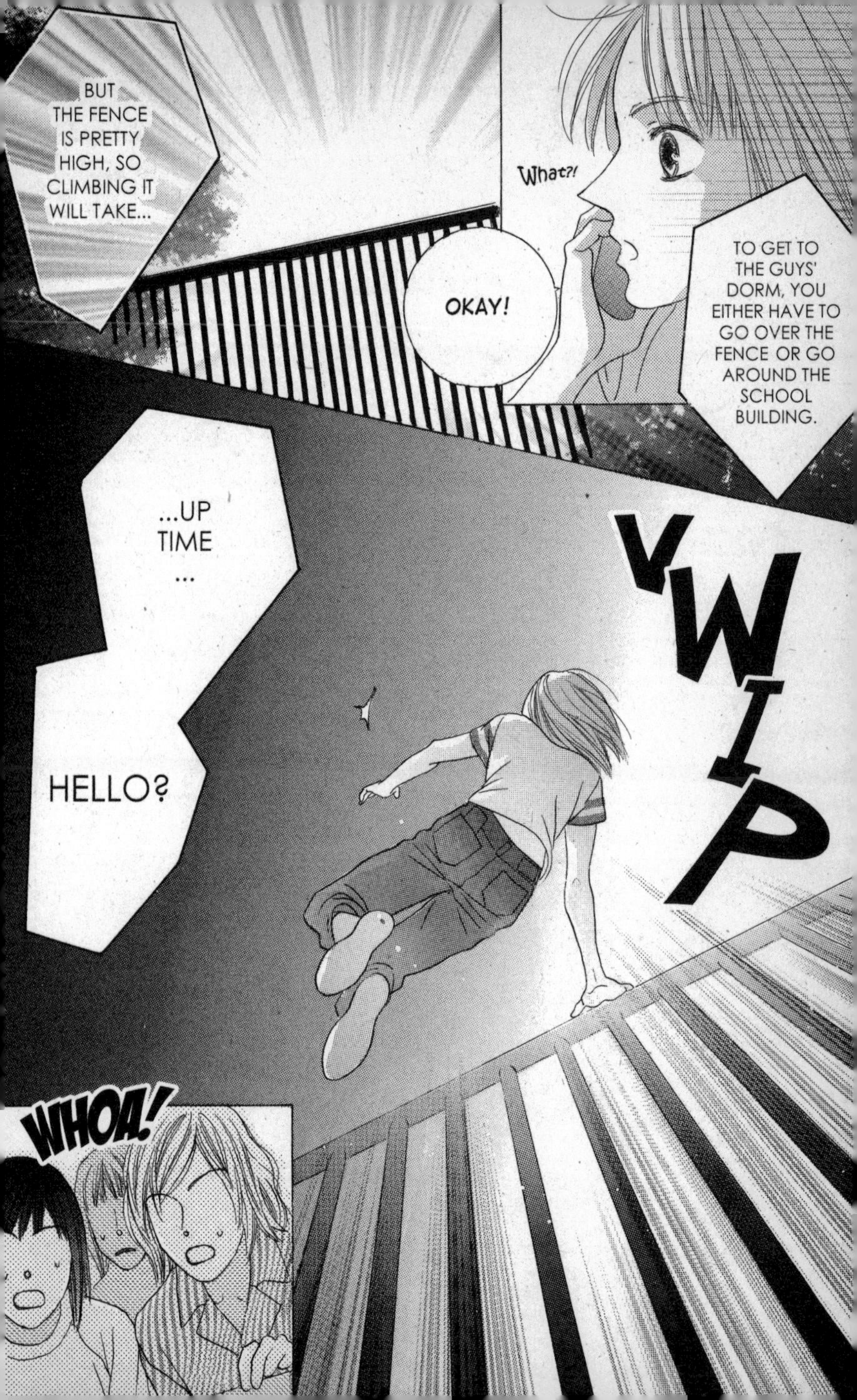
What?!
TO GET TO THE GUYS' DORM, YOU EITHER HAVE TO GO OVER THE FENCE OR GO AROUND THE SCHOOL BUILDING.
OKAY!
BUT THE FENCE IS PRETTY HIGH, SO CLIMBING IT WILL TAKE...
VWIP
...UP TIME ...
HELLO?
WHOA!

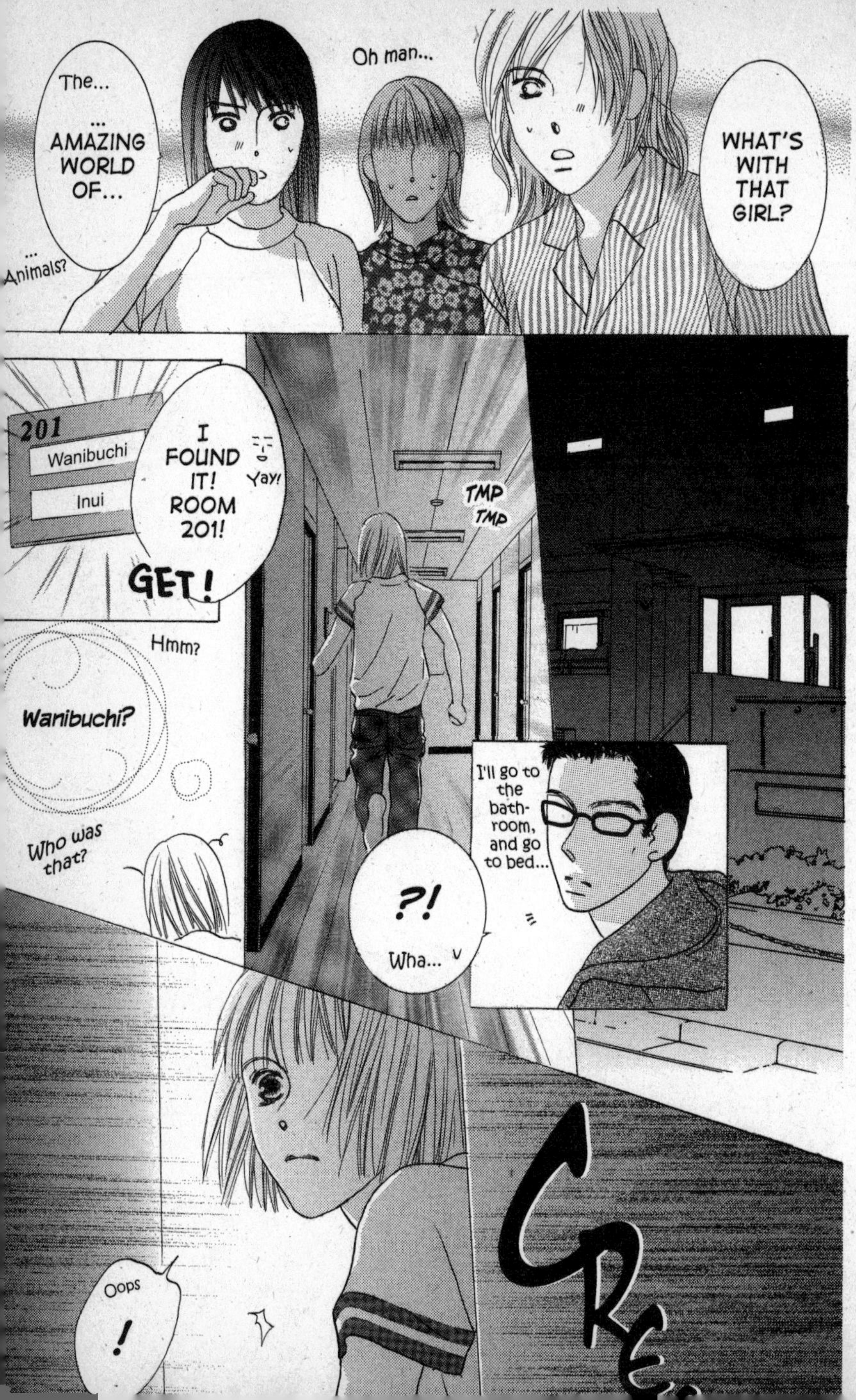

WHAT'S WITH THAT GIRL?
Oh man...
The... ...AMAZING WORLD OF...
...Animals?
I'll go to the bath-room, and go to bed...
TMP TMP
201
Wanibuchi
Inui
I FOUND IT! ROOM 201!
Yay!
GET!
Hmm?
Wanibuchi?
Who was that?
?! Wha...
CRE...
Oops
!

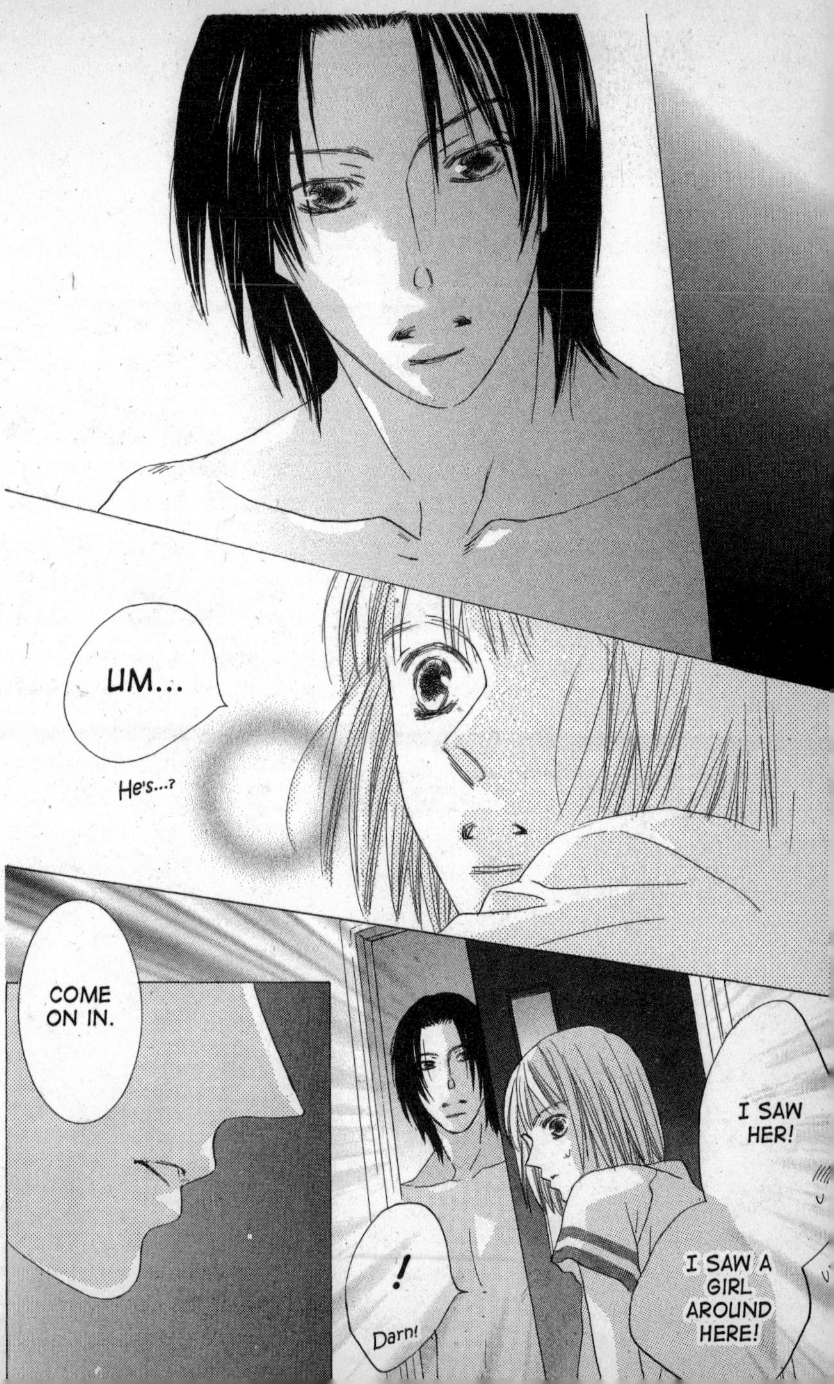
UM...
He's...?
I SAW HER!
I SAW A GIRL AROUND HERE!
!
Darn!
COME ON IN.

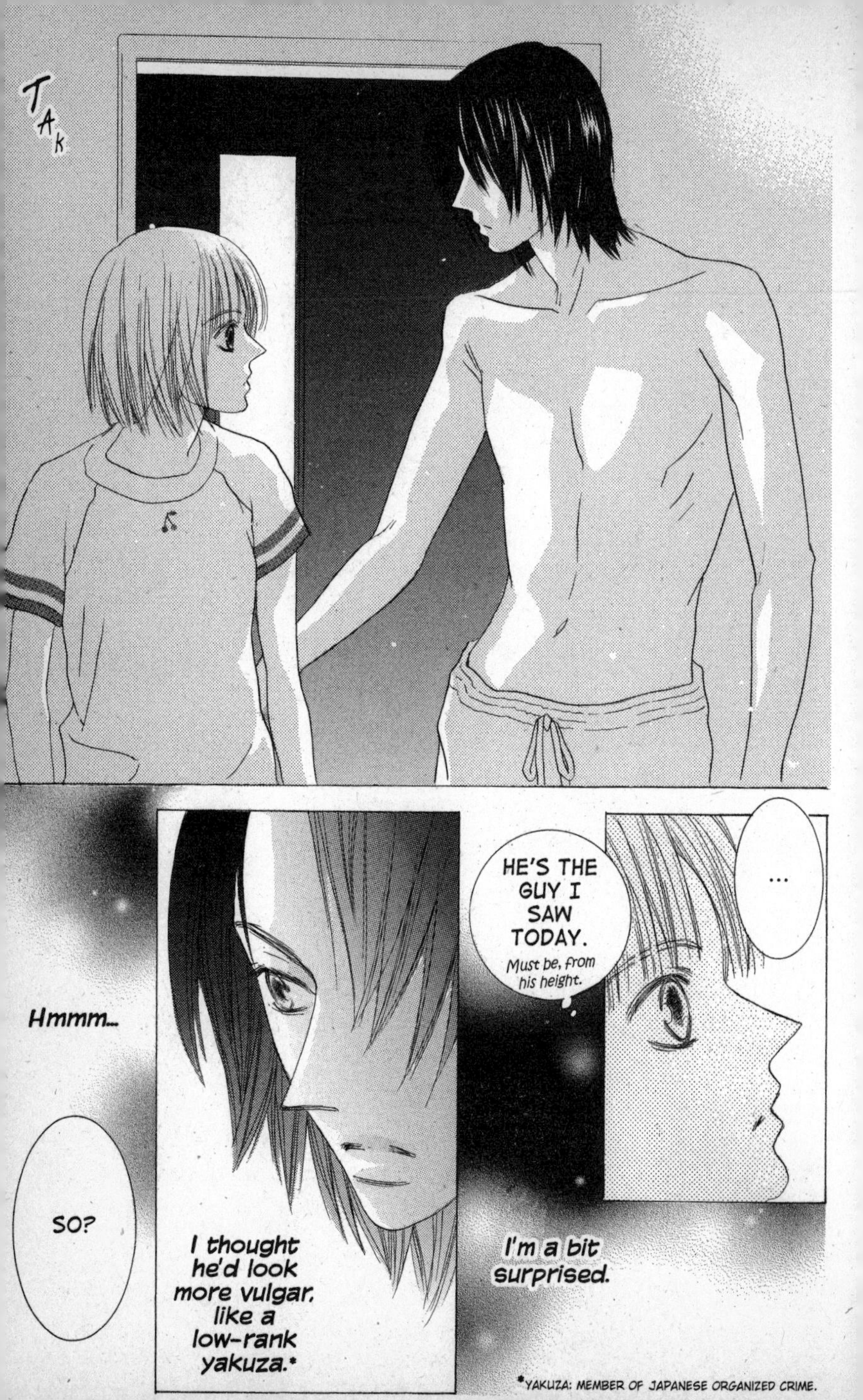
TAK
...
HE'S THE GUY I SAW TODAY.
Must be, from his height.
I'm a bit surprised.
I thought he'd look more vulgar, like a low-rank yakuza.*
Hmmm...
SO?

*YAKUZA: MEMBER OF JAPANESE ORGANIZED CRIME.

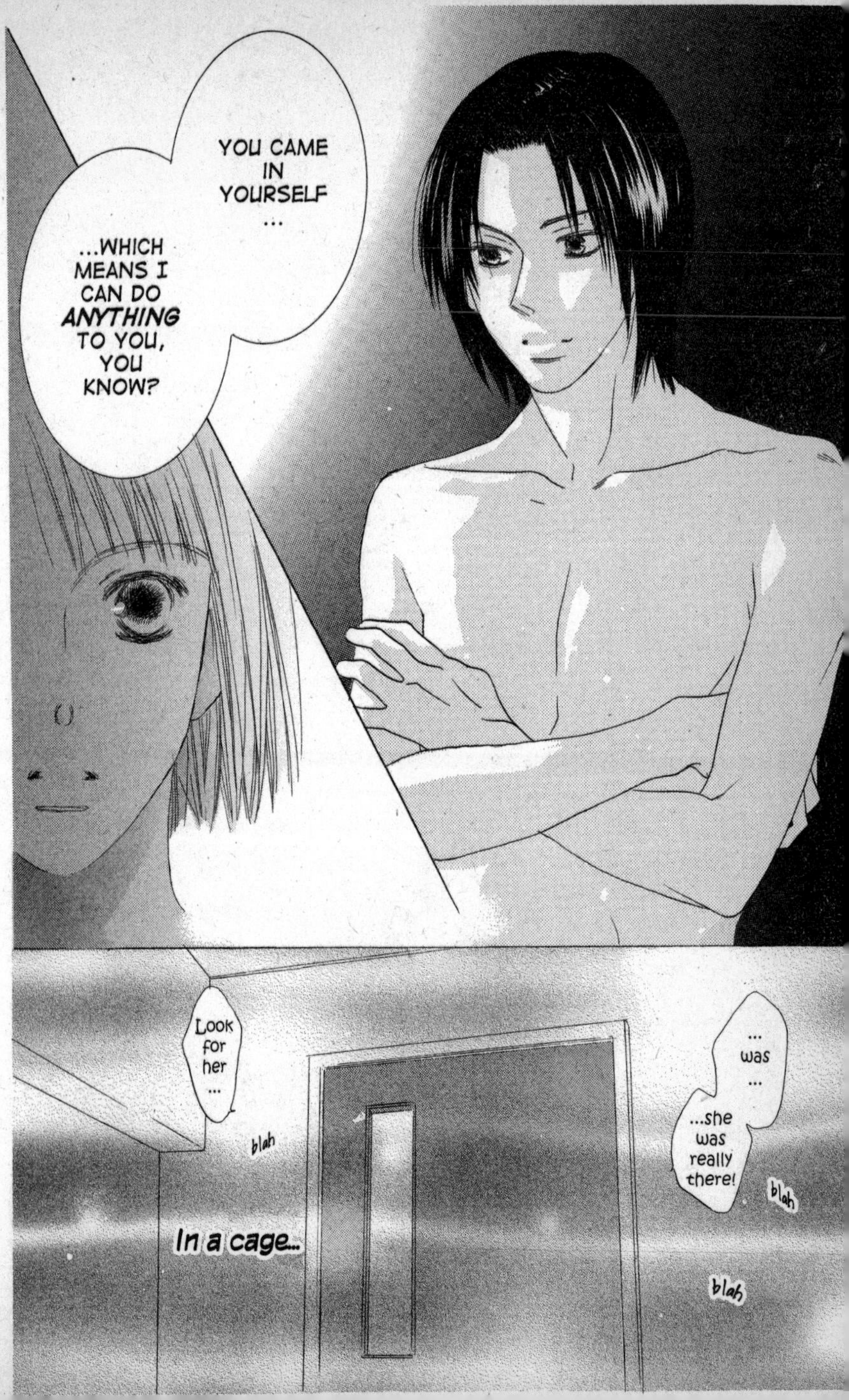

YOU CAME IN YOURSELF ...
...WHICH MEANS I CAN DO ANYTHING TO YOU, YOU KNOW?
... was ...
...she was really there!
blah
Look for her ...
blah
blah
In a cage...

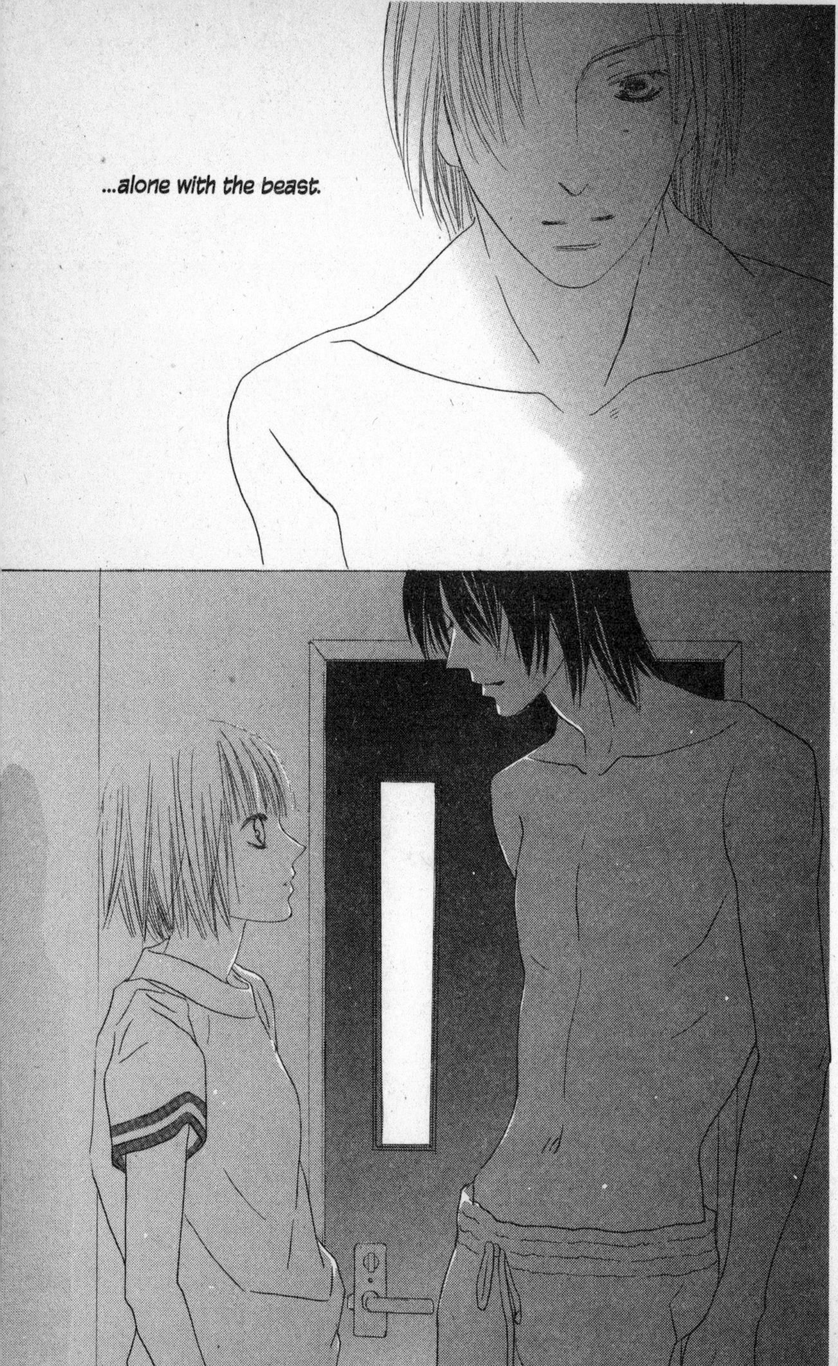
...alone with the beast.

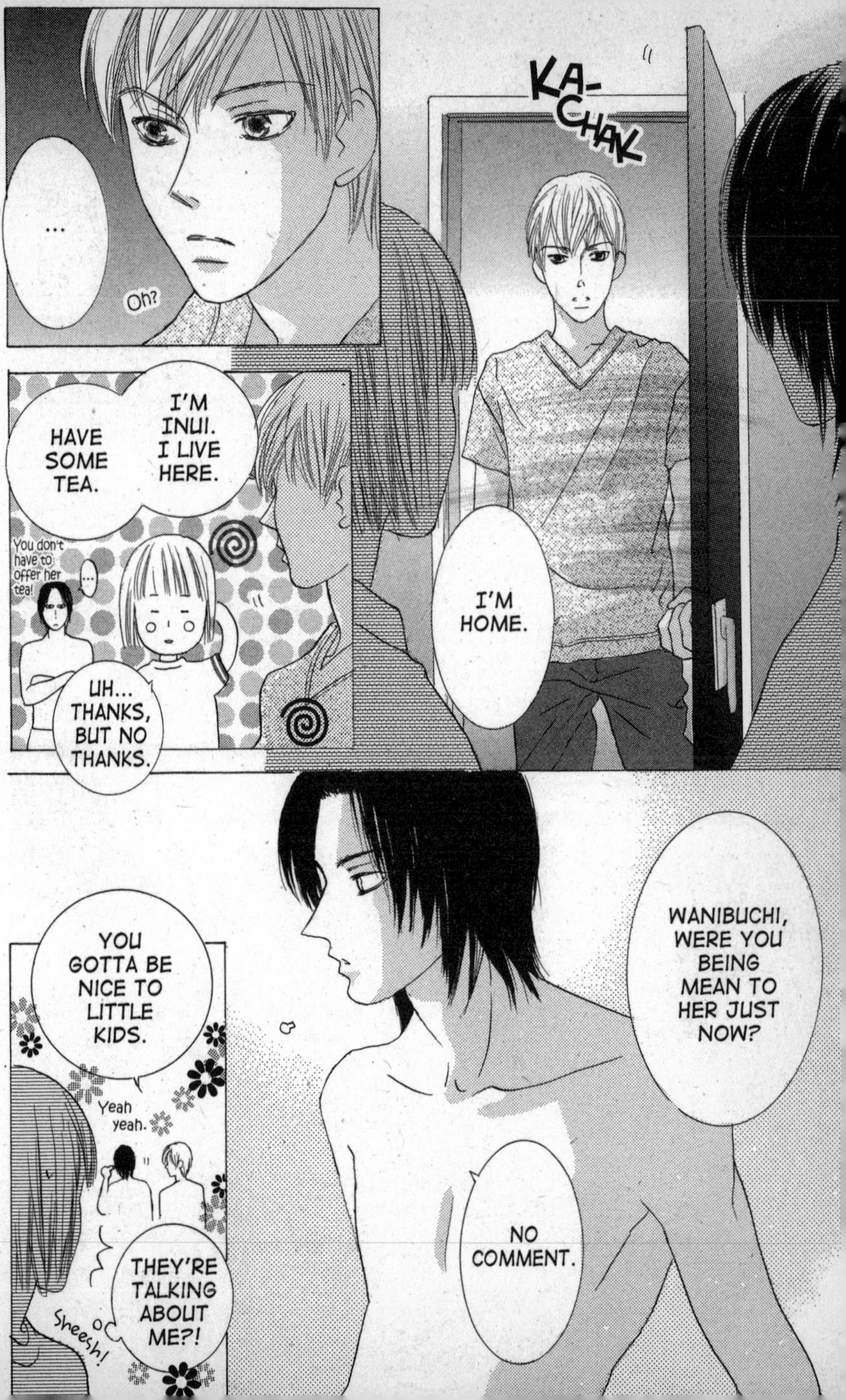
KA-CHAK
I'M HOME.
...
Oh?
I'M INUI. I LIVE HERE.
HAVE SOME TEA.
You don't have to offer her tea!
UH... THANKS, BUT NO THANKS.
WANIBUCHI, WERE YOU BEING MEAN TO HER JUST NOW?
NO COMMENT.
YOU GOTTA BE NICE TO LITTLE KIDS.
Yeah yeah.
THEY'RE TALKING ABOUT ME?!
Sheesh!

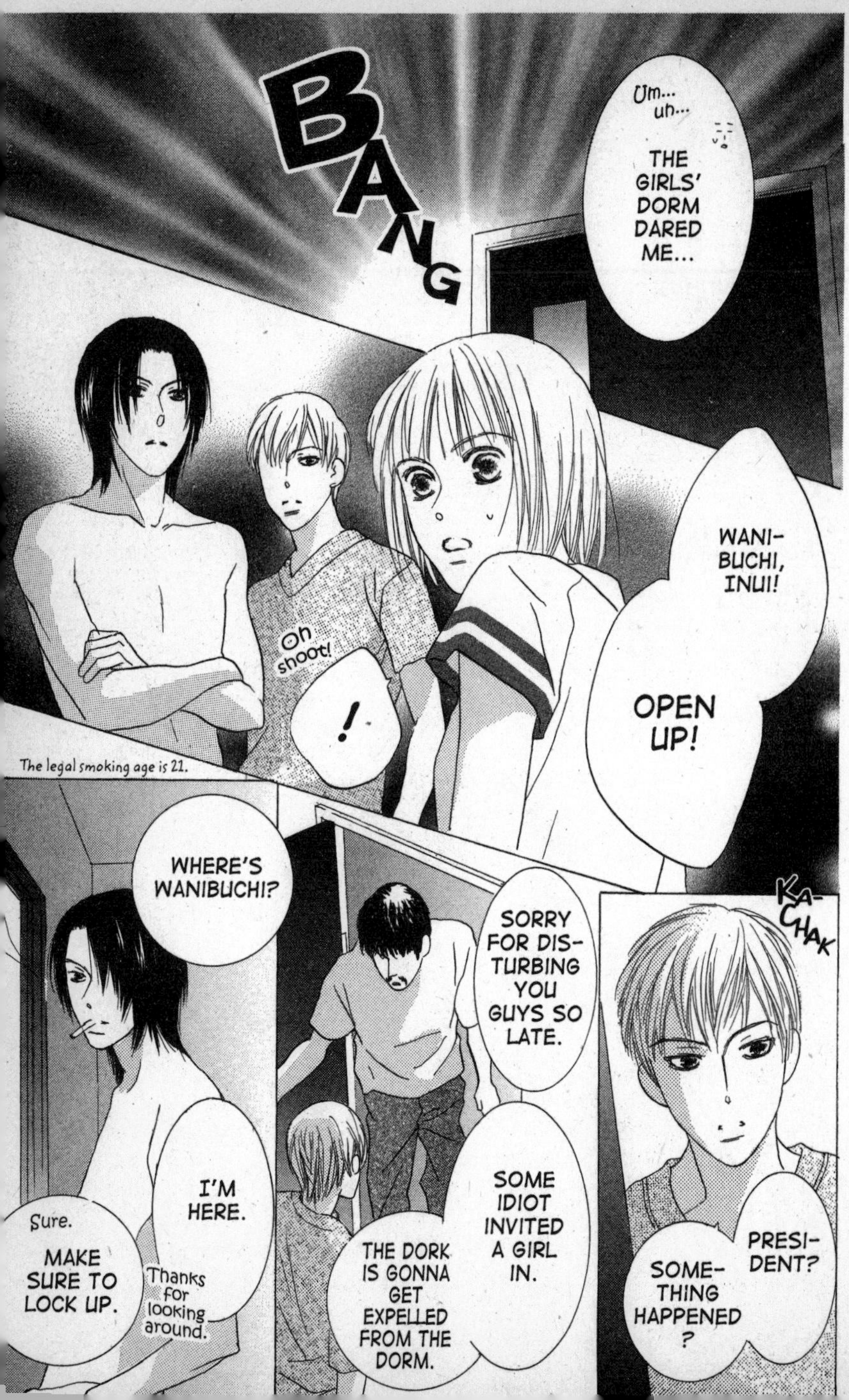
BANG
Um... uh...
THE GIRLS' DORM DARED ME...
WANI-BUCHI, INUI!
OPEN UP!
Oh shoot!
!
The legal smoking age is 21.
KA-CHAK
PRESI-DENT?
SOME-THING HAPPENED?
SORRY FOR DIS-TURBING YOU GUYS SO LATE.
SOME IDIOT INVITED A GIRL IN.
THE DORK IS GONNA GET EXPELLED FROM THE DORM.
WHERE'S WANIBUCHI?
I'M HERE.
Thanks for looking around.
Sure.
MAKE SURE TO LOCK UP.

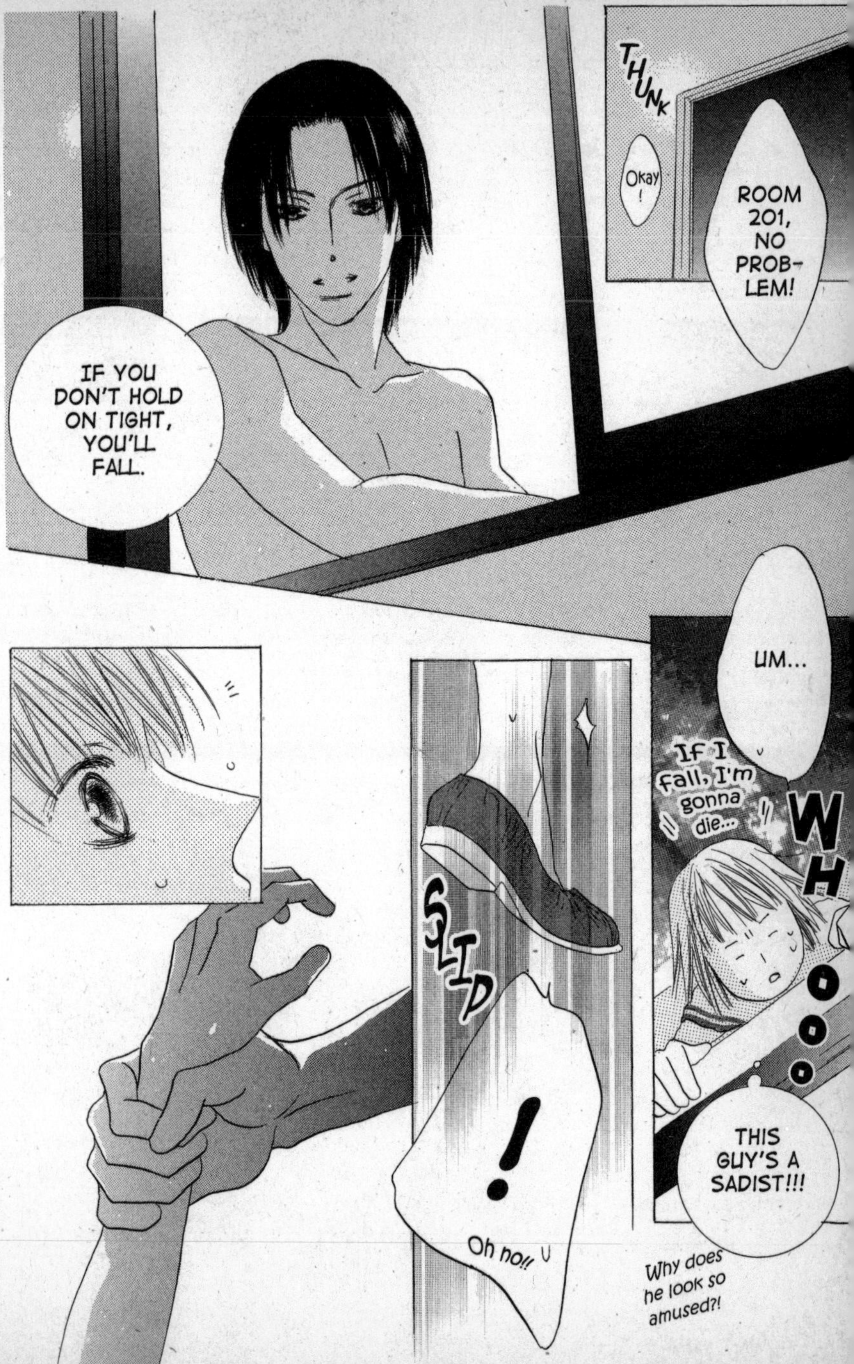
THUNK
ROOM 201, NO PROB-LEM!
Okay!
IF YOU DON'T HOLD ON TIGHT, YOU'LL FALL.
UM...
If I fall, I'm gonna die...
WH...
THIS GUY'S A SADIST!!!
Why does he look so amused?!
SLIP
!
Oh no!!

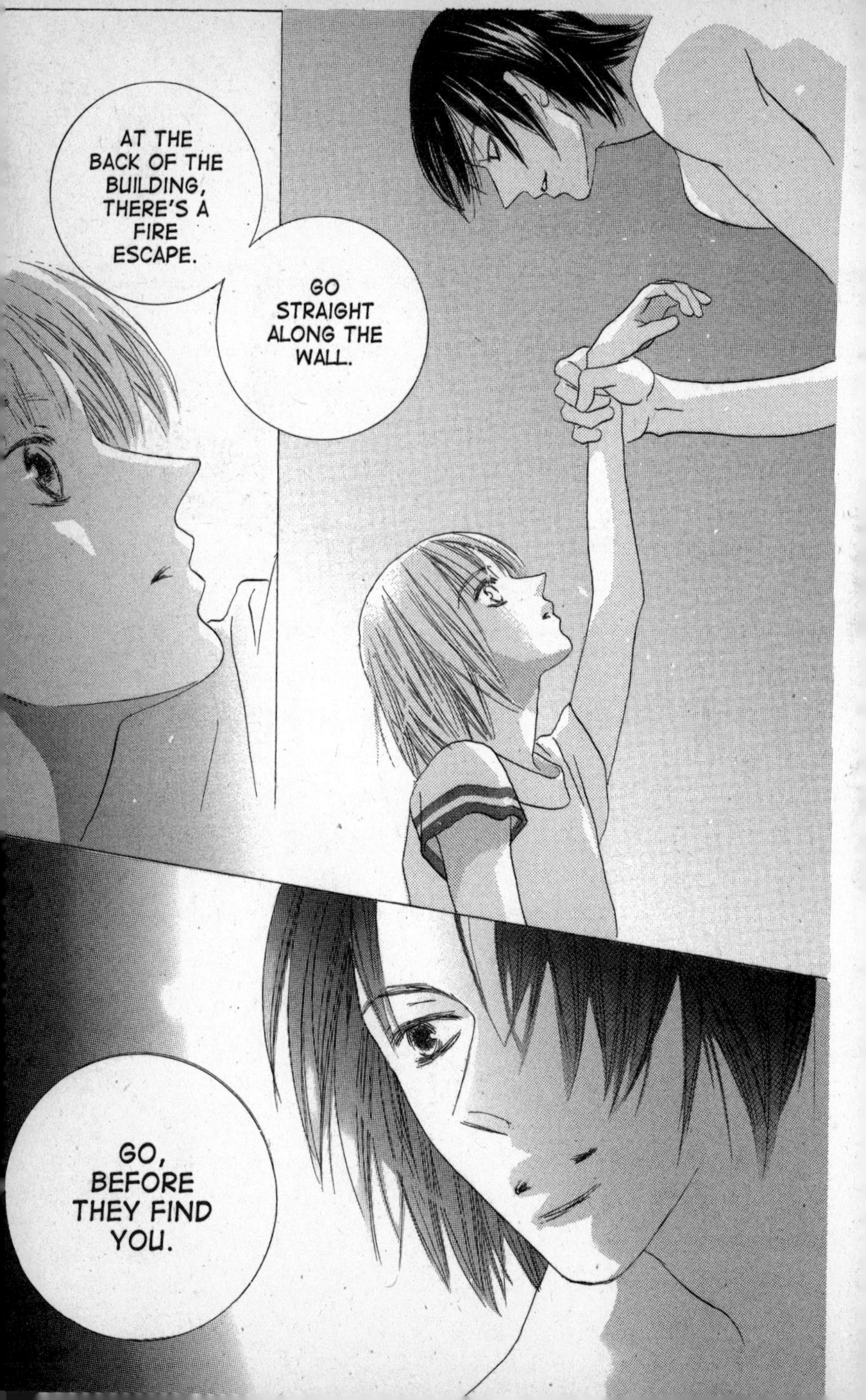
AT THE BACK OF THE BUILDING, THERE'S A FIRE ESCAPE.
GO STRAIGHT ALONG THE WALL.
GO, BEFORE THEY FIND YOU.

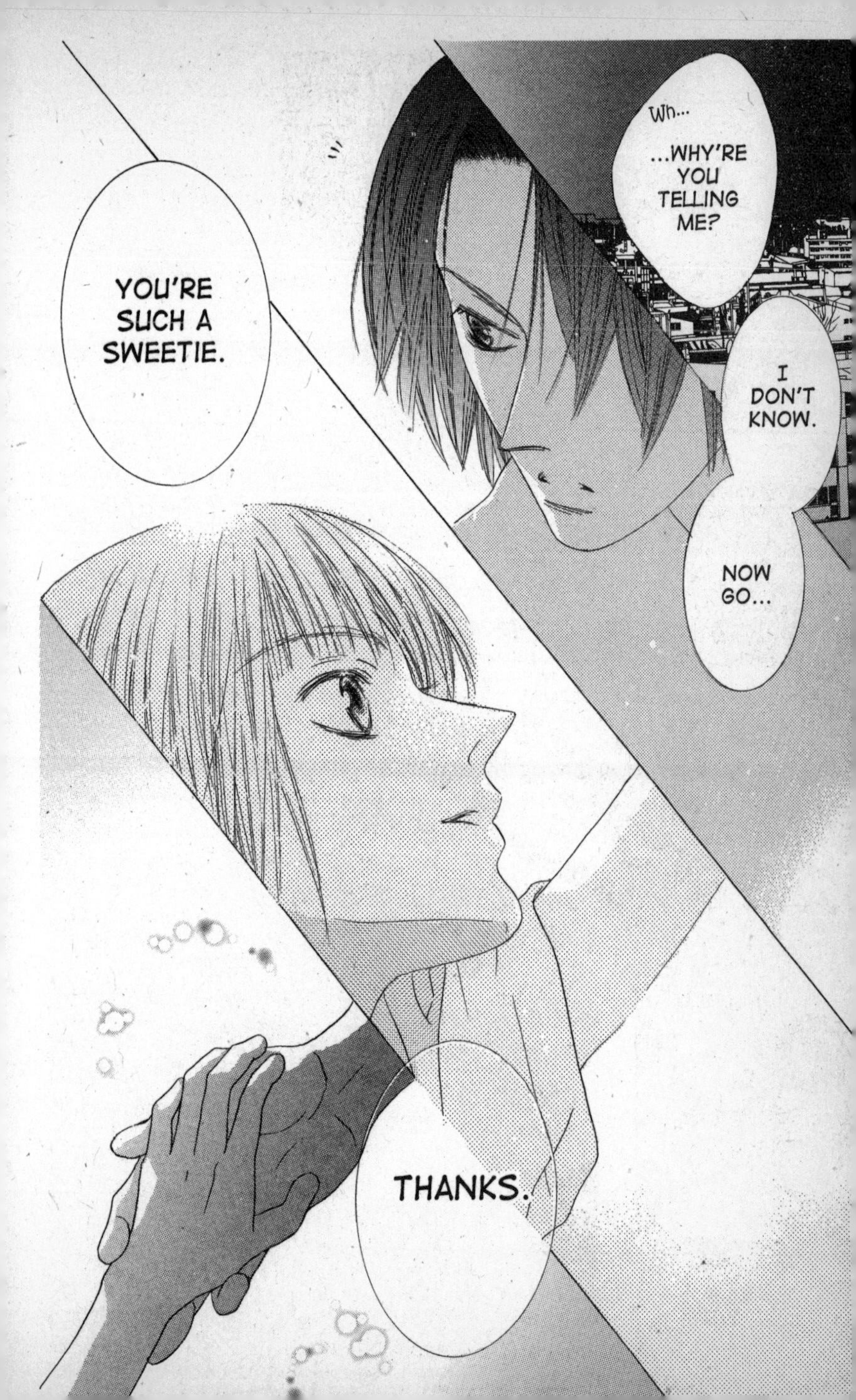
Wh...
...WHY'RE YOU TELLING ME?
I DON'T KNOW.
NOW GO...
YOU'RE SUCH A SWEETIE.
THANKS.

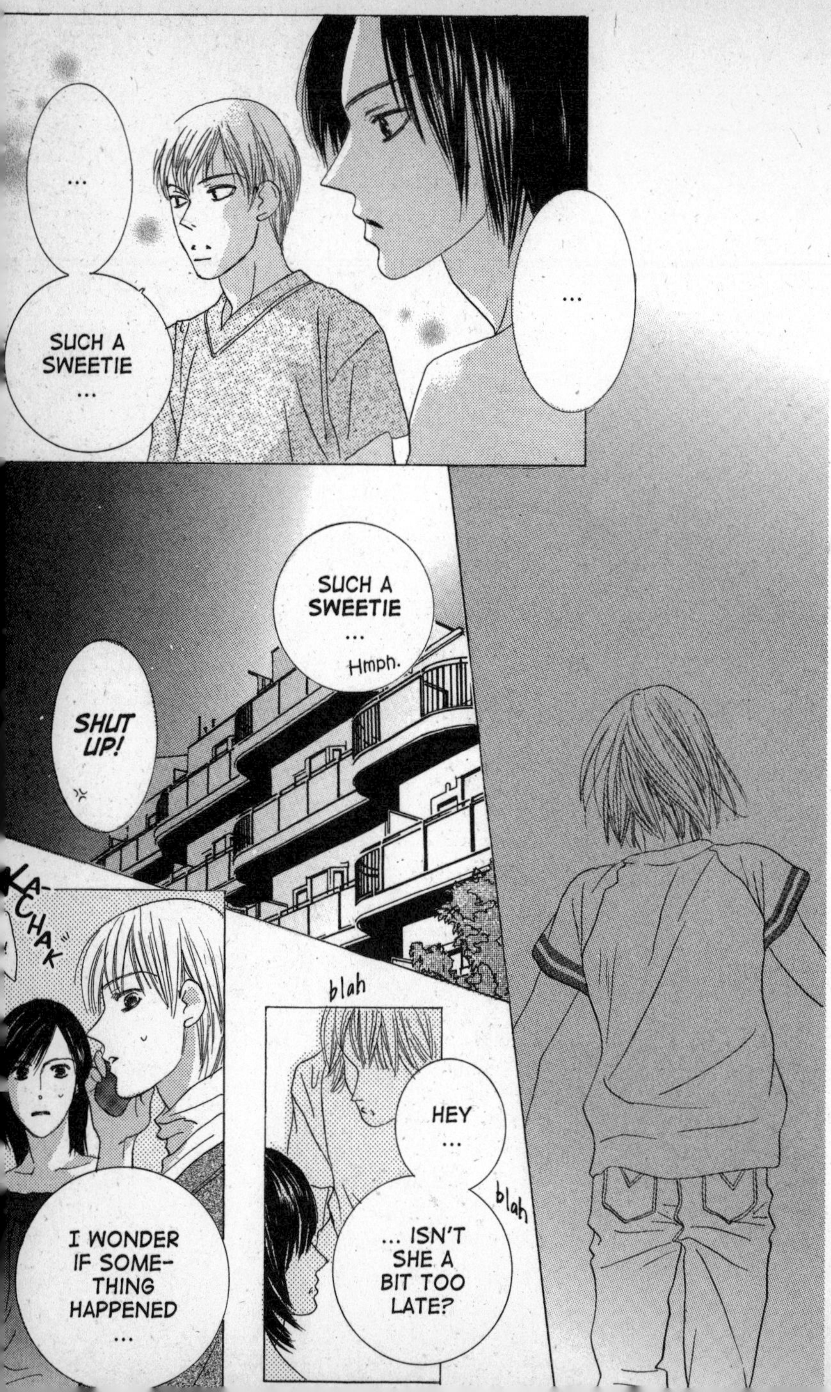
...
...
SUCH A SWEETIE ...
SUCH A SWEETIE ...
Hmph.
SHUT UP!
blah
HEY ...
blah
... ISN'T SHE A BIT TOO LATE?
KA-CHAK
I WONDER IF SOME-THING HAPPENED ...

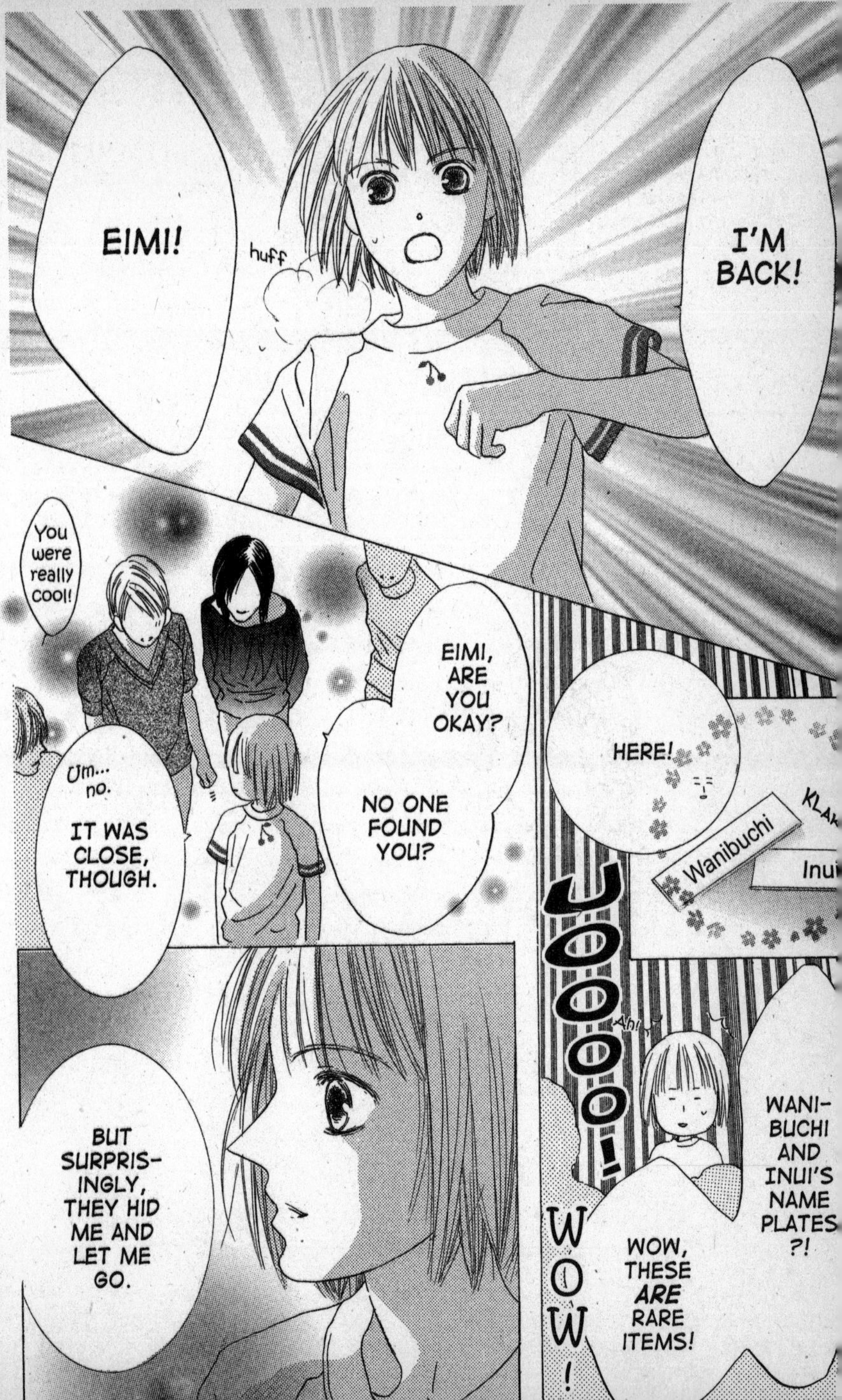
I'M BACK!
huff
EIMI!
EIMI, ARE YOU OKAY?
NO ONE FOUND YOU?
You were really cool!
Um... no.
IT WAS CLOSE, THOUGH.
BUT SURPRIS-INGLY, THEY HID ME AND LET ME GO.
HERE!
KLA
Wanibuchi
Inui
WOOOOO!
WOW!
Ah!
WANI-BUCHI AND INUI'S NAME PLATES?!
WOW, THESE ARE RARE ITEMS!

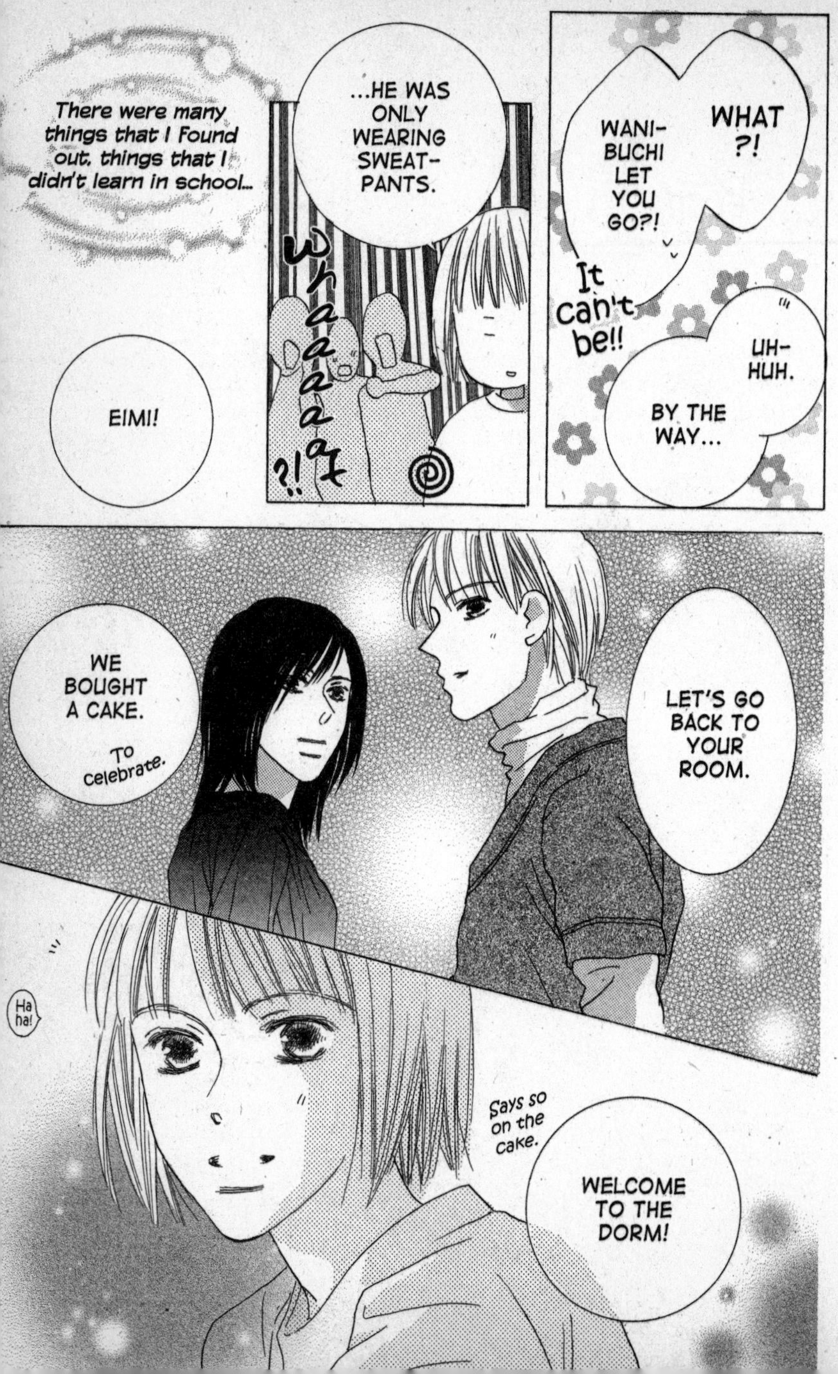
WHAT?!
WANI-BUCHI LET YOU GO?!
It can't be!!
UH-HUH.
BY THE WAY...
...HE WAS ONLY WEARING SWEAT-PANTS.
Whaaaaaat?!
There were many things that I found out, things that I didn't learn in school...
EIMI!
LET'S GO BACK TO YOUR ROOM.
WE BOUGHT A CAKE.
To celebrate.
Ha ha!
Says so on the cake.
WELCOME TO THE DORM!

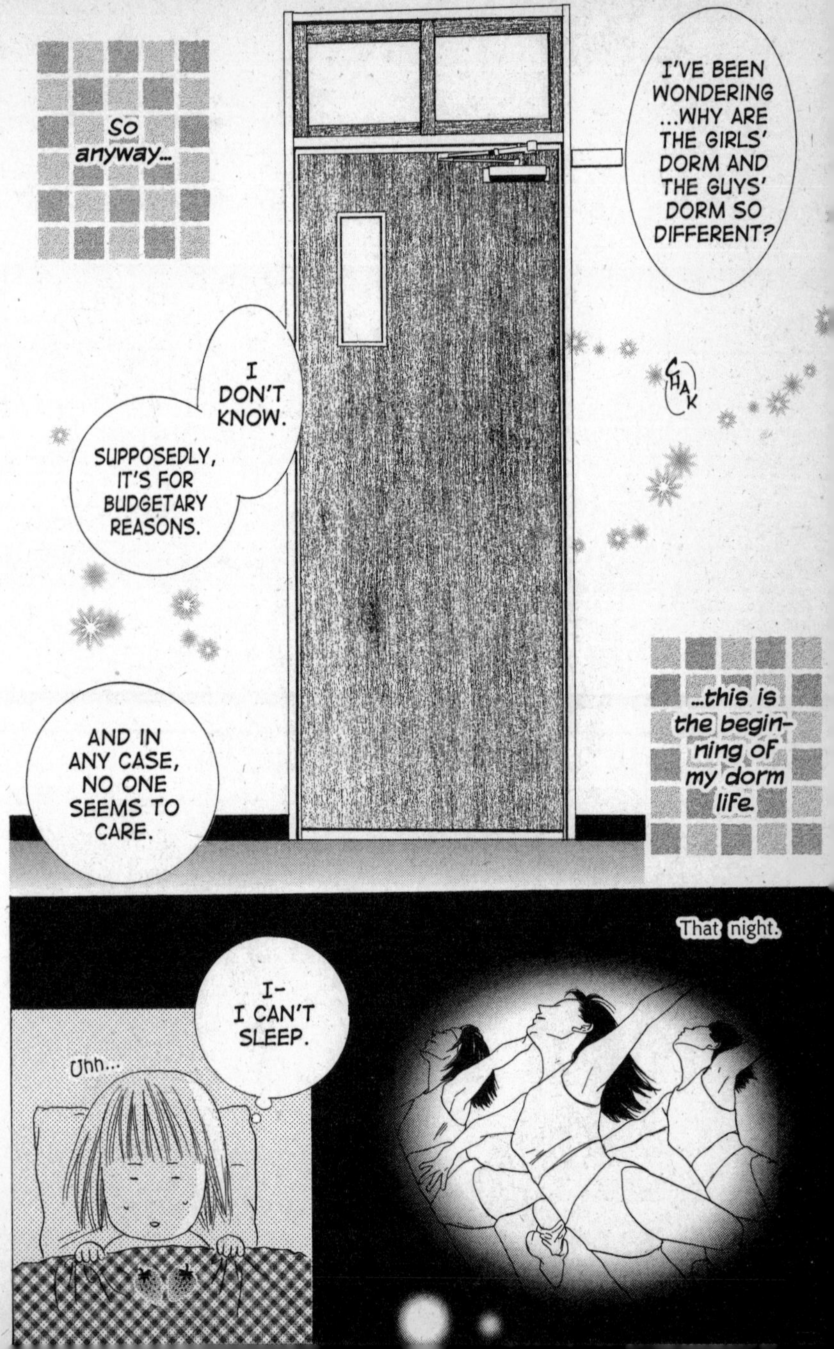
I'VE BEEN WONDERING ...WHY ARE THE GIRLS' DORM AND THE GUYS' DORM SO DIFFERENT?
CHAK
I DON'T KNOW.
SUPPOSEDLY, IT'S FOR BUDGETARY REASONS.
AND IN ANY CASE, NO ONE SEEMS TO CARE.
So anyway...
...this is the begin-ning of my dorm life.
That night.
I- I CAN'T SLEEP.
Uhh...

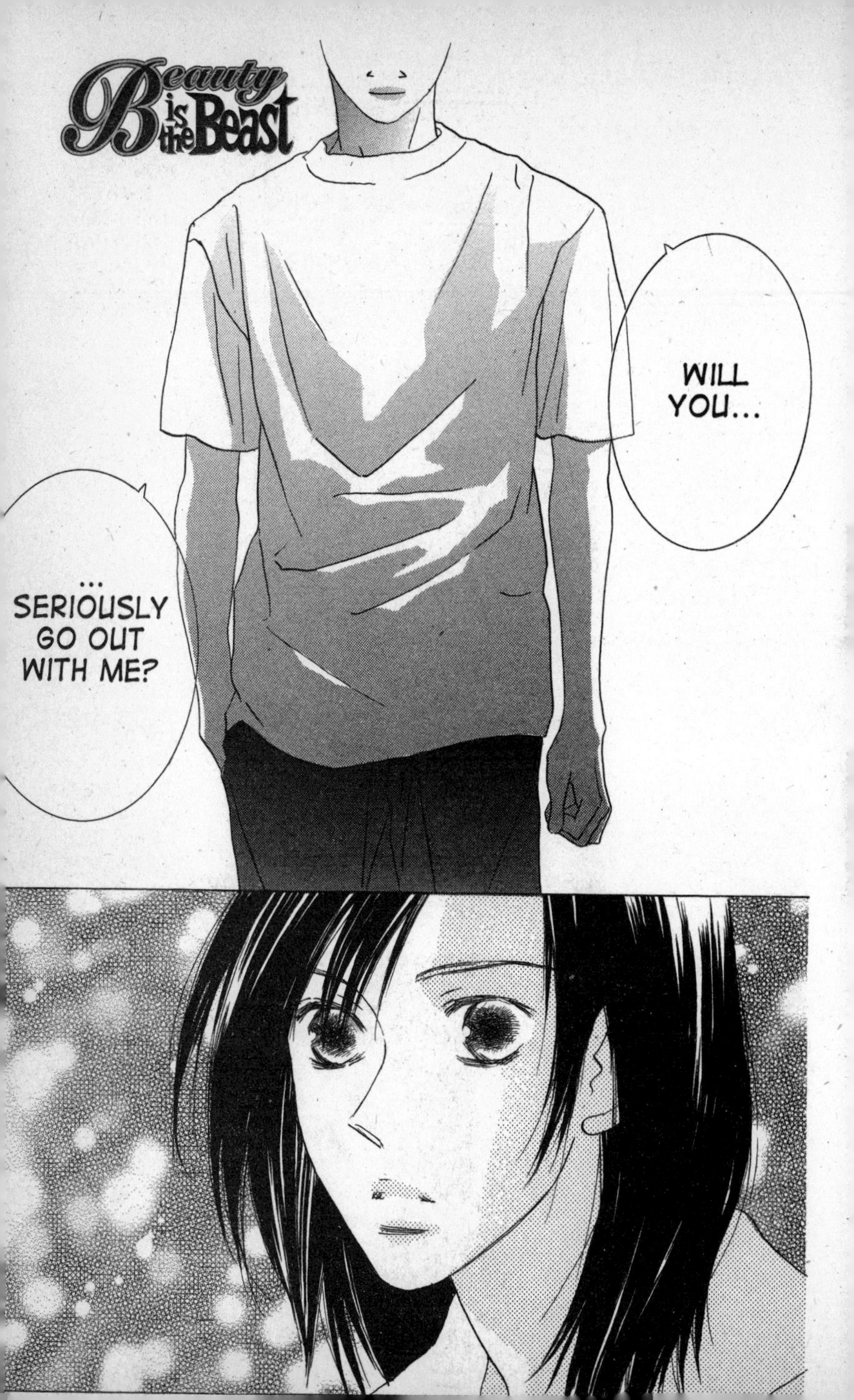
Beauty is the Beast
WILL YOU...
...SERIOUSLY GO OUT WITH ME?

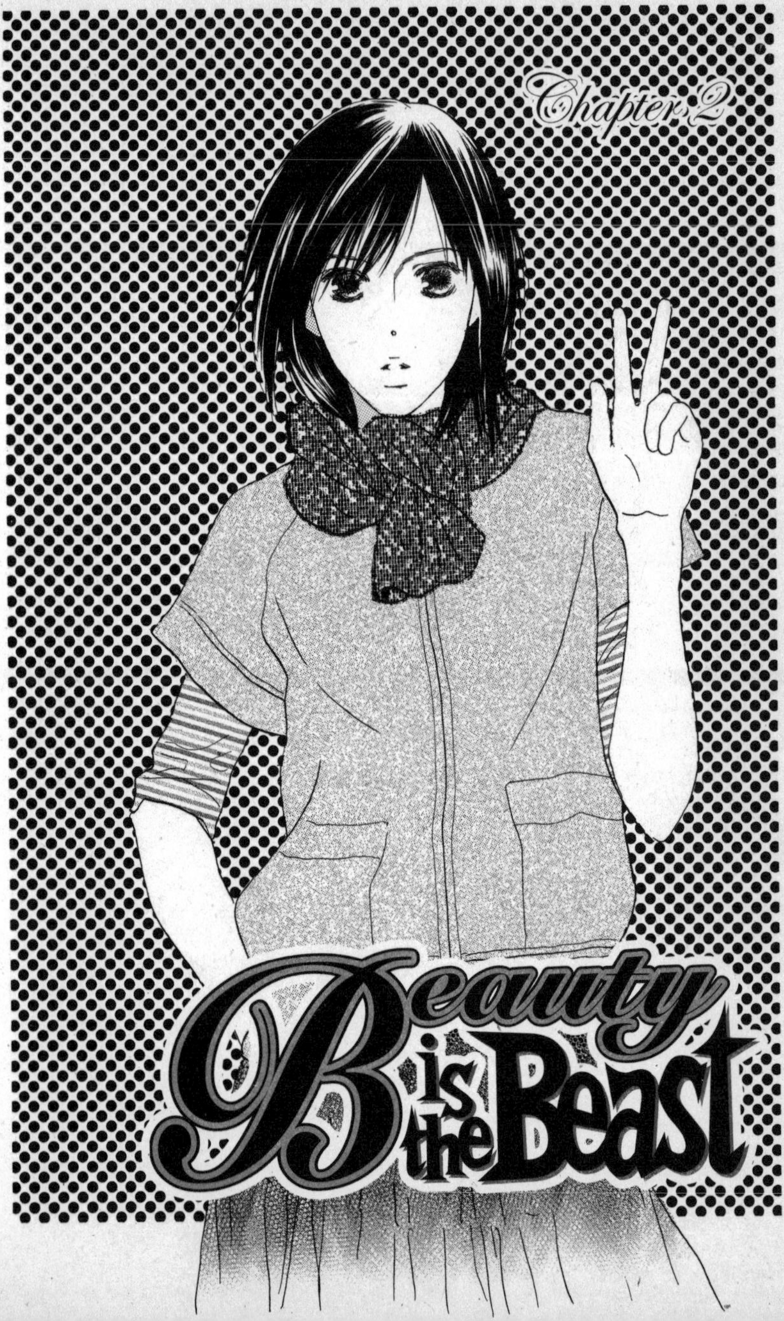
Chapter 2
Beauty is the Beast

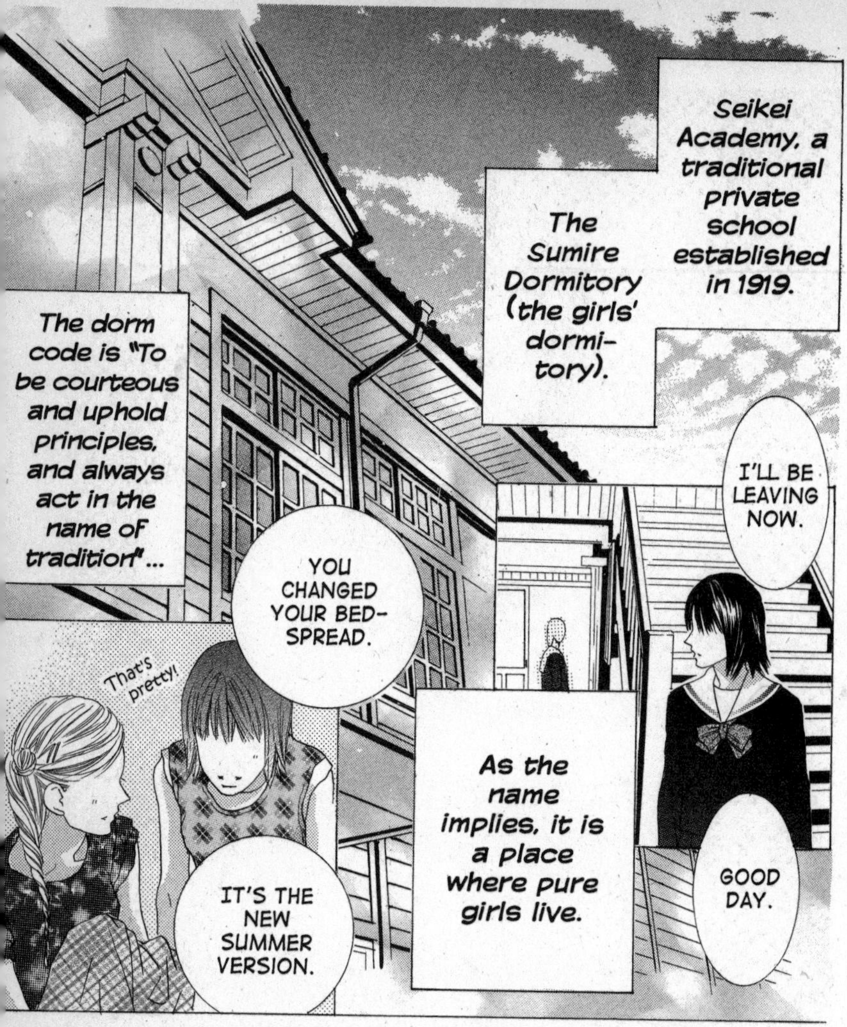
Seikei Academy, a traditional private school established in 1919.
The Sumire Dormitory (the girls' dormitory).
The dorm code is "To be courteous and uphold principles, and always act in the name of tradition"...
I'LL BE LEAVING NOW.
GOOD DAY.
As the name implies, it is a place where pure girls live.
YOU CHANGED YOUR BED-SPREAD.
That's pretty!
IT'S THE NEW SUMMER VERSION.

A Must-have for Dorm Life 1: Washbowl

It's useful when taking baths, when washing your face, and doing your laundry. ☆

LaLa decided to make some goodies to commemorate the start of this series. I wanted them to make a washbowl, but I thought, "Would young girls really want a washbowl?" (I should've realized it earlier.) And so my suggestion was scrapped. If you're thinking "What?! I want a washbowl!!" please let me know. (☺)

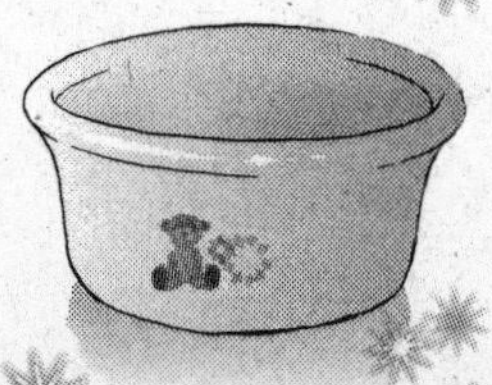

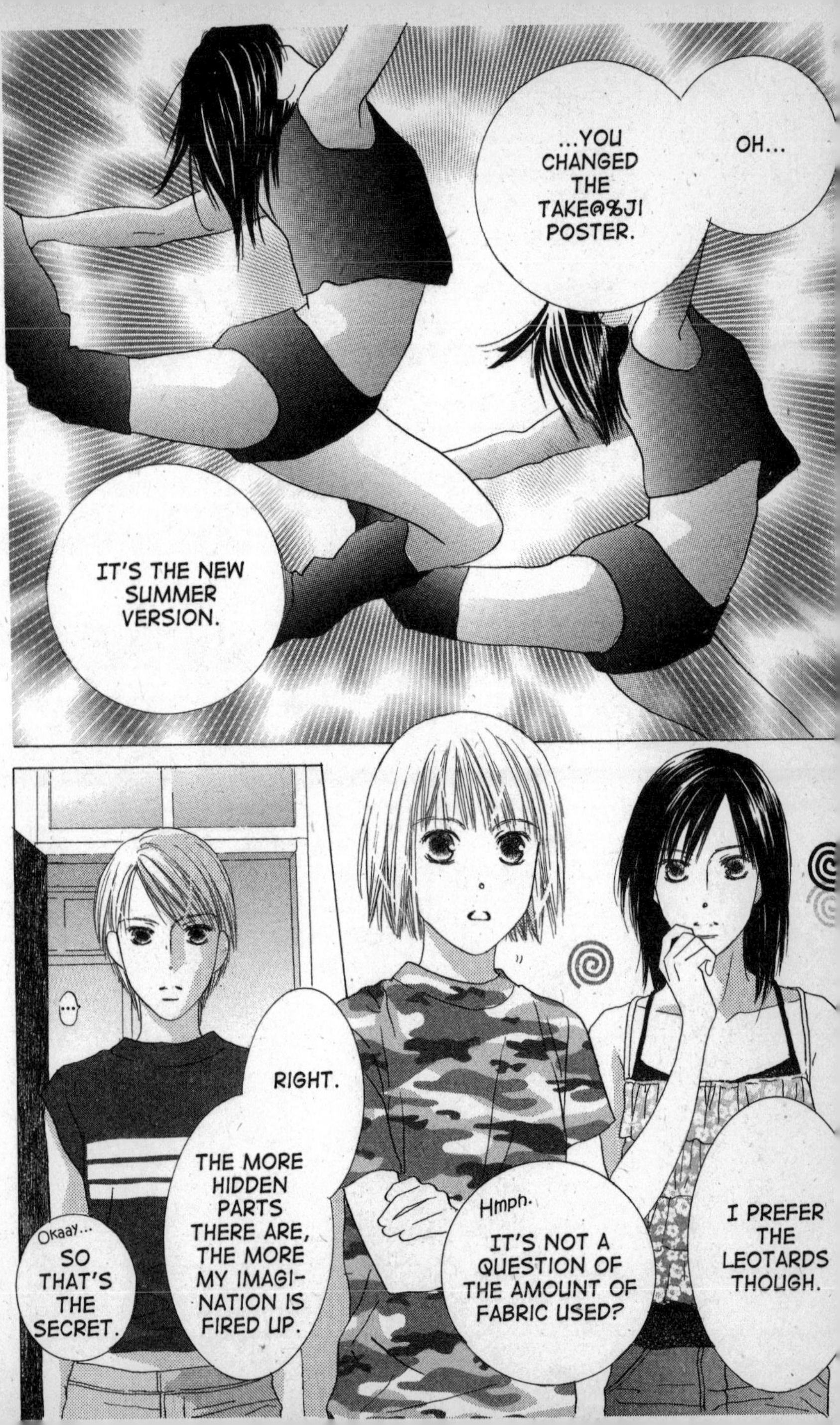

OH...
...YOU CHANGED THE TAKE@%JI POSTER.
IT'S THE NEW SUMMER VERSION.
I PREFER THE LEOTARDS THOUGH.
Hmph.
IT'S NOT A QUESTION OF THE AMOUNT OF FABRIC USED?
RIGHT.
THE MORE HIDDEN PARTS THERE ARE, THE MORE MY IMAGINATION IS FIRED UP.
...
Okaay...
SO THAT'S THE SECRET.

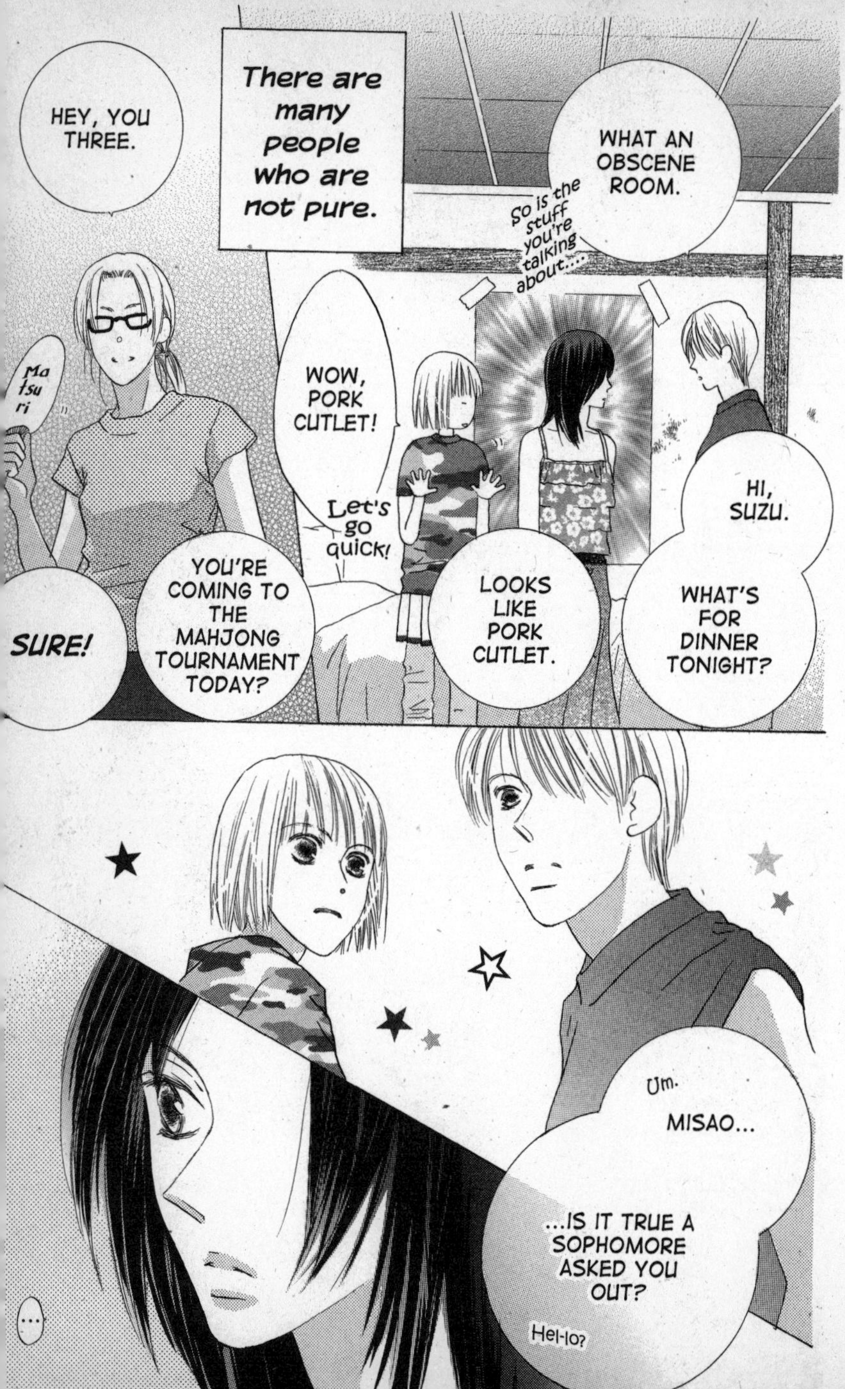
WHAT AN OBSCENE ROOM.
So is the stuff you're talking about...
There are many people who are not pure.
HEY, YOU THREE.
Matsuri
HI, SUZU.
WHAT'S FOR DINNER TONIGHT?
LOOKS LIKE PORK CUTLET.
WOW, PORK CUTLET!
Let's go quick!
YOU'RE COMING TO THE MAHJONG TOURNAMENT TODAY?
SURE!
Um.
MISAO...
...IS IT TRUE A SOPHOMORE ASKED YOU OUT?
Hel-lo?
...

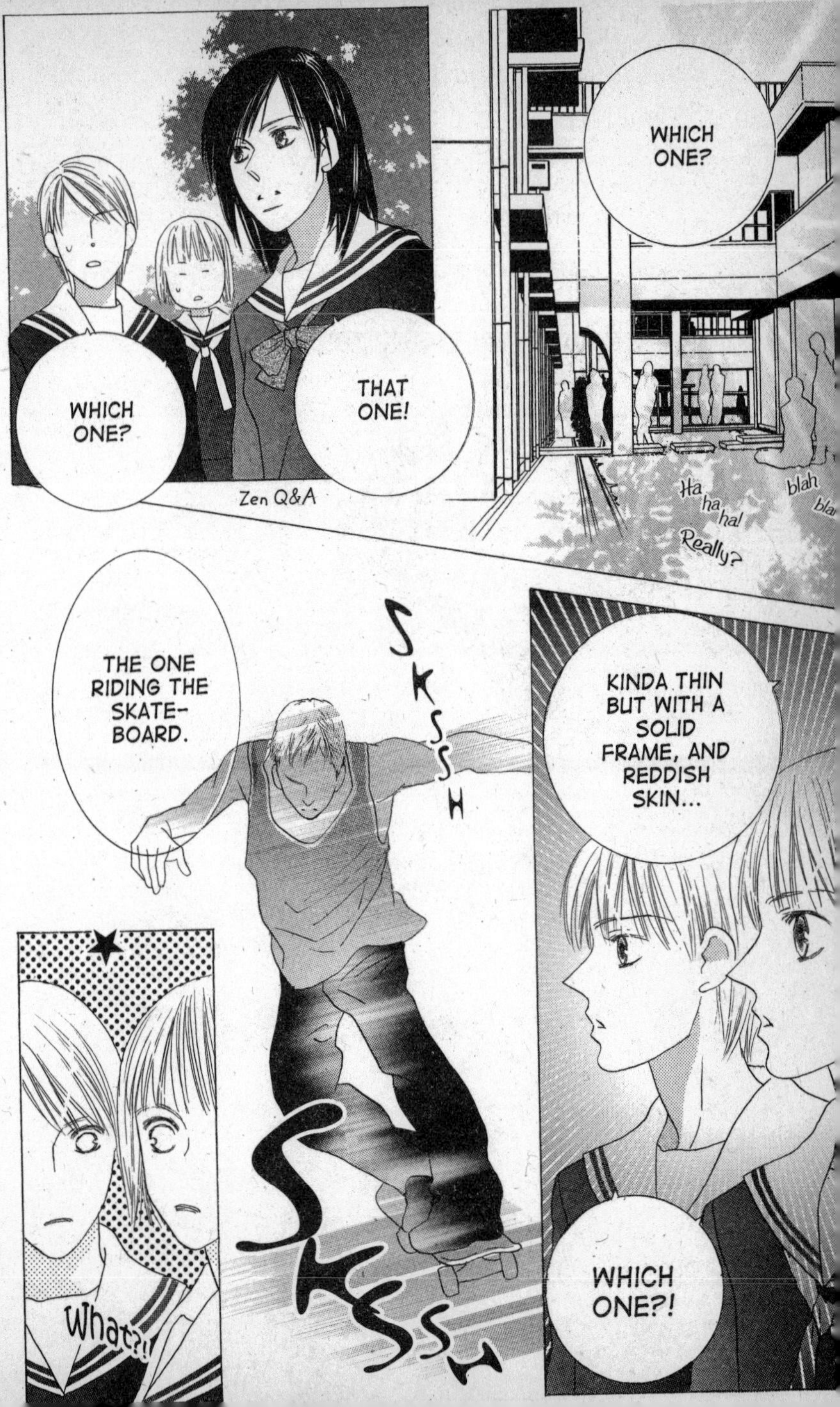
WHICH ONE?
Ha ha ha!
Really?
blah
THAT ONE!
WHICH ONE?
Zen Q&A
KINDA THIN BUT WITH A SOLID FRAME, AND REDDISH SKIN...
WHICH ONE?!
THE ONE RIDING THE SKATE-BOARD.
SKSSH
SKSSH
What?!

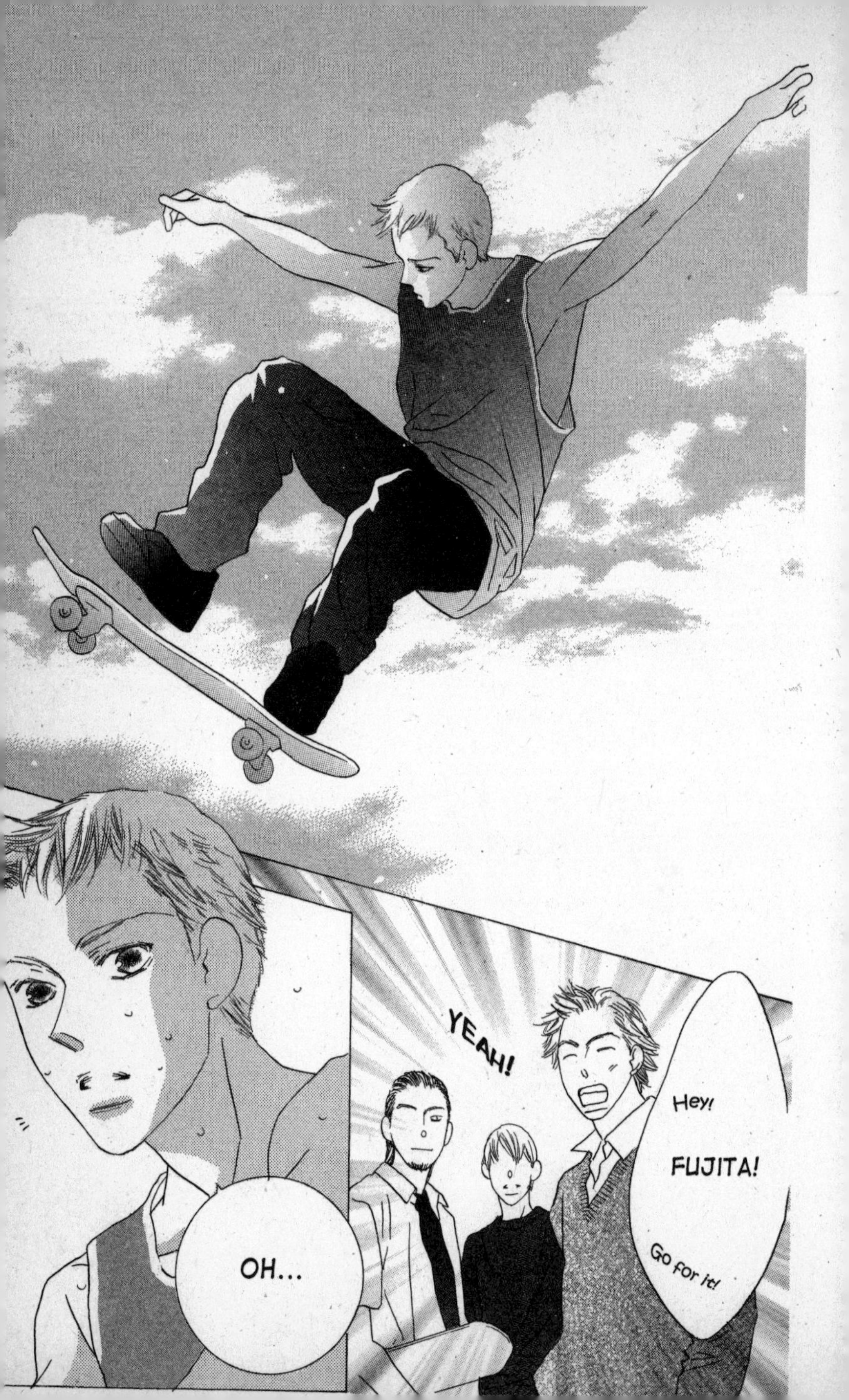
Hey! FUJITA! Go for it!
YEAH!
OH...

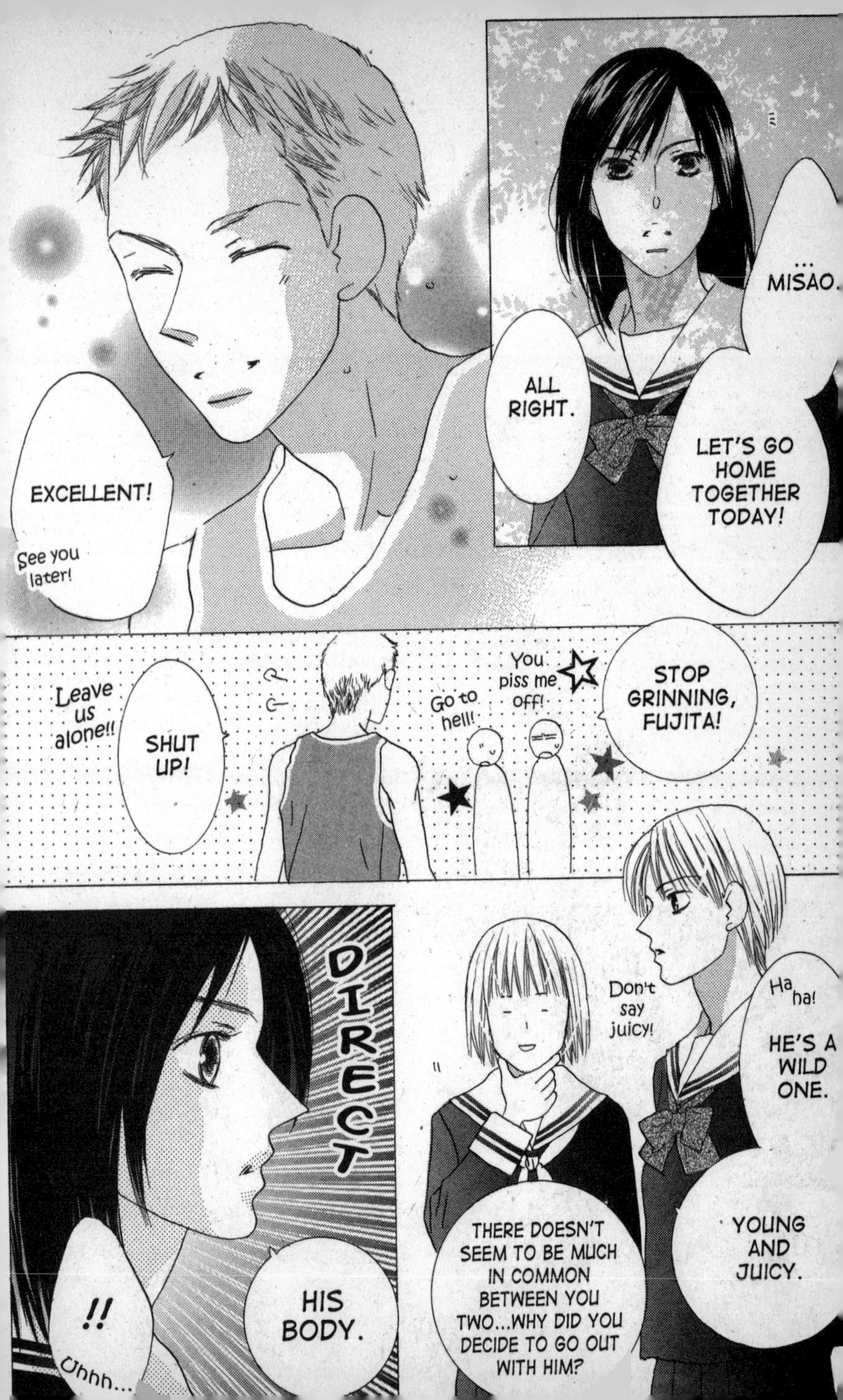

...MISAO.
LET'S GO HOME TOGETHER TODAY!
ALL RIGHT.
EXCELLENT!
See you later!
STOP GRINNING, FUJITA!
You piss me off!
Go to hell!
SHUT UP!
Leave us alone!!
Ha ha!
HE'S A WILD ONE.
YOUNG AND JUICY.
Don't say juicy!
THERE DOESN'T SEEM TO BE MUCH IN COMMON BETWEEN YOU TWO...WHY DID YOU DECIDE TO GO OUT WITH HIM?
DIRECT
HIS BODY.
!!
Uhhh...

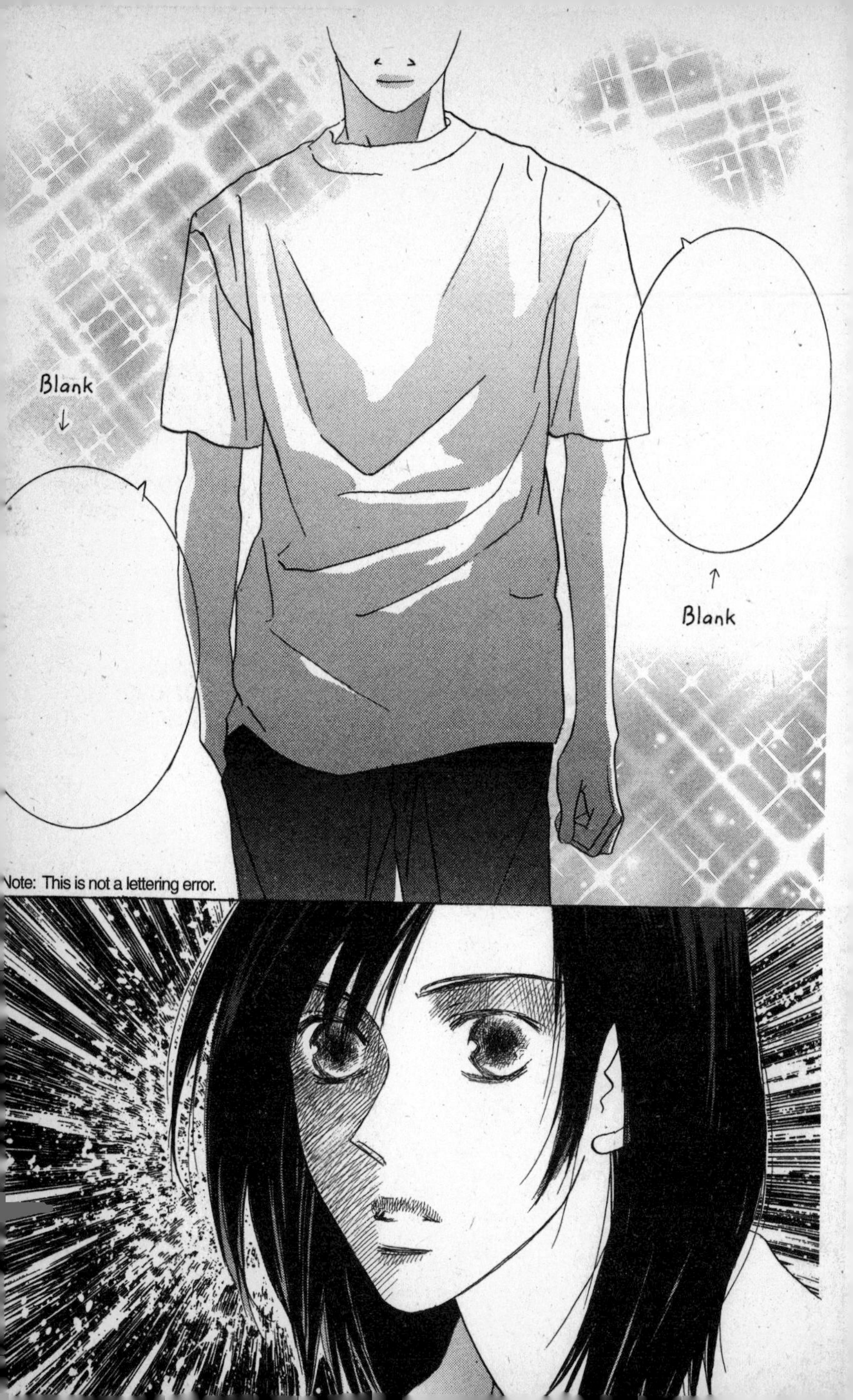
Blank
Blank
Note: This is not a lettering error.

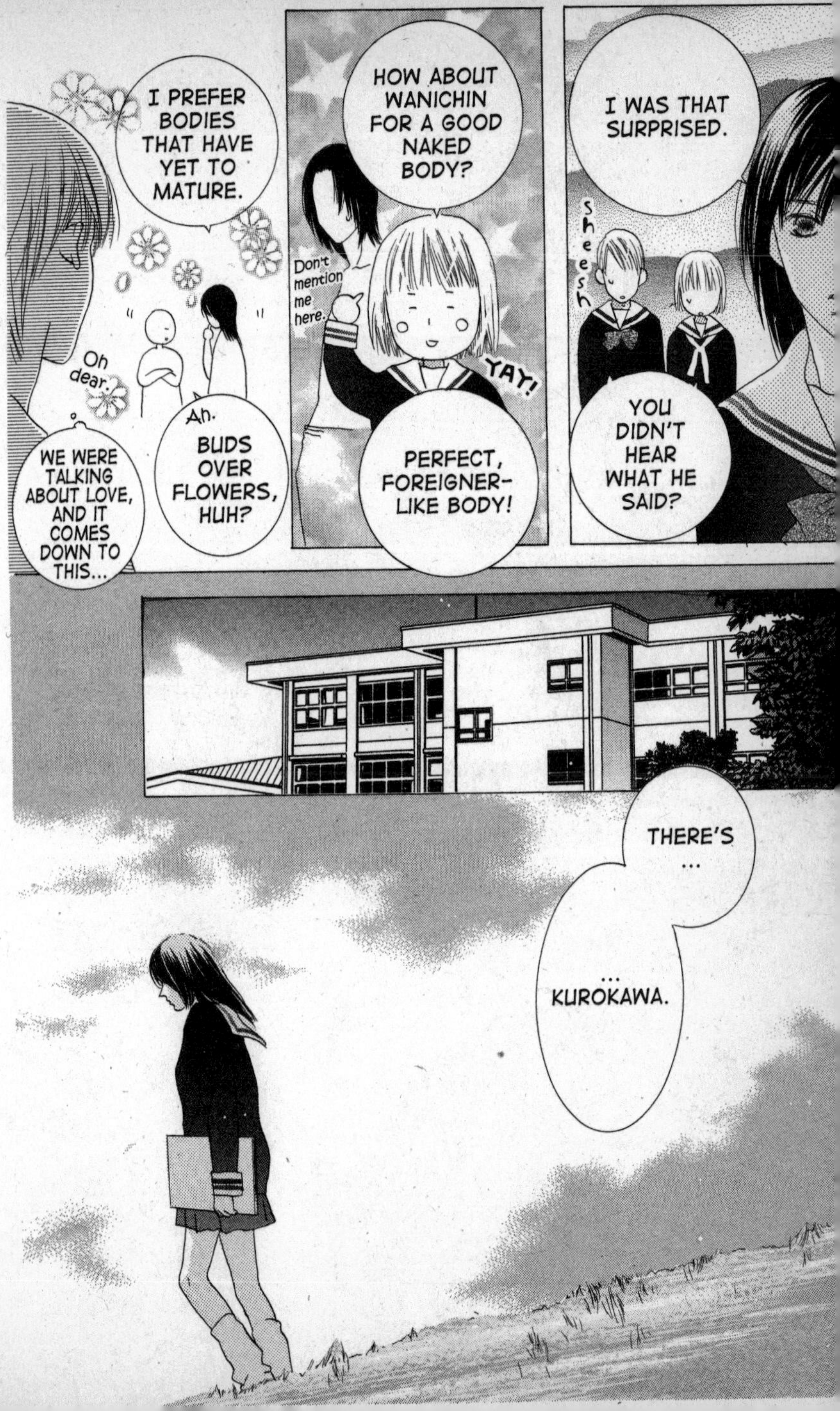
I WAS THAT SURPRISED.
Sheesh
YOU DIDN'T HEAR WHAT HE SAID?
HOW ABOUT WANICHIN FOR A GOOD NAKED BODY?
Don't mention me here.
YAY!
PERFECT, FOREIGNER-LIKE BODY!
I PREFER BODIES THAT HAVE YET TO MATURE.
Oh dear.
Ah.
BUDS OVER FLOWERS, HUH?
WE WERE TALKING ABOUT LOVE, AND IT COMES DOWN TO THIS...
THERE'S ...
... KUROKAWA.

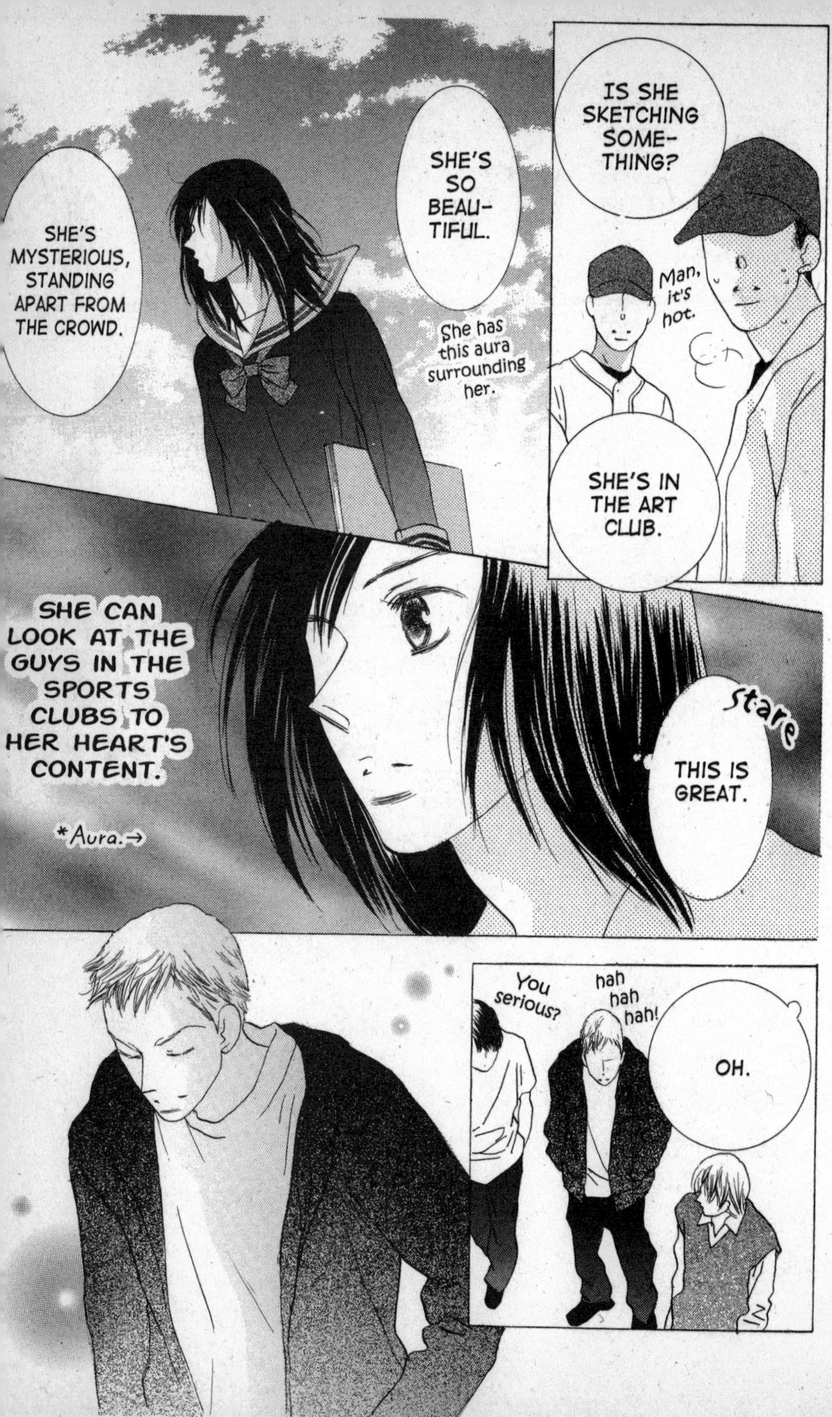
IS SHE SKETCHING SOMETHING?
Man, it's hot.
SHE'S IN THE ART CLUB.
SHE'S SO BEAUTIFUL.
She has this aura surrounding her.
SHE'S MYSTERIOUS, STANDING APART FROM THE CROWD.
Stare
THIS IS GREAT.
SHE CAN LOOK AT THE GUYS IN THE SPORTS CLUBS TO HER HEART'S CONTENT.
*Aura.→
OH.
hah hah hah!
You serious?

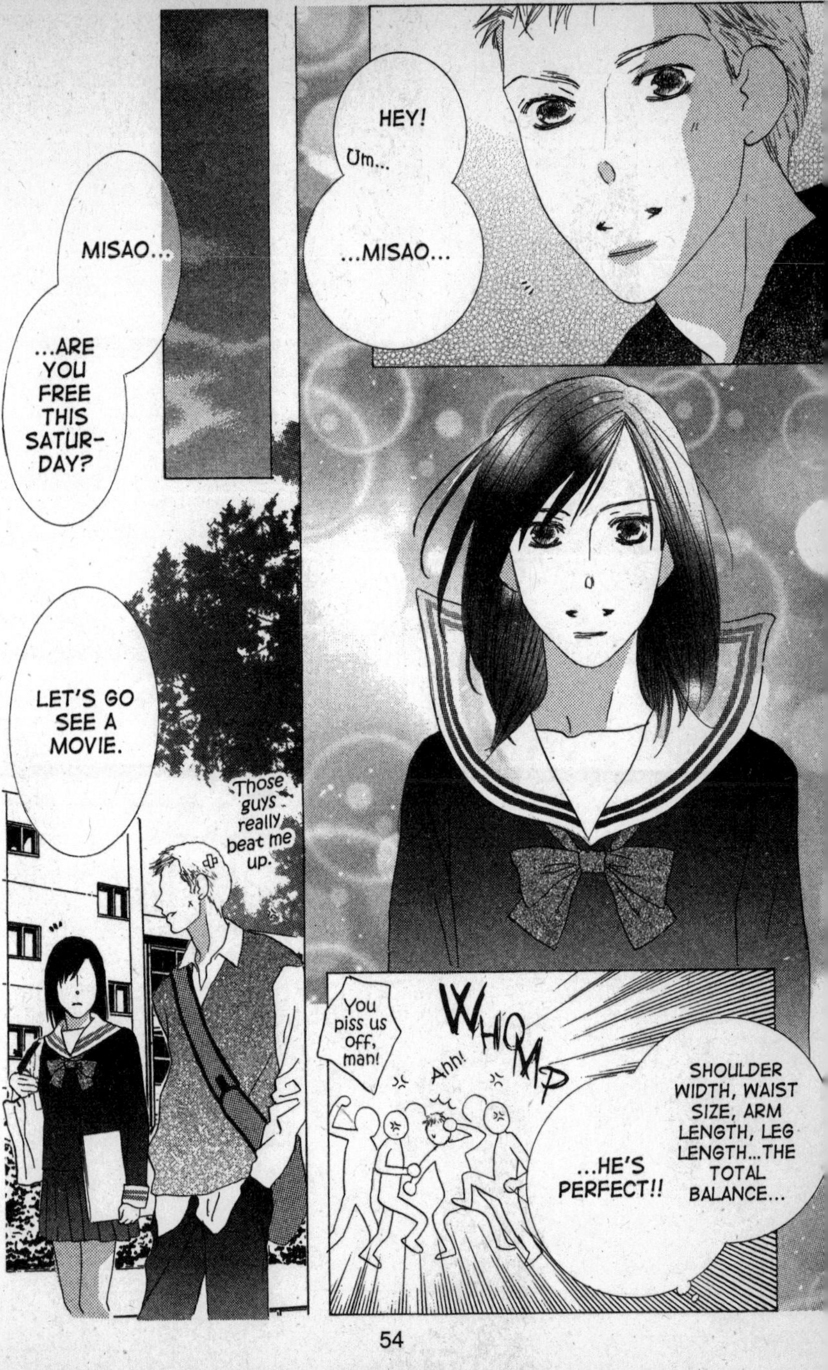
HEY!
Um...
...MISAO...
MISAO...
...ARE YOU FREE THIS SATUR-DAY?
LET'S GO SEE A MOVIE.
Those guys really beat me up.
SHOULDER WIDTH, WAIST SIZE, ARM LENGTH, LEG LENGTH...THE TOTAL BALANCE...
...HE'S PERFECT!!
WHOMP
You piss us off, man!
Ahh!

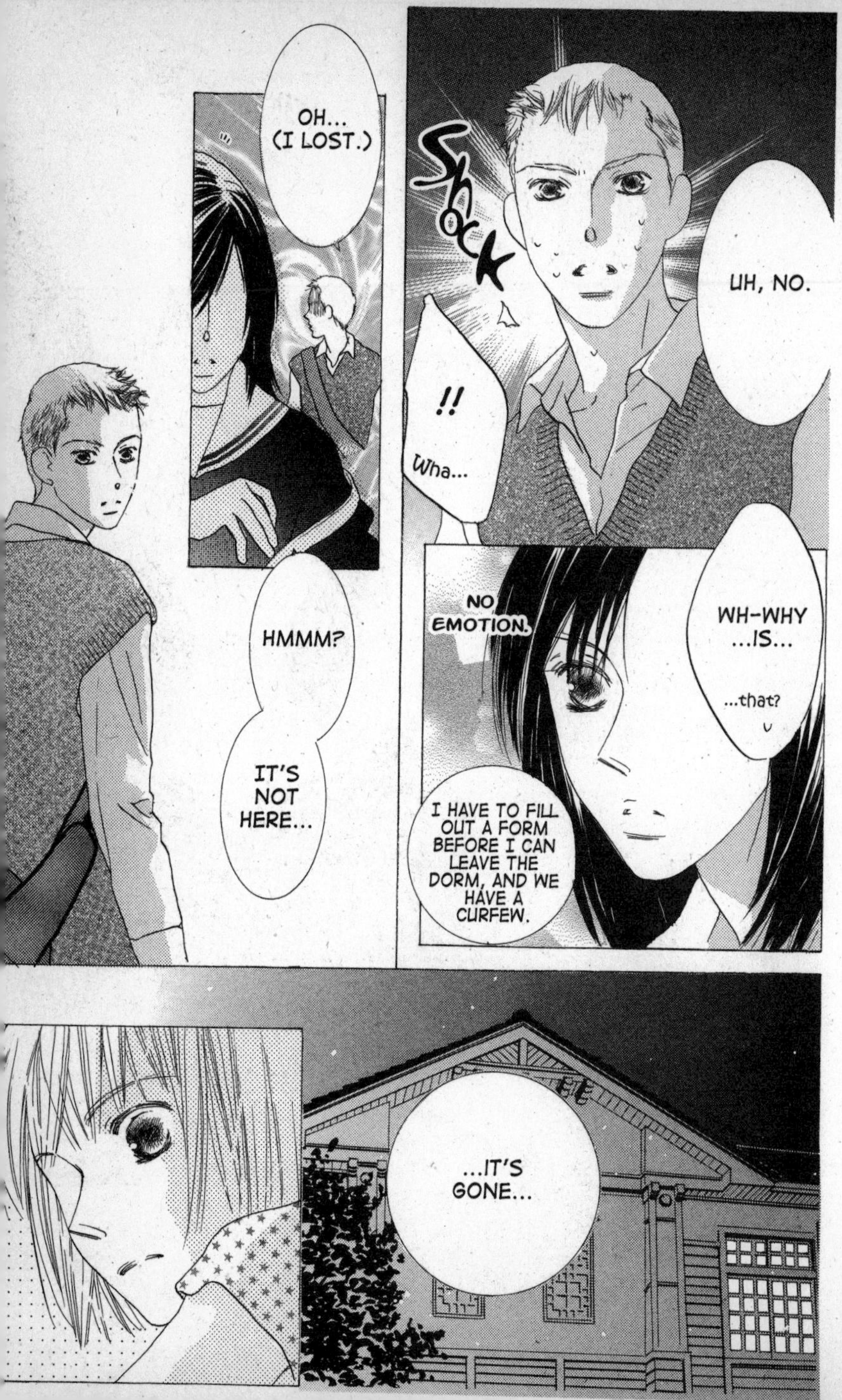
UH, NO.
SHOCK
!!
Wha...
OH... (I LOST.)
WH-WHY ...IS...
...that?
NO EMOTION.
I HAVE TO FILL OUT A FORM BEFORE I CAN LEAVE THE DORM, AND WE HAVE A CURFEW.
HMMM?
IT'S NOT HERE...
...IT'S GONE...

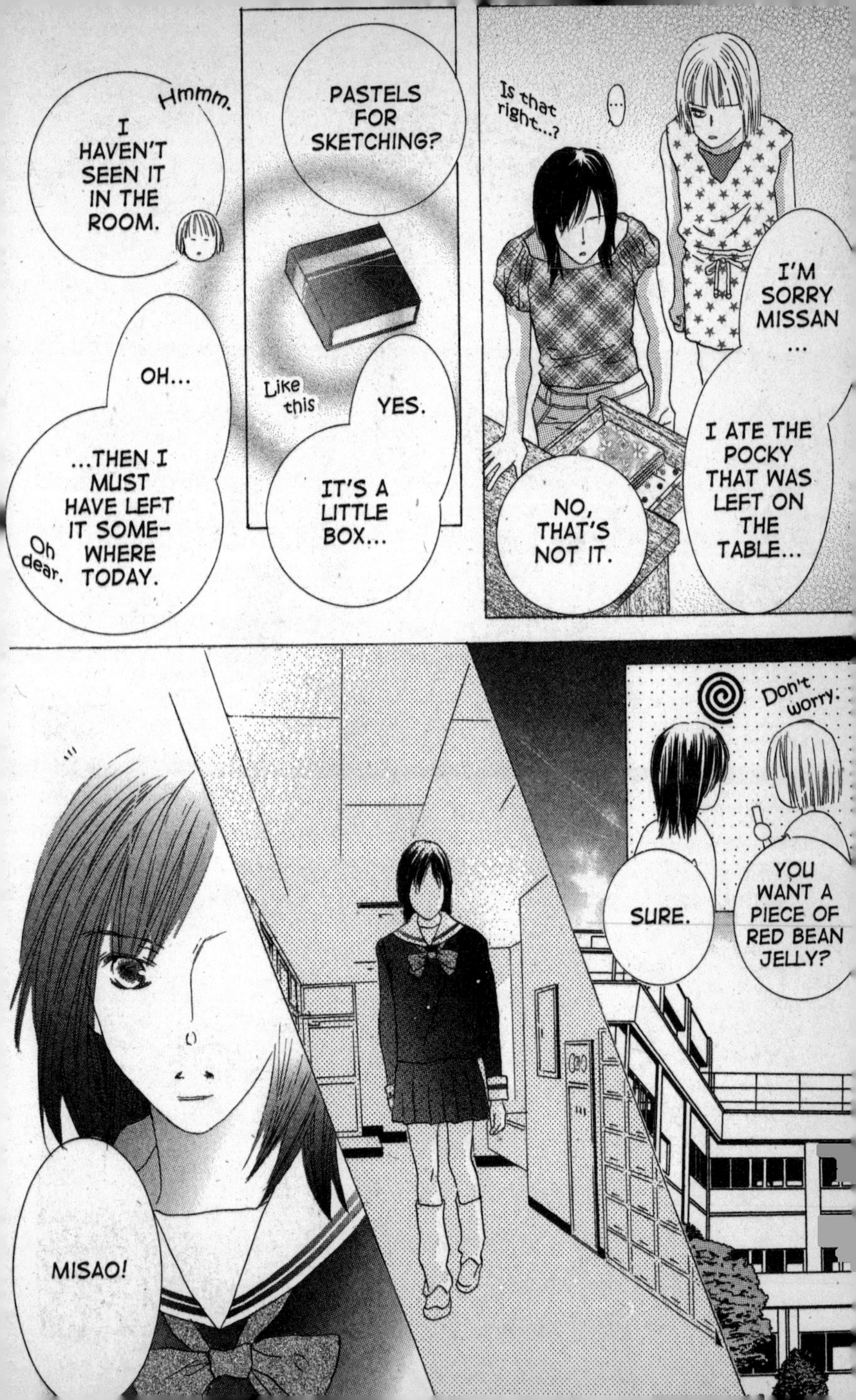
I'M SORRY MISSAN ...
I ATE THE POCKY THAT WAS LEFT ON THE TABLE...
NO, THAT'S NOT IT.
...
Is that right...?
PASTELS FOR SKETCHING?
YES.
IT'S A LITTLE BOX...
Like this
Hmmm.
I HAVEN'T SEEN IT IN THE ROOM.
OH...
...THEN I MUST HAVE LEFT IT SOME-WHERE TODAY.
Oh dear.
Don't worry.
YOU WANT A PIECE OF RED BEAN JELLY?
SURE.
MISAO!

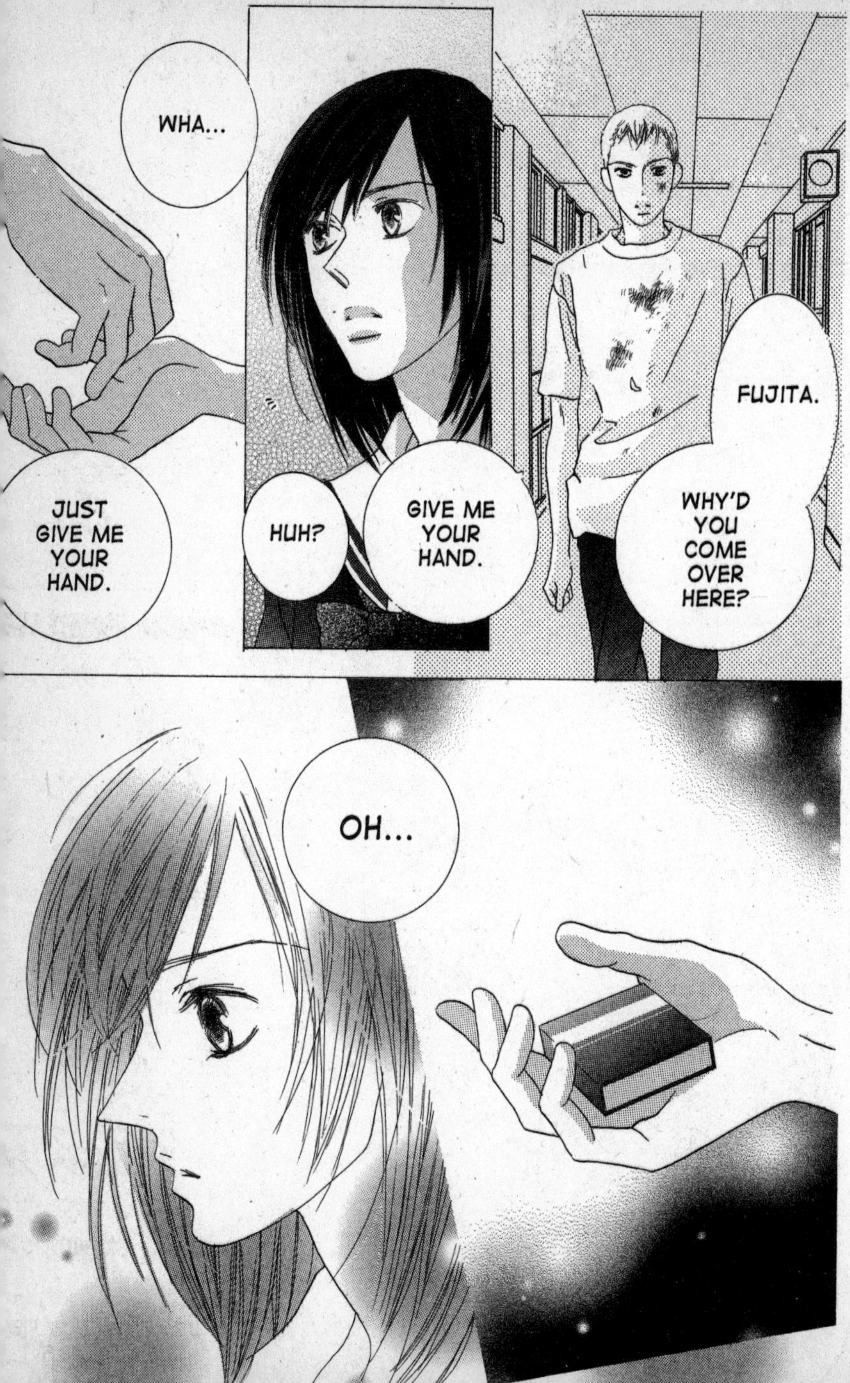
FUJITA.
WHY'D YOU COME OVER HERE?
GIVE ME YOUR HAND.
HUH?
WHA...
JUST GIVE ME YOUR HAND.
OH...

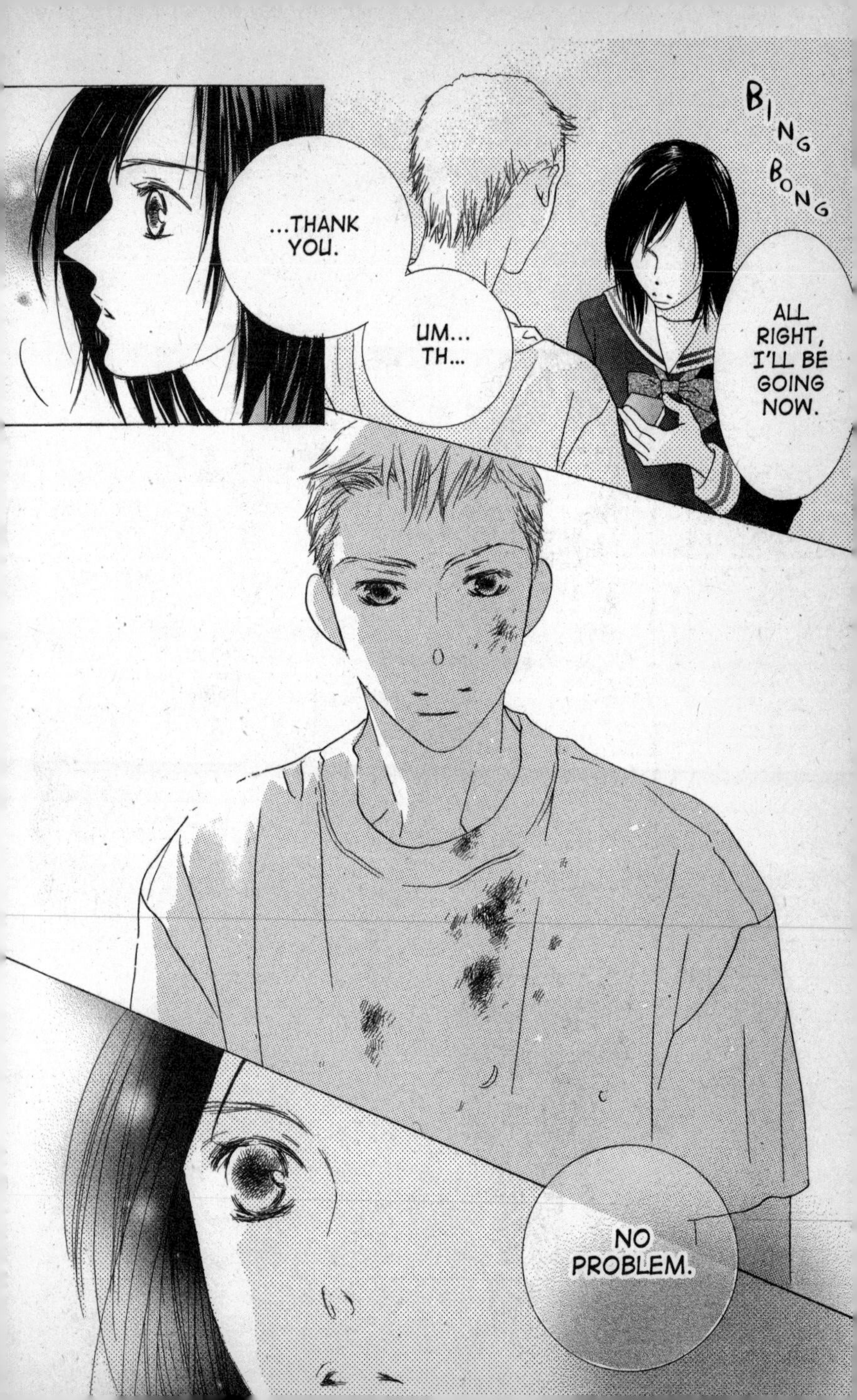
BING BONG
ALL RIGHT, I'LL BE GOING NOW.
UM... TH...
...THANK YOU.
NO PROBLEM.

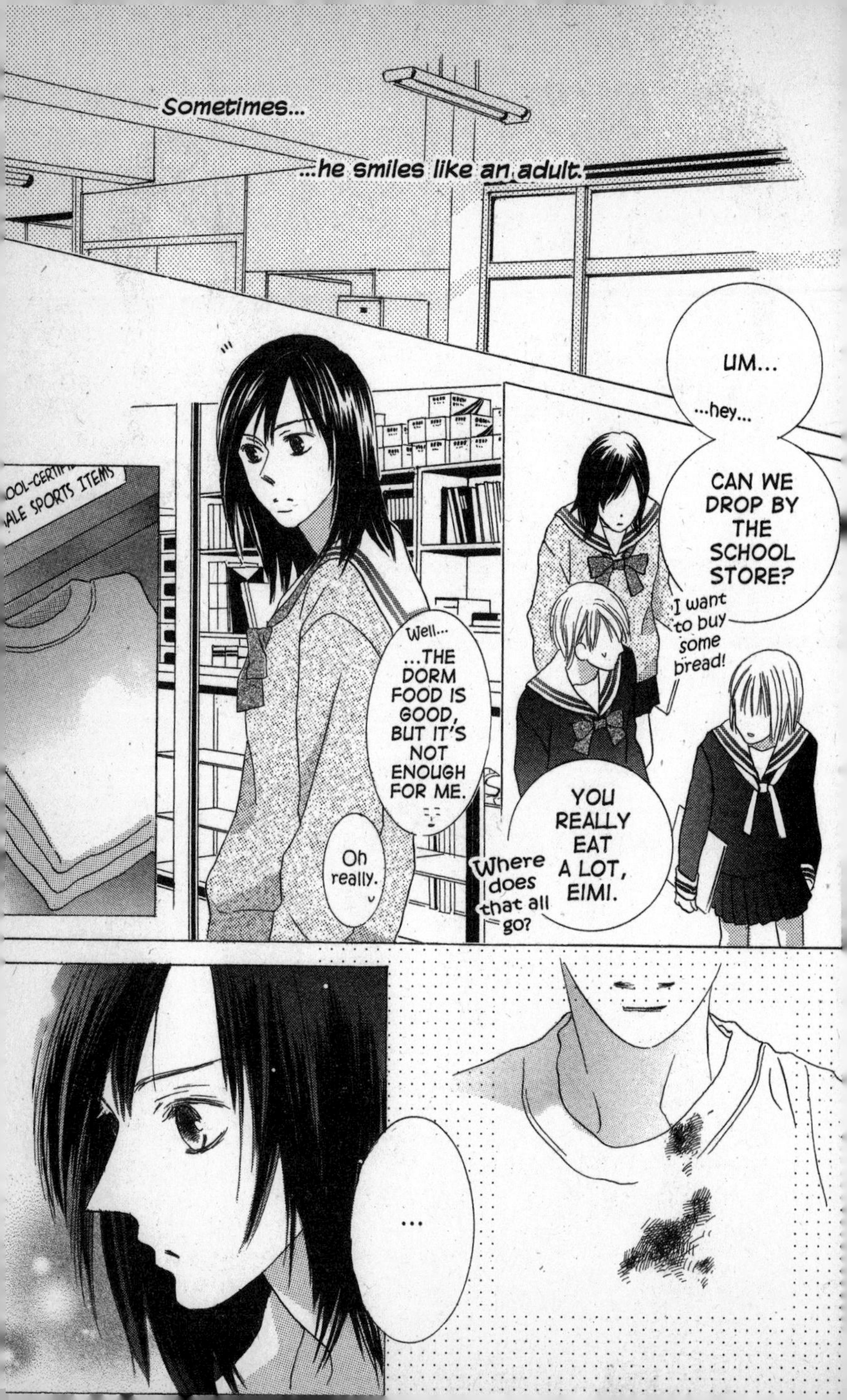
Sometimes...
...he smiles like an adult.
UM...
...hey...
CAN WE DROP BY THE SCHOOL STORE?
I want to buy some bread!
YOU REALLY EAT A LOT, EIMI.
Where does that all go?
Well...
...THE DORM FOOD IS GOOD, BUT IT'S NOT ENOUGH FOR ME.
Oh really.
...

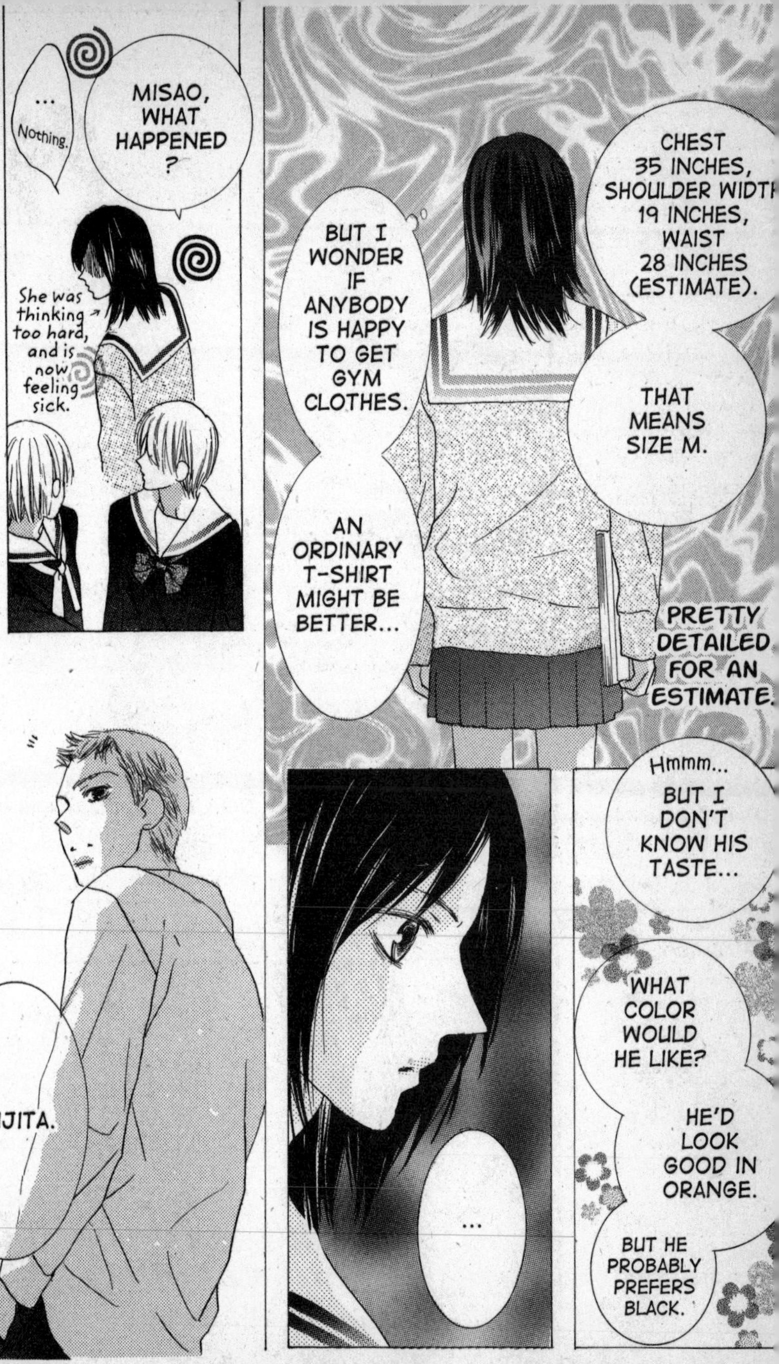
CHEST 35 INCHES, SHOULDER WIDTH 19 INCHES, WAIST 28 INCHES (ESTIMATE).
THAT MEANS SIZE M.
BUT I WONDER IF ANYBODY IS HAPPY TO GET GYM CLOTHES.
AN ORDINARY T-SHIRT MIGHT BE BETTER...
PRETTY DETAILED FOR AN ESTIMATE.
MISAO, WHAT HAPPENED?
... Nothing.
She was thinking too hard, and is now feeling sick.
Hmmm... BUT I DON'T KNOW HIS TASTE...
WHAT COLOR WOULD HE LIKE?
HE'D LOOK GOOD IN ORANGE.
BUT HE PROBABLY PREFERS BLACK.
...
FUJITA.

2

I forgot to mention earlier, but this story, "Beauty Is the Beast," was created from my experiences living in a dorm for three years in senior high school.

The original plot featured three sisters (Misao was the eldest sister, Suzu the second sister), and the story was centered on their school lives. If I'd drawn that, the manga might have turned out differently.

The dorm I lived in was pretty old. There were no air conditioners, the walls were thin, and it was a hassle living there. But I'm speechless now that I'm making a living drawing a manga based on those experiences! (↑ I'm over-reacting...)

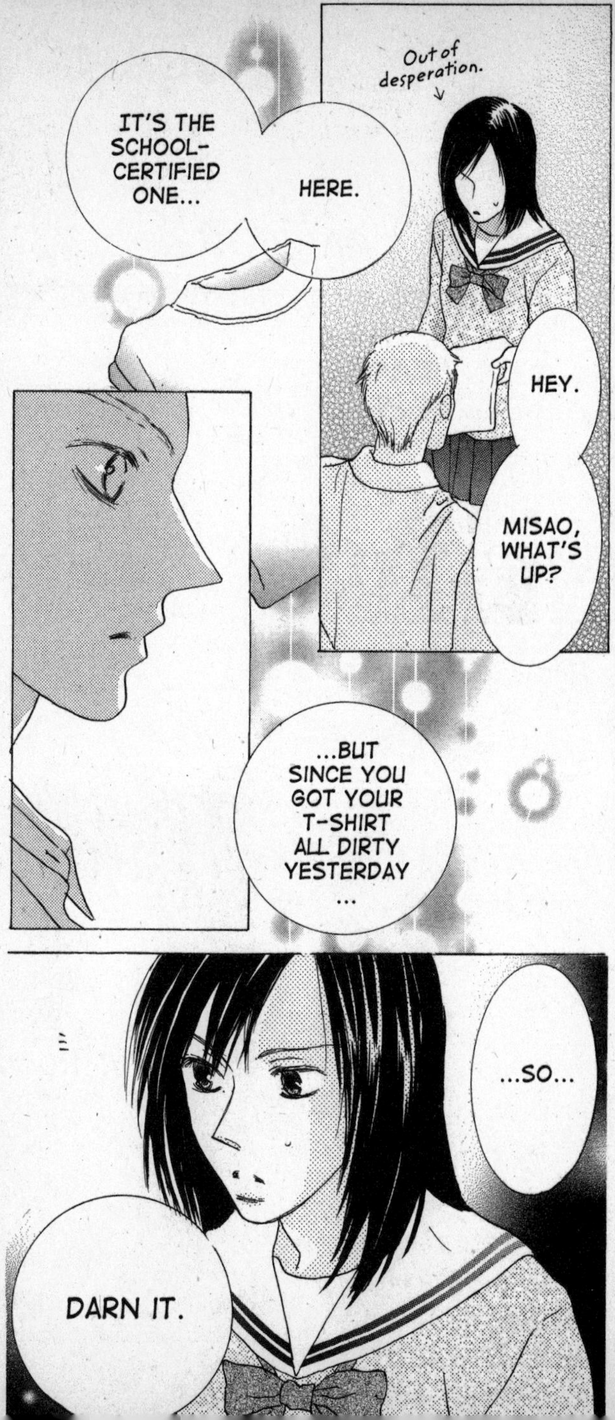
Out of desperation.
HERE.
IT'S THE SCHOOL-CERTIFIED ONE...
HEY.
MISAO, WHAT'S UP?
...BUT SINCE YOU GOT YOUR T-SHIRT ALL DIRTY YESTERDAY...
...SO...
DARN IT.

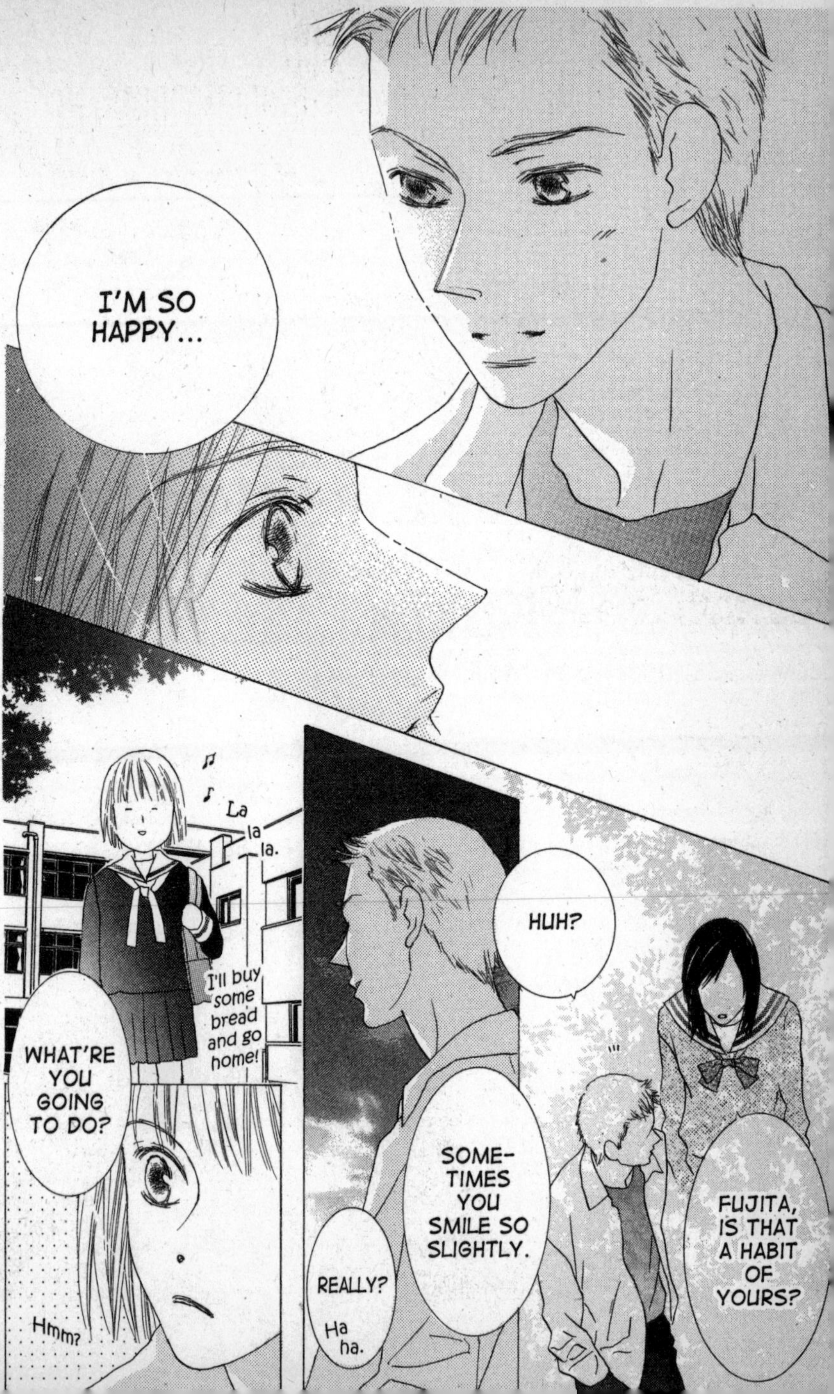
I'M SO HAPPY...
FUJITA, IS THAT A HABIT OF YOURS?
HUH?
SOME-TIMES YOU SMILE SO SLIGHTLY.
REALLY?
Ha ha.
La la la.
I'll buy some bread and go home!
WHAT'RE YOU GOING TO DO?
Hmm?

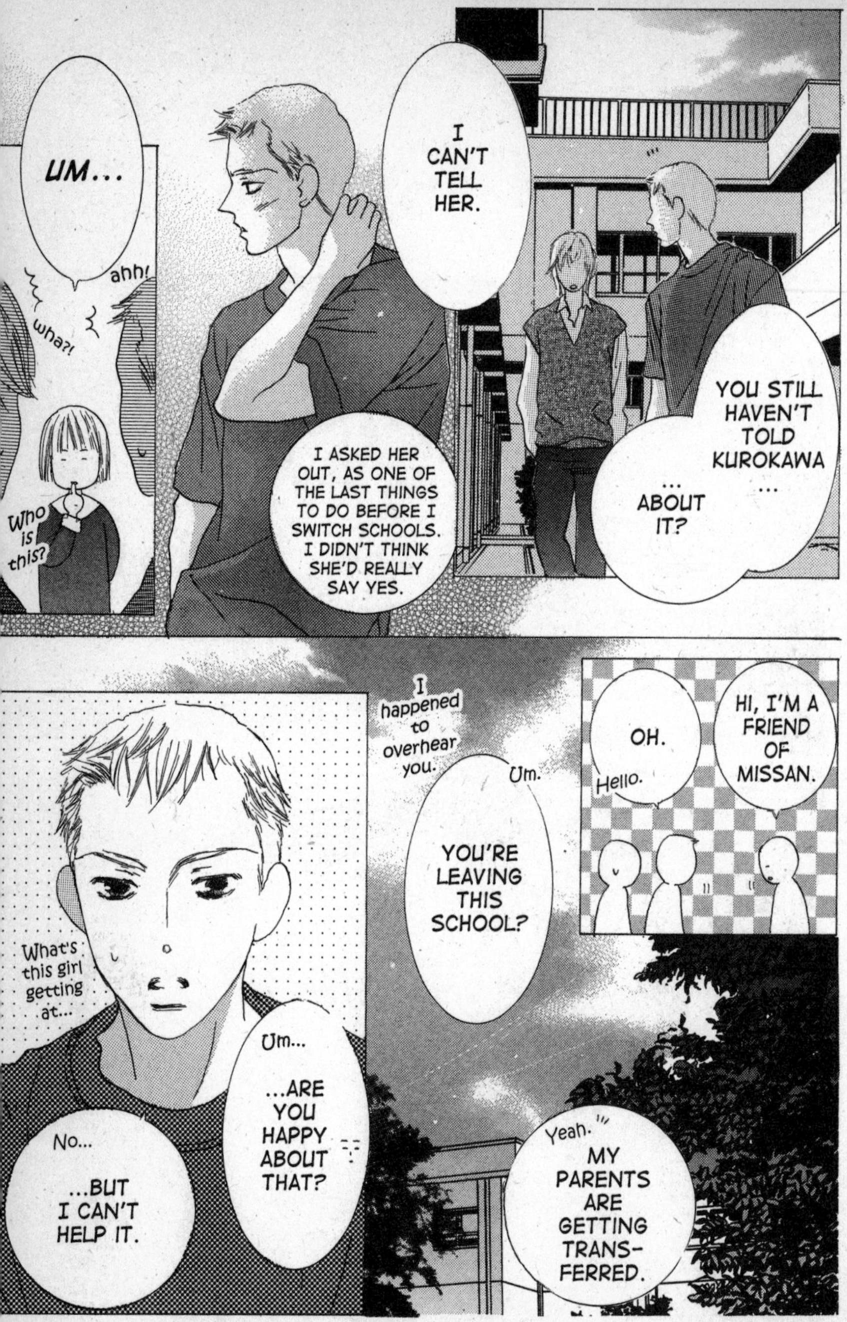
YOU STILL HAVEN'T TOLD KUROKAWA ...
... ABOUT IT?
I CAN'T TELL HER.
I ASKED HER OUT, AS ONE OF THE LAST THINGS TO DO BEFORE I SWITCH SCHOOLS. I DIDN'T THINK SHE'D REALLY SAY YES.
UM...
ahh!
wha?!
Who is this?
HI, I'M A FRIEND OF MISSAN.
OH.
Hello.
I happened to overhear you.
Um.
YOU'RE LEAVING THIS SCHOOL?
Yeah.
MY PARENTS ARE GETTING TRANS-FERRED.
Um...
...ARE YOU HAPPY ABOUT THAT?
What's this girl getting at...
No...
...BUT I CAN'T HELP IT.

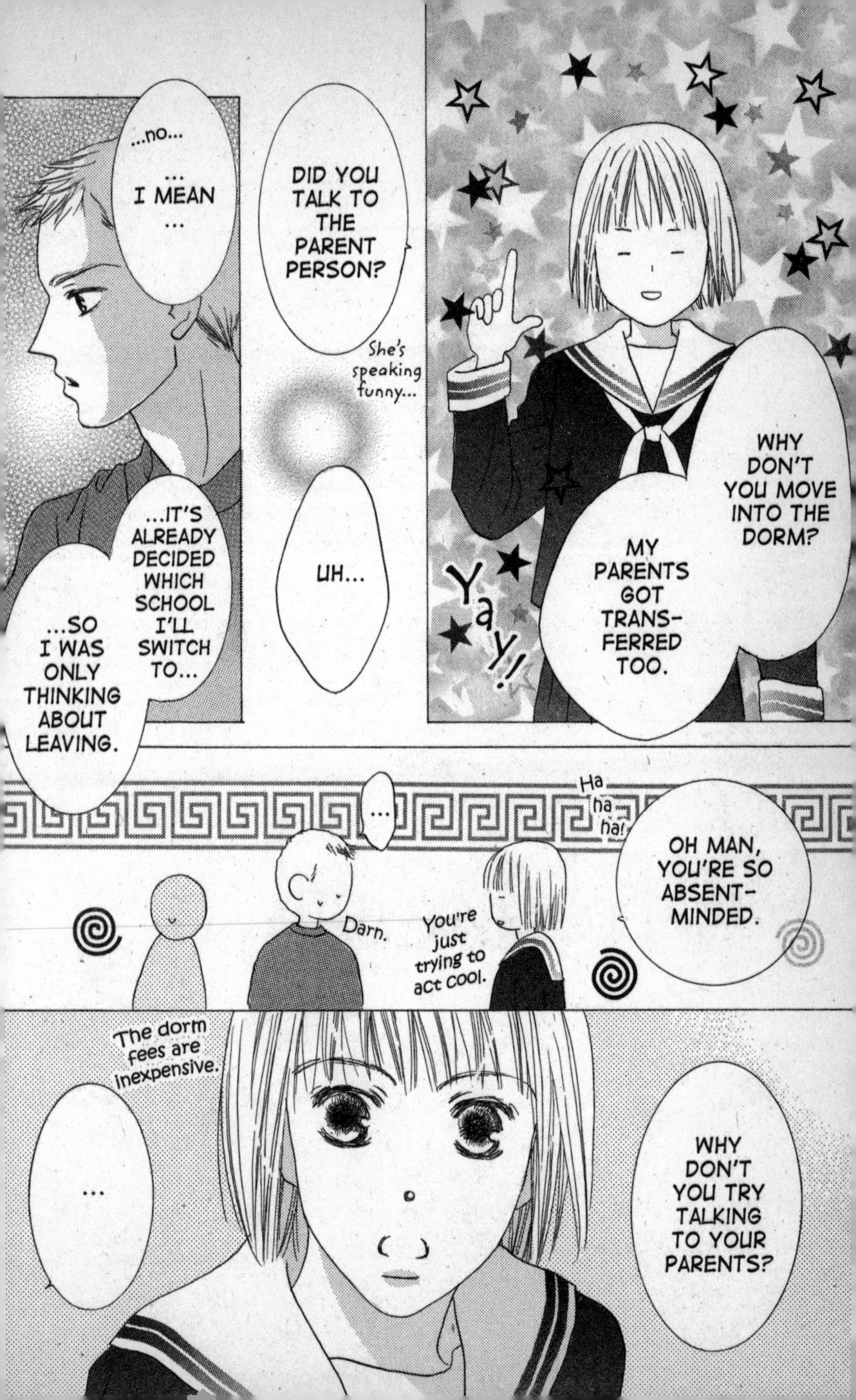
WHY DON'T YOU MOVE INTO THE DORM?
MY PARENTS GOT TRANS-FERRED TOO.
Yay!
DID YOU TALK TO THE PARENT PERSON?
She's speaking funny...
UH...
...no...
... I MEAN ...
...IT'S ALREADY DECIDED WHICH SCHOOL I'LL SWITCH TO...
...SO I WAS ONLY THINKING ABOUT LEAVING.
OH MAN, YOU'RE SO ABSENT-MINDED.
Ha ha ha!
You're just trying to act cool.
Darn.
...
WHY DON'T YOU TRY TALKING TO YOUR PARENTS?
The dorm fees are inexpensive.
...

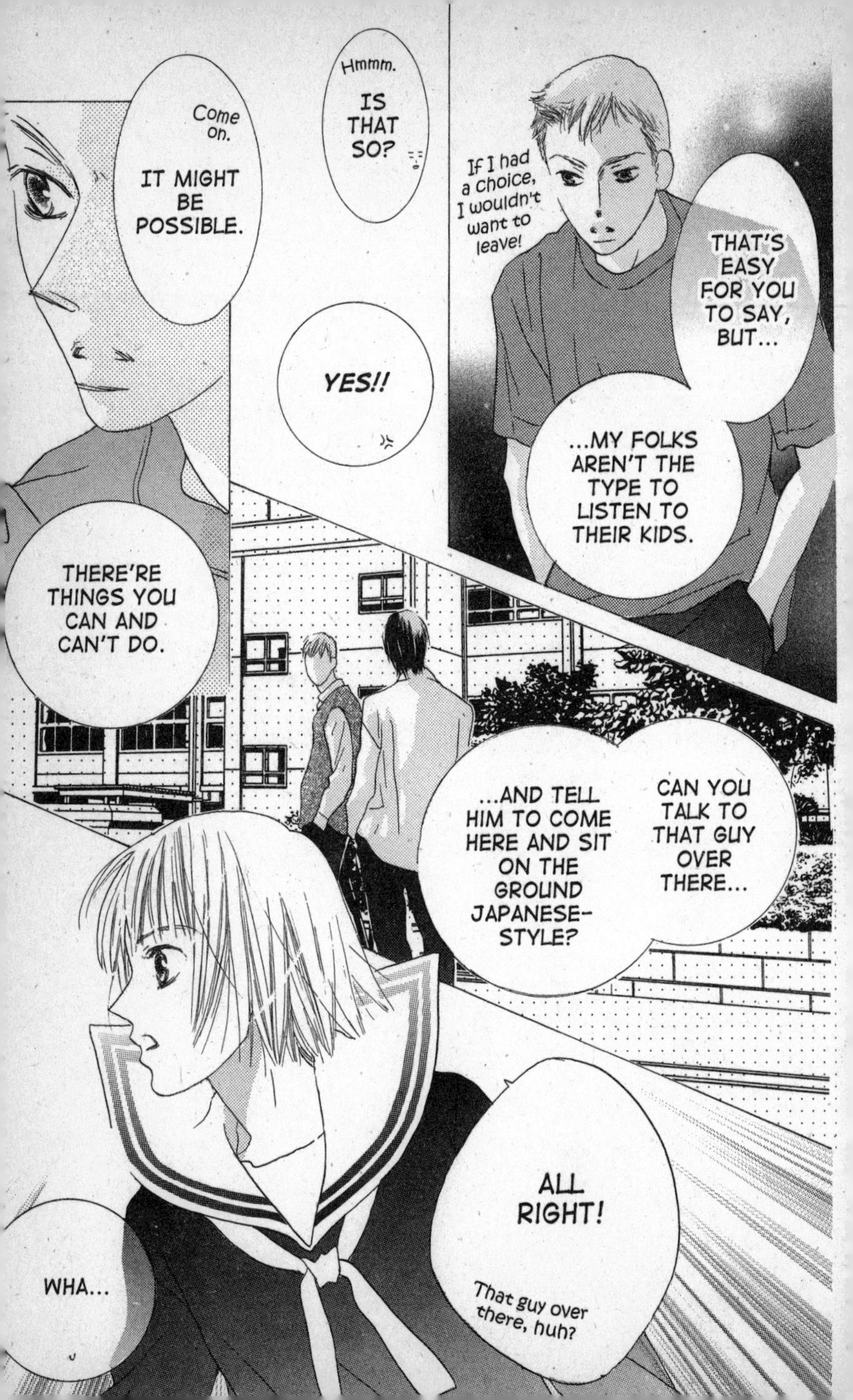
THAT'S EASY FOR YOU TO SAY, BUT...
...MY FOLKS AREN'T THE TYPE TO LISTEN TO THEIR KIDS.
If I had a choice, I wouldn't want to leave!
Hmmm.
IS THAT SO?
YES!!
Come on.
IT MIGHT BE POSSIBLE.
THERE'RE THINGS YOU CAN AND CAN'T DO.
CAN YOU TALK TO THAT GUY OVER THERE...
...AND TELL HIM TO COME HERE AND SIT ON THE GROUND JAPANESE-STYLE?
ALL RIGHT!
That guy over there, huh?
WHA...

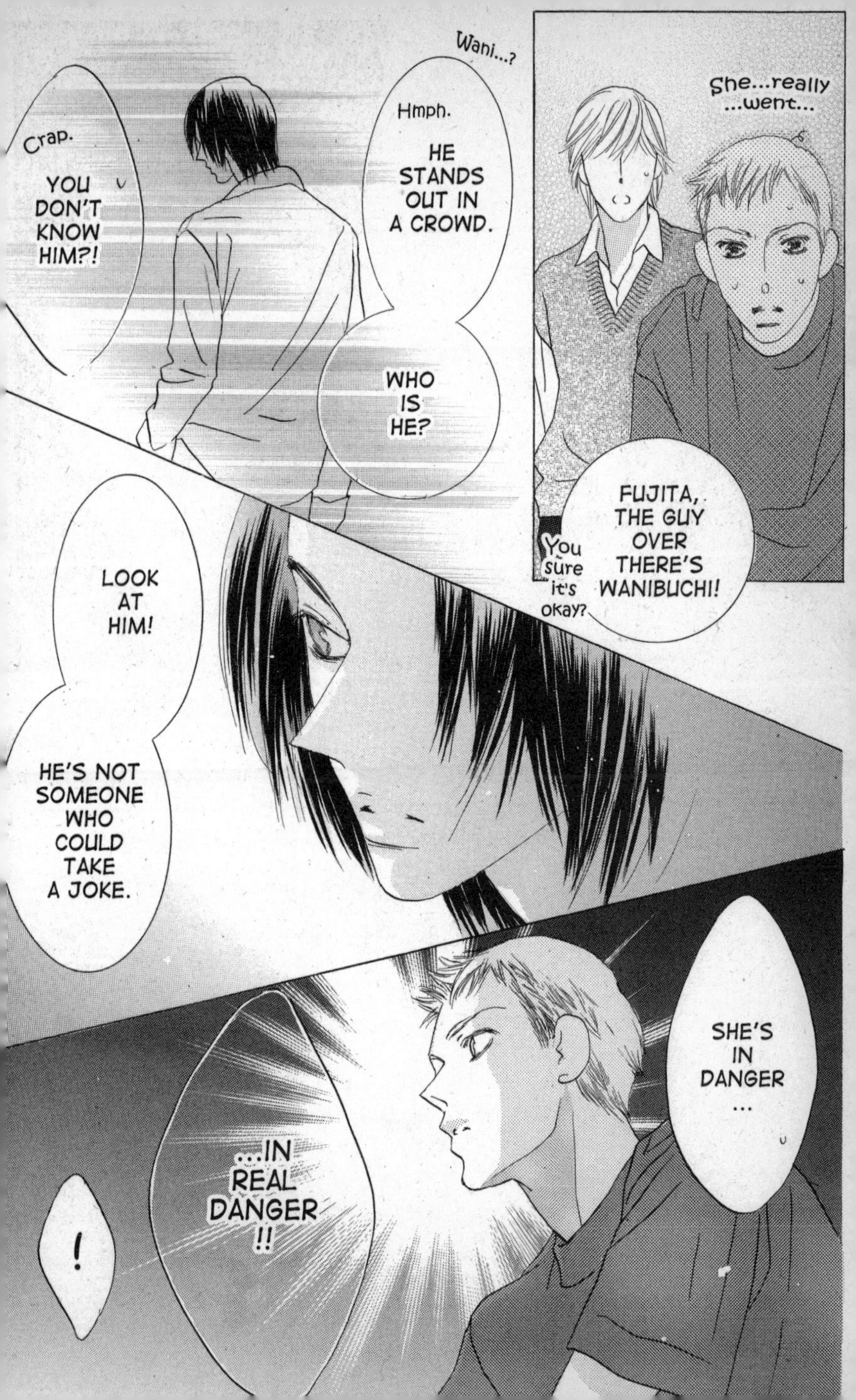
She...really ...went...
FUJITA, THE GUY OVER THERE'S WANIBUCHI!
You sure it's okay?
Wani...?
Hmph.
HE STANDS OUT IN A CROWD.
WHO IS HE?
Crap.
YOU DON'T KNOW HIM?!
LOOK AT HIM!
HE'S NOT SOMEONE WHO COULD TAKE A JOKE.
SHE'S IN DANGER ...
...IN REAL DANGER !!
!

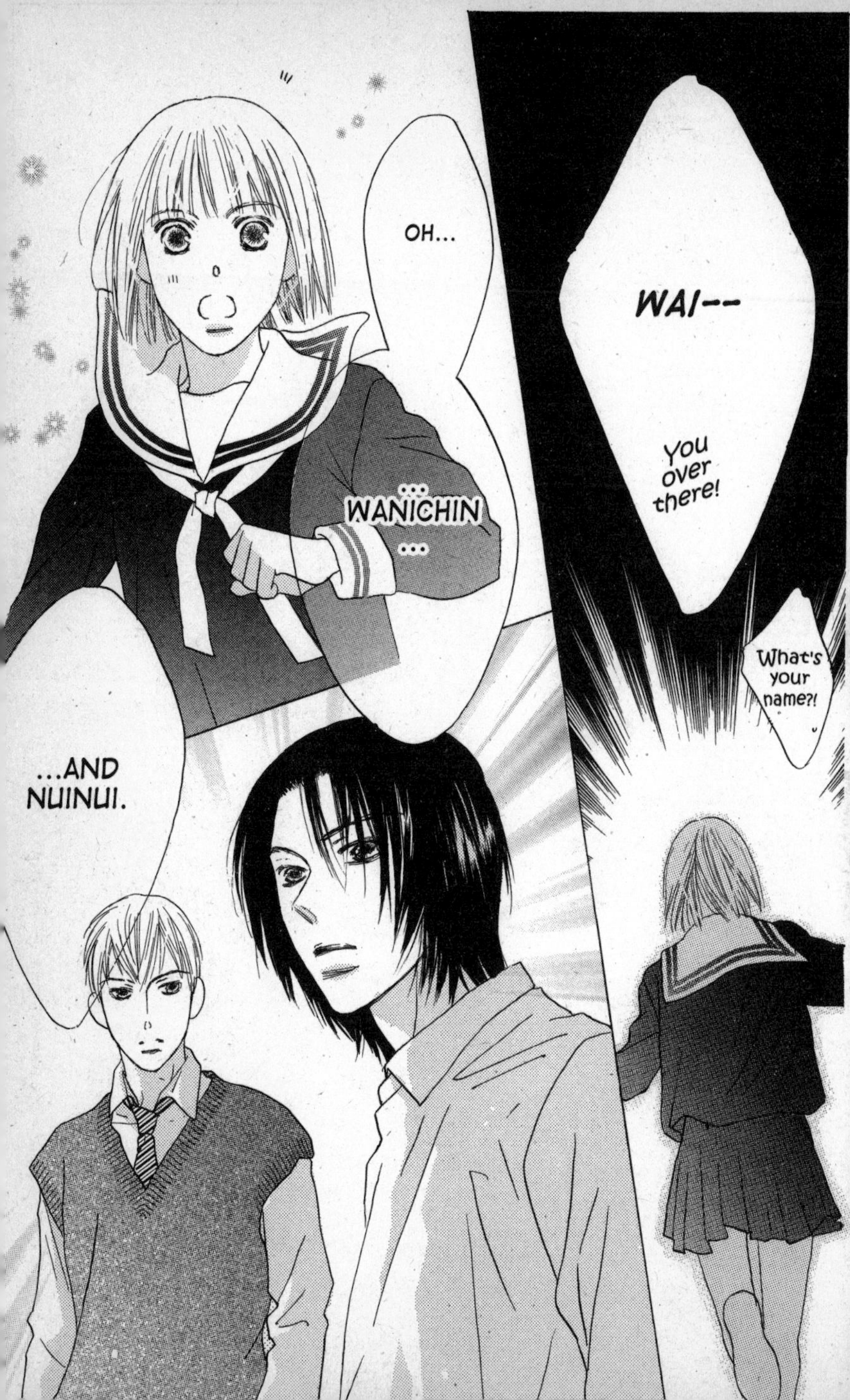
WAI--
You over there!
What's your name?!
OH...
...WANICHIN...
...AND NUINUI.

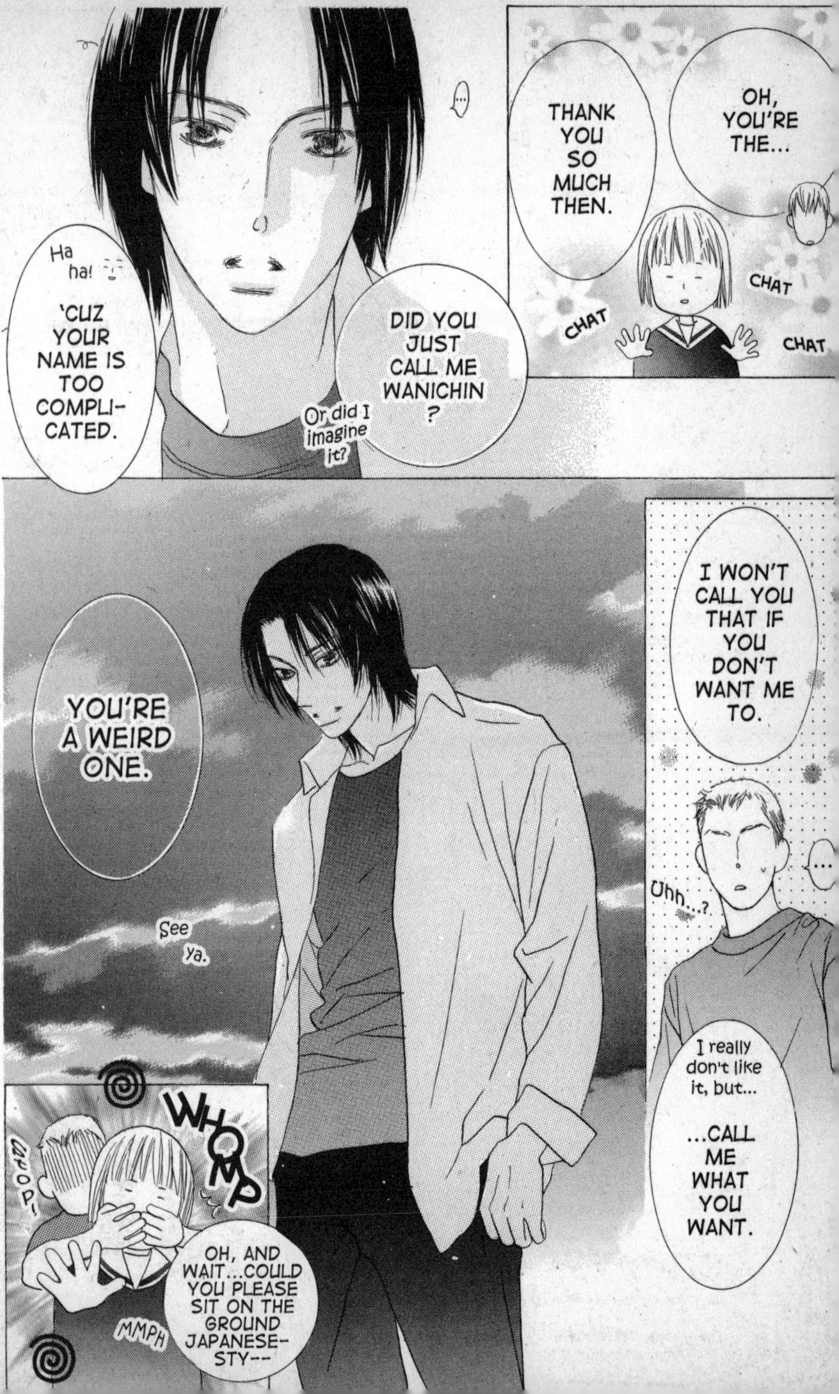

OH, YOU'RE THE...
THANK YOU SO MUCH THEN.
CHAT
CHAT
CHAT
...
DID YOU JUST CALL ME WANICHIN?
Or did I imagine it?
Ha ha!
'CUZ YOUR NAME IS TOO COMPLI-CATED.
I WON'T CALL YOU THAT IF YOU DON'T WANT ME TO.
...
Uhh...?
I really don't like it, but...
...CALL ME WHAT YOU WANT.
YOU'RE A WEIRD ONE.
See ya.
WHOMP
STOP!
OH, AND WAIT...COULD YOU PLEASE SIT ON THE GROUND JAPANESE-STY--
MMPH

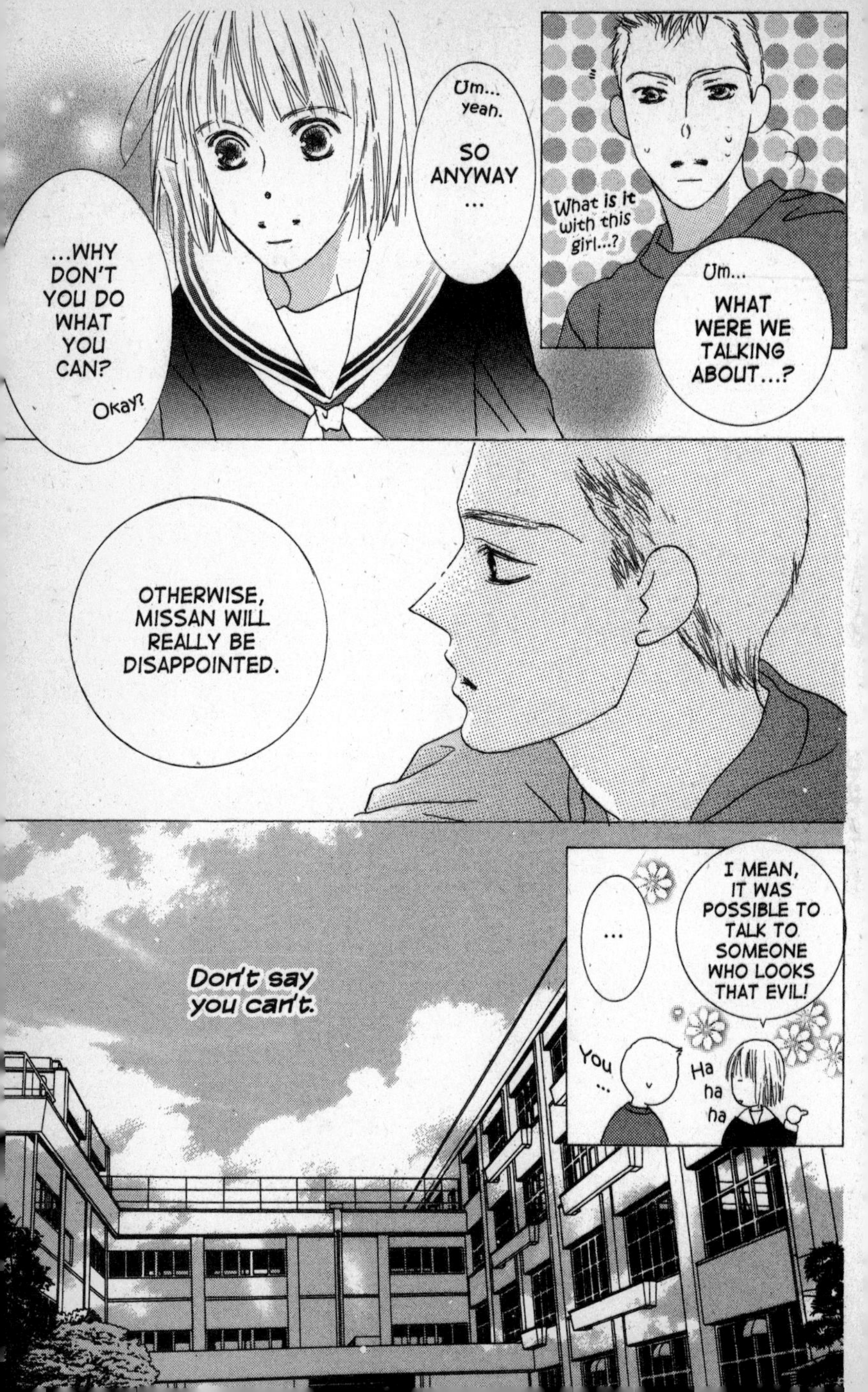
What is it with this girl...?
Um... WHAT WERE WE TALKING ABOUT...?
Um... yeah. SO ANYWAY ...
...WHY DON'T YOU DO WHAT YOU CAN?
Okay?
OTHERWISE, MISSAN WILL REALLY BE DISAPPOINTED.
I MEAN, IT WAS POSSIBLE TO TALK TO SOMEONE WHO LOOKS THAT EVIL!
Ha ha ha
...
You ...
Don't say you can't.

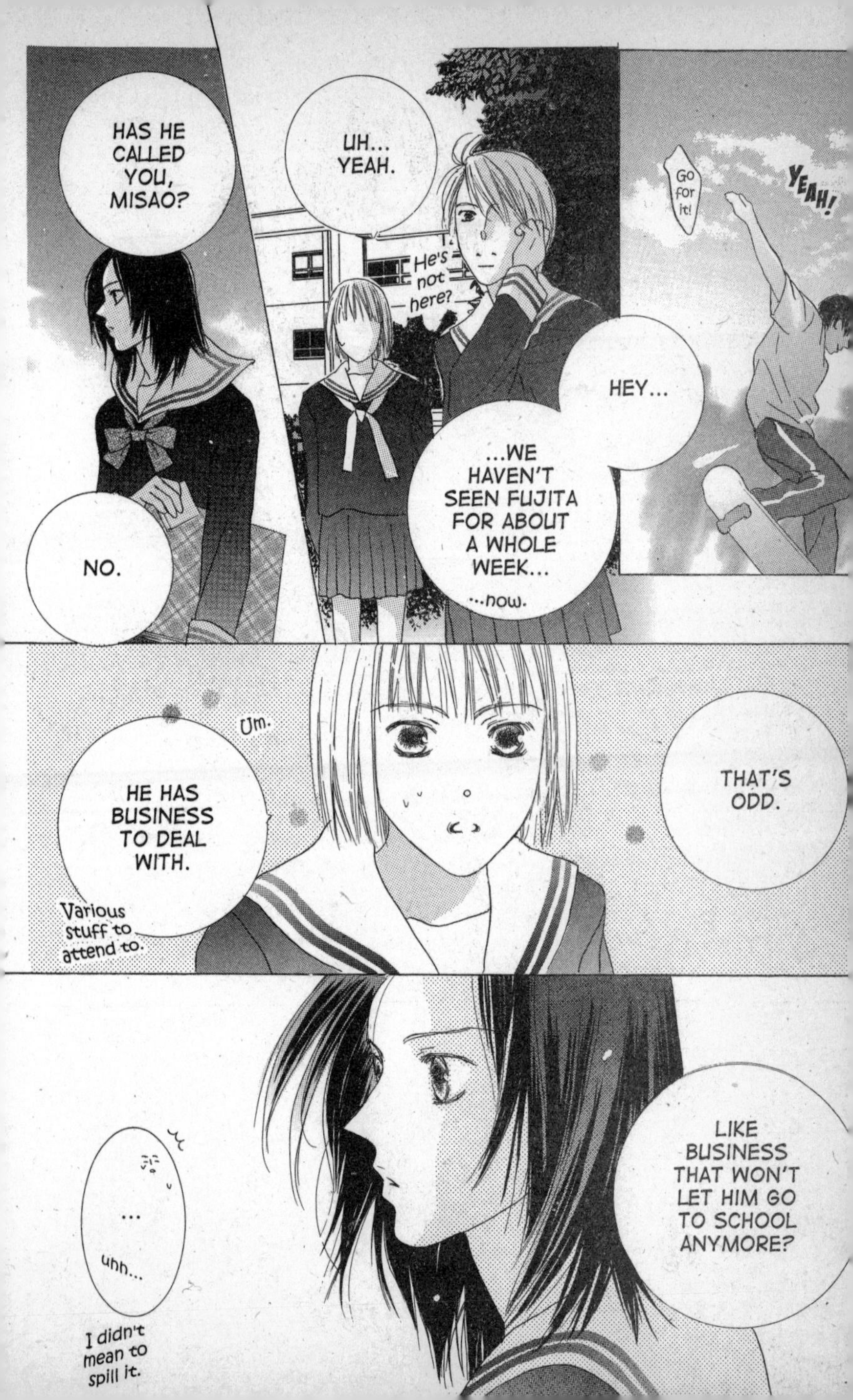
YEAH!
Go for it!
HEY...
...WE HAVEN'T SEEN FUJITA FOR ABOUT A WHOLE WEEK...
...now.
He's not here?
UH... YEAH.
HAS HE CALLED YOU, MISAO?
NO.
THAT'S ODD.
Um.
HE HAS BUSINESS TO DEAL WITH.
Various stuff to attend to.
LIKE BUSINESS THAT WON'T LET HIM GO TO SCHOOL ANYMORE?
...
unn...
I didn't mean to spill it.

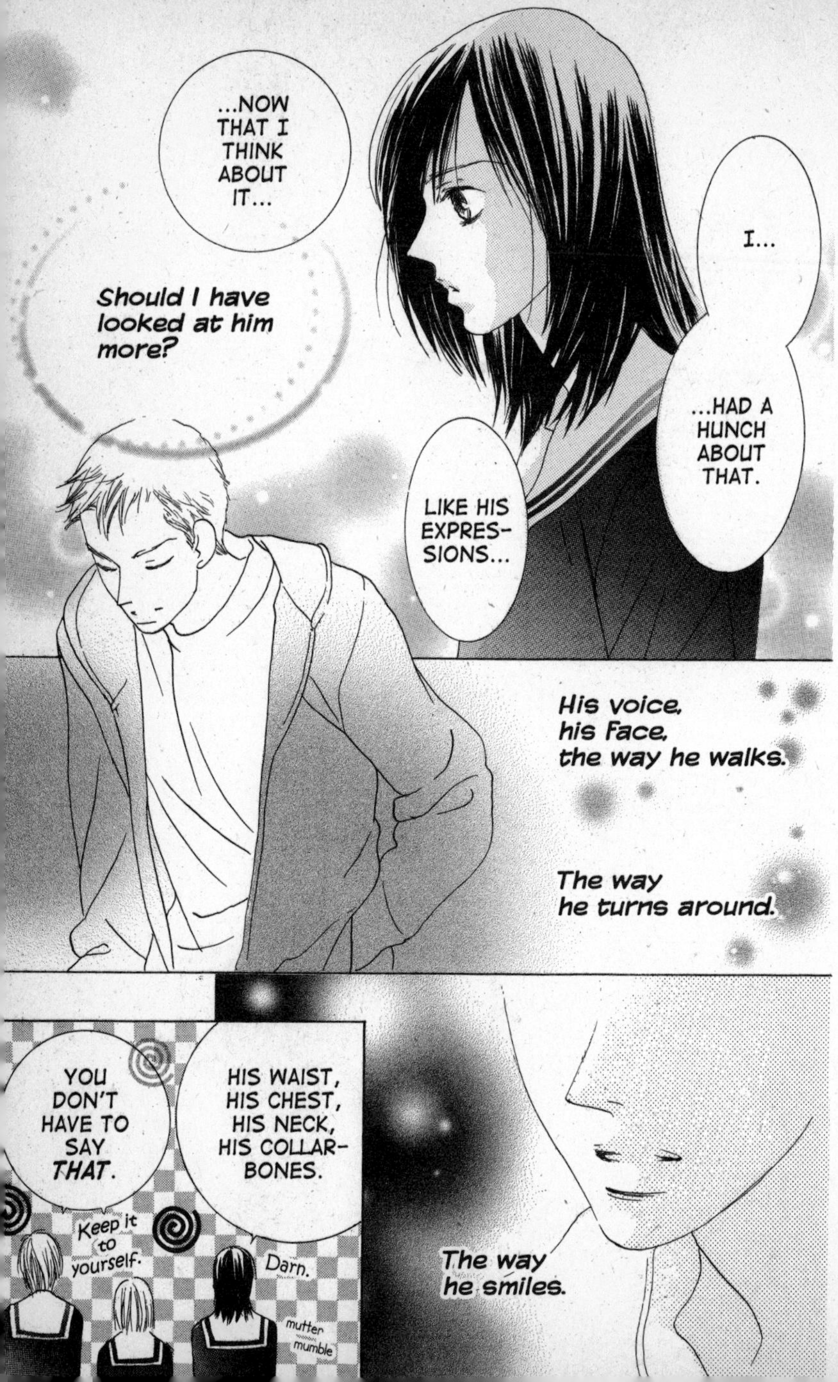
I...
...HAD A HUNCH ABOUT THAT.
...NOW THAT I THINK ABOUT IT...
Should I have looked at him more?
LIKE HIS EXPRES-SIONS...
His voice, his face, the way he walks.
The way he turns around.
The way he smiles.
HIS WAIST, HIS CHEST, HIS NECK, HIS COLLAR-BONES.
YOU DON'T HAVE TO SAY THAT.
Keep it to yourself.
Darn.
mutter mumble

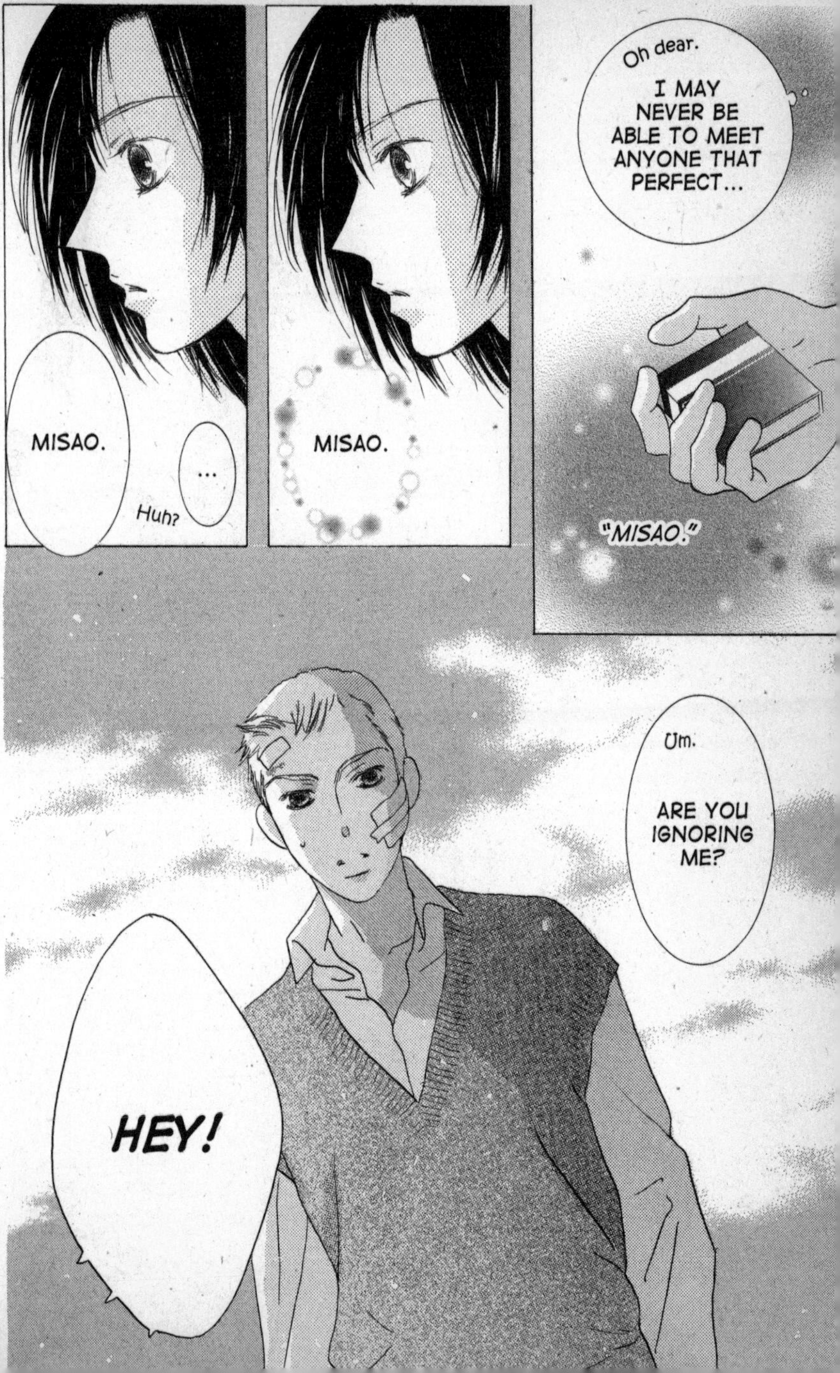
Oh dear.
I MAY NEVER BE ABLE TO MEET ANYONE THAT PERFECT...
"MISAO."
MISAO.
MISAO.
...
Huh?
Um.
ARE YOU IGNORING ME?
HEY!

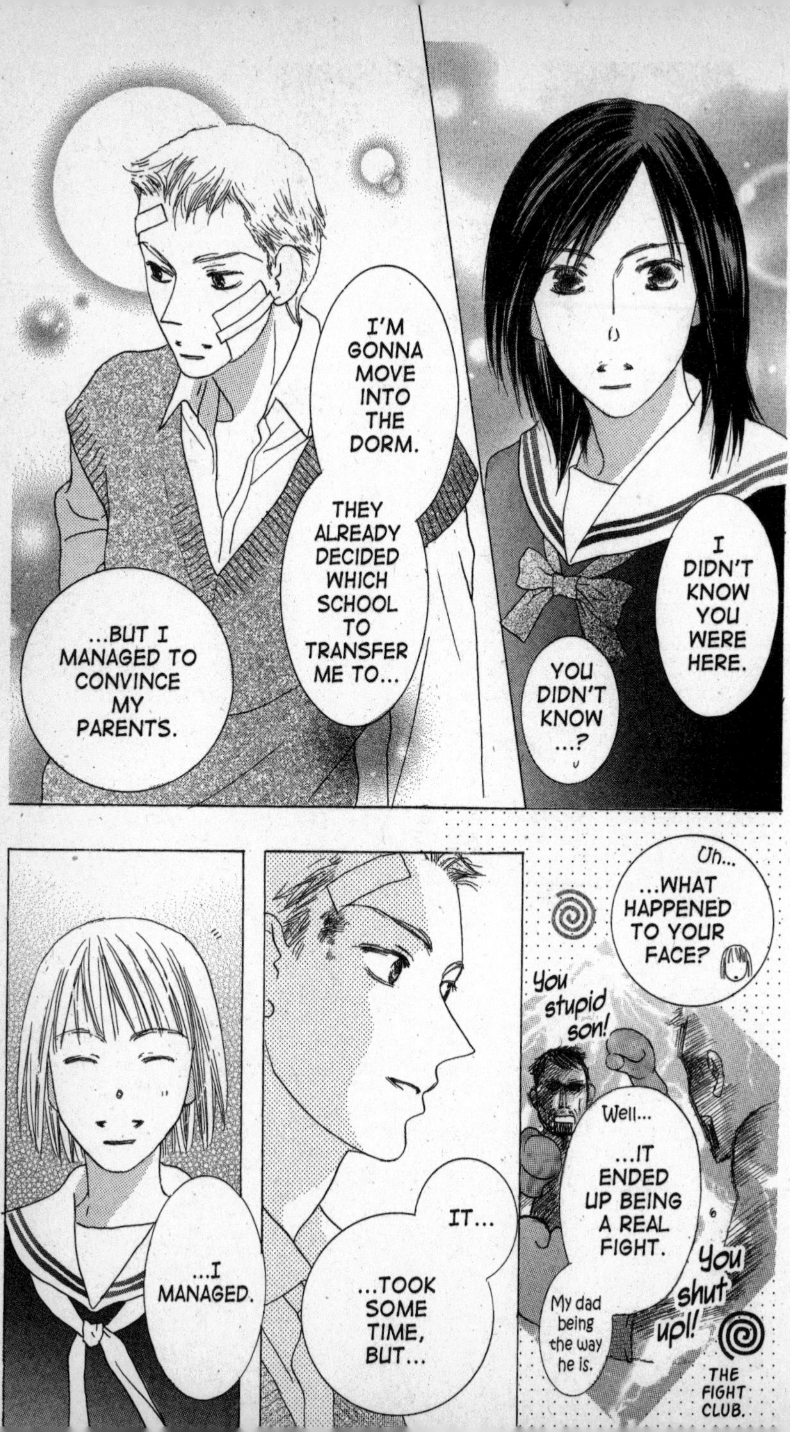
I DIDN'T KNOW YOU WERE HERE.
YOU DIDN'T KNOW ...?
I'M GONNA MOVE INTO THE DORM.
THEY ALREADY DECIDED WHICH SCHOOL TO TRANSFER ME TO...
...BUT I MANAGED TO CONVINCE MY PARENTS.
Uh...
...WHAT HAPPENED TO YOUR FACE?
You stupid son!
Well...
...IT ENDED UP BEING A REAL FIGHT.
You shut up!
My dad being the way he is.
THE FIGHT CLUB.
IT...
...TOOK SOME TIME, BUT...
...I MANAGED.

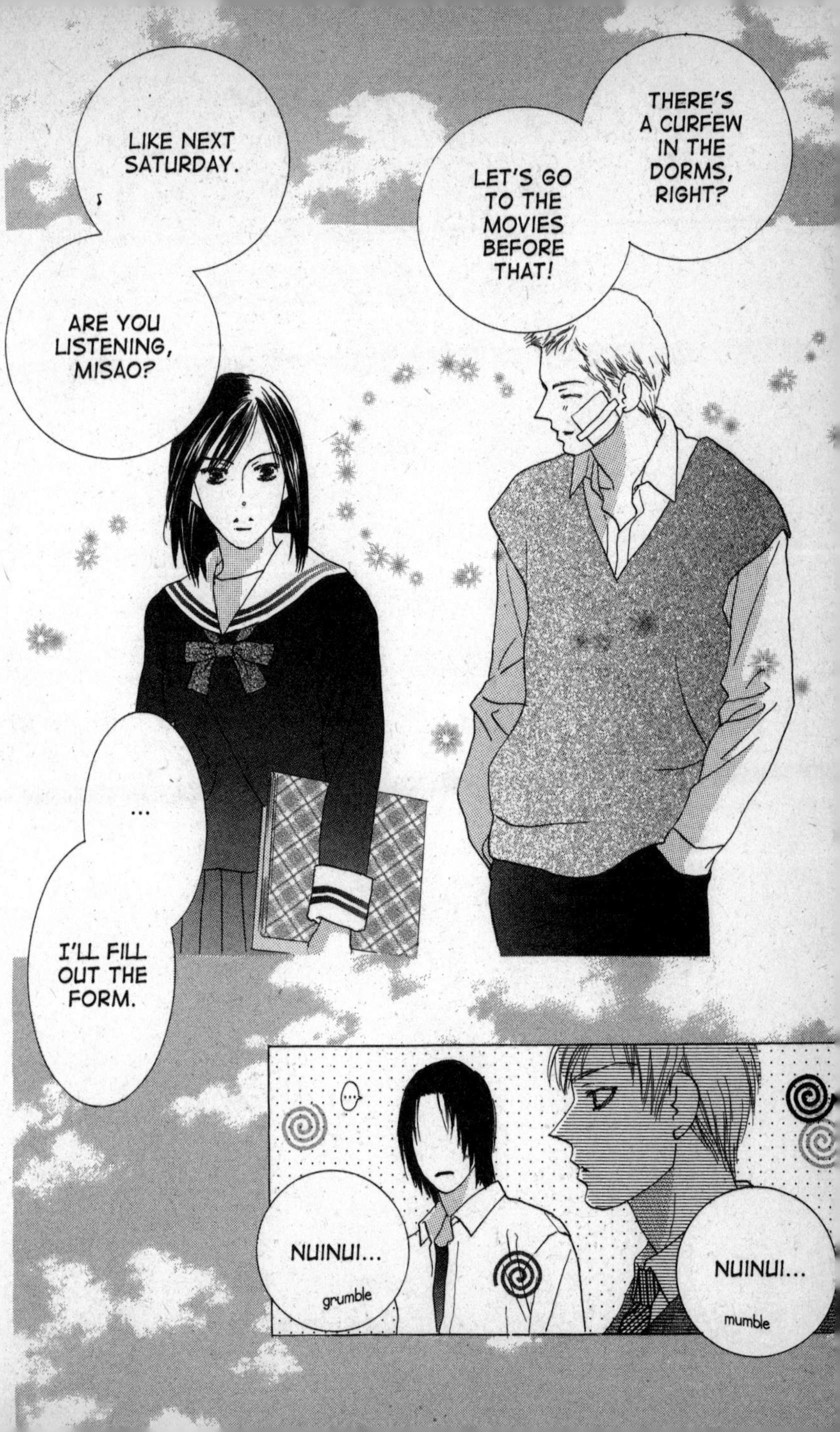
THERE'S A CURFEW IN THE DORMS, RIGHT?
LET'S GO TO THE MOVIES BEFORE THAT!
LIKE NEXT SATURDAY.
ARE YOU LISTENING, MISAO?
...
I'LL FILL OUT THE FORM.
NUINUI...
mumble
NUINUI...
grumble
...

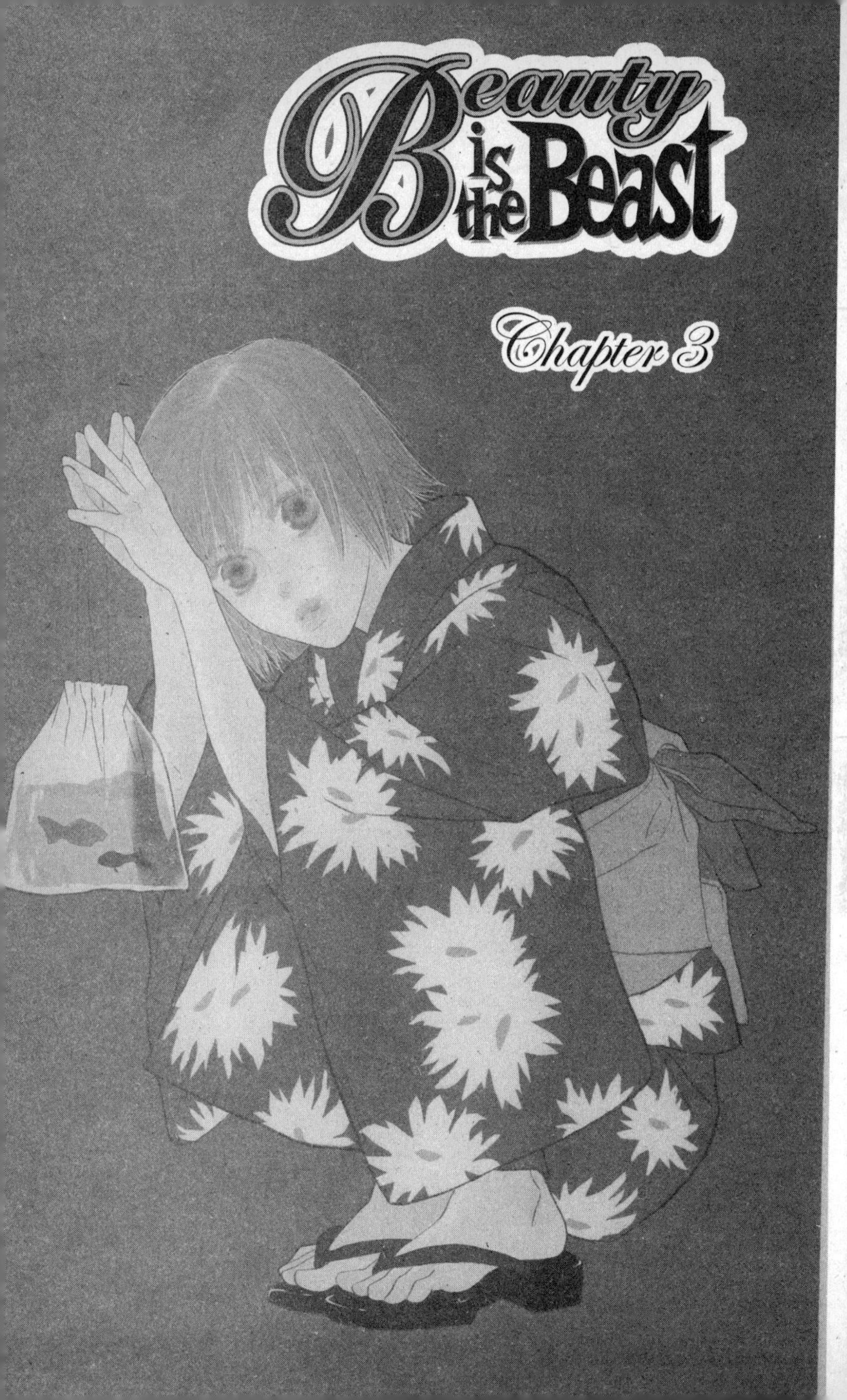
Beauty is the Beast
Chapter 3

BEAUTY
IS THE
BEAST

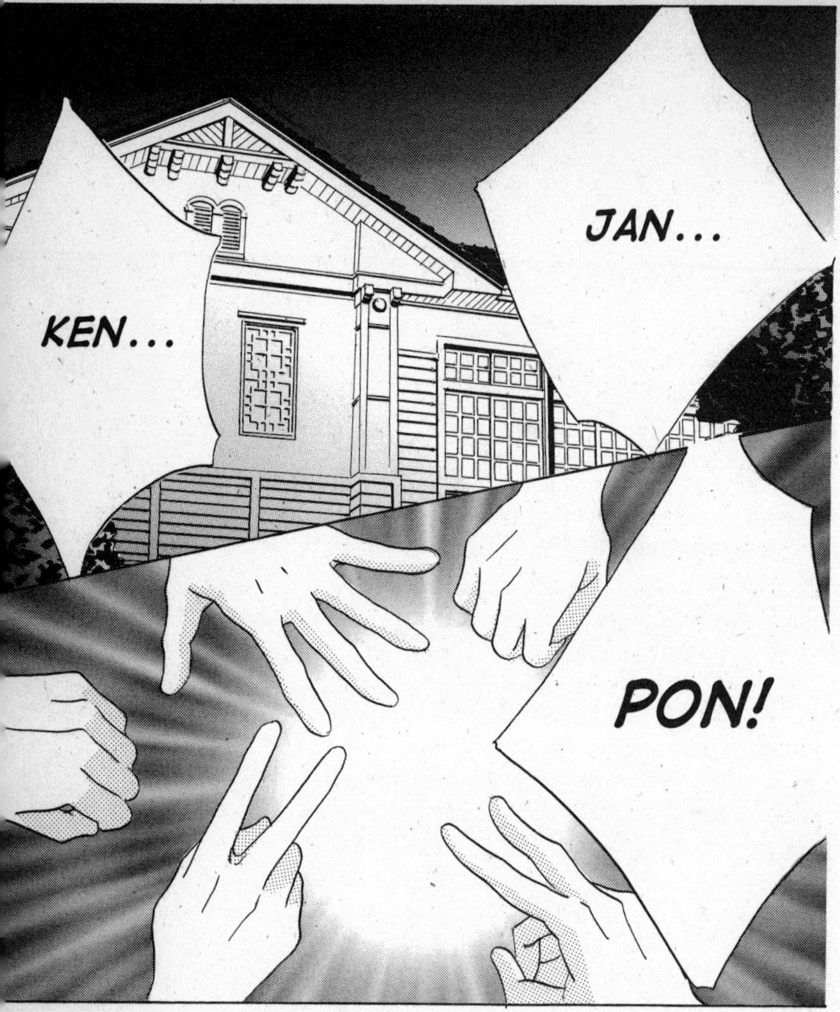
JAN...
KEN...
PON!

A Must-have for Dorm Life 2: Snacks

They are good when you're hungry. They are also effective when you are negotiating. For example, "I'd like you to do my meal duties..."
(I think that I learned the basic principals of social life in the dorm...)

I guess there aren't many people who get angry when they receive something to eat.

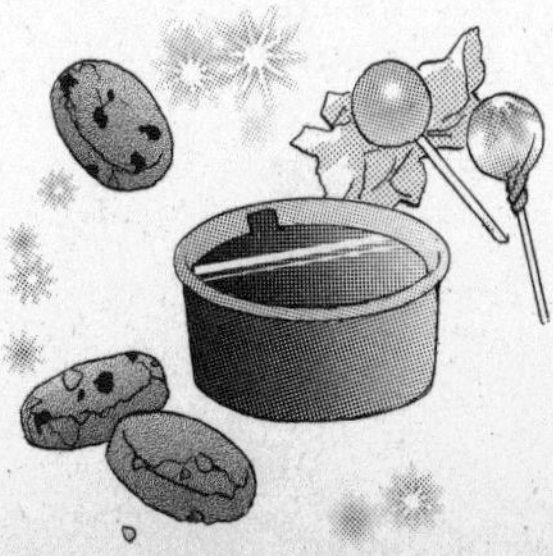

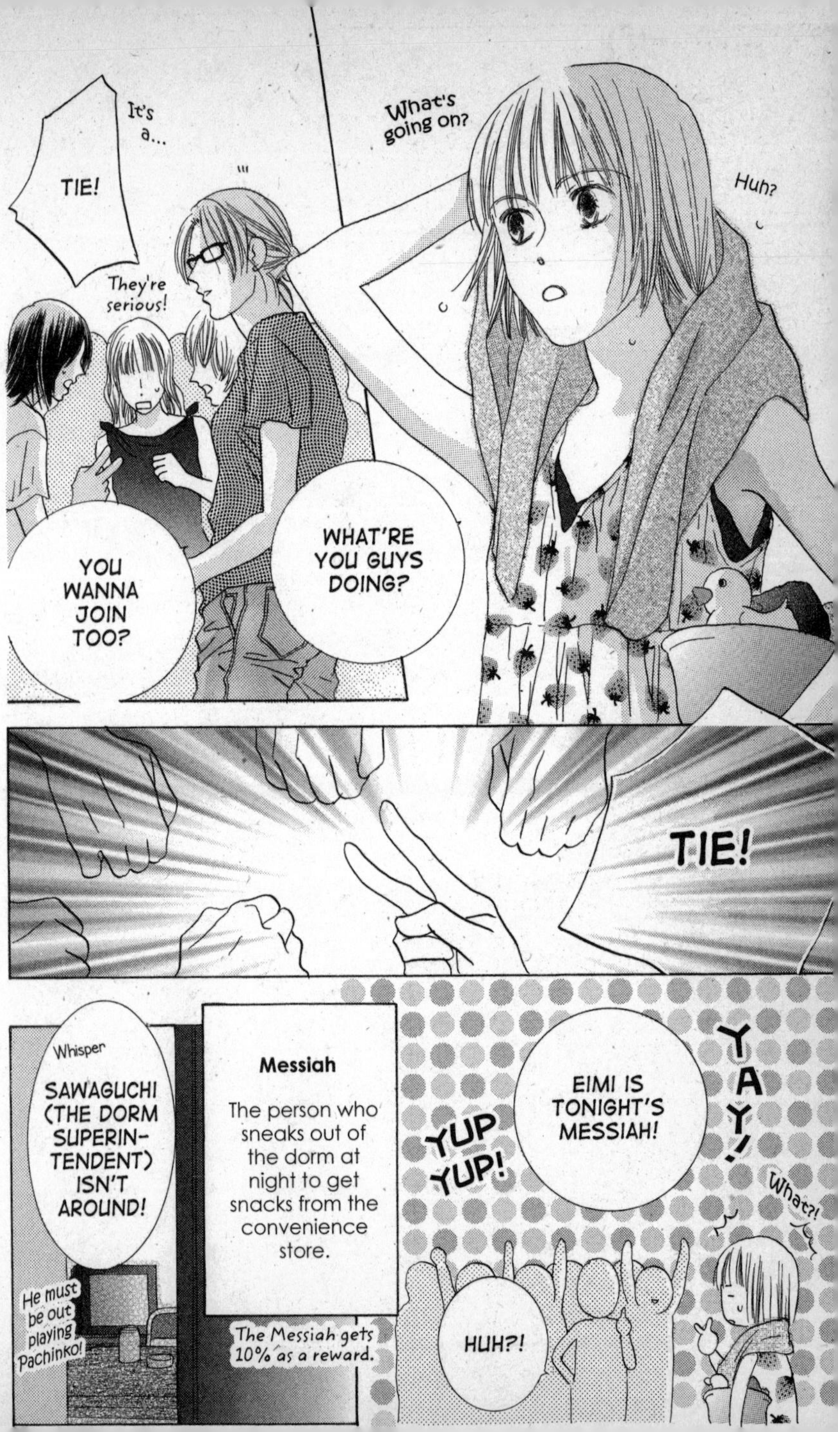
Huh?
What's going on?
WHAT'RE YOU GUYS DOING?
YOU WANNA JOIN TOO?
It's a...
TIE!
They're serious!
TIE!
EIMI IS TONIGHT'S MESSIAH!
YAY!
YUP YUP!
What?!
HUH?!
Messiah
The person who sneaks out of the dorm at night to get snacks from the convenience store.
The Messiah gets 10% as a reward.
Whisper
SAWAGUCHI (THE DORM SUPERIN-TENDENT) ISN'T AROUND!
He must be out playing Pachinko!

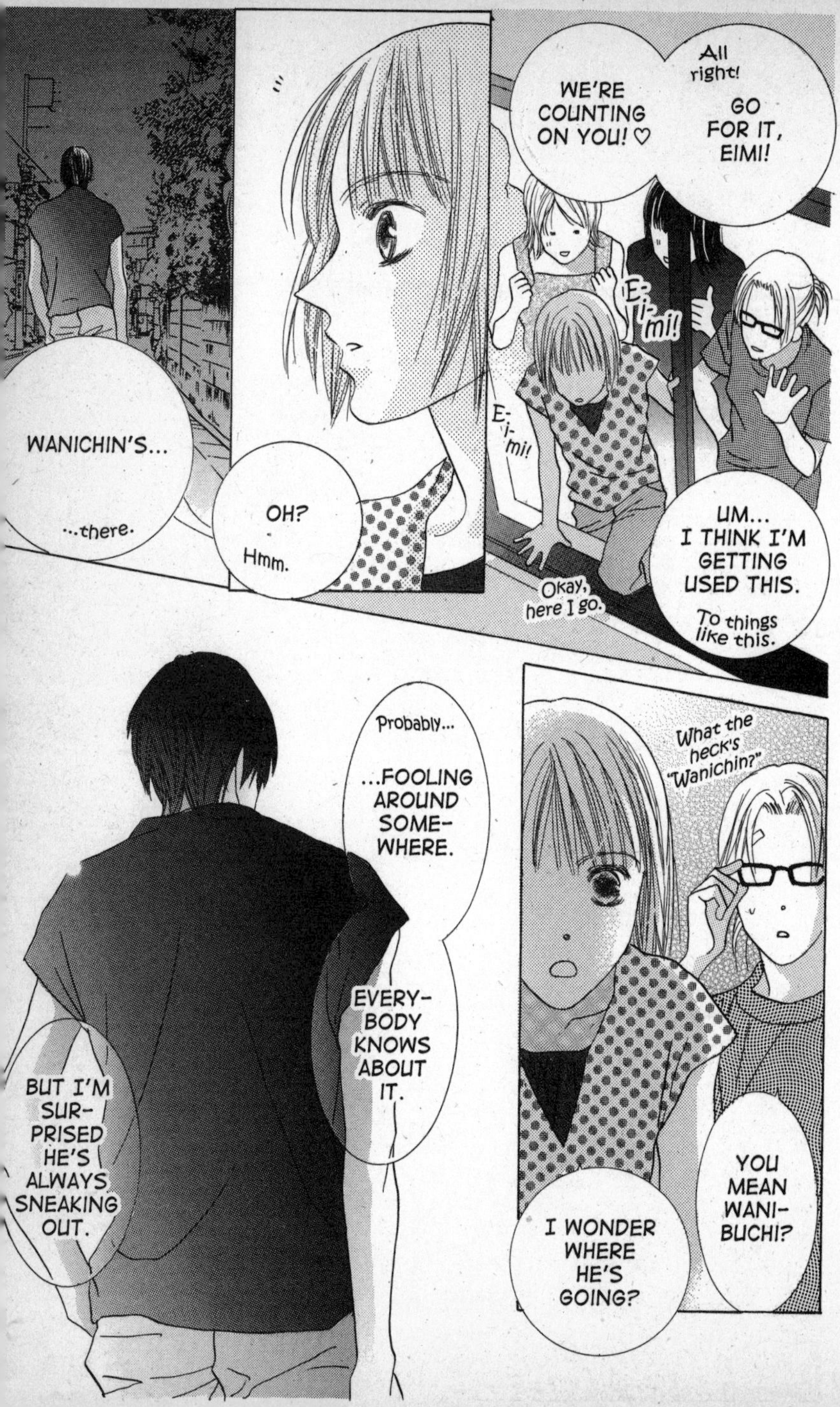
All right! GO FOR IT, EIMI!
WE'RE COUNTING ON YOU! ♡
E-i-mi!
E-i-mi!
UM... I THINK I'M GETTING USED THIS.
To things like this.
Okay, here I go.
OH?
Hmm.
WANICHIN'S...
...there.
What the heck's "Wanichin?"
YOU MEAN WANI-BUCHI?
I WONDER WHERE HE'S GOING?
Probably...
...FOOLING AROUND SOME-WHERE.
EVERY-BODY KNOWS ABOUT IT.
BUT I'M SUR-PRISED HE'S ALWAYS SNEAKING OUT.

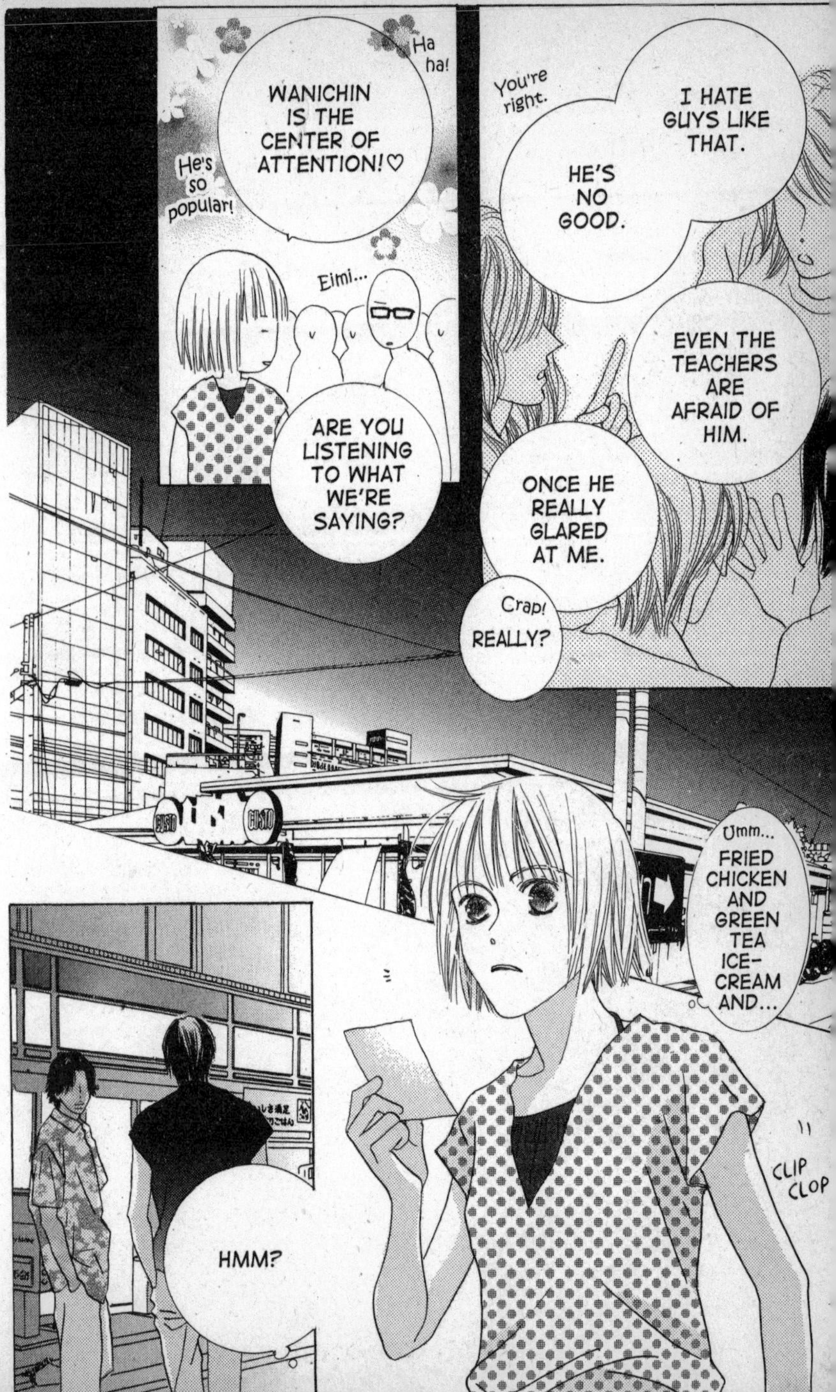
I HATE GUYS LIKE THAT.
You're right.
HE'S NO GOOD.
EVEN THE TEACHERS ARE AFRAID OF HIM.
ONCE HE REALLY GLARED AT ME.
Crap!
REALLY?
Ha ha!
WANICHIN IS THE CENTER OF ATTENTION!♡
He's so popular!
Eimi...
ARE YOU LISTENING TO WHAT WE'RE SAYING?
Umm...
FRIED CHICKEN AND GREEN TEA ICE-CREAM AND...
CLIP CLOP
HMM?

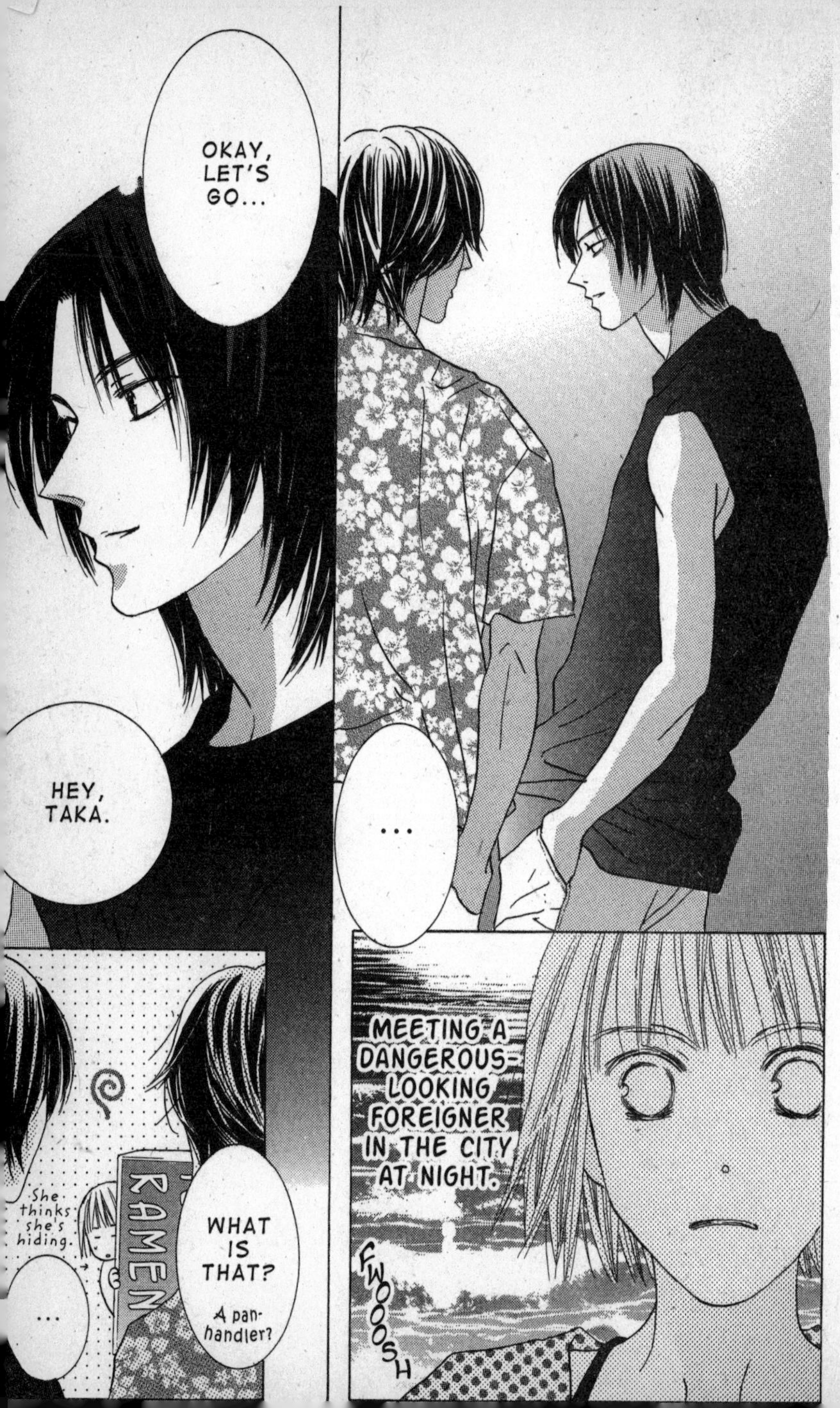
...
OKAY, LET'S GO...
HEY, TAKA.
MEETING A DANGEROUS-LOOKING FOREIGNER IN THE CITY AT NIGHT.
FWOOOSH
WHAT IS THAT?
A pan-handler?
RAMEN
She thinks she's hiding.
...

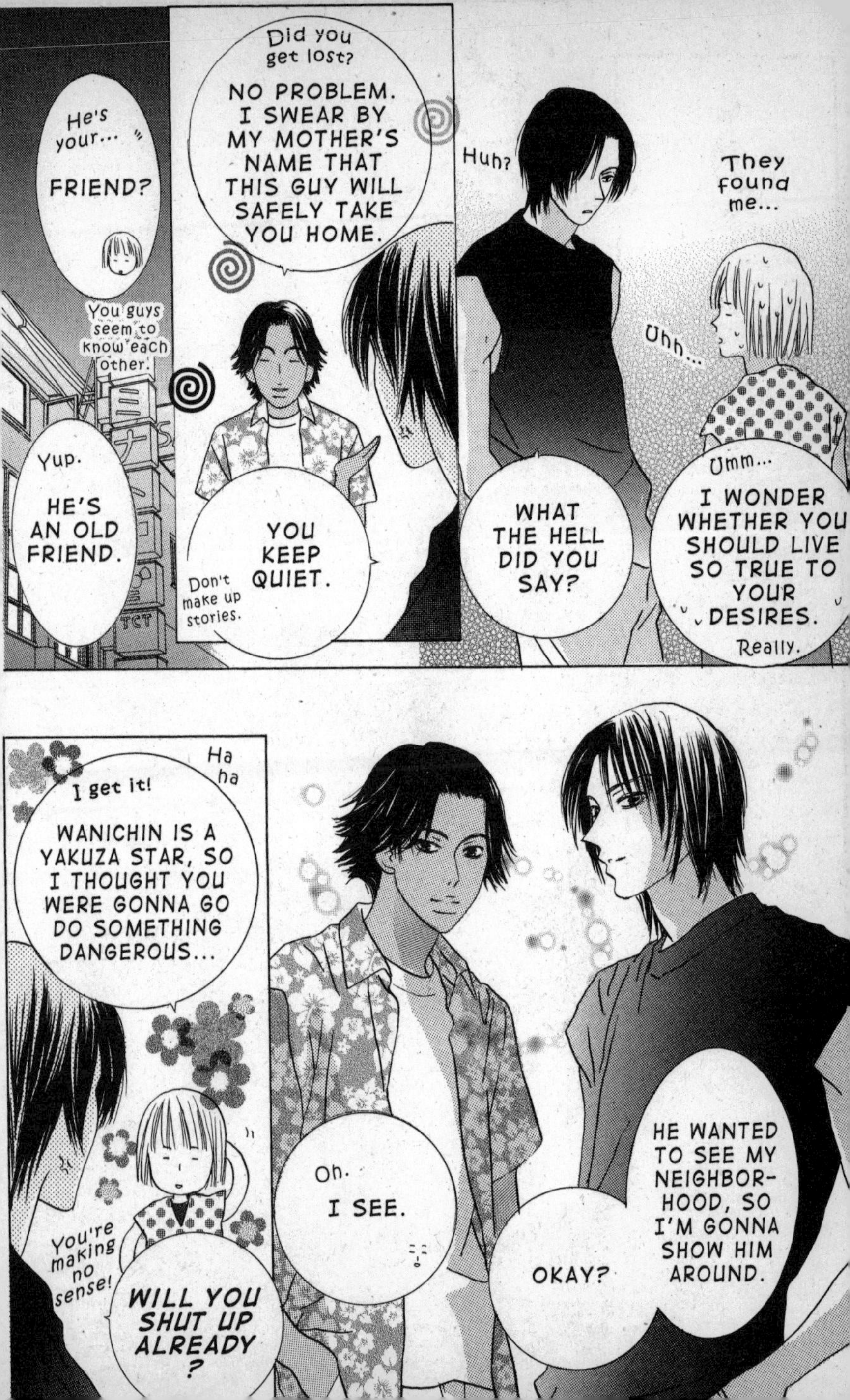
They found me...
Uhh...
Huh?
Umm... I WONDER WHETHER YOU SHOULD LIVE SO TRUE TO YOUR DESIRES.
Really.
WHAT THE HELL DID YOU SAY?
Did you get lost?
NO PROBLEM. I SWEAR BY MY MOTHER'S NAME THAT THIS GUY WILL SAFELY TAKE YOU HOME.
YOU KEEP QUIET.
Don't make up stories.
He's your...
FRIEND?
You guys seem to know each other.
Yup.
HE'S AN OLD FRIEND.
HE WANTED TO SEE MY NEIGHBORHOOD, SO I'M GONNA SHOW HIM AROUND.
OKAY?
Oh.
I SEE.
Ha ha
I get it!
WANICHIN IS A YAKUZA STAR, SO I THOUGHT YOU WERE GONNA GO DO SOMETHING DANGEROUS...
You're making no sense!
WILL YOU SHUT UP ALREADY?

3

After I started this series, I was having problems finding good information on wooden school buildings, but thanks to my acquaintances, I was able to visit a school. It was so wonderful, I couldn't help smiling widely when I looked at it.

The corridors and staircases had wood floors, and the windows had beautiful decorative frames.

Usually, school buildings look the same everywhere, but this one was in a class by itself. It is a very old building, so the teachers are always jumpy every time a typhoon comes. (☺)

The backgrounds of the dorms in this work are based on the photographs I took then.

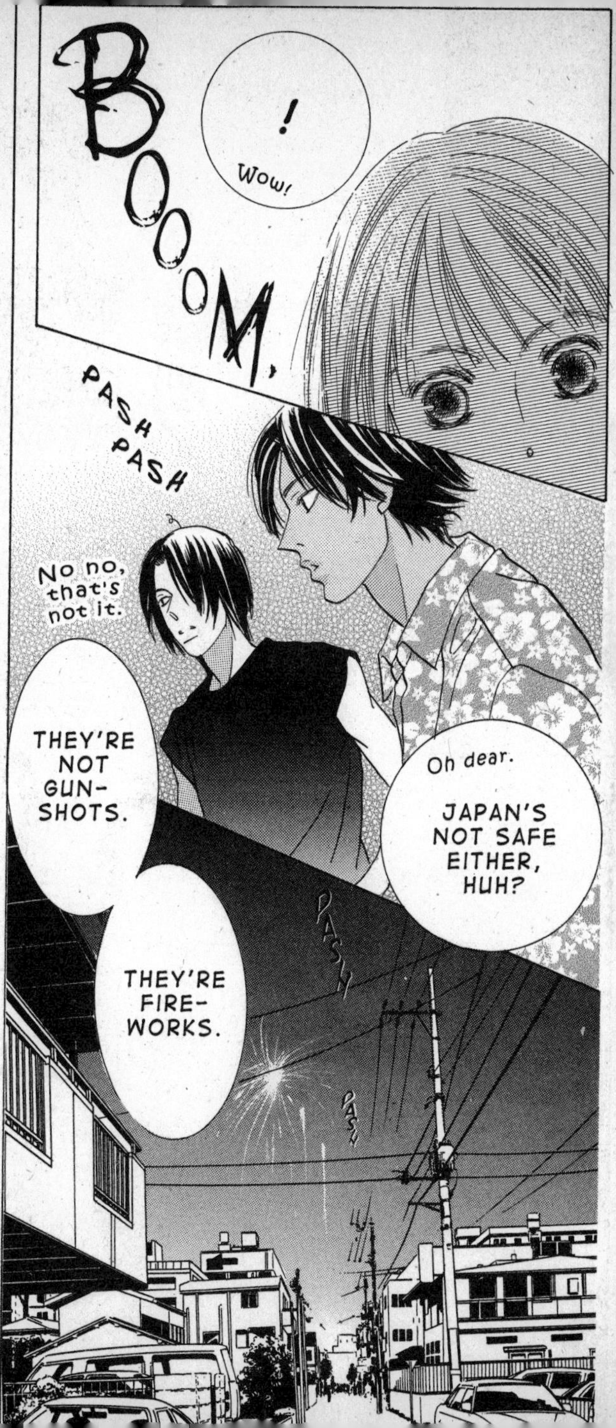

BOOOM
!
Wow!
PASH PASH
Oh dear.
JAPAN'S NOT SAFE EITHER, HUH?
No no, that's not it.
THEY'RE NOT GUN-SHOTS.
THEY'RE FIRE-WORKS.

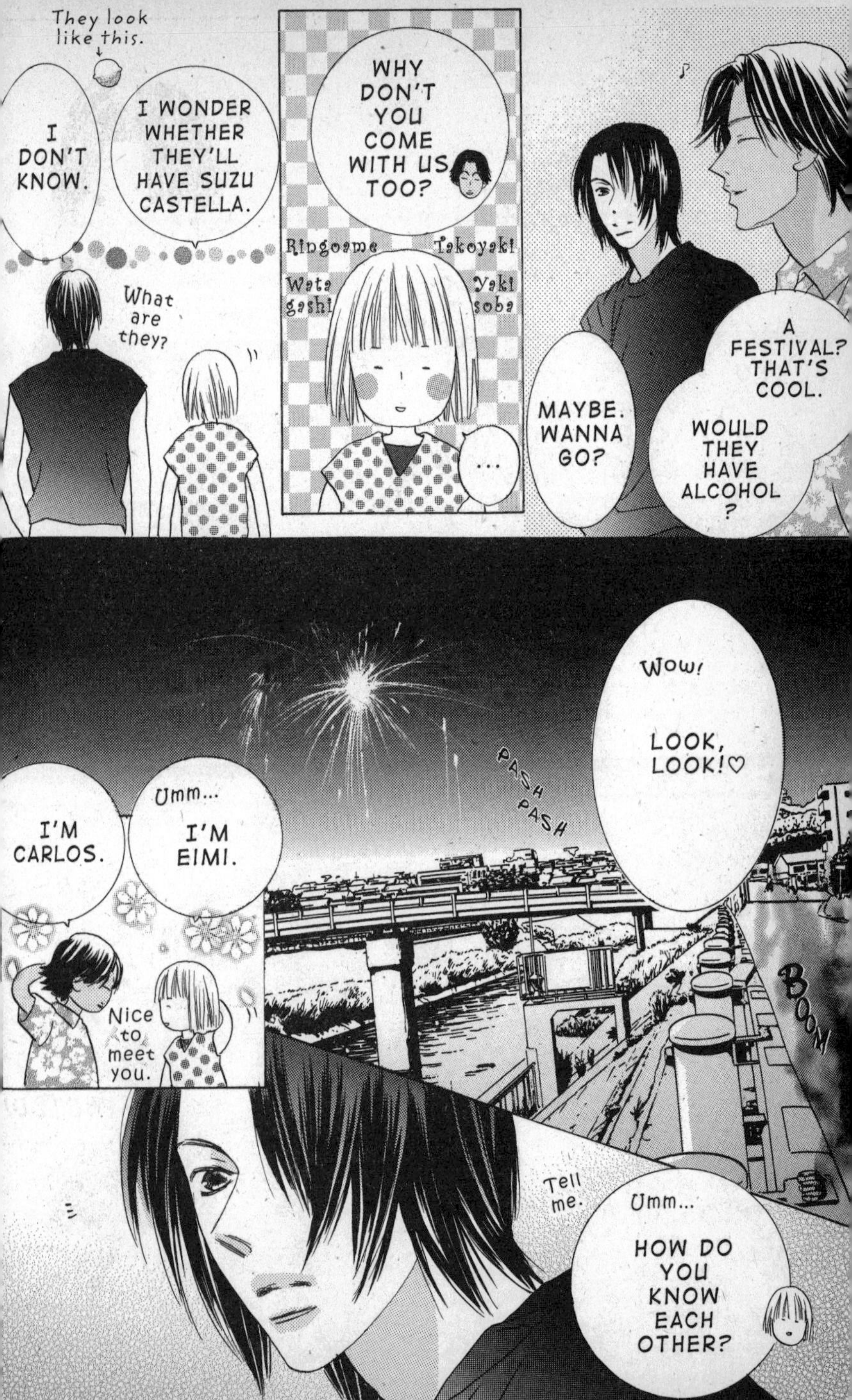
A FESTIVAL? THAT'S COOL.
WOULD THEY HAVE ALCOHOL?
MAYBE. WANNA GO?
WHY DON'T YOU COME WITH US TOO?
Ringoame
Takoyaki
Wata gashi
Yaki soba
...
I WONDER WHETHER THEY'LL HAVE SUZU CASTELLA.
I DON'T KNOW.
They look like this.
What are they?
Wow!
LOOK, LOOK!♡
PASH PASH
BOOM
Umm...
I'M EIMI.
I'M CARLOS.
Nice to meet you.
Tell me.
Umm...
HOW DO YOU KNOW EACH OTHER?

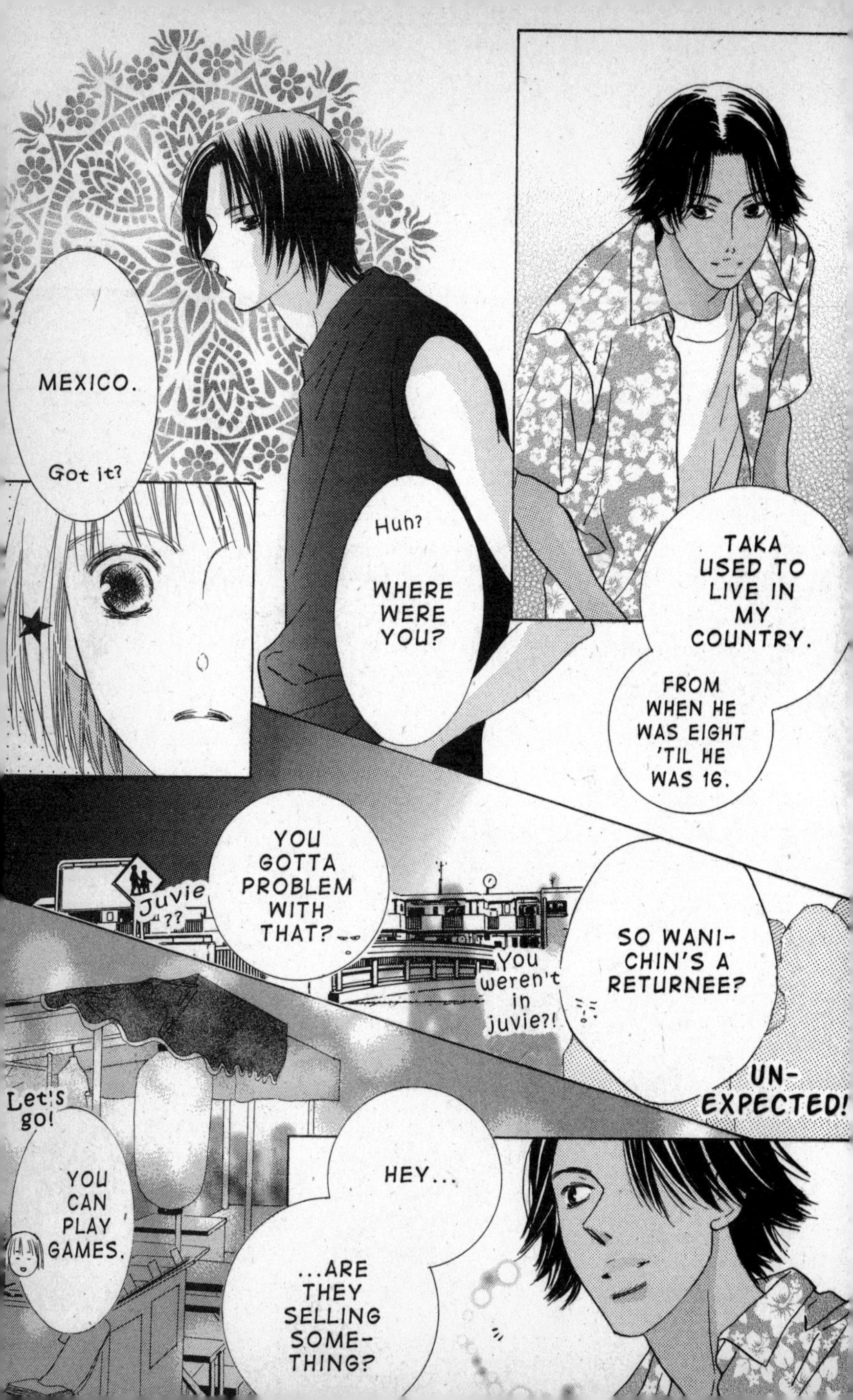
TAKA USED TO LIVE IN MY COUNTRY.
FROM WHEN HE WAS EIGHT 'TIL HE WAS 16.
Huh?
WHERE WERE YOU?
MEXICO.
Got it?
SO WANI-CHIN'S A RETURNEE?
UN-EXPECTED!
You weren't in juvie?!
YOU GOTTA PROBLEM WITH THAT?
Juvie ??
HEY...
...ARE THEY SELLING SOMETHING?
Let's go!
YOU CAN PLAY GAMES.

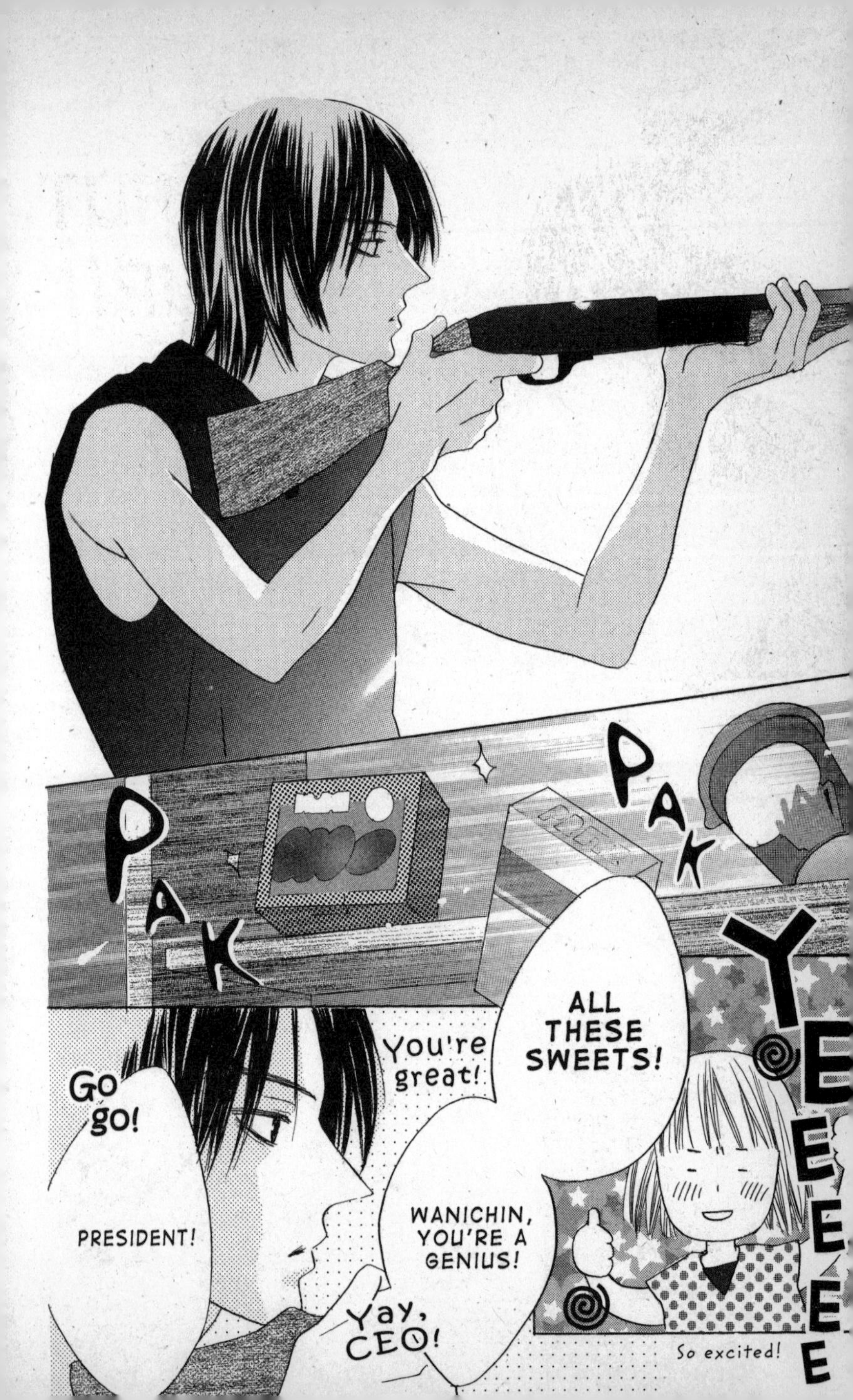
PAK
PAK
YEEEEE
ALL THESE SWEETS!
You're great!
Go go!
PRESIDENT!
WANICHIN, YOU'RE A GENIUS!
Yay, CEO!
So excited!

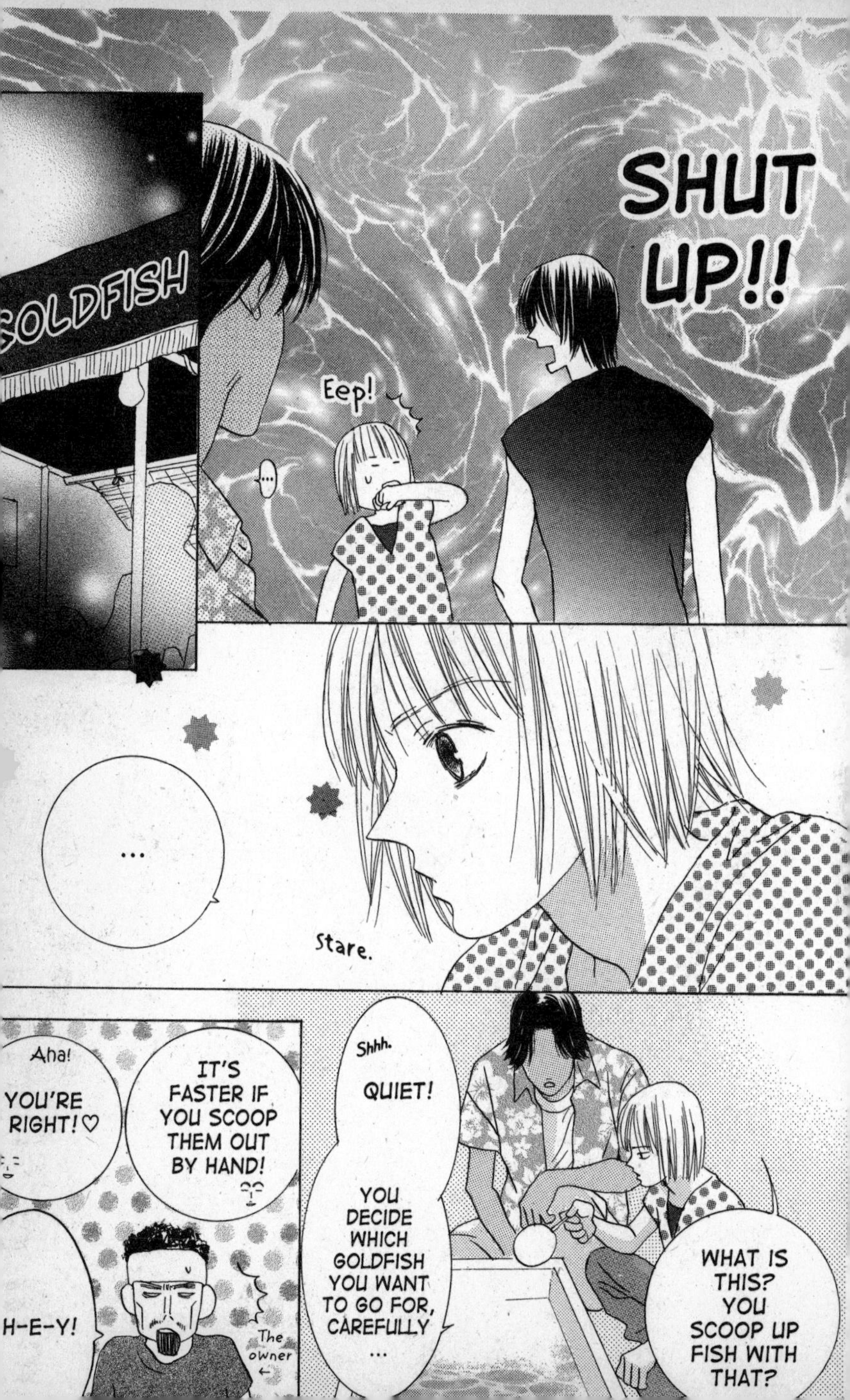
SHUT UP!!
Eep!
...
GOLDFISH
...
Stare.
WHAT IS THIS? YOU SCOOP UP FISH WITH THAT?
Shhh.
QUIET!
YOU DECIDE WHICH GOLDFISH YOU WANT TO GO FOR, CAREFULLY ...
IT'S FASTER IF YOU SCOOP THEM OUT BY HAND!
Aha!
YOU'RE RIGHT! ♡
H-E-Y!
The owner ←

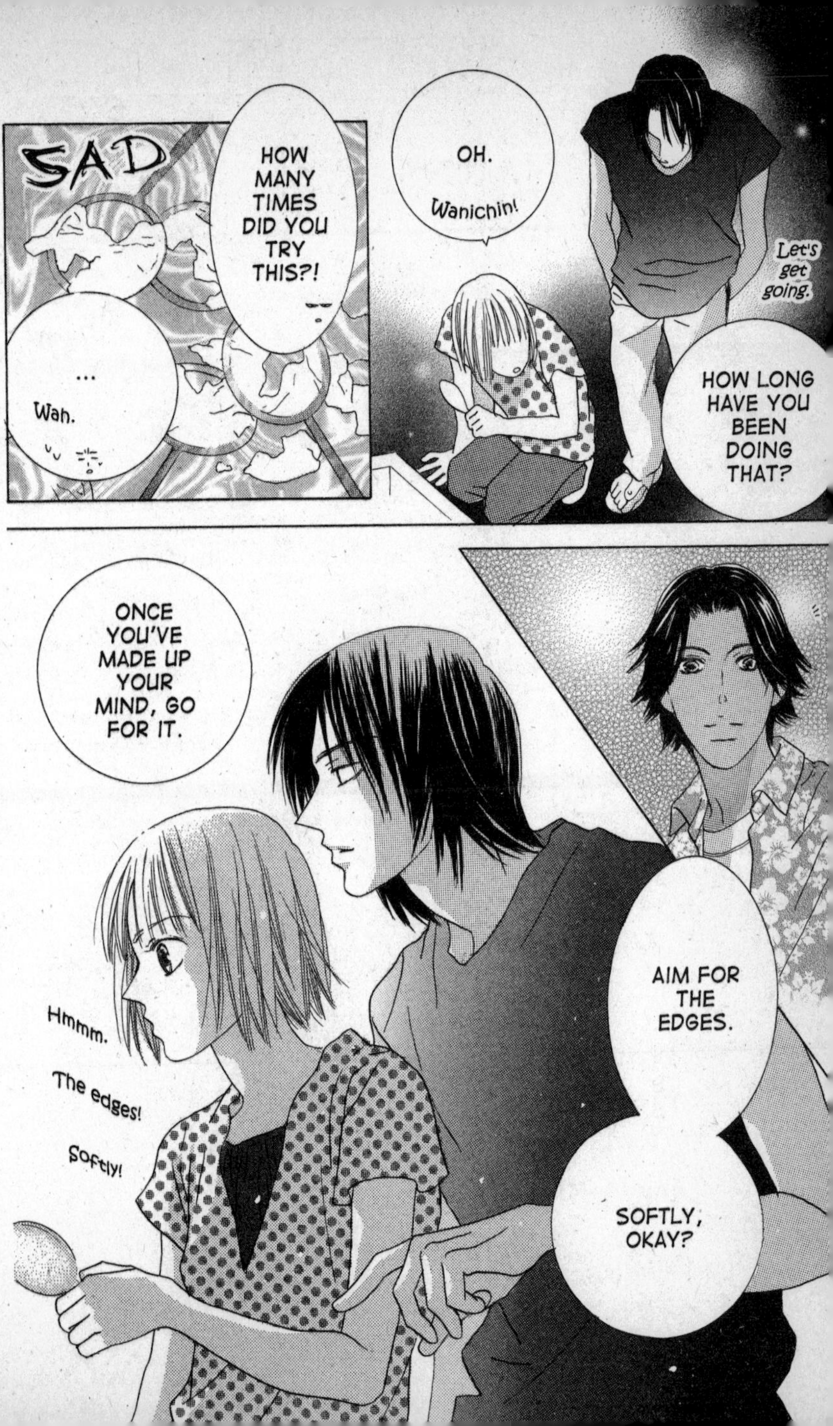
Let's get going.
HOW LONG HAVE YOU BEEN DOING THAT?
OH.
Wanichin!
HOW MANY TIMES DID YOU TRY THIS?!
SAD
...
Wah.
AIM FOR THE EDGES.
SOFTLY, OKAY?
ONCE YOU'VE MADE UP YOUR MIND, GO FOR IT.
Hmmm.
The edges!
Softly!

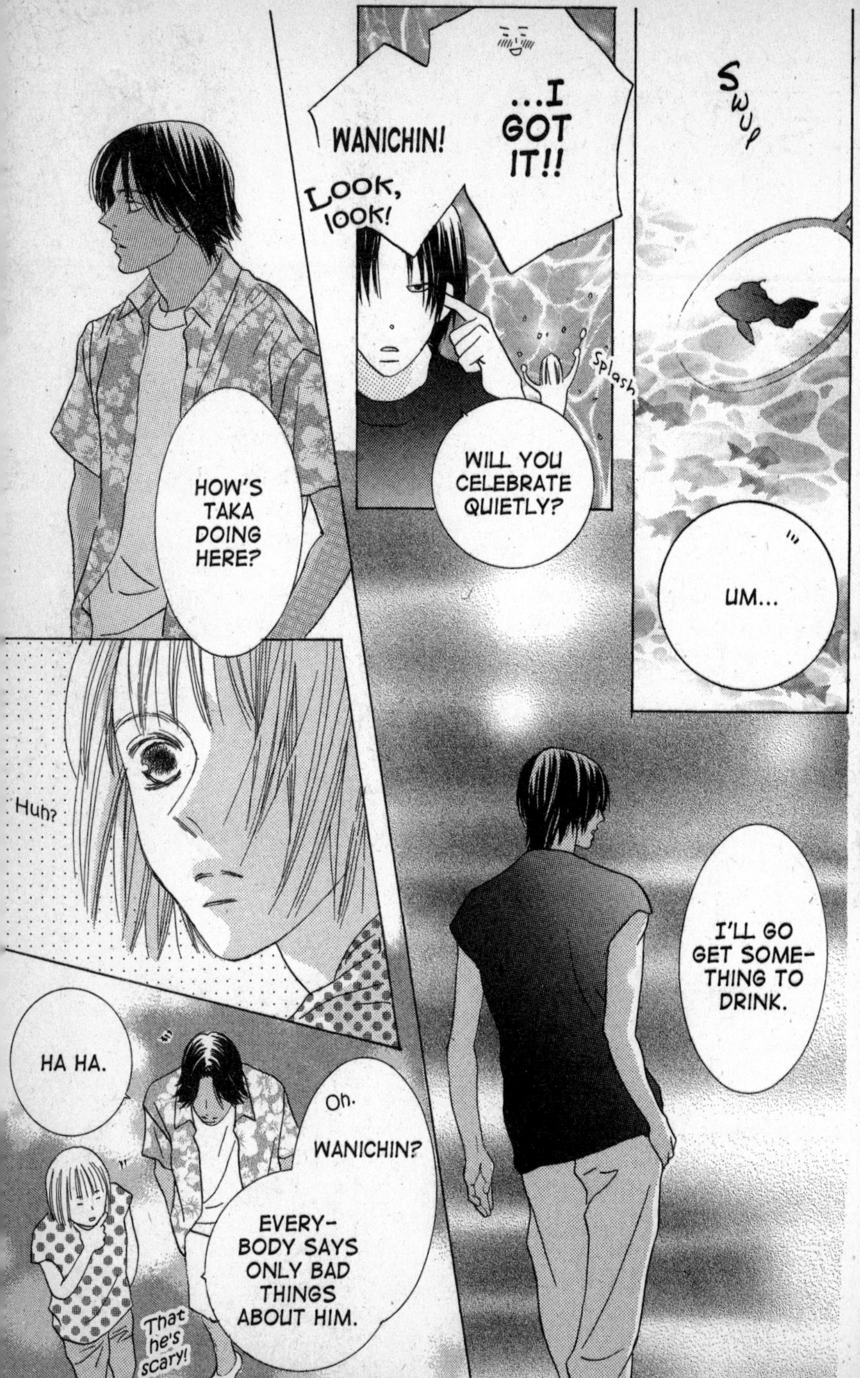
Swul
Um...
...I got it!!
Wanichin!
Look, look!
Splash
Will you celebrate quietly?
How's Taka doing here?
I'll go get some-thing to drink.
Huh?
Oh.
Wanichin?
Every-body says only bad things about him.
That he's scary!
Ha ha.

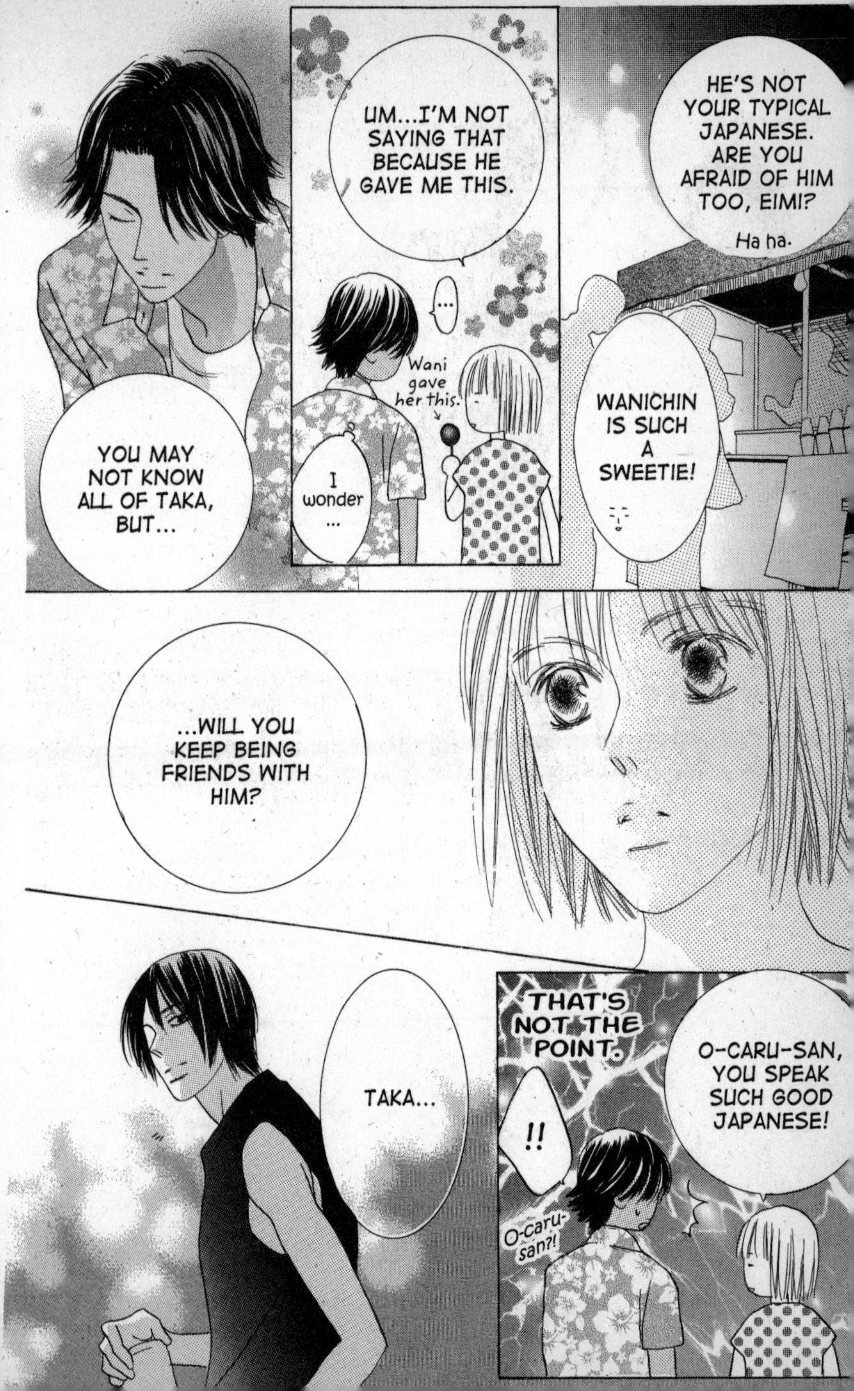
HE'S NOT YOUR TYPICAL JAPANESE. ARE YOU AFRAID OF HIM TOO, EIMI?
Ha ha.
WANICHIN IS SUCH A SWEETIE!
UM...I'M NOT SAYING THAT BECAUSE HE GAVE ME THIS.
...
Wani gave her this.
I wonder ...
YOU MAY NOT KNOW ALL OF TAKA, BUT...
...WILL YOU KEEP BEING FRIENDS WITH HIM?
O-CARU-SAN, YOU SPEAK SUCH GOOD JAPANESE!
THAT'S NOT THE POINT.
!!
O-caru-san?!
TAKA...

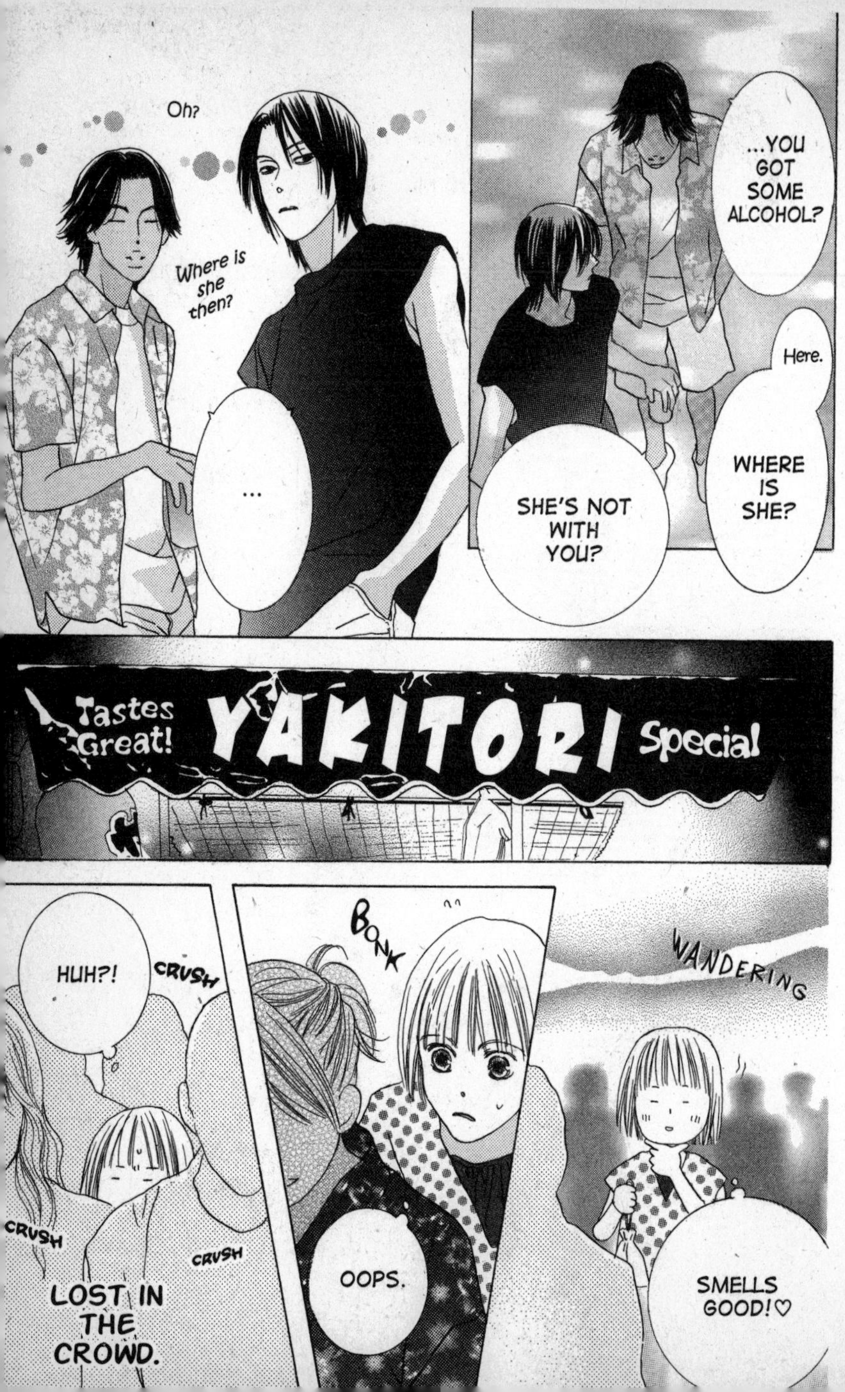
...YOU GOT SOME ALCOHOL?
Here.
WHERE IS SHE?
SHE'S NOT WITH YOU?
Oh?
Where is she then?
...
Tastes Great!
YAKITORI
Special
WANDERING
SMELLS GOOD!♡
BONK
OOPS.
HUH?!
CRUSH
CRUSH
CRUSH
LOST IN THE CROWD.

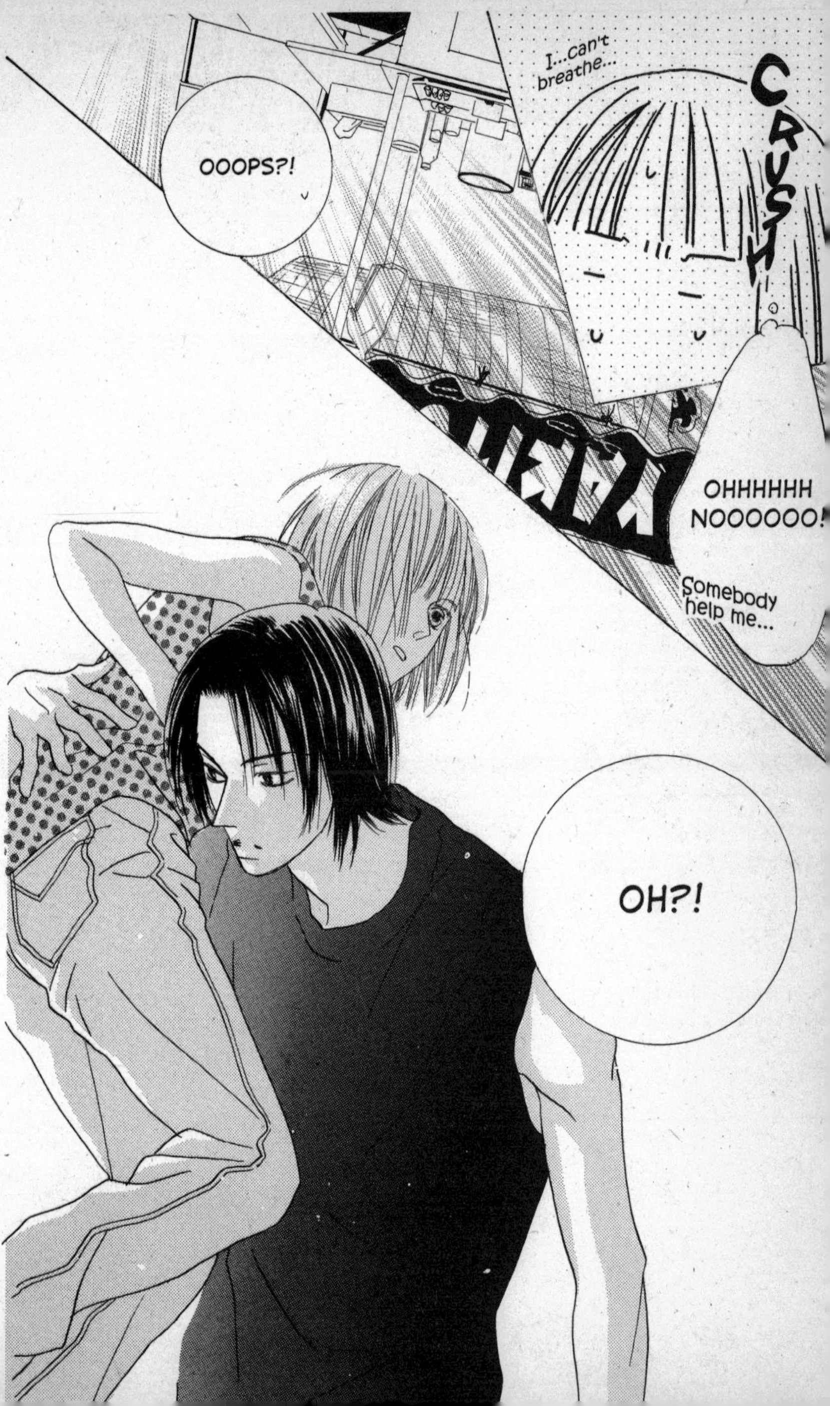
I...can't breathe...
CRUSH
OOOPS?!
OHHHHHH NOOOOOO!
Somebody help me...
OH?!

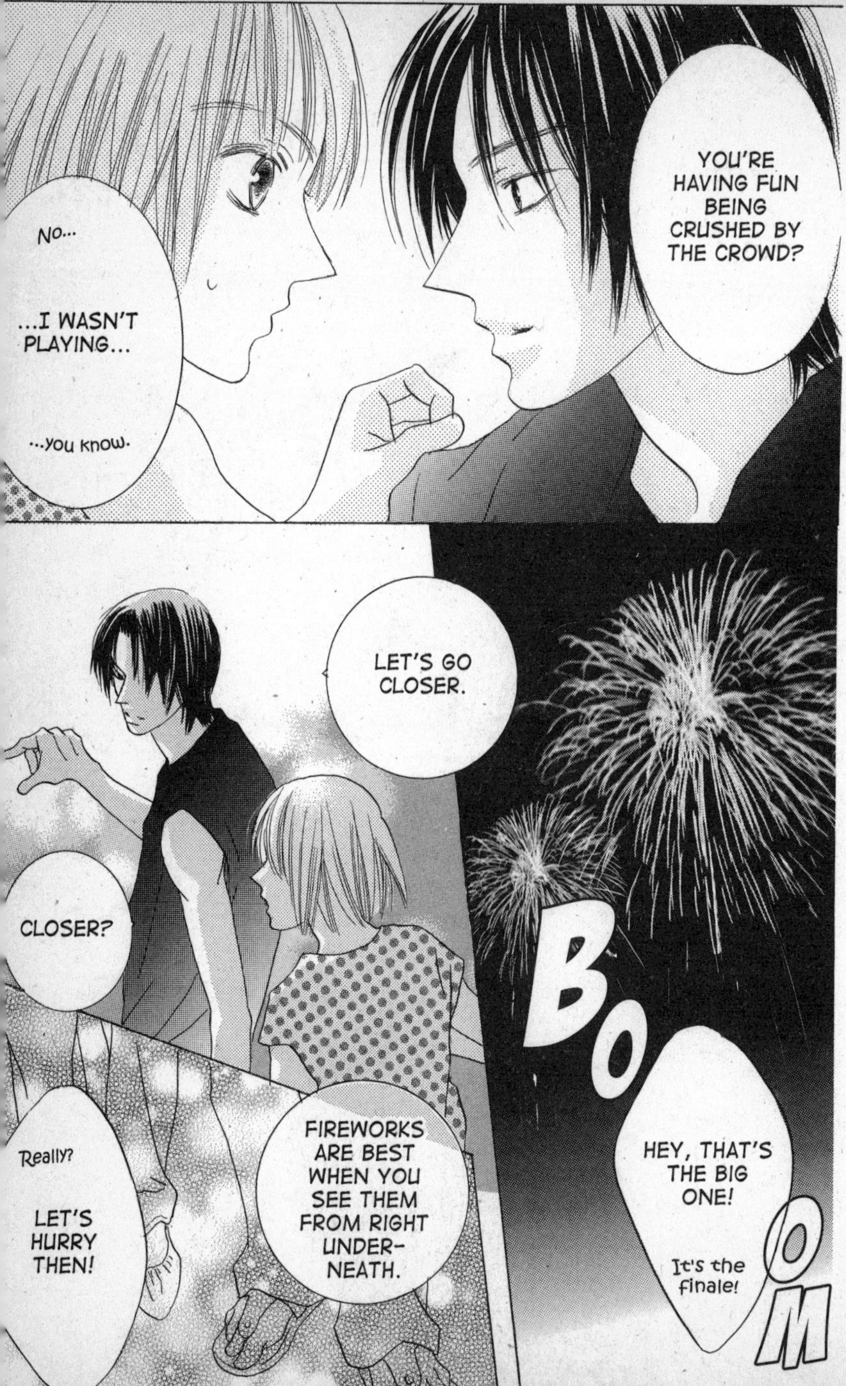
YOU'RE HAVING FUN BEING CRUSHED BY THE CROWD?
No... ...I WASN'T PLAYING... ...you know.
BOOOM
HEY, THAT'S THE BIG ONE!
It's the finale!
LET'S GO CLOSER.
CLOSER?
FIREWORKS ARE BEST WHEN YOU SEE THEM FROM RIGHT UNDER-NEATH.
Really?
LET'S HURRY THEN!

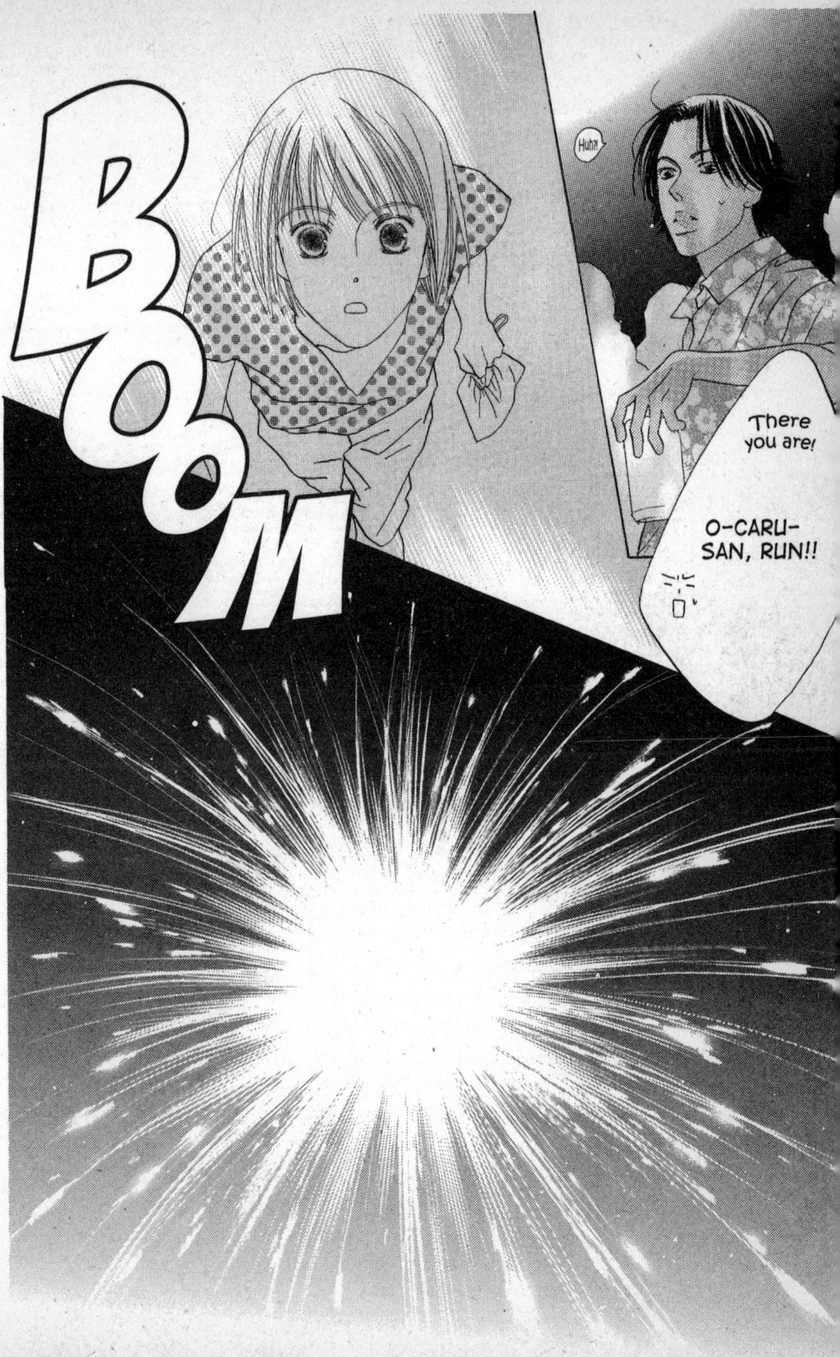
Huh?!
There you are!
O-CARU-SAN, RUN!!
BOOM

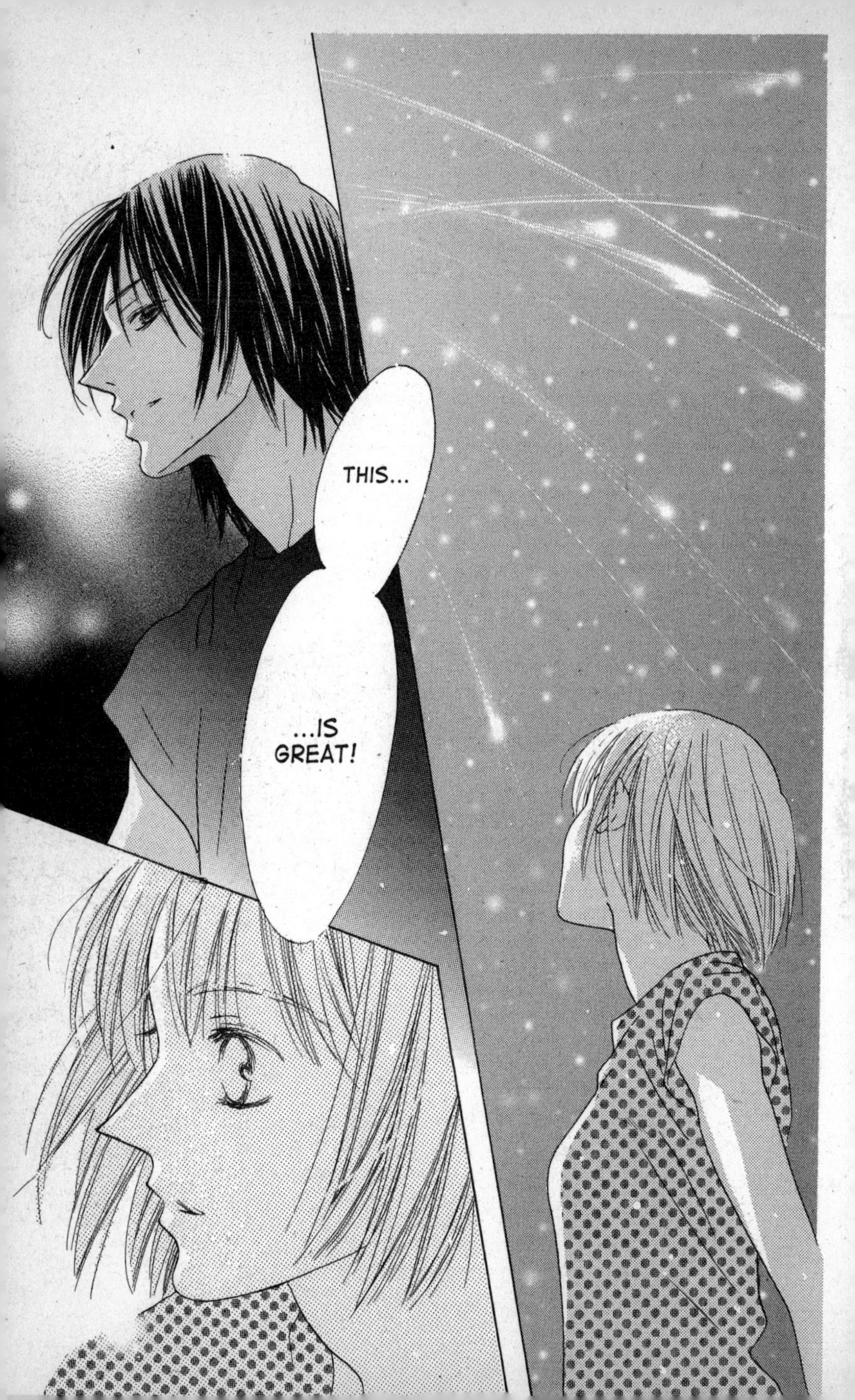
THIS...
...IS GREAT!

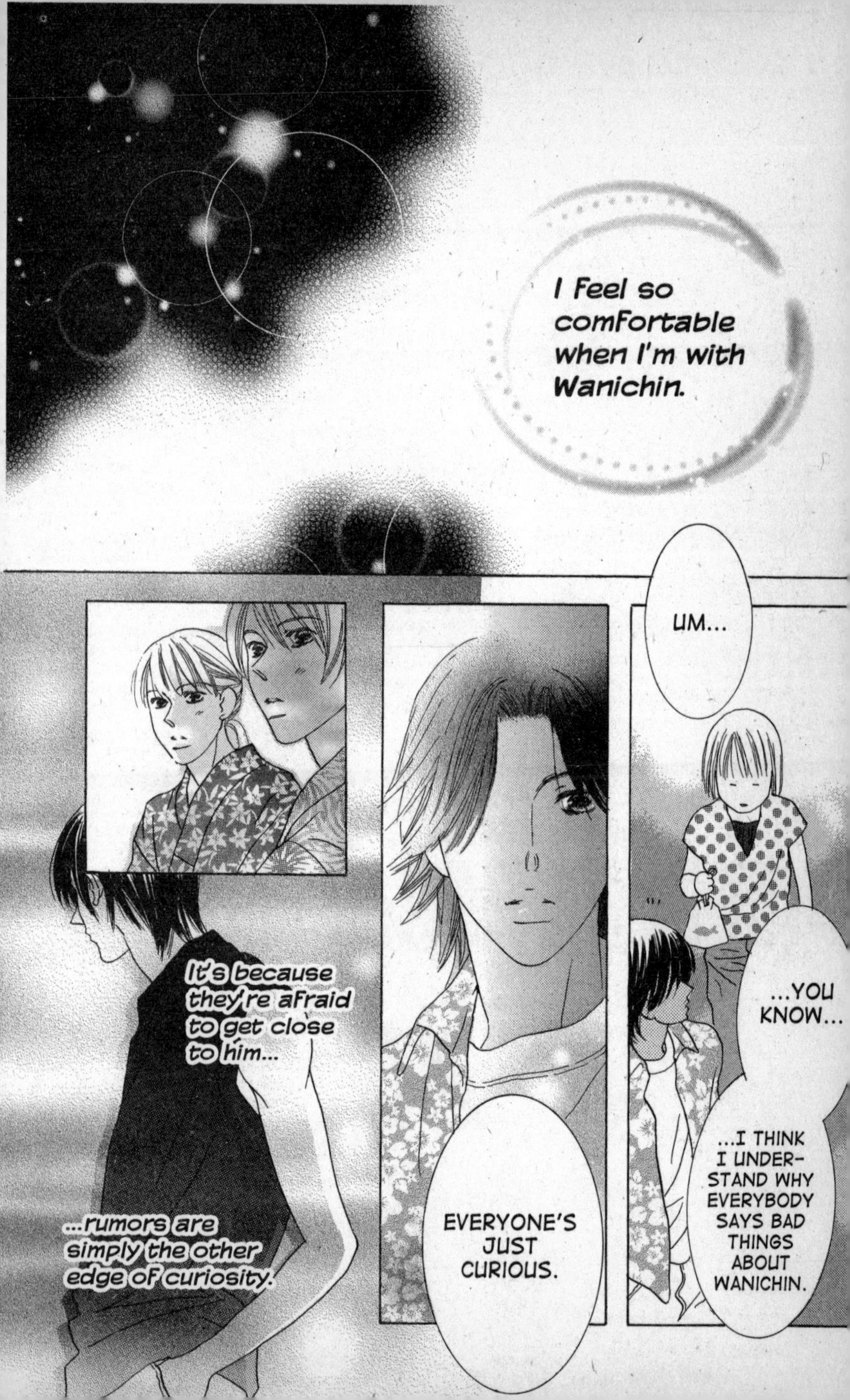
I Feel so comfortable when I'm with Wanichin.
UM...
...YOU KNOW...
...I THINK I UNDERSTAND WHY EVERYBODY SAYS BAD THINGS ABOUT WANICHIN.
EVERYONE'S JUST CURIOUS.
It's because they're afraid to get close to him...
...rumors are simply the other edge of curiosity.

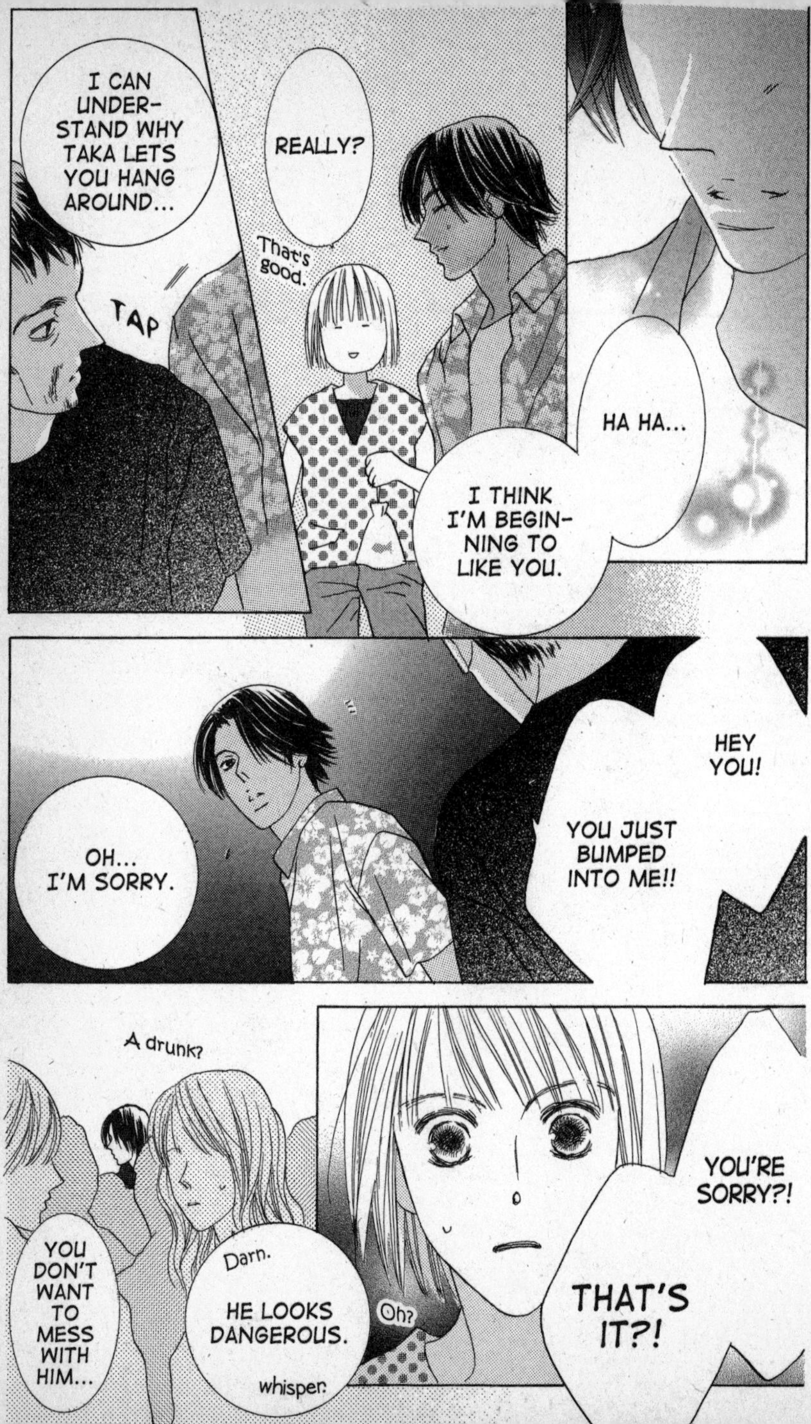
I CAN UNDER-STAND WHY TAKA LETS YOU HANG AROUND...
REALLY?
That's good.
TAP
HA HA...
I THINK I'M BEGIN-NING TO LIKE YOU.
HEY YOU!
YOU JUST BUMPED INTO ME!!
OH... I'M SORRY.
A drunk?
YOU DON'T WANT TO MESS WITH HIM...
Darn.
HE LOOKS DANGEROUS.
whisper.
Oh?
YOU'RE SORRY?!
THAT'S IT?!

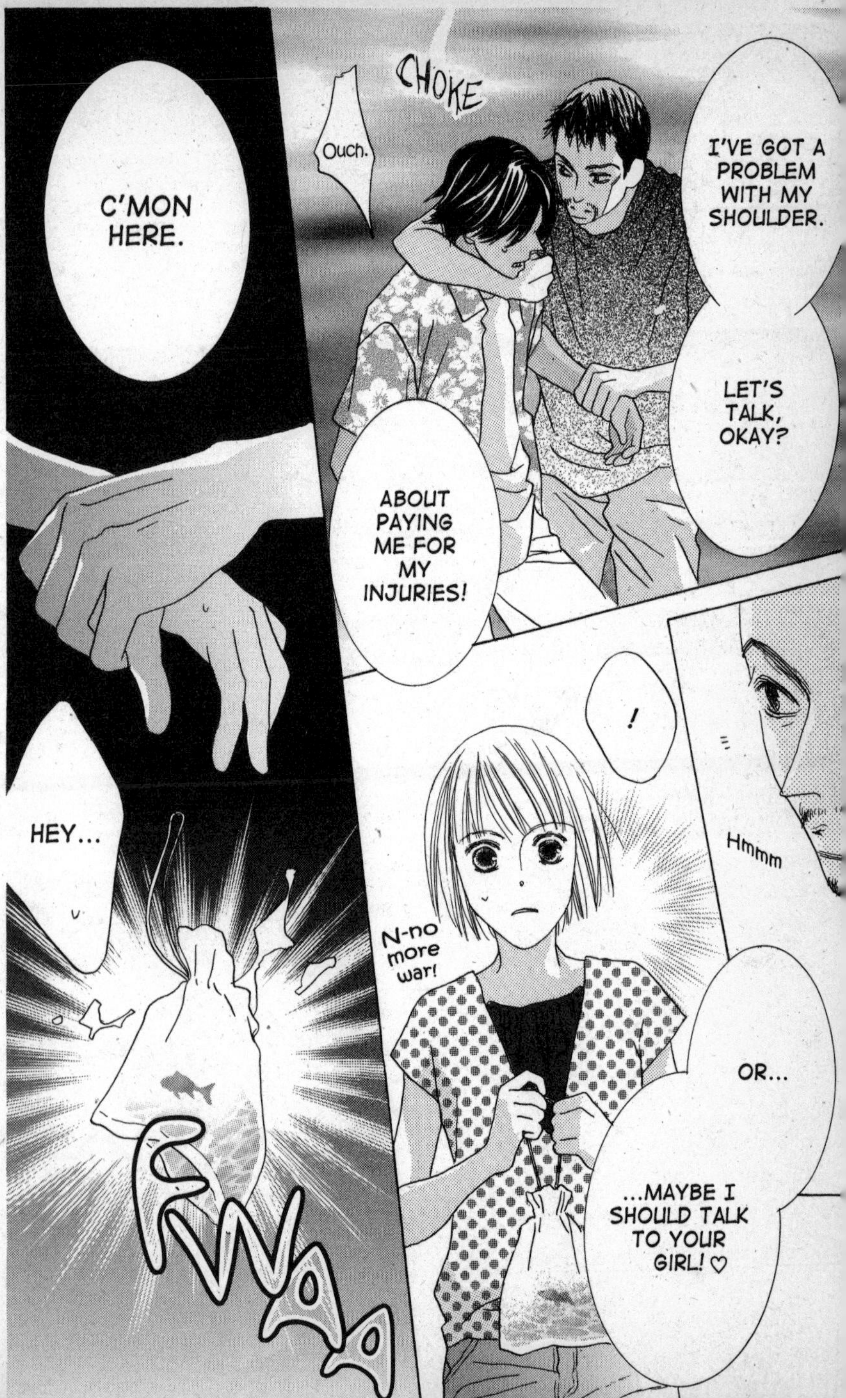
I'VE GOT A PROBLEM WITH MY SHOULDER.
LET'S TALK, OKAY?
CHOKE
Ouch.
ABOUT PAYING ME FOR MY INJURIES!
C'MON HERE.
Hmmm
!
OR...
...MAYBE I SHOULD TALK TO YOUR GIRL! ♡
N-no more war!
HEY...
FWAA

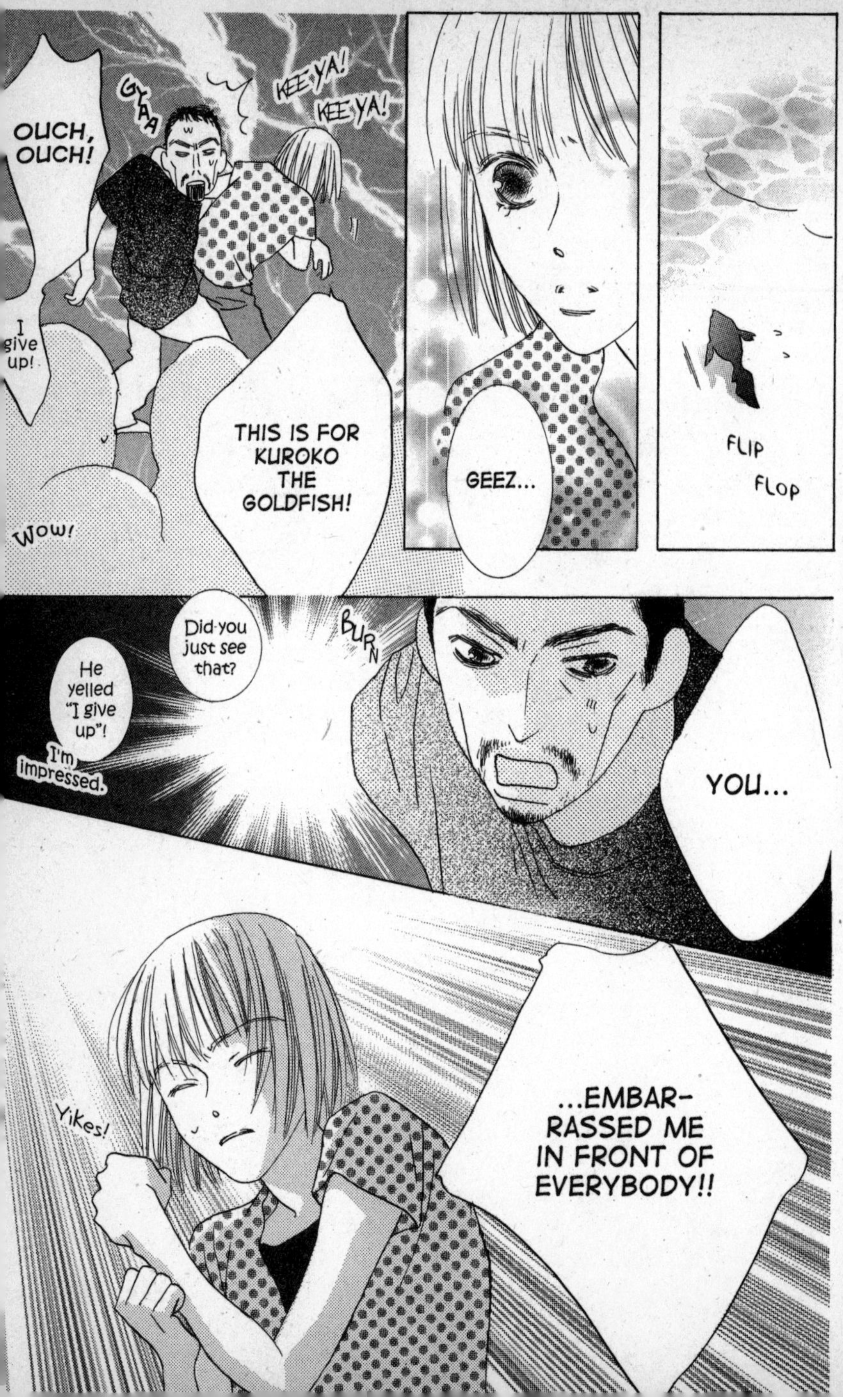
FLIP
FLOP
GEEZ...
THIS IS FOR KUROKO THE GOLDFISH!
KEE YA!
KEE YA!
GYAA
OUCH, OUCH!
I give up!
WOW!
YOU...
BURN
Did you just see that?
He yelled "I give up"!
I'm impressed.
...EMBAR-RASSED ME IN FRONT OF EVERYBODY!!
Yikes!

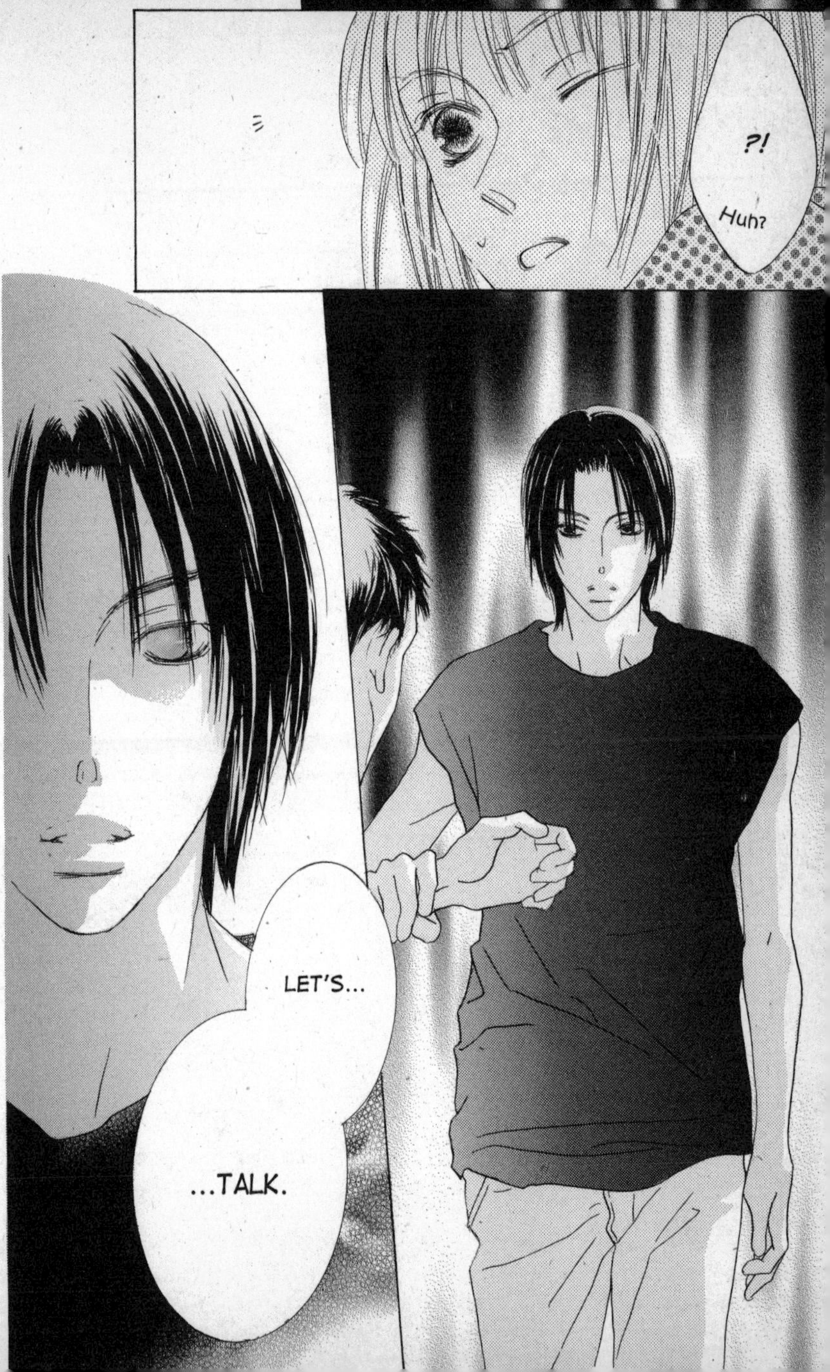
?!
Huh?
LET'S...
...TALK.

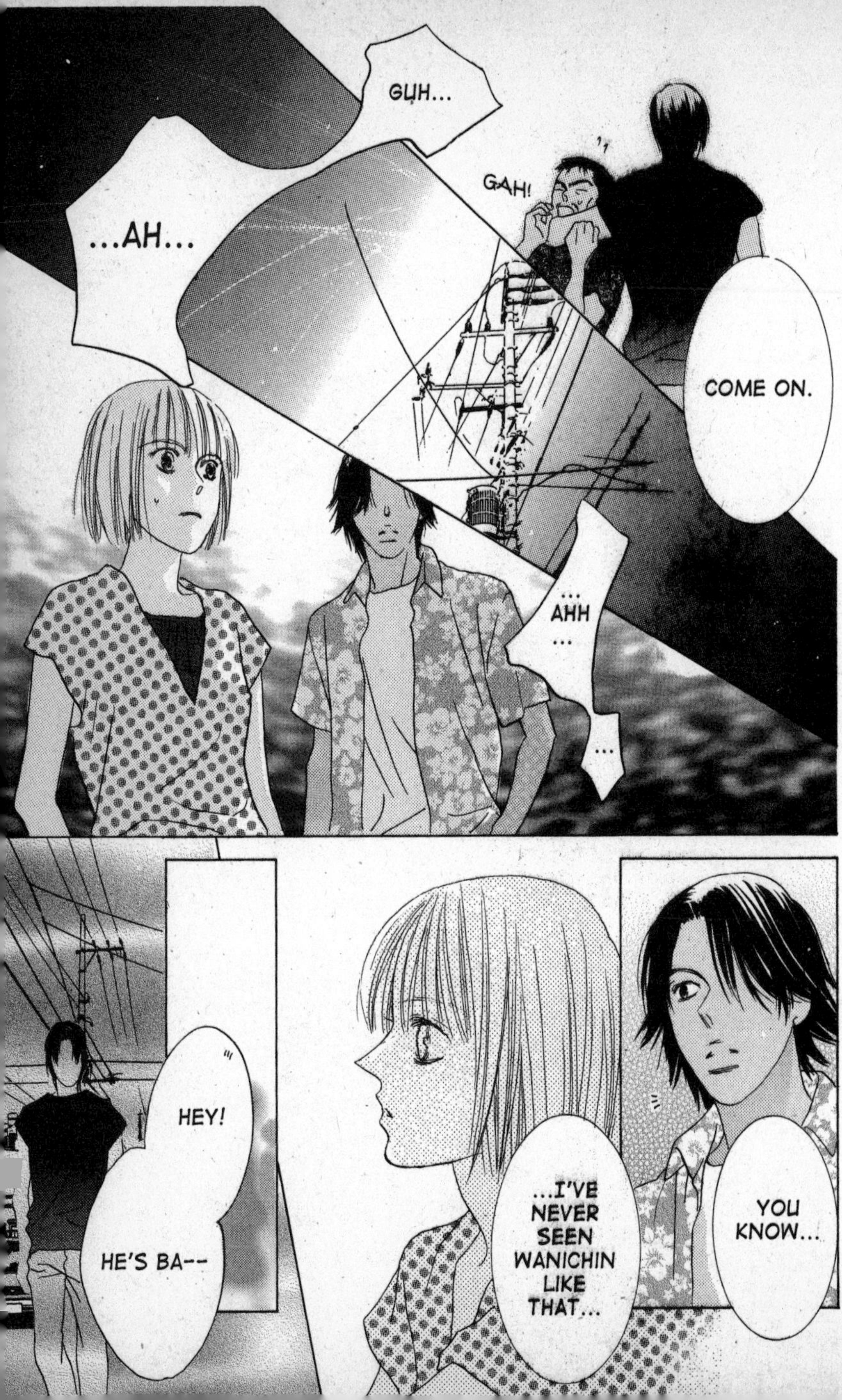
GUH...
...AH...
GAH!
COME ON.
...
AHH
...
...
YOU KNOW...
...I'VE NEVER SEEN WANICHIN LIKE THAT...
HEY!
HE'S BA--

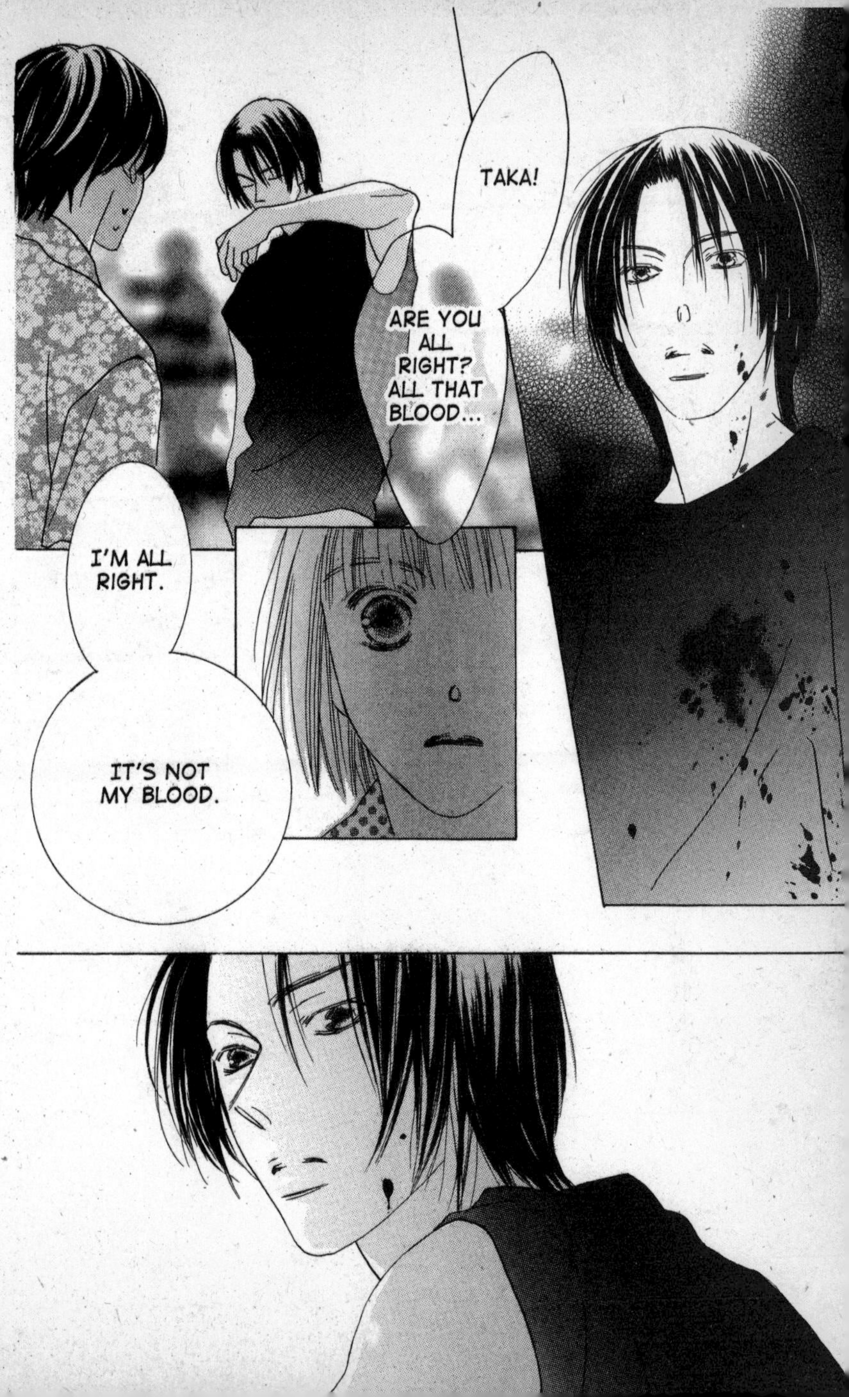
TAKA!
ARE YOU ALL RIGHT? ALL THAT BLOOD...
I'M ALL RIGHT.
IT'S NOT MY BLOOD.

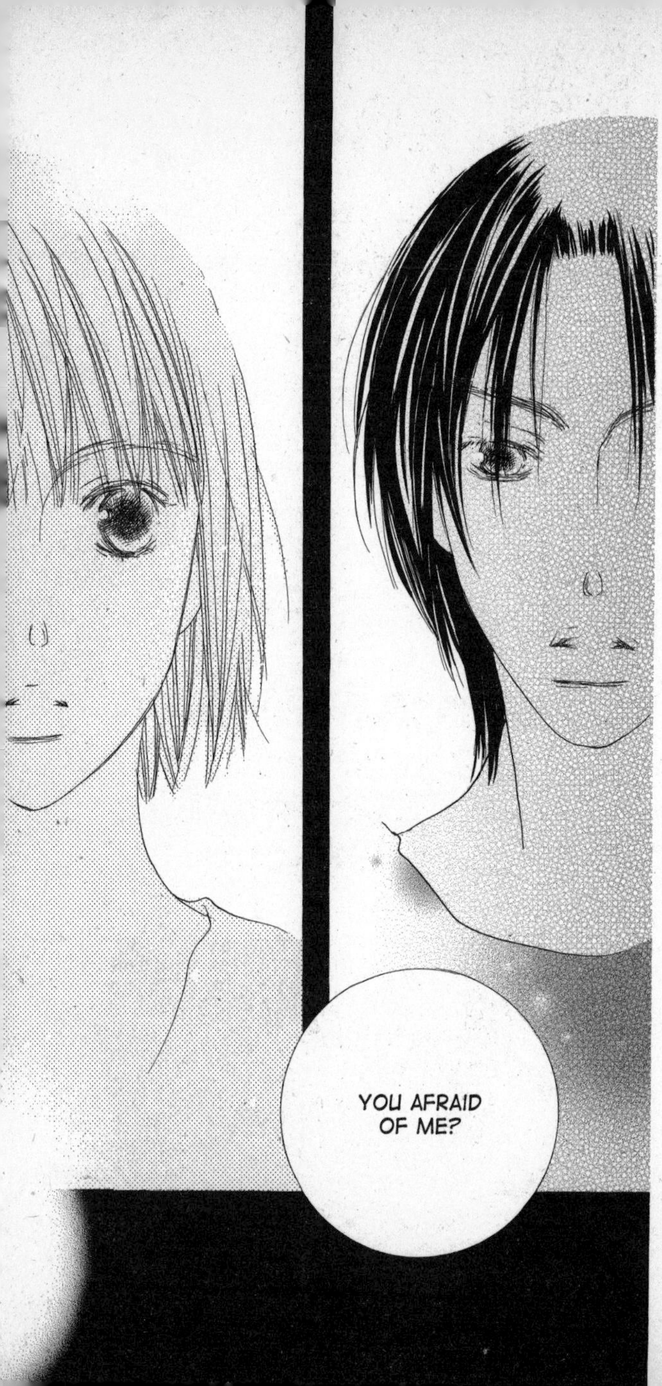
YOU AFRAID OF ME?

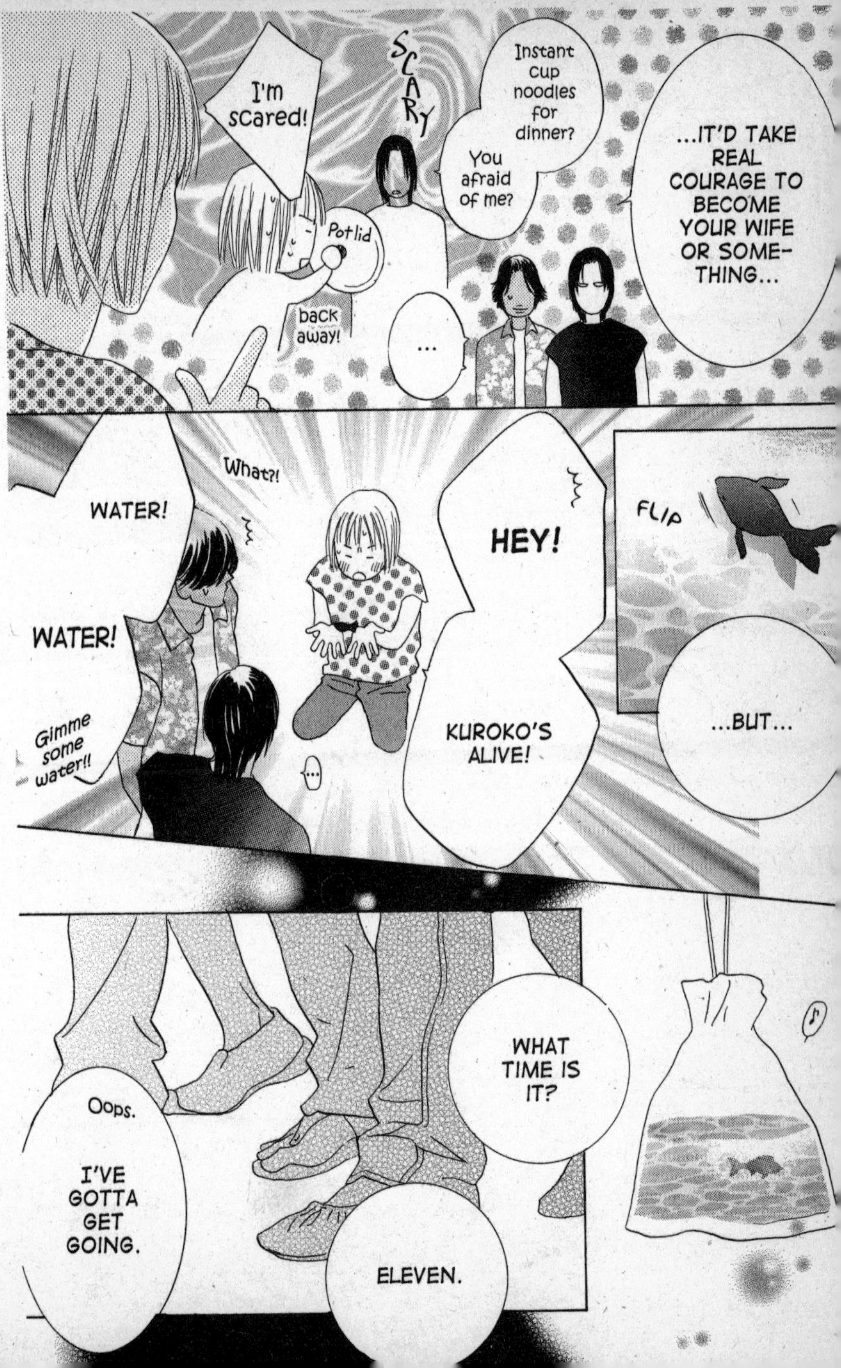
...IT'D TAKE REAL COURAGE TO BECOME YOUR WIFE OR SOME-THING...
Instant cup noodles for dinner?
You afraid of me?
SCARY
I'm scared!
Potlid
back away!
...
FLIP
...BUT...
HEY!
KUROKO'S ALIVE!
What?!
WATER!
WATER!
Gimme some water!!
...
WHAT TIME IS IT?
ELEVEN.
Oops.
I'VE GOTTA GET GOING.

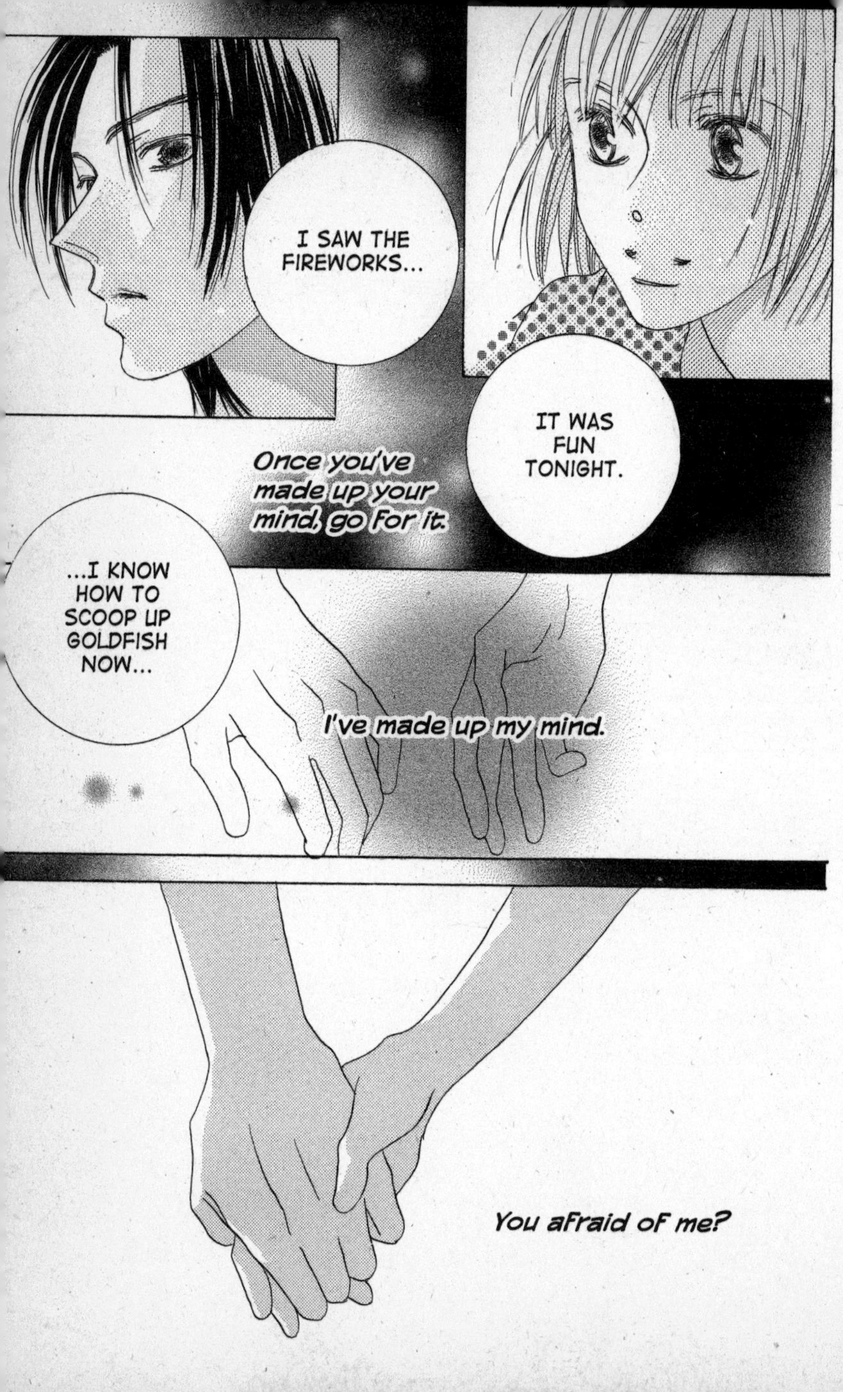
I SAW THE FIREWORKS...
IT WAS FUN TONIGHT.
Once you've made up your mind, go for it.
...I KNOW HOW TO SCOOP UP GOLDFISH NOW...
I've made up my mind.
You afraid of me?

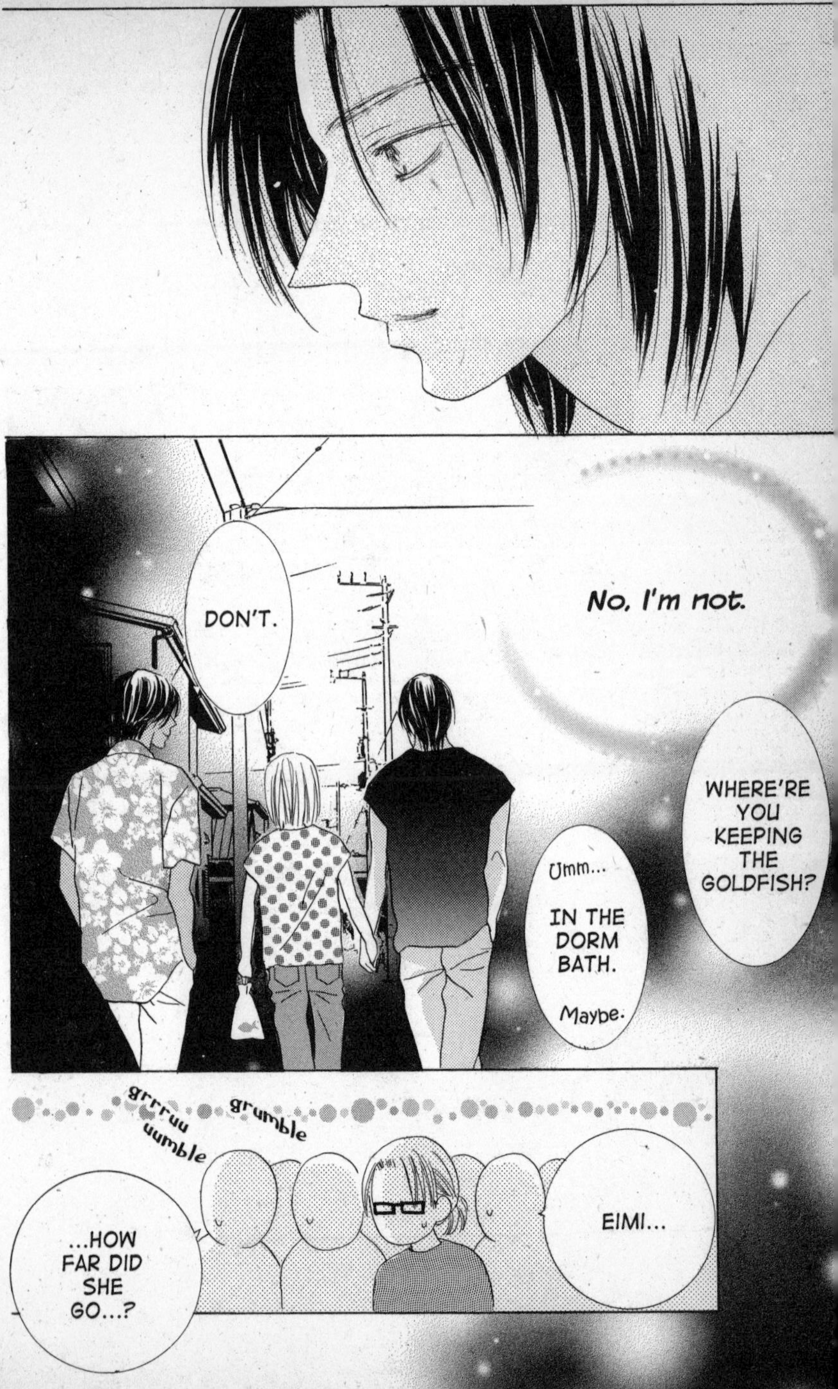
No, I'm not.
DON'T.
WHERE'RE YOU KEEPING THE GOLDFISH?
Umm... IN THE DORM BATH. Maybe.
grumble
grrruu uumble
EIMI...
...HOW FAR DID SHE GO...?

BEAUTY
IS THE
BEAST

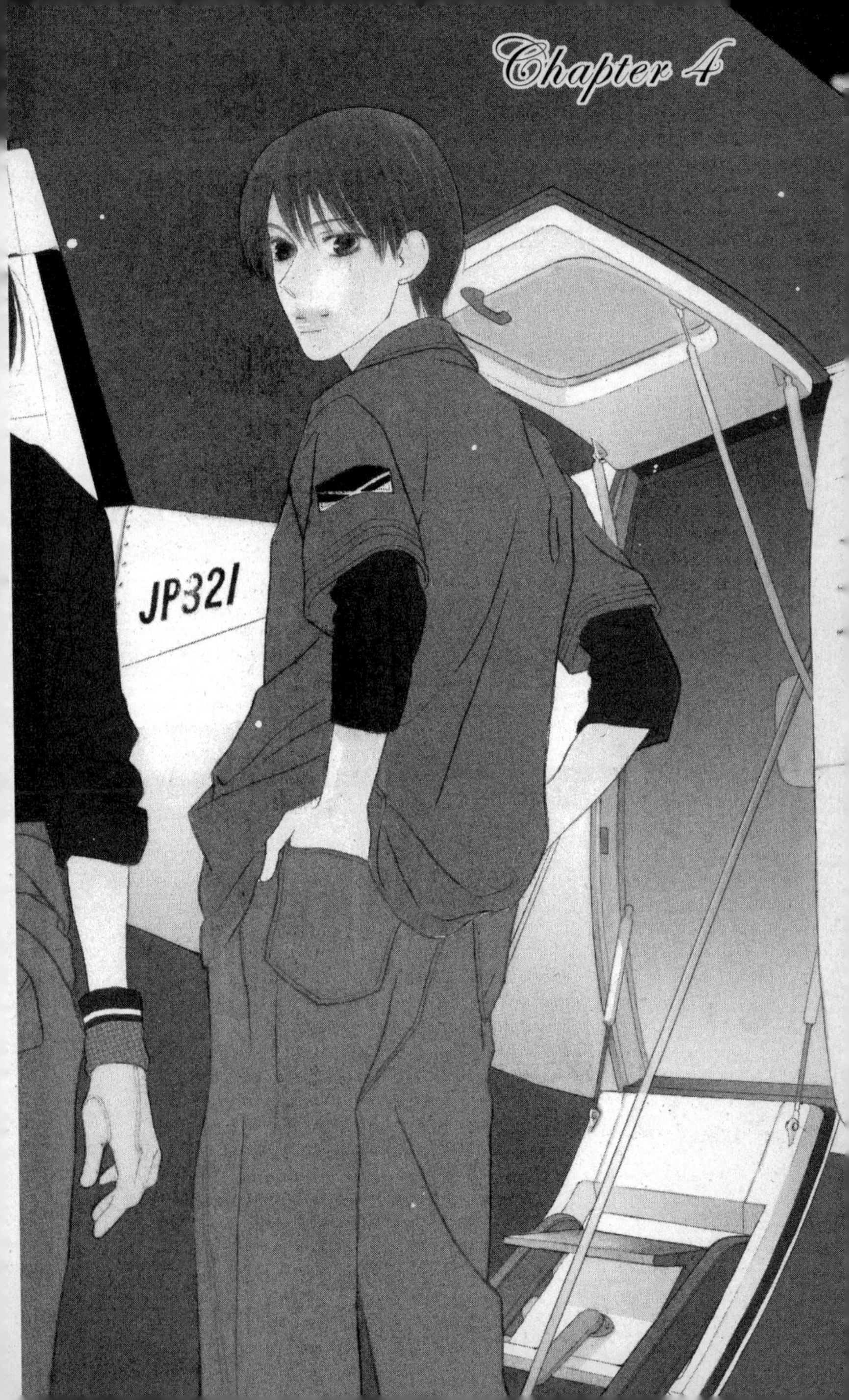
Chapter 4
JP321

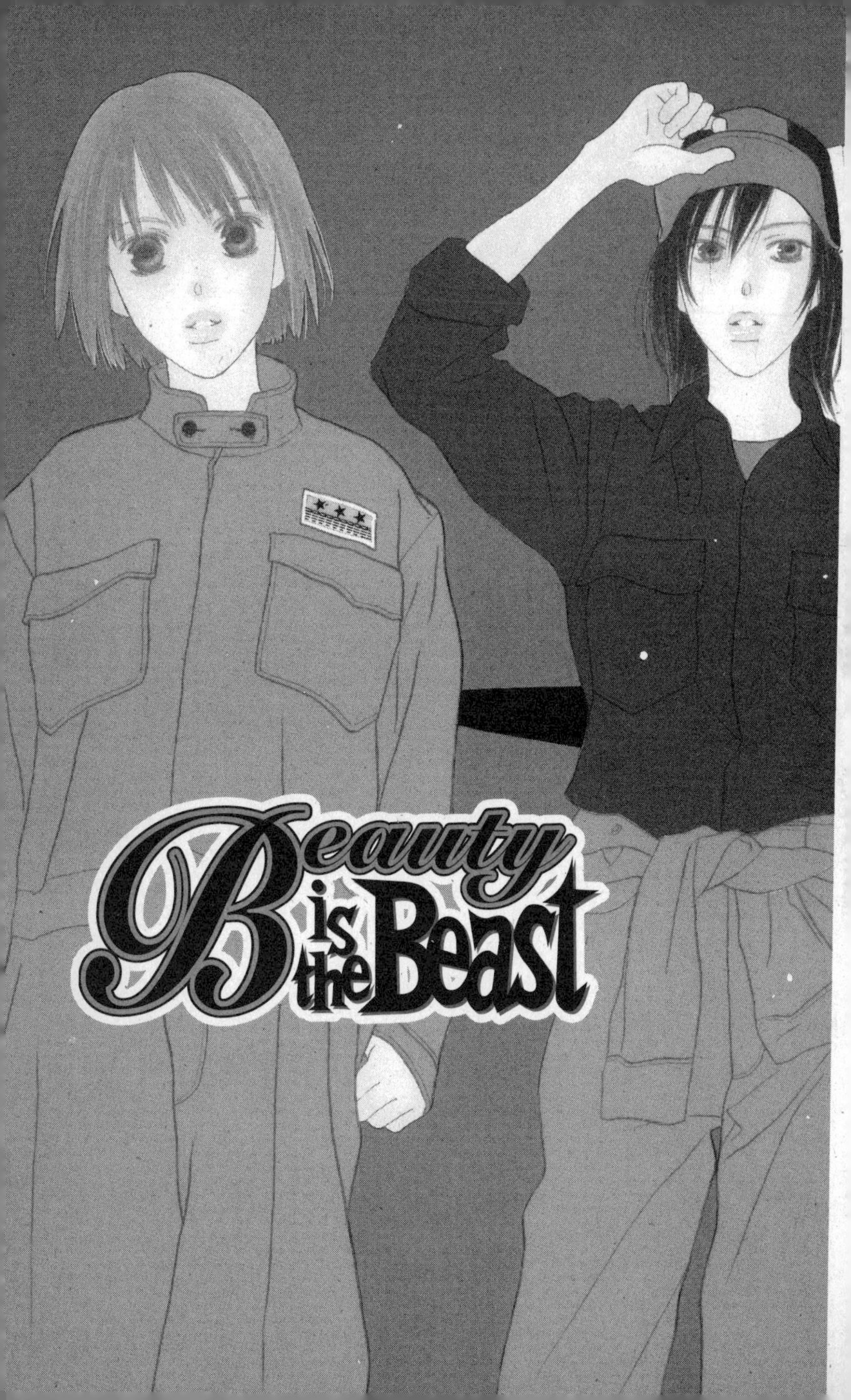
Beauty is the Beast

BEAUTY
IS THE
BEAST

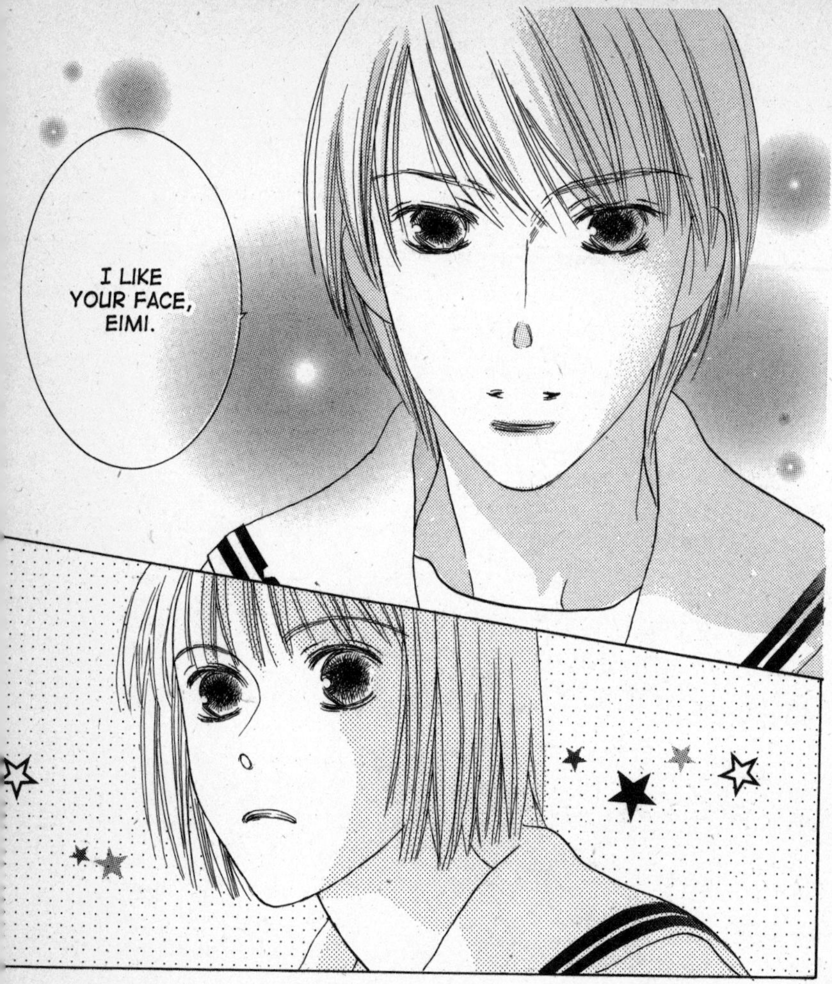
I LIKE YOUR FACE, EIMI.

A Must-have for Dorm Life 3: Alarm Clocks

You need a loud one, because no one wakes you up.
But if it's too loud, your neighbors will scold you, so it's difficult.
I had a friend who had real trouble waking up in the morning, so she used a super-loud alarm clock, and woke up under the pressure of having to shut it off quickly. (I kinda respected her for that.)

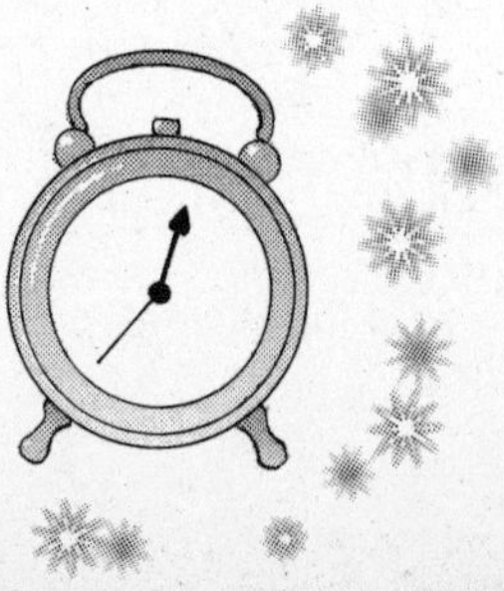

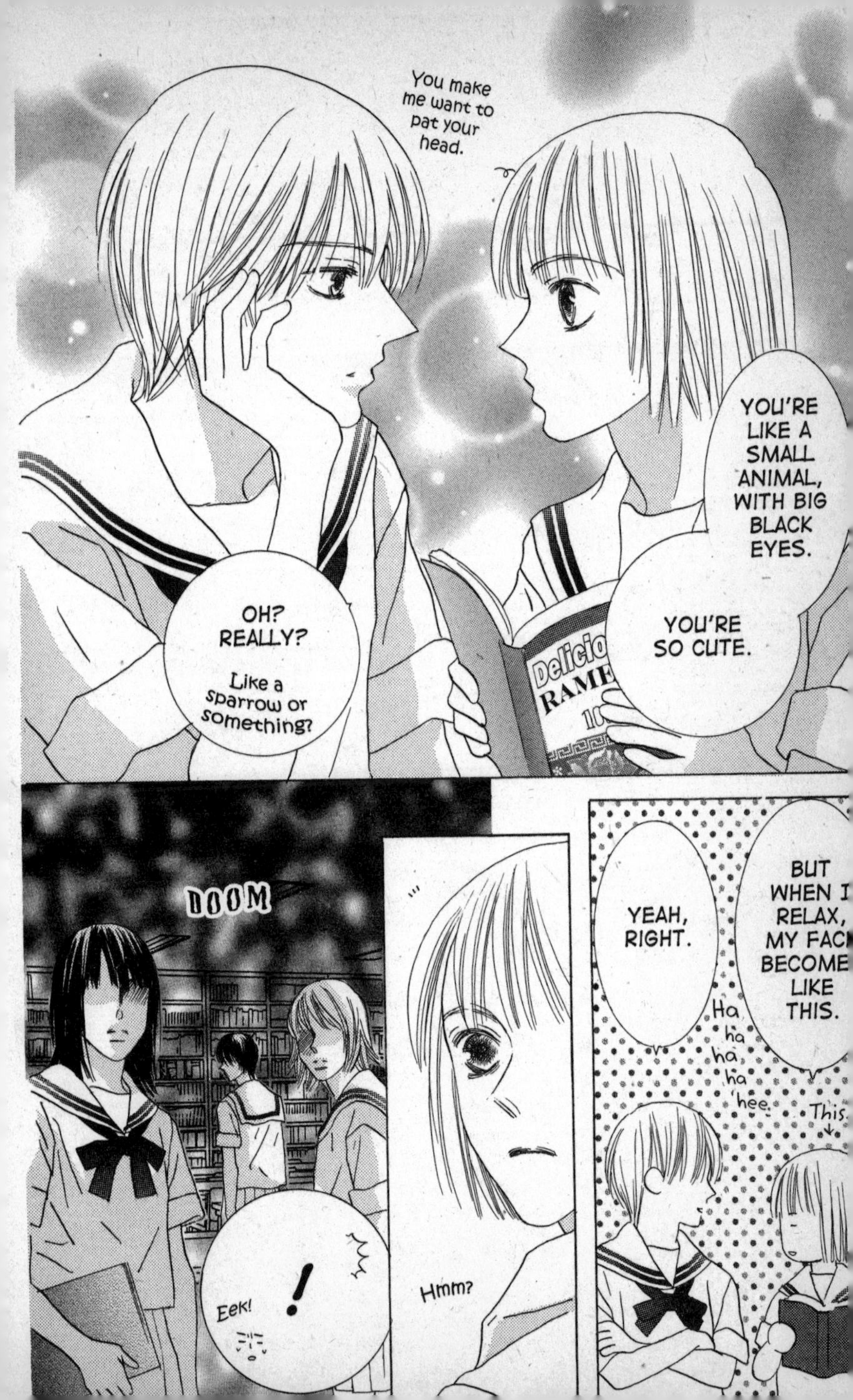
You make me want to pat your head.
YOU'RE LIKE A SMALL ANIMAL, WITH BIG BLACK EYES.
YOU'RE SO CUTE.
OH? REALLY?
Like a sparrow or something?
BUT WHEN I RELAX, MY FAC BECOME LIKE THIS.
YEAH, RIGHT.
Ha ha ha ha hee.
This.
...
Hmm?
DOOM
!
Eek!

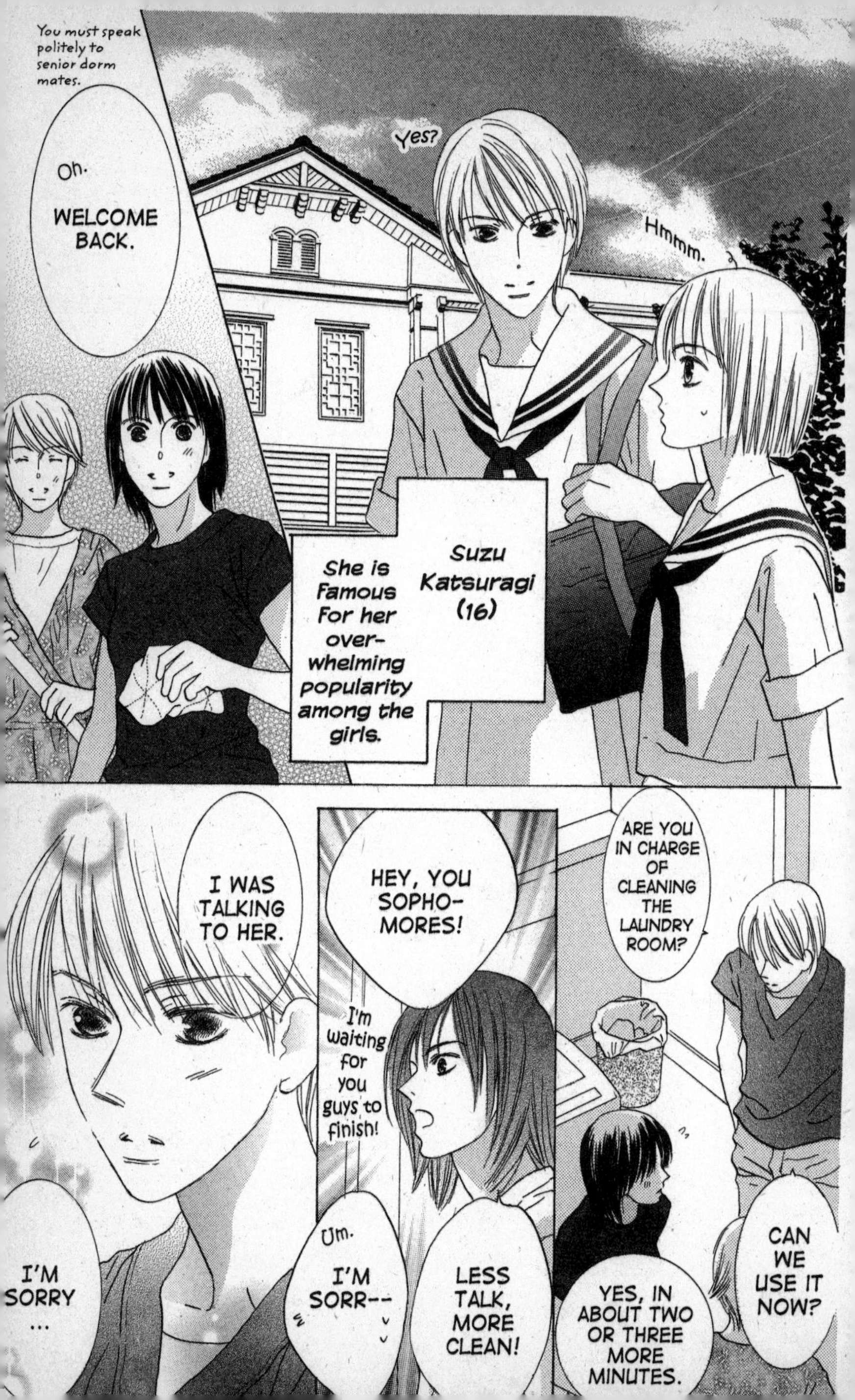
Hmmm.
Yes?
Suzu Katsuragi (16)
She is famous for her over-whelming popularity among the girls.
Oh.
WELCOME BACK.
You must speak politely to senior dorm mates.
ARE YOU IN CHARGE OF CLEANING THE LAUNDRY ROOM?
CAN WE USE IT NOW?
YES, IN ABOUT TWO OR THREE MORE MINUTES.
HEY, YOU SOPHO-MORES!
I'm waiting for you guys to finish!
Um.
I'M SORR--
LESS TALK, MORE CLEAN!
I WAS TALKING TO HER.
I'M SORRY ...

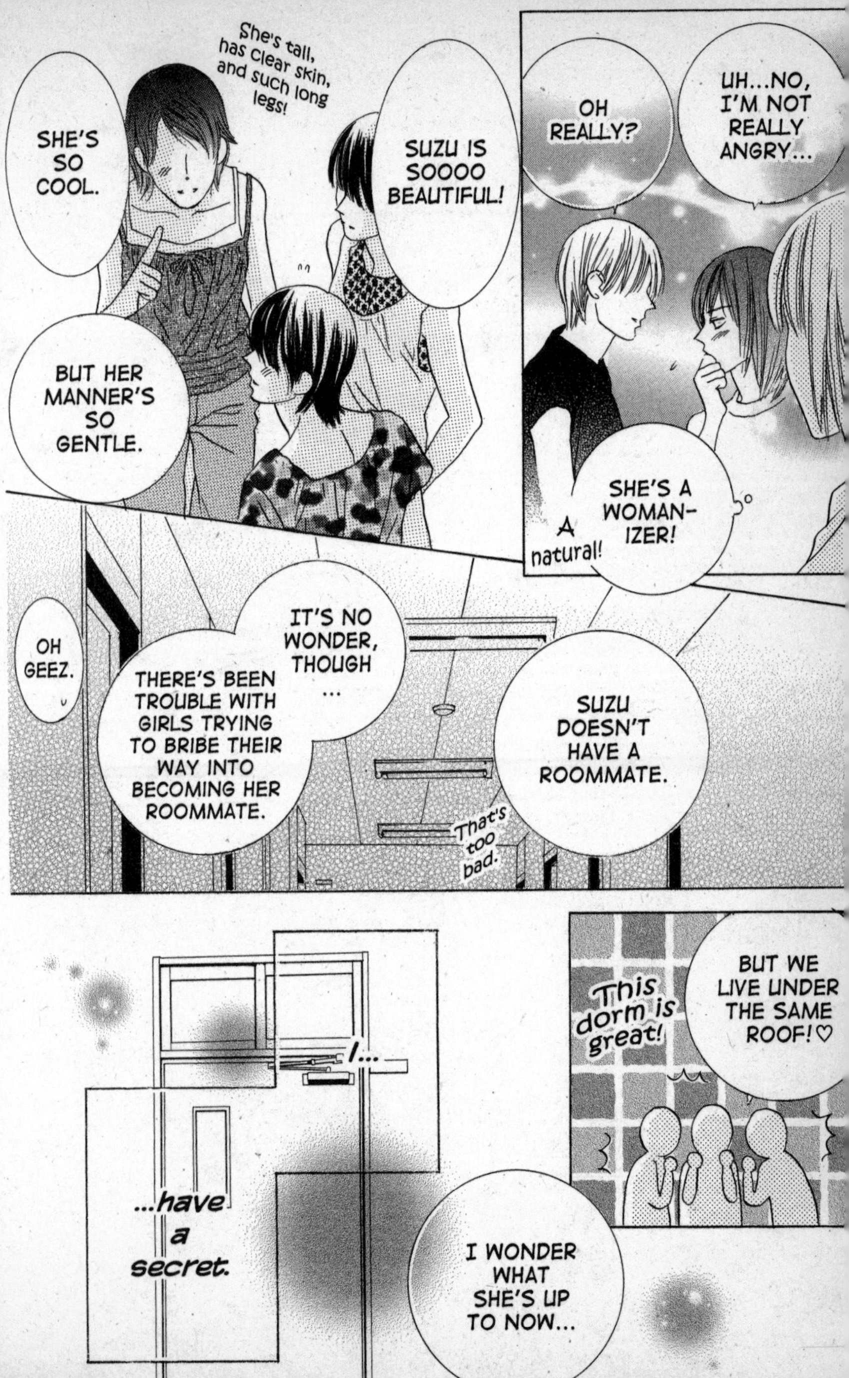
UH...NO, I'M NOT REALLY ANGRY...
OH REALLY?
SHE'S A WOMAN-IZER!
A natural!
SUZU IS SOOOO BEAUTIFUL!
She's tall, has clear skin, and such long legs!
SHE'S SO COOL.
BUT HER MANNER'S SO GENTLE.
SUZU DOESN'T HAVE A ROOMMATE.
That's too bad.
IT'S NO WONDER, THOUGH ...
THERE'S BEEN TROUBLE WITH GIRLS TRYING TO BRIBE THEIR WAY INTO BECOMING HER ROOMMATE.
OH GEEZ.
BUT WE LIVE UNDER THE SAME ROOF!♡
This dorm is great!
I WONDER WHAT SHE'S UP TO NOW...
I...
...have a secret.

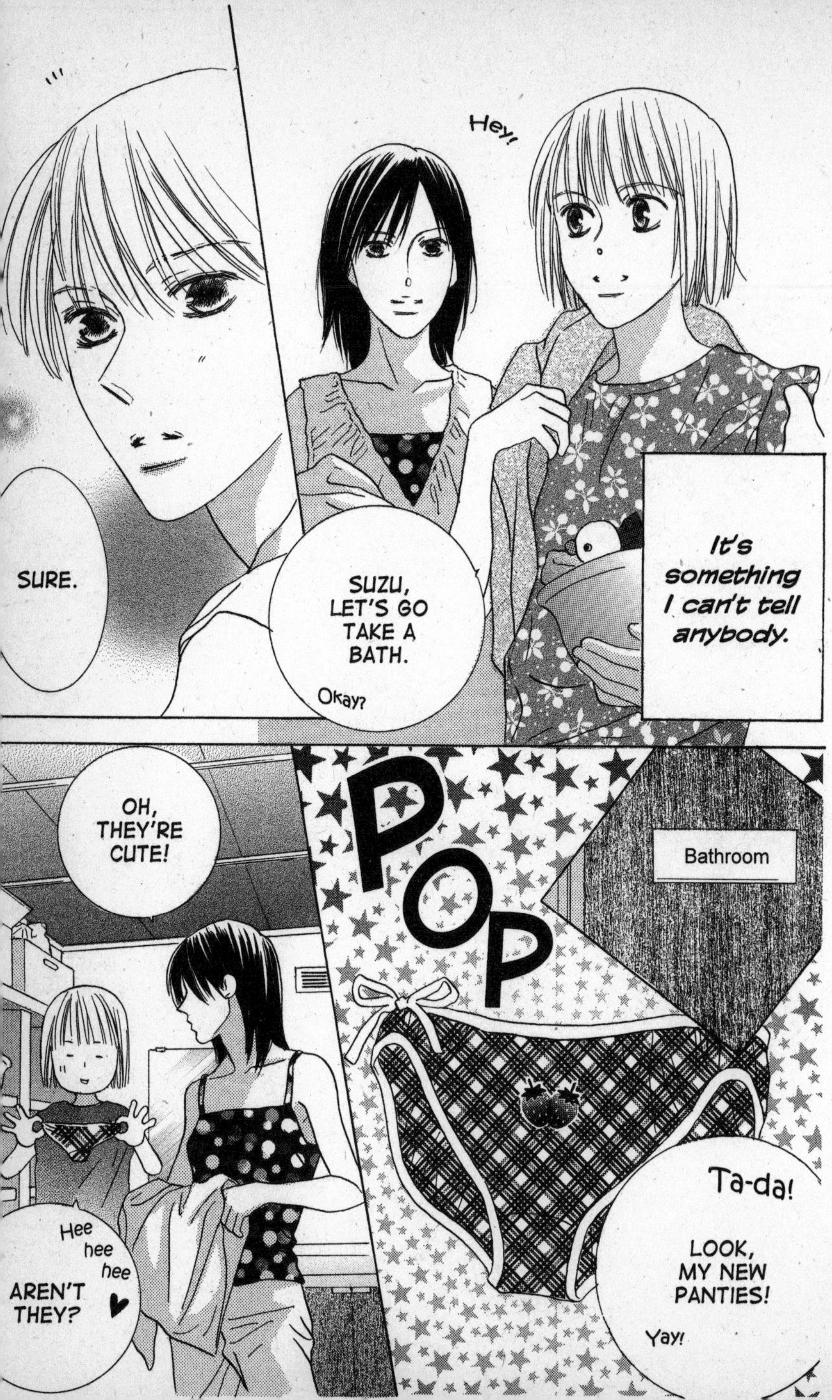

Hey!
It's something I can't tell anybody.
SUZU, LET'S GO TAKE A BATH.
Okay?
SURE.
Bathroom
POP
Ta-da!
LOOK, MY NEW PANTIES!
Yay!
OH, THEY'RE CUTE!
Hee hee hee
AREN'T THEY?

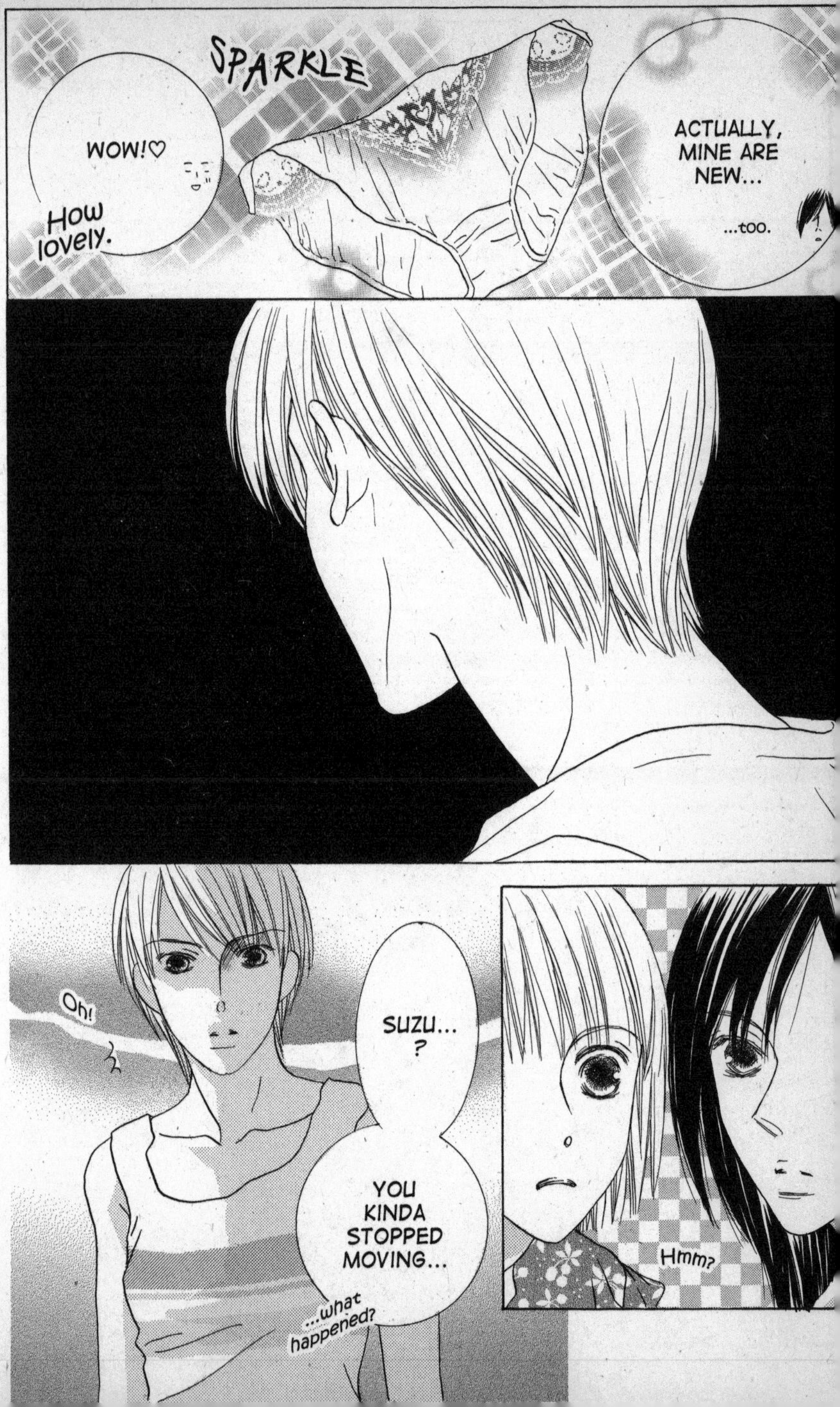
ACTUALLY, MINE ARE NEW...
...too.
SPARKLE
WOW!♡
How lovely.
Hmm?
Oh!
SUZU...?
YOU KINDA STOPPED MOVING...
...what happened?

4

You can't hide anything when you're living in a dorm, so everyone seemed to know what kind of underwear you liked (☺).

I used wear a "babashatsu" I brought from home. It was black, with gold threads woven in it (...now that I think about, that was something...), so girls called me "Bar Madam..." ♡

My roommate really loved underwear (and small, cute things), and even now, she gives me lots of panties that she's carefully selected as my birthday gift...(tears)

Thank you, my friend!!

A "babashatsu" is a thin undershirt (could be with or without sleeves) that you wear under your clothes in winter. —Ed.

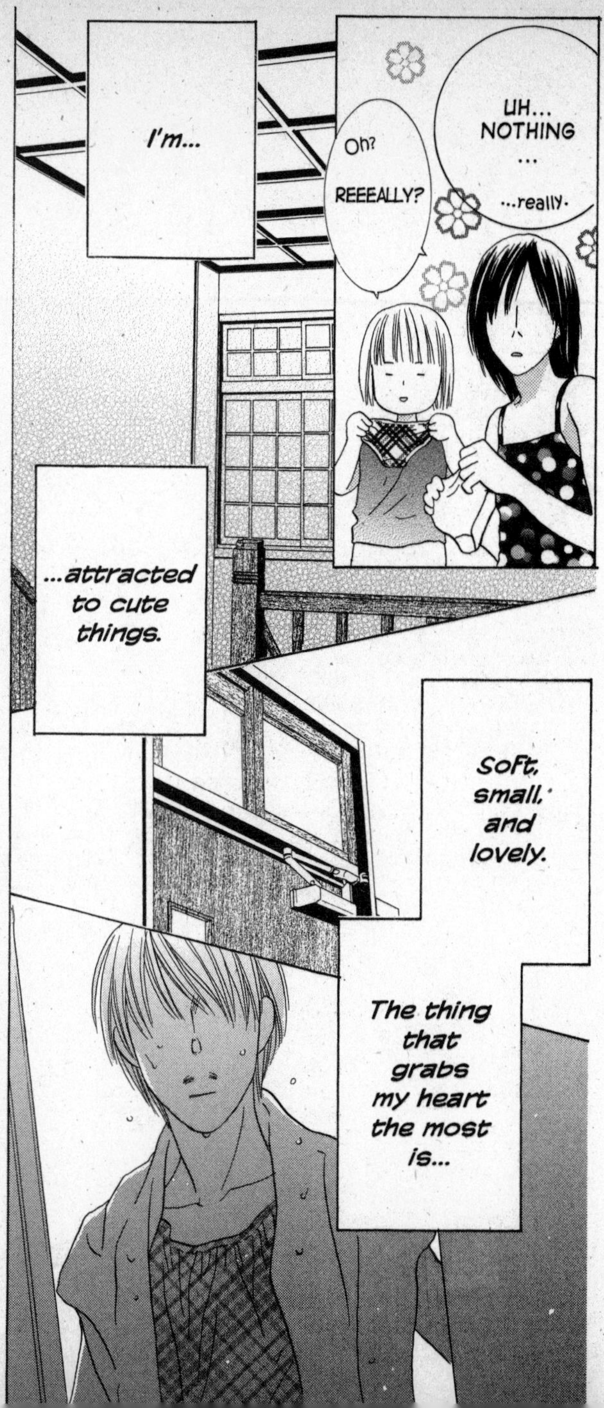
UH... NOTHING ... ...really.
Oh? REEEALLY?
I'm...
...attracted to cute things.
Soft, small, and lovely.
The thing that grabs my heart the most is...

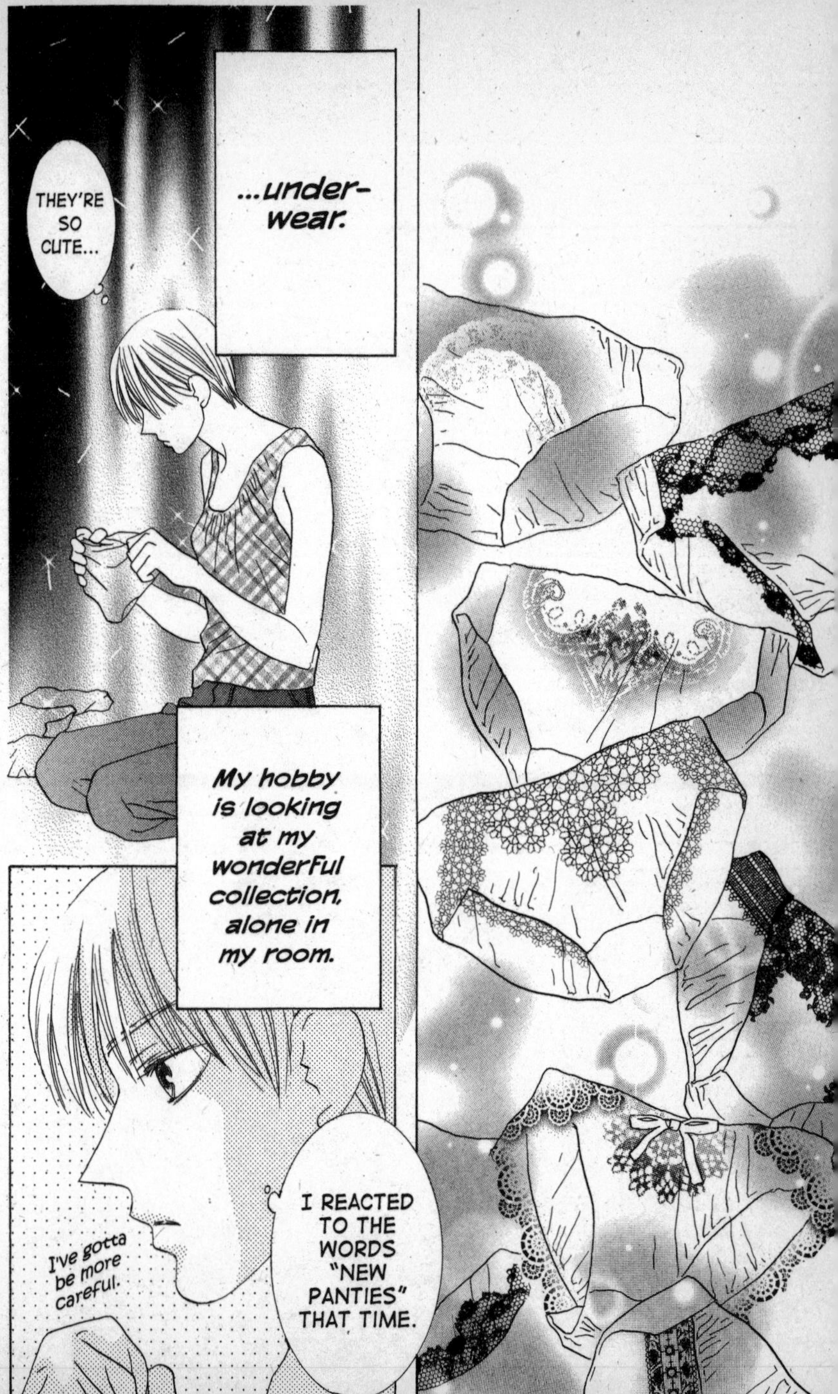
...under-wear.
THEY'RE SO CUTE...
My hobby is looking at my wonderful collection, alone in my room.
I REACTED TO THE WORDS "NEW PANTIES" THAT TIME.
I've gotta be more careful.

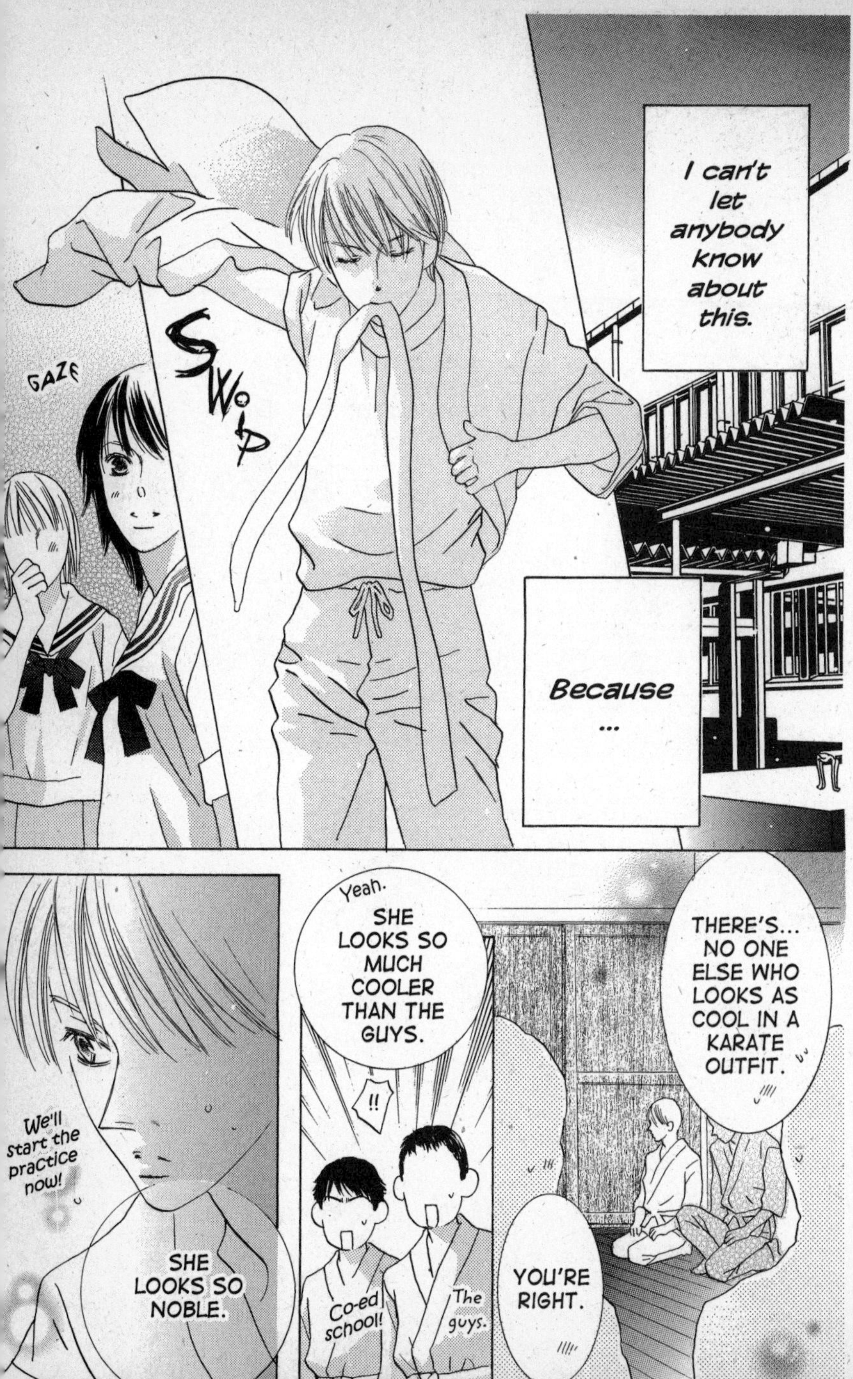
I can't let anybody know about this.
Because ...
SWOOP
GAZE
THERE'S... NO ONE ELSE WHO LOOKS AS COOL IN A KARATE OUTFIT.
YOU'RE RIGHT.
Yeah.
SHE LOOKS SO MUCH COOLER THAN THE GUYS.
!!
The guys.
Co-ed school!
We'll start the practice now!
SHE LOOKS SO NOBLE.

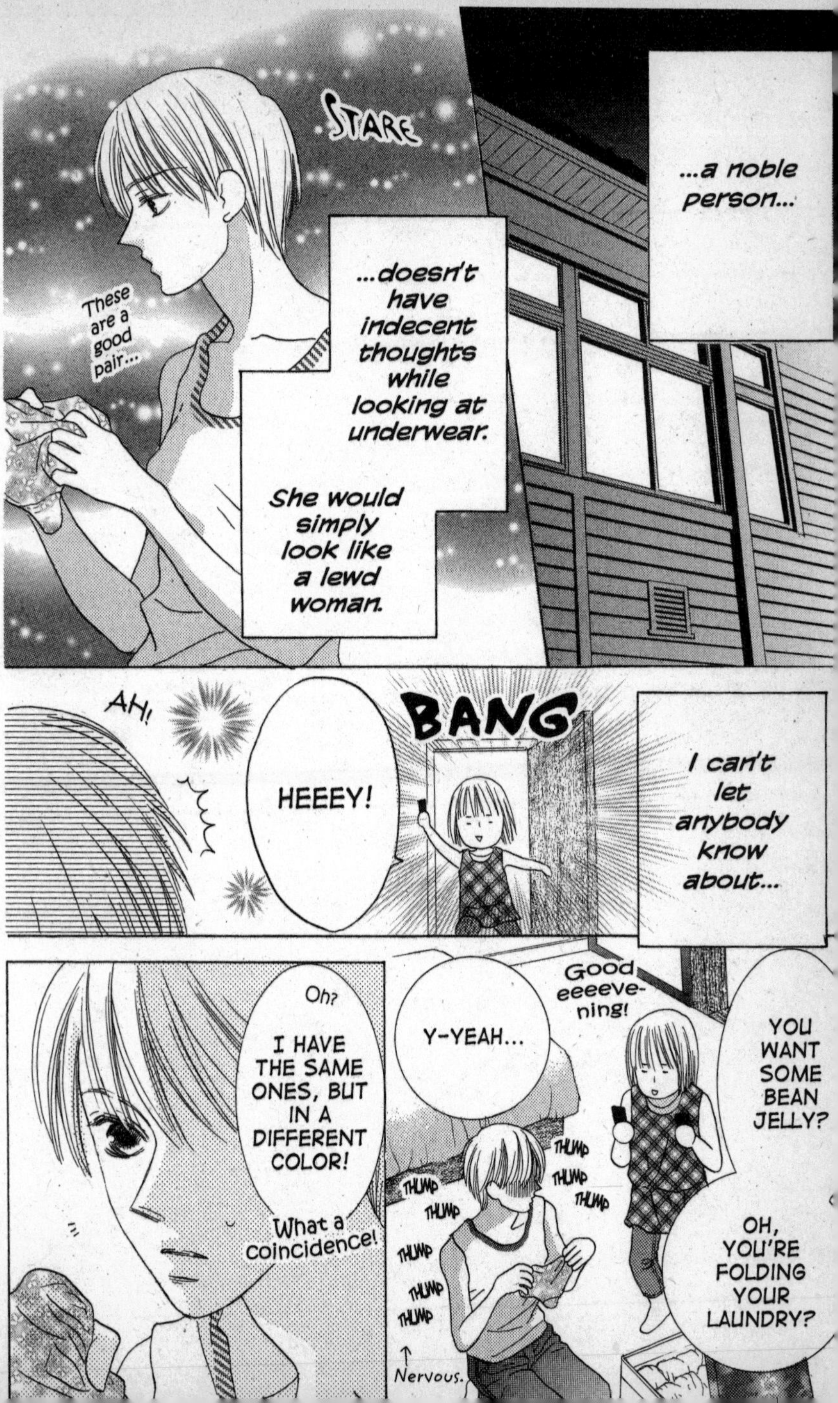
...a noble person...
...doesn't have indecent thoughts while looking at underwear.
She would simply look like a lewd woman.
STARE
These are a good pair...
I can't let anybody know about...
BANG
HEEEY!
AH!
Good eeeeve-ning!
YOU WANT SOME BEAN JELLY?
OH, YOU'RE FOLDING YOUR LAUNDRY?
Y-YEAH...
THUMP THUMP THUMP
THUMP THUMP THUMP THUMP THUMP THUMP
Nervous.
Oh?
I HAVE THE SAME ONES, BUT IN A DIFFERENT COLOR!
What a coincidence!

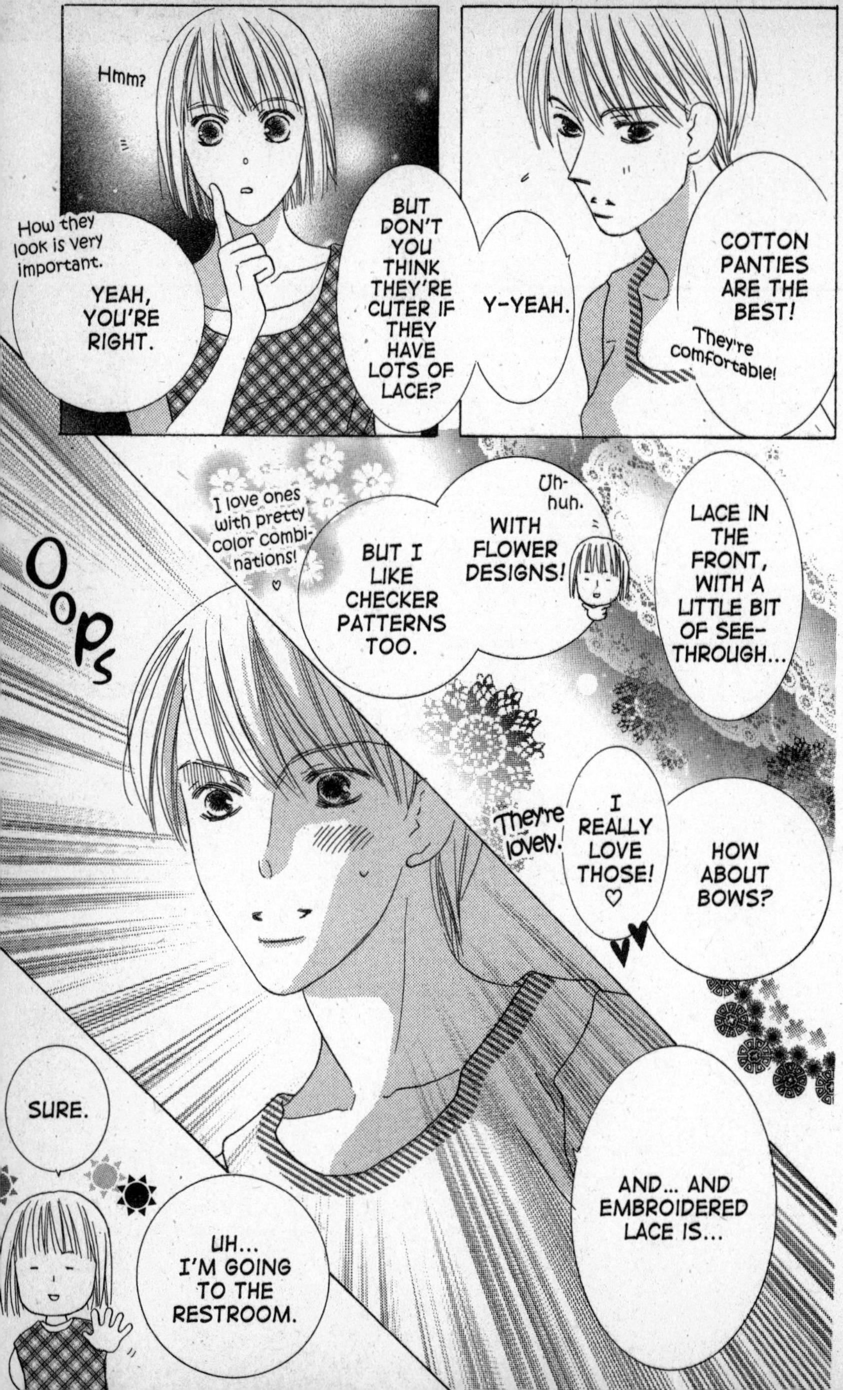
COTTON PANTIES ARE THE BEST!
They're comfortable!
Y-YEAH.
BUT DON'T YOU THINK THEY'RE CUTER IF THEY HAVE LOTS OF LACE?
Hmm?
YEAH, YOU'RE RIGHT.
How they look is very important.
LACE IN THE FRONT, WITH A LITTLE BIT OF SEE-THROUGH...
Uh-huh.
WITH FLOWER DESIGNS!
BUT I LIKE CHECKER PATTERNS TOO.
I love ones with pretty color combinations! ♡
HOW ABOUT BOWS?
I REALLY LOVE THOSE! ♡
They're lovely.
Oops
AND... AND EMBROIDERED LACE IS...
UH... I'M GOING TO THE RESTROOM.
SURE.

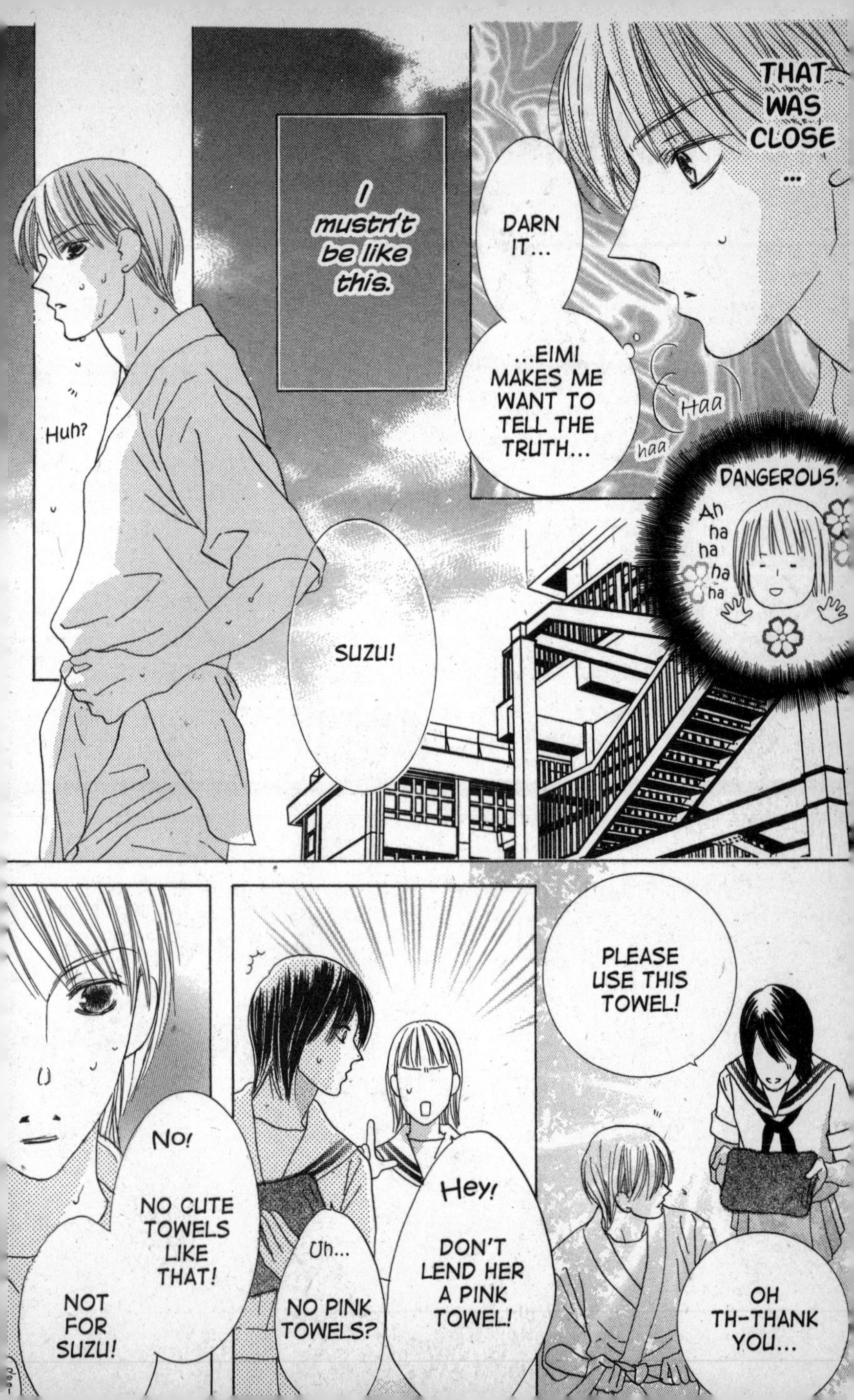
THAT WAS CLOSE...
DARN IT...
...EIMI MAKES ME WANT TO TELL THE TRUTH...
Haa haa
DANGEROUS.
Ah ha ha ha ha
I mustn't be like this.
SUZU!
Huh?
PLEASE USE THIS TOWEL!
OH TH-THANK YOU...
Hey!
DON'T LEND HER A PINK TOWEL!
Uh...
NO PINK TOWELS?
No!
NO CUTE TOWELS LIKE THAT!
NOT FOR SUZU!

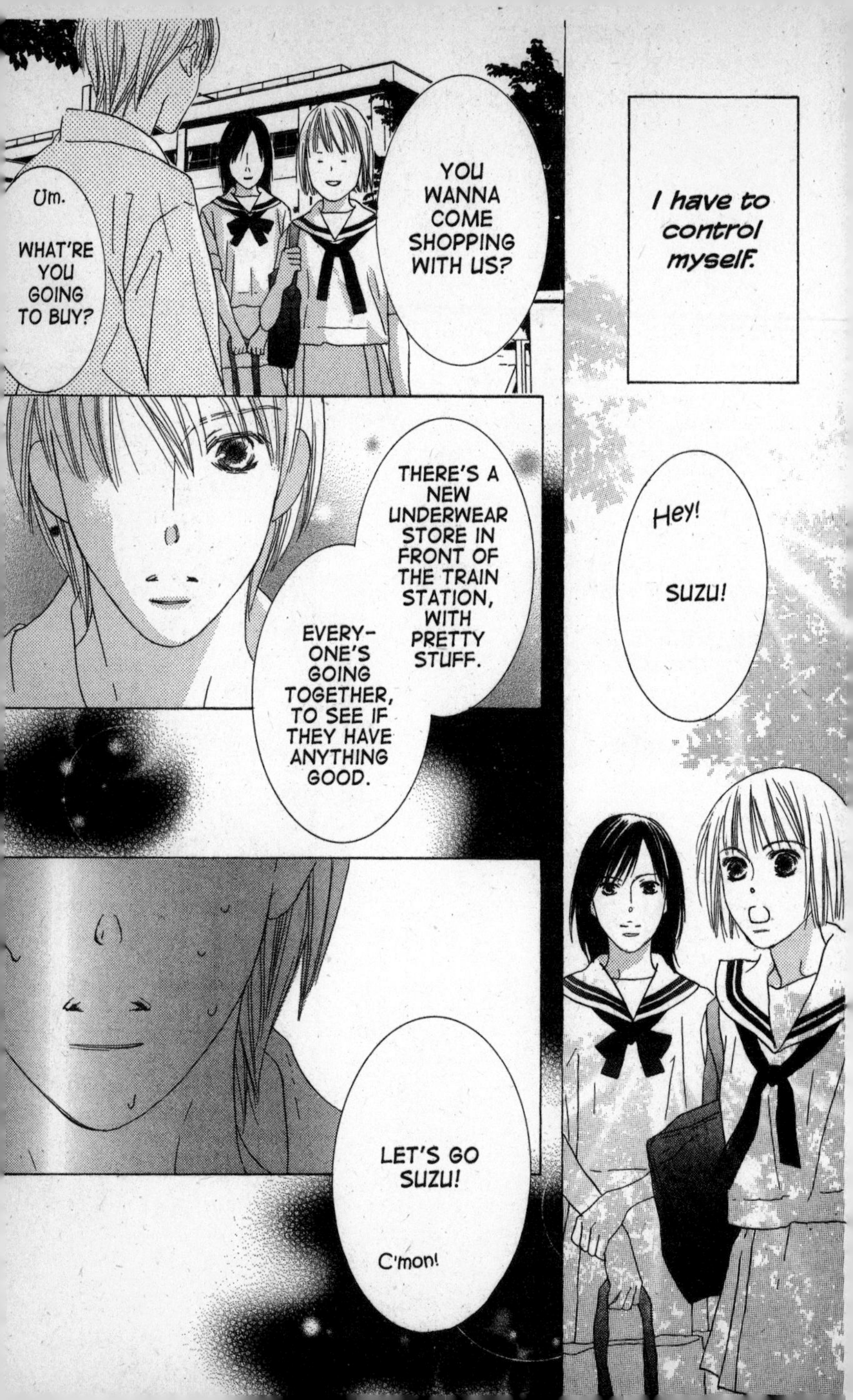
I have to control myself.
Hey! Suzu!
YOU WANNA COME SHOPPING WITH US?
Um. WHAT'RE YOU GOING TO BUY?
THERE'S A NEW UNDERWEAR STORE IN FRONT OF THE TRAIN STATION, WITH PRETTY STUFF.
EVERY-ONE'S GOING TOGETHER, TO SEE IF THEY HAVE ANYTHING GOOD.
LET'S GO SUZU!
C'mon!

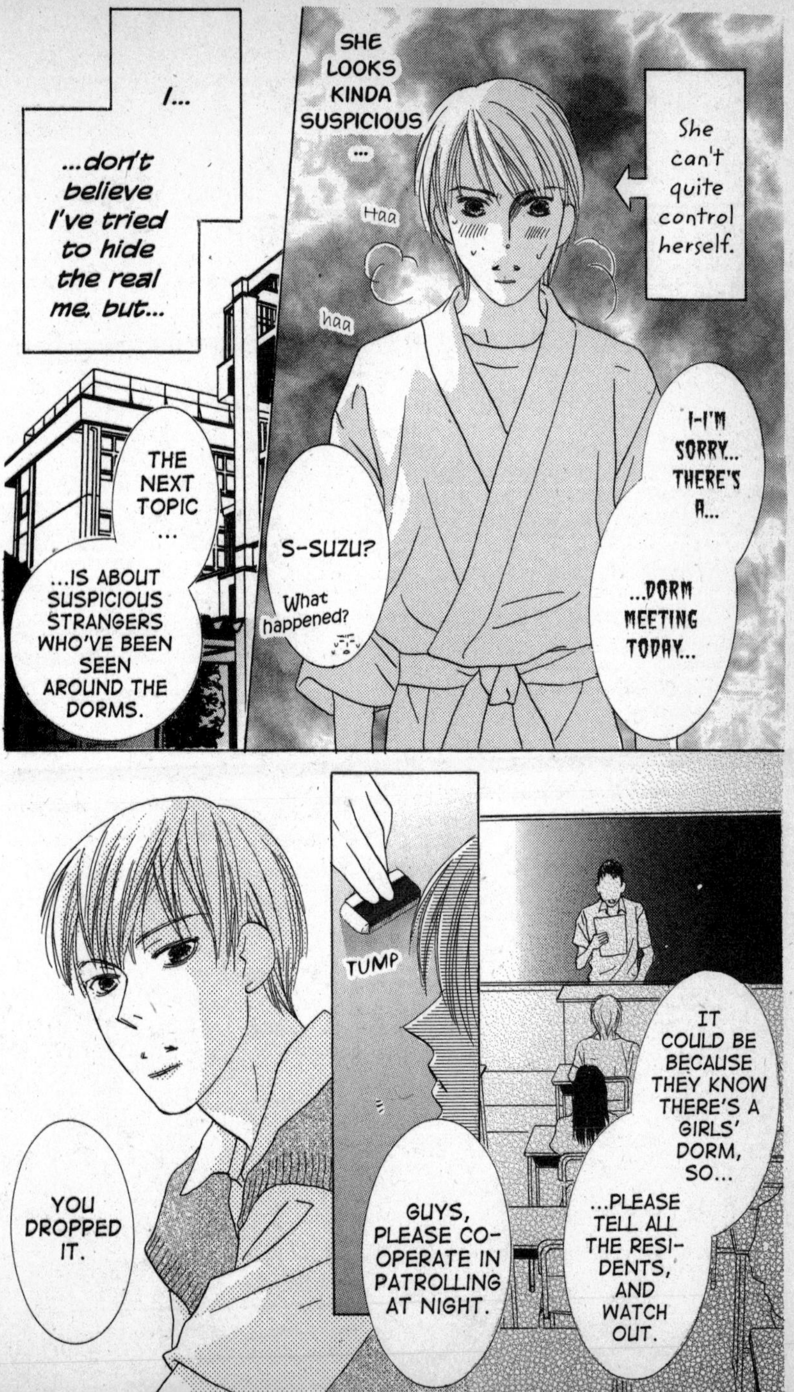
SHE LOOKS KINDA SUSPICIOUS ...
She can't quite control herself.
Haa
haa
I-I'M SORRY... THERE'S A...
...DORM MEETING TODAY...
S-SUZU?
What happened?
I...
...don't believe I've tried to hide the real me, but...
THE NEXT TOPIC ...
...IS ABOUT SUSPICIOUS STRANGERS WHO'VE BEEN SEEN AROUND THE DORMS.
IT COULD BE BECAUSE THEY KNOW THERE'S A GIRLS' DORM, SO...
...PLEASE TELL ALL THE RESI-DENTS, AND WATCH OUT.
GUYS, PLEASE CO-OPERATE IN PATROLLING AT NIGHT.
TUMP
YOU DROPPED IT.

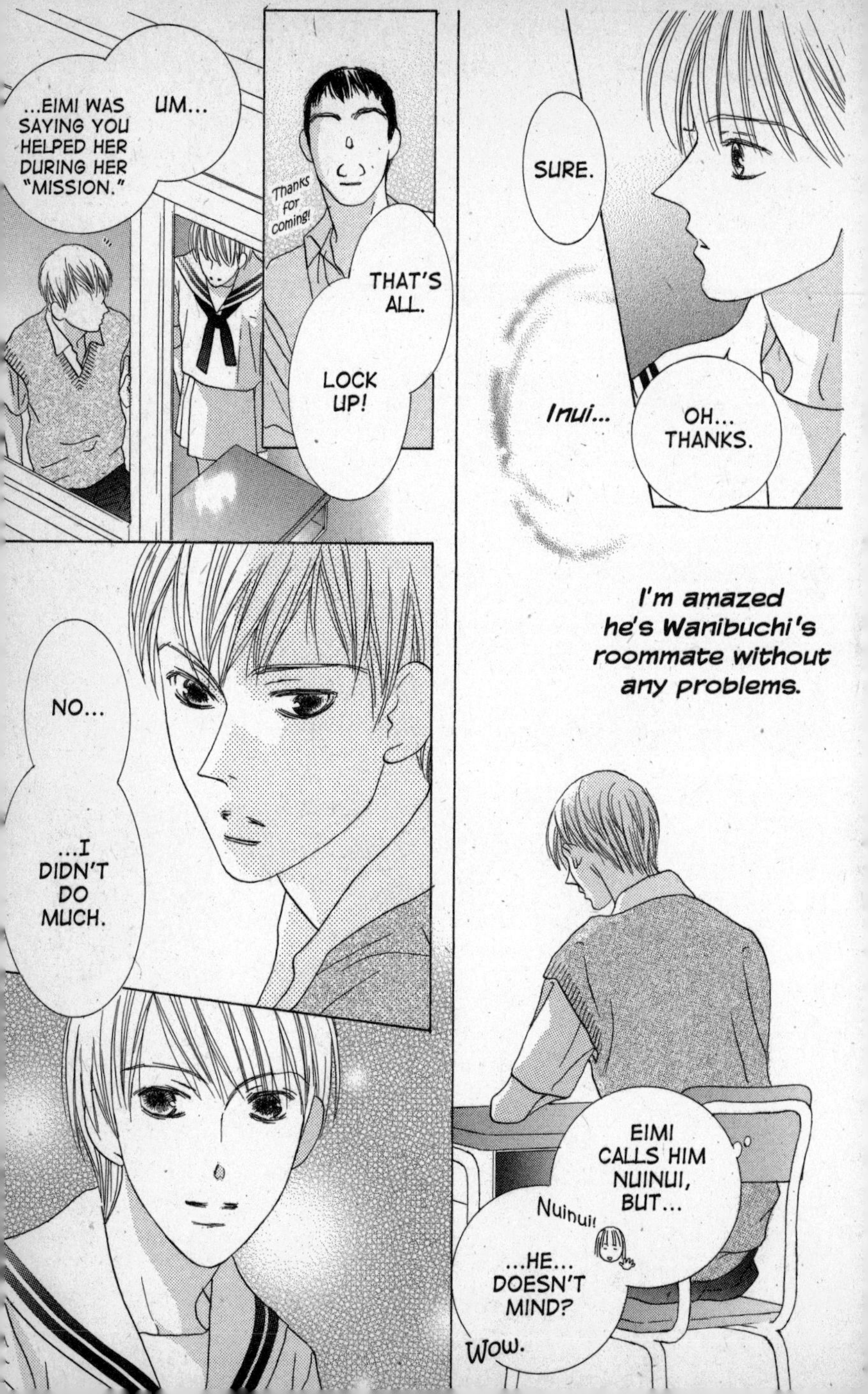
SURE.
OH... THANKS.
Inui...
UM...
...EIMI WAS SAYING YOU HELPED HER DURING HER "MISSION."
Thanks for coming!
THAT'S ALL.
LOCK UP!
NO...
...I DIDN'T DO MUCH.
I'm amazed he's Wanibuchi's roommate without any problems.
EIMI CALLS HIM NUINUI, BUT...
Nuinui!
...HE... DOESN'T MIND?
Wow.

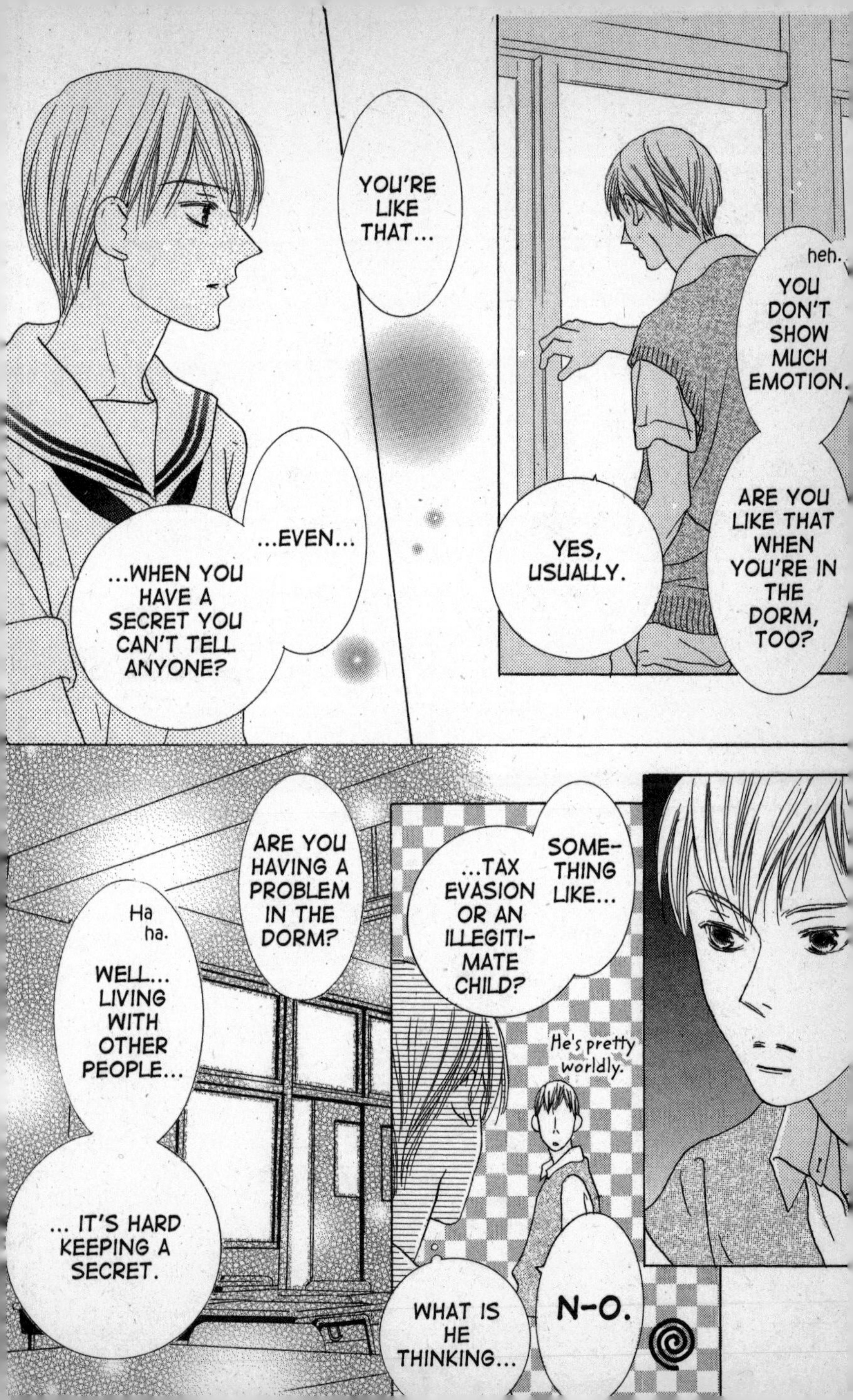
heh.
YOU DON'T SHOW MUCH EMOTION.
ARE YOU LIKE THAT WHEN YOU'RE IN THE DORM, TOO?
YES, USUALLY.
YOU'RE LIKE THAT...
...EVEN...
...WHEN YOU HAVE A SECRET YOU CAN'T TELL ANYONE?
SOME-THING LIKE...
...TAX EVASION OR AN ILLEGITI-MATE CHILD?
He's pretty worldly.
N-O.
WHAT IS HE THINKING...
ARE YOU HAVING A PROBLEM IN THE DORM?
Ha ha.
WELL... LIVING WITH OTHER PEOPLE...
... IT'S HARD KEEPING A SECRET.

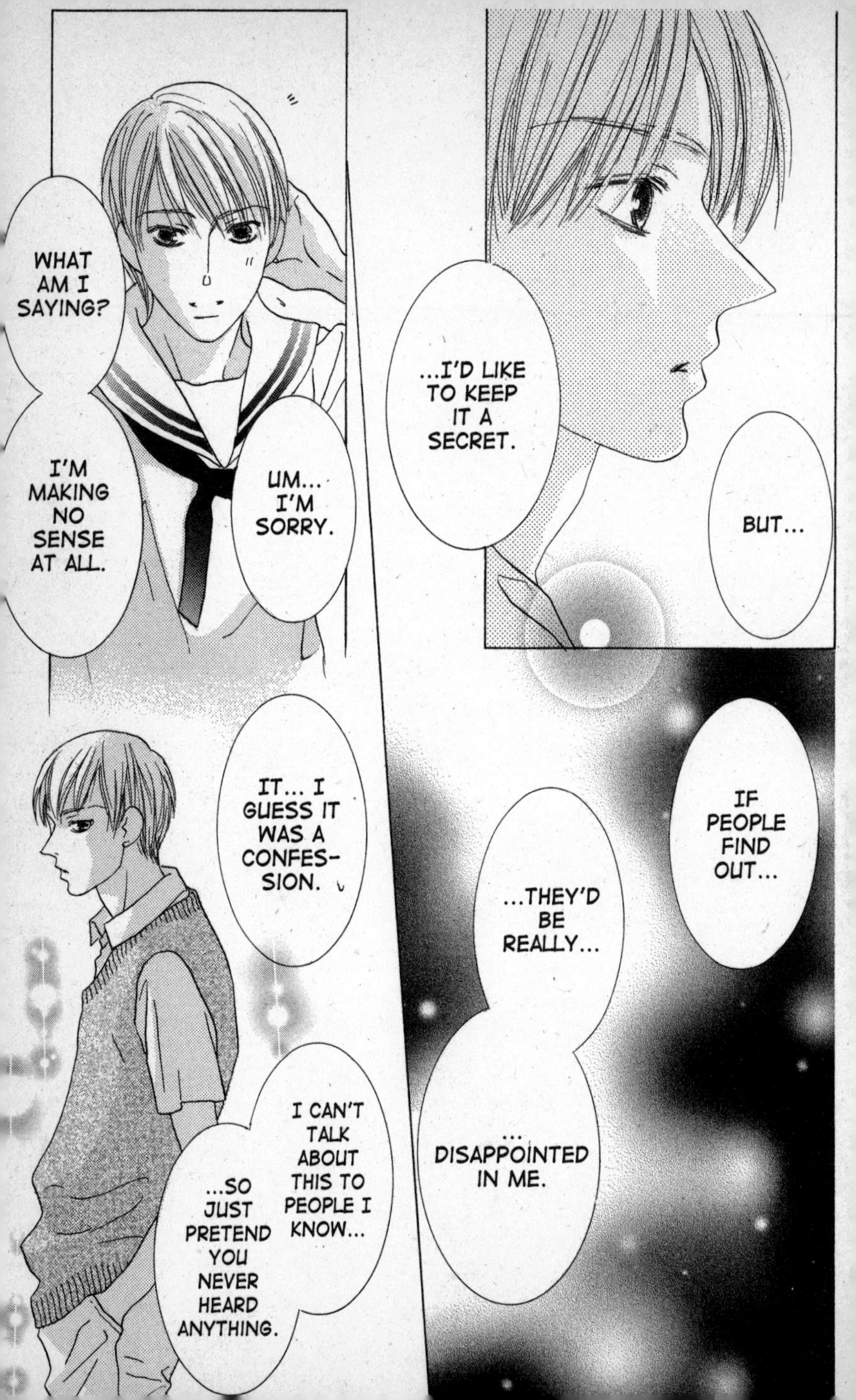
BUT...
...I'D LIKE TO KEEP IT A SECRET.
UM... I'M SORRY.
WHAT AM I SAYING?
I'M MAKING NO SENSE AT ALL.
IF PEOPLE FIND OUT...
...THEY'D BE REALLY...
...DISAPPOINTED IN ME.
IT... I GUESS IT WAS A CONFESSION.
I CAN'T TALK ABOUT THIS TO PEOPLE I KNOW...
...SO JUST PRETEND YOU NEVER HEARD ANYTHING.

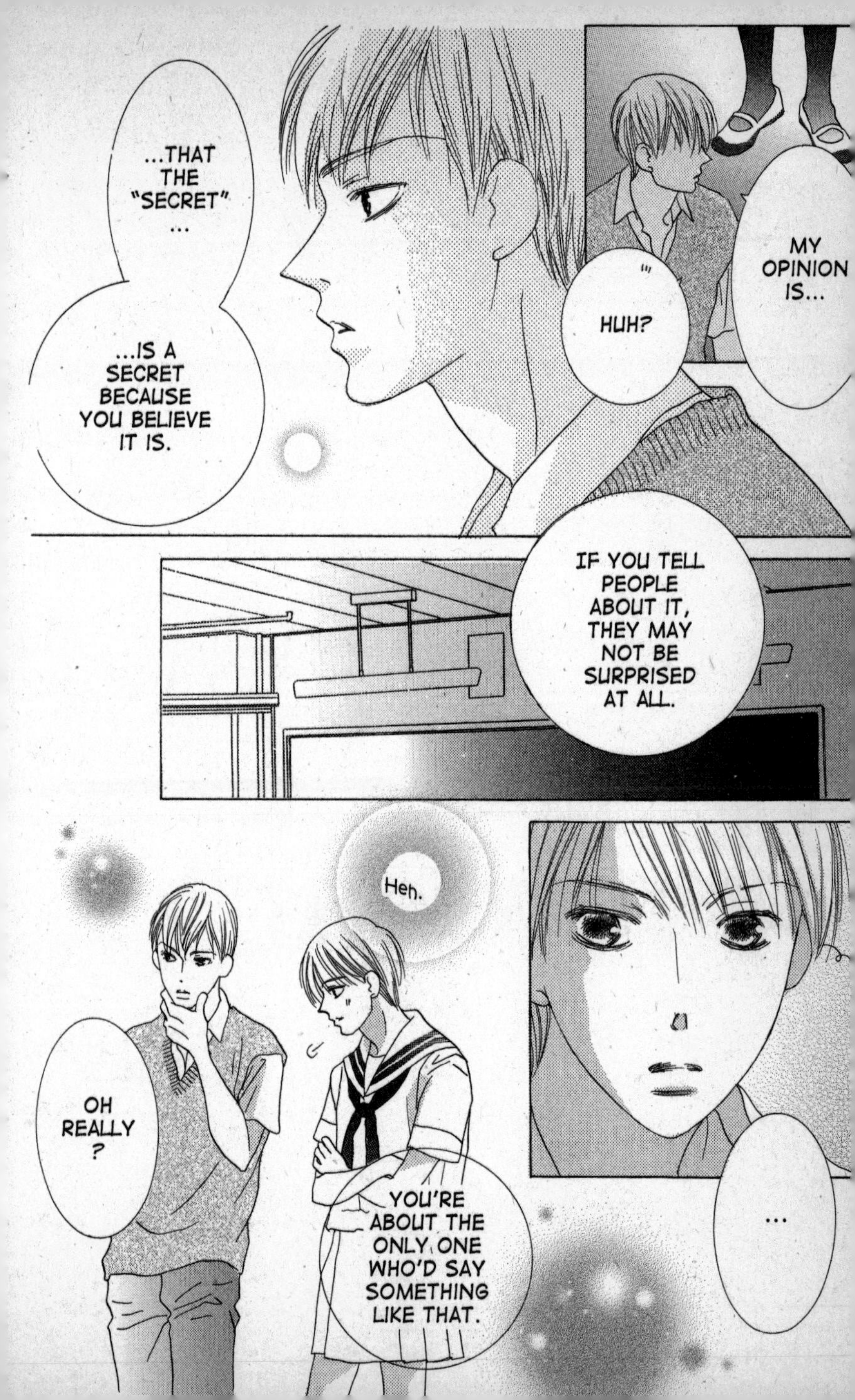
MY OPINION IS...
HUH?
...THAT THE "SECRET" ...
...IS A SECRET BECAUSE YOU BELIEVE IT IS.
IF YOU TELL PEOPLE ABOUT IT, THEY MAY NOT BE SURPRISED AT ALL.
...
Heh.
YOU'RE ABOUT THE ONLY ONE WHO'D SAY SOMETHING LIKE THAT.
OH REALLY ?

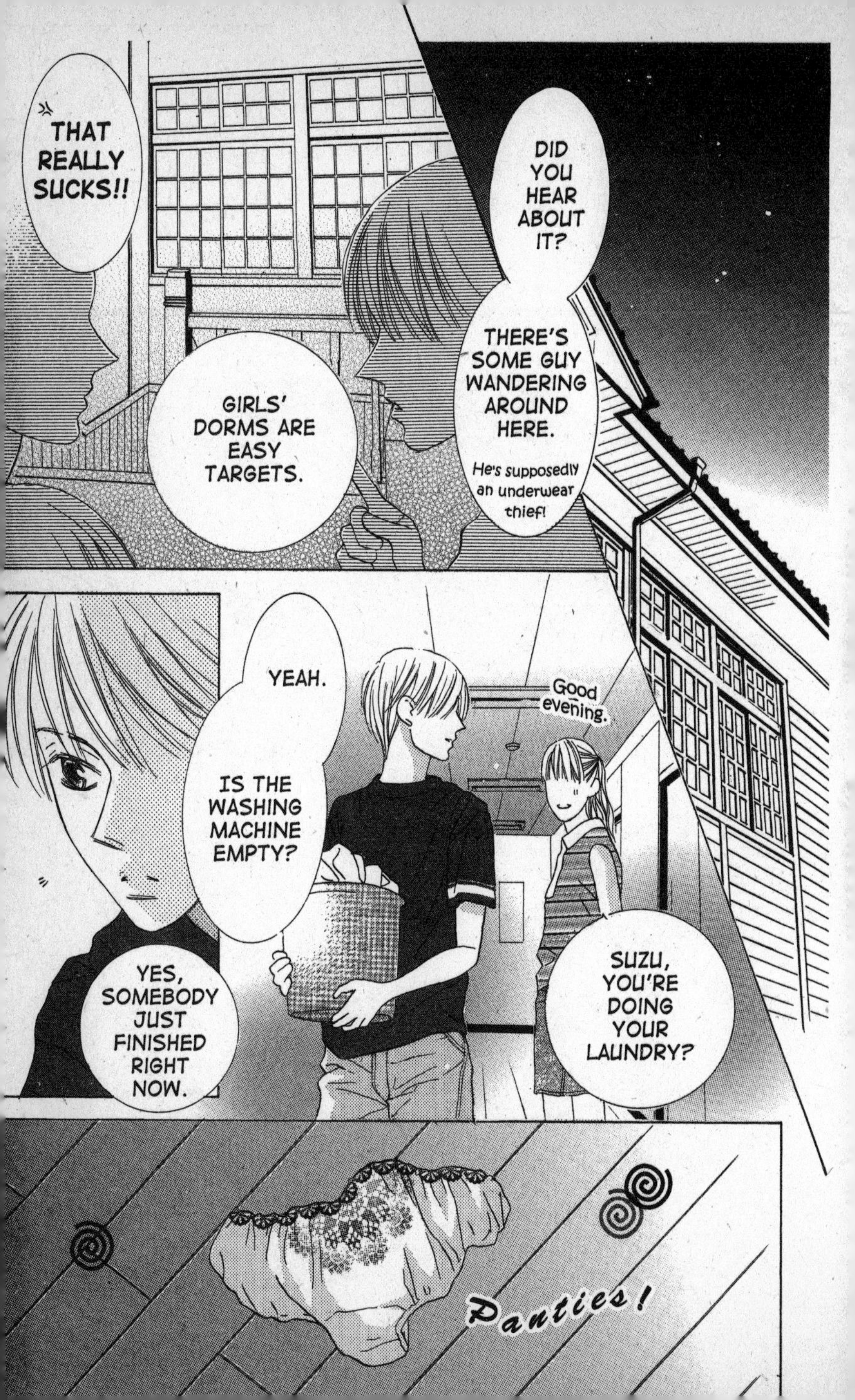
DID YOU HEAR ABOUT IT?
THERE'S SOME GUY WANDERING AROUND HERE.
He's supposedly an underwear thief!
GIRLS' DORMS ARE EASY TARGETS.
THAT REALLY SUCKS!!
Good evening.
SUZU, YOU'RE DOING YOUR LAUNDRY?
YEAH.
IS THE WASHING MACHINE EMPTY?
YES, SOMEBODY JUST FINISHED RIGHT NOW.
Panties!

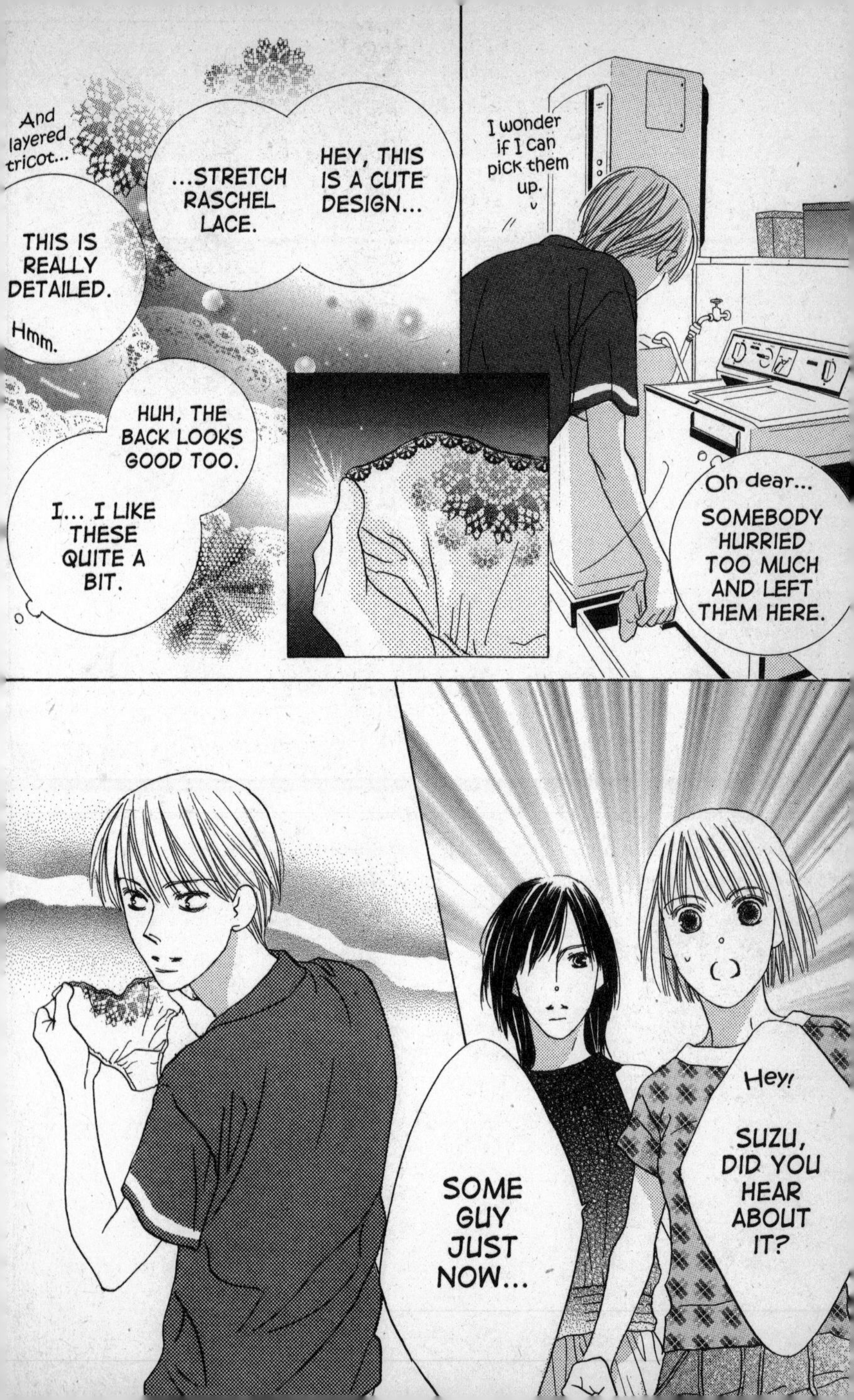
I wonder if I can pick them up.
Oh dear... SOMEBODY HURRIED TOO MUCH AND LEFT THEM HERE.
HEY, THIS IS A CUTE DESIGN...
...STRETCH RASCHEL LACE.
And layered tricot...
THIS IS REALLY DETAILED.
Hmm.
HUH, THE BACK LOOKS GOOD TOO.
I... I LIKE THESE QUITE A BIT.
Hey!
SUZU, DID YOU HEAR ABOUT IT?
SOME GUY JUST NOW...

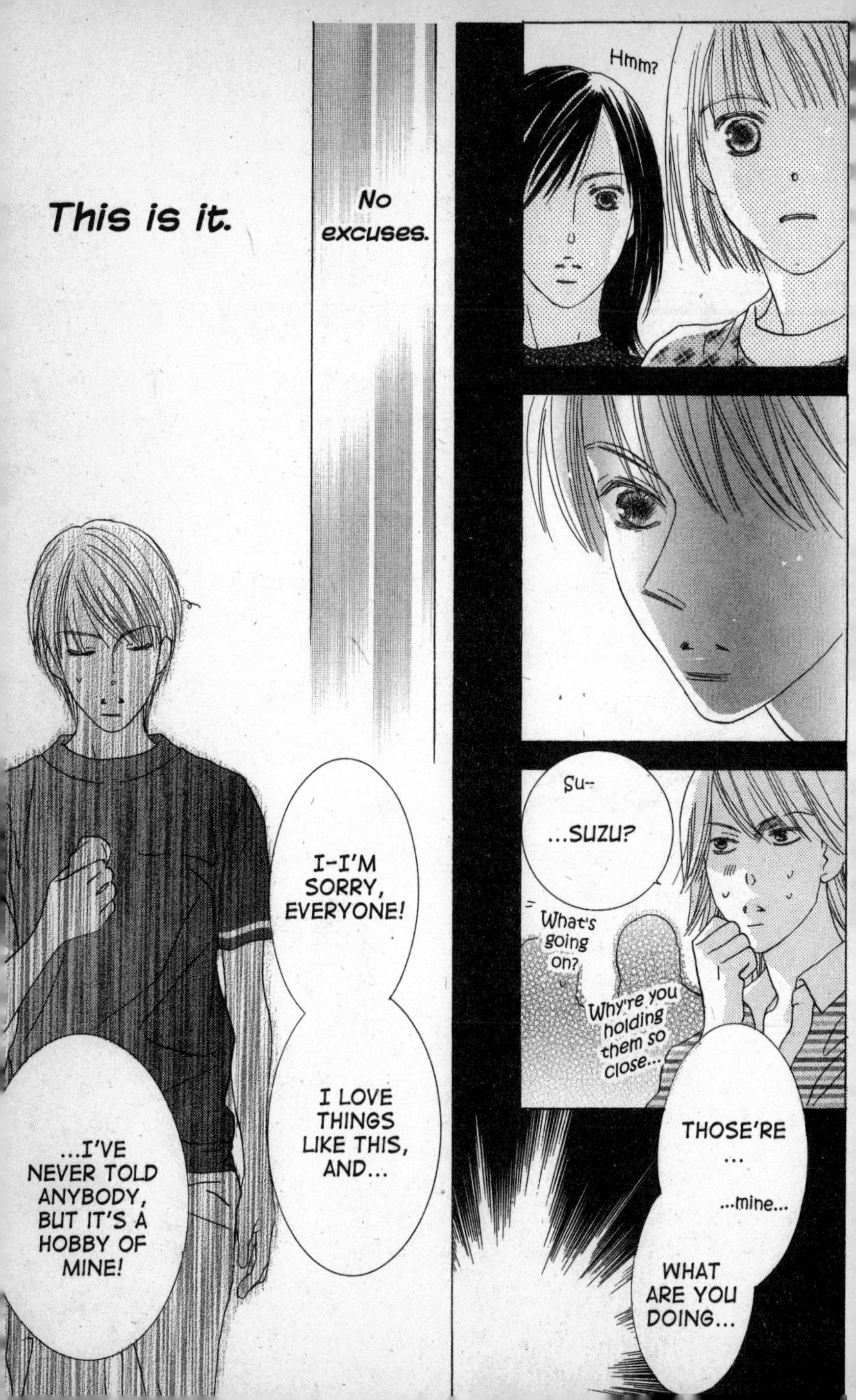
Hmm?
Su--
...SUZU?
What's going on?
Why're you holding them so close...
THOSE'RE ...
...mine...
WHAT ARE YOU DOING...
No excuses.
This is it.
I-I'M SORRY, EVERYONE!
I LOVE THINGS LIKE THIS, AND...
...I'VE NEVER TOLD ANYBODY, BUT IT'S A HOBBY OF MINE!

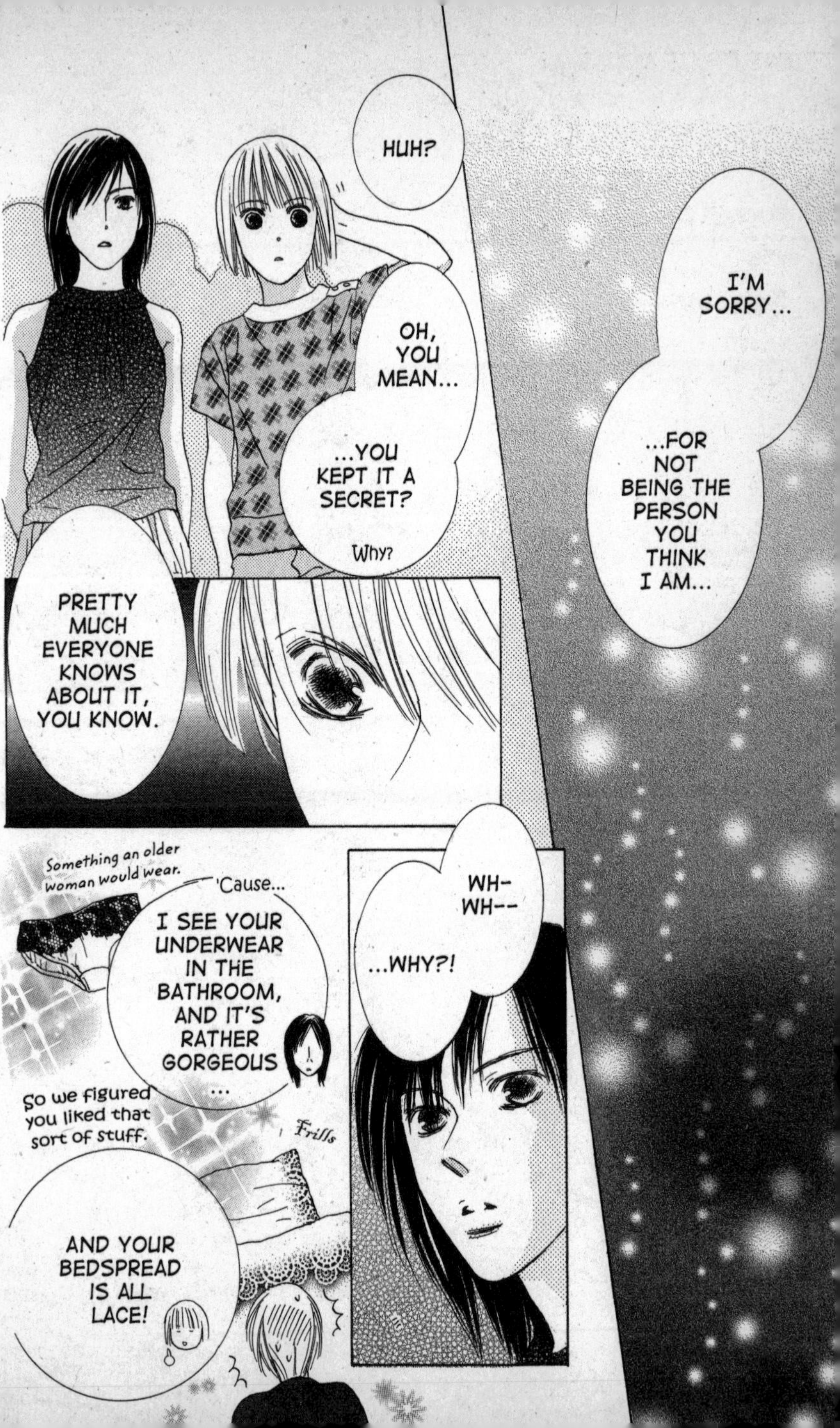
I'M SORRY...
...FOR NOT BEING THE PERSON YOU THINK I AM...
HUH?
OH, YOU MEAN...
...YOU KEPT IT A SECRET?
Why?
PRETTY MUCH EVERYONE KNOWS ABOUT IT, YOU KNOW.
WH-WH--
...WHY?!
'Cause...
I SEE YOUR UNDERWEAR IN THE BATHROOM, AND IT'S RATHER GORGEOUS...
Something an older woman would wear.
So we figured you liked that sort of stuff.
Frills
AND YOUR BEDSPREAD IS ALL LACE!

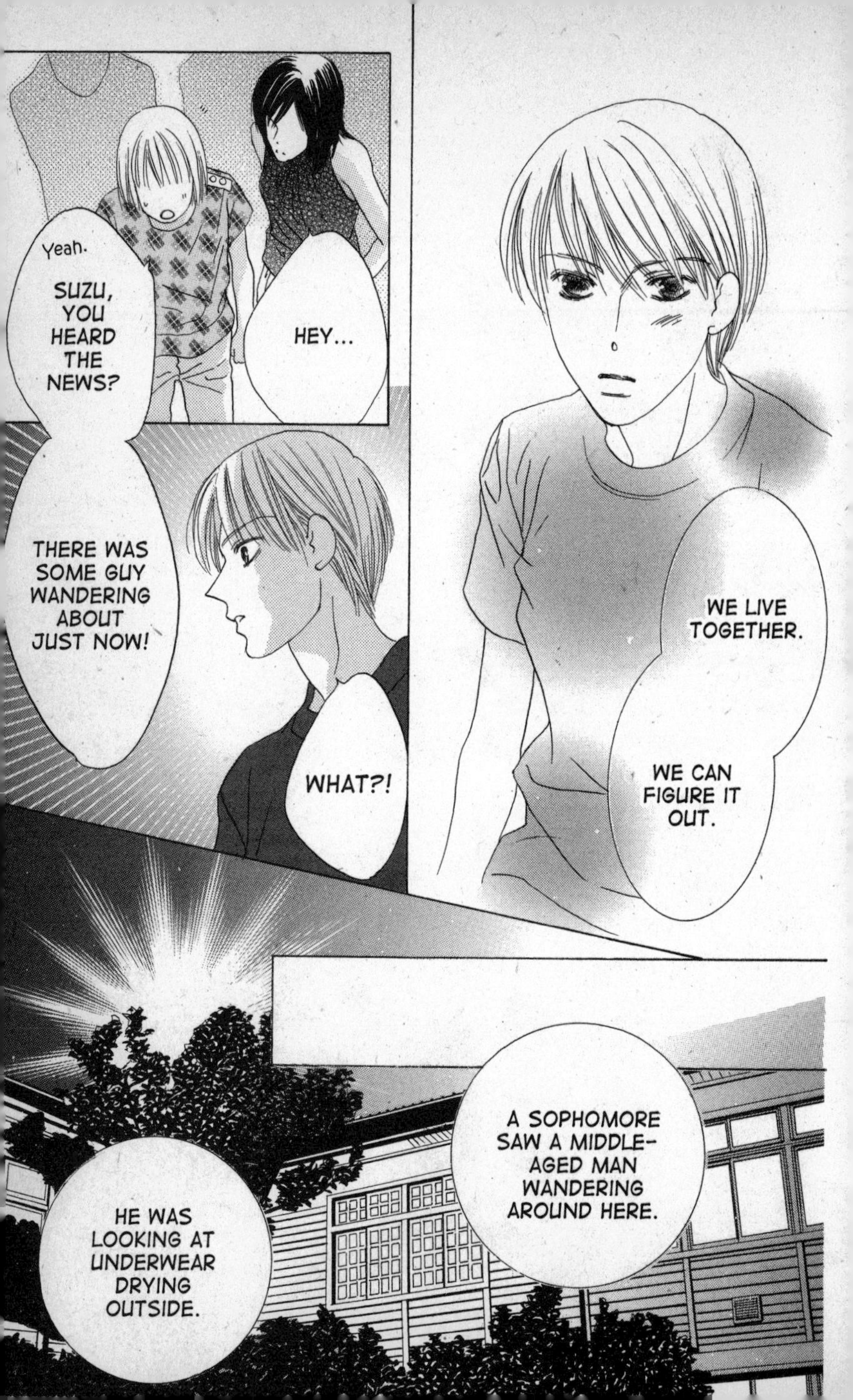
WE LIVE TOGETHER.
WE CAN FIGURE IT OUT.
HEY...
Yeah.
SUZU, YOU HEARD THE NEWS?
THERE WAS SOME GUY WANDERING ABOUT JUST NOW!
WHAT?!
A SOPHOMORE SAW A MIDDLE-AGED MAN WANDERING AROUND HERE.
HE WAS LOOKING AT UNDERWEAR DRYING OUTSIDE.

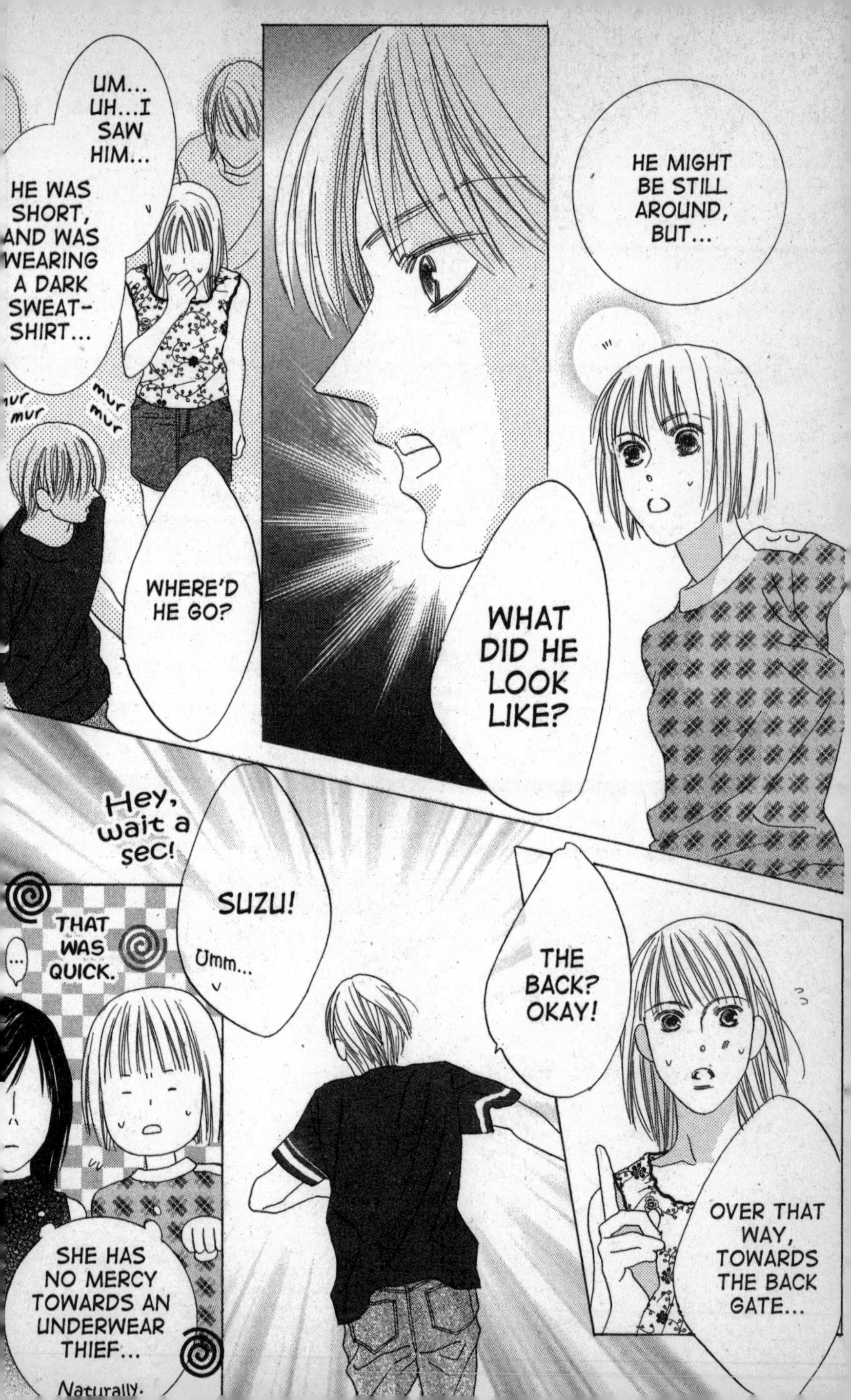

HE MIGHT BE STILL AROUND, BUT...
WHAT DID HE LOOK LIKE?
WHERE'D HE GO?
UM... UH...I SAW HIM...
HE WAS SHORT, AND WAS WEARING A DARK SWEAT-SHIRT...
mur mur
mur mur
OVER THAT WAY, TOWARDS THE BACK GATE...
THE BACK? OKAY!
SUZU!
Umm...
Hey, wait a sec!
THAT WAS QUICK.
...
SHE HAS NO MERCY TOWARDS AN UNDERWEAR THIEF...
Naturally.

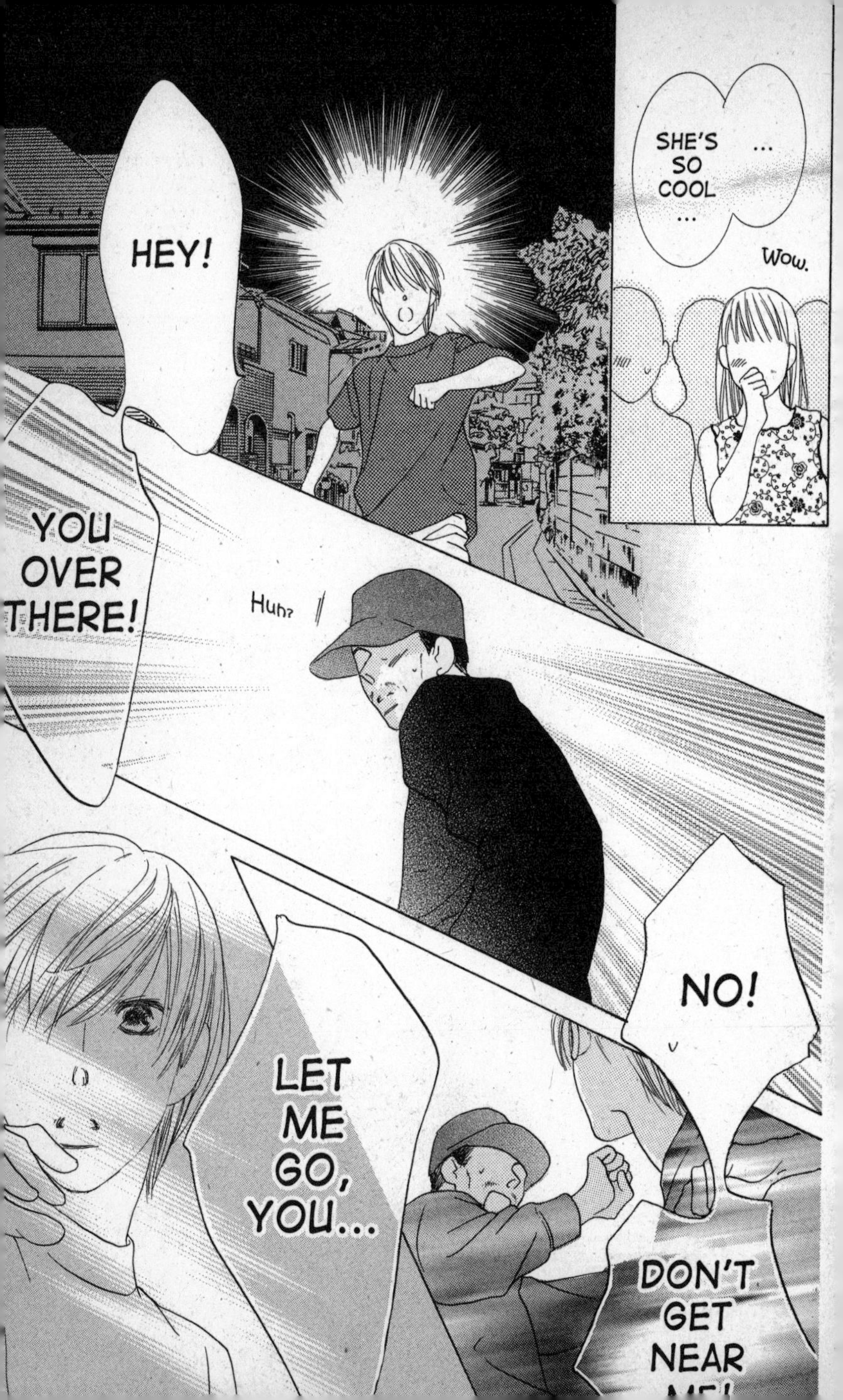

SHE'S ... SO COOL ...
Wow.
HEY!
YOU OVER THERE!
Huh?
NO!
LET ME GO, YOU...
DON'T GET NEAR

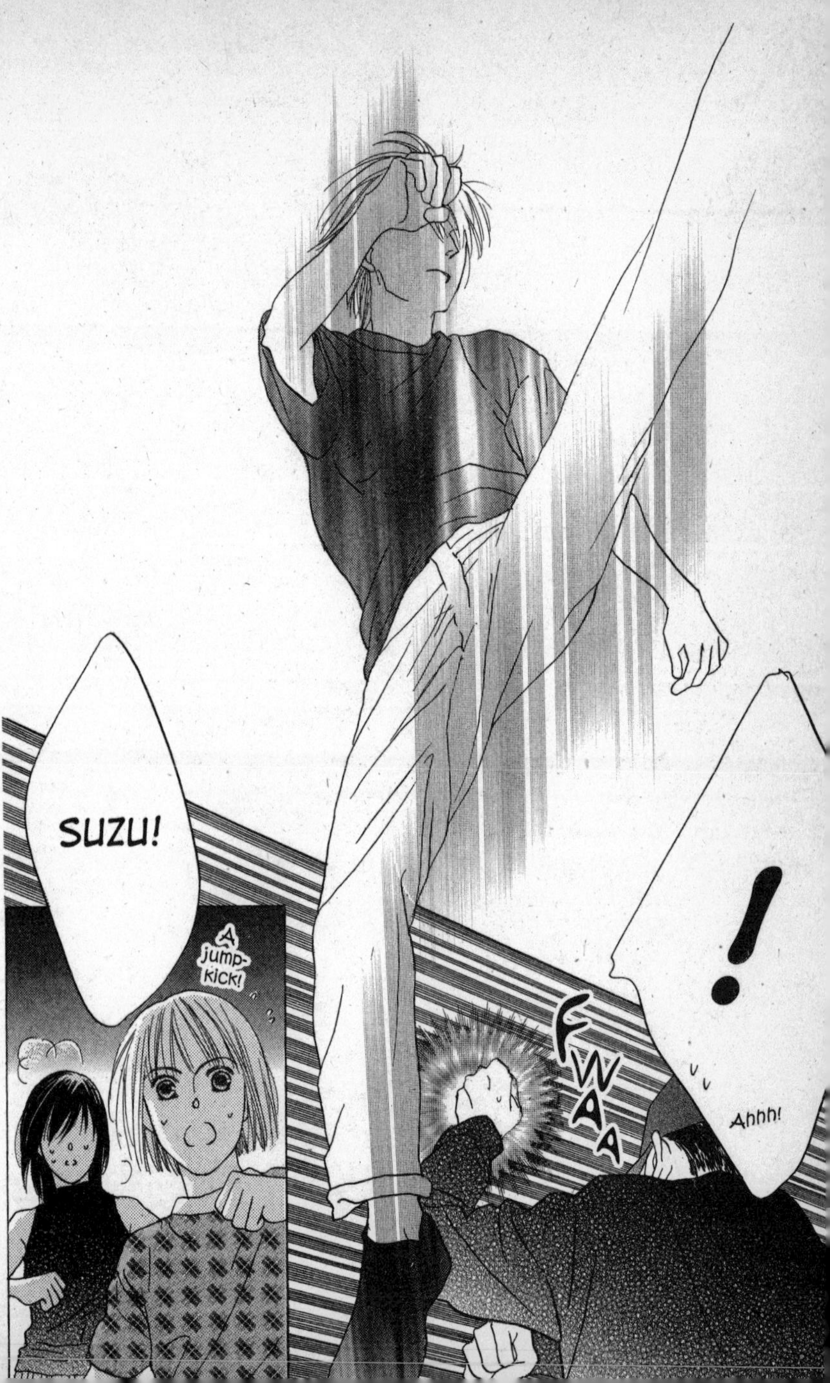
!
Ahhh!
FWAA
SUZU!
A jump-kick!

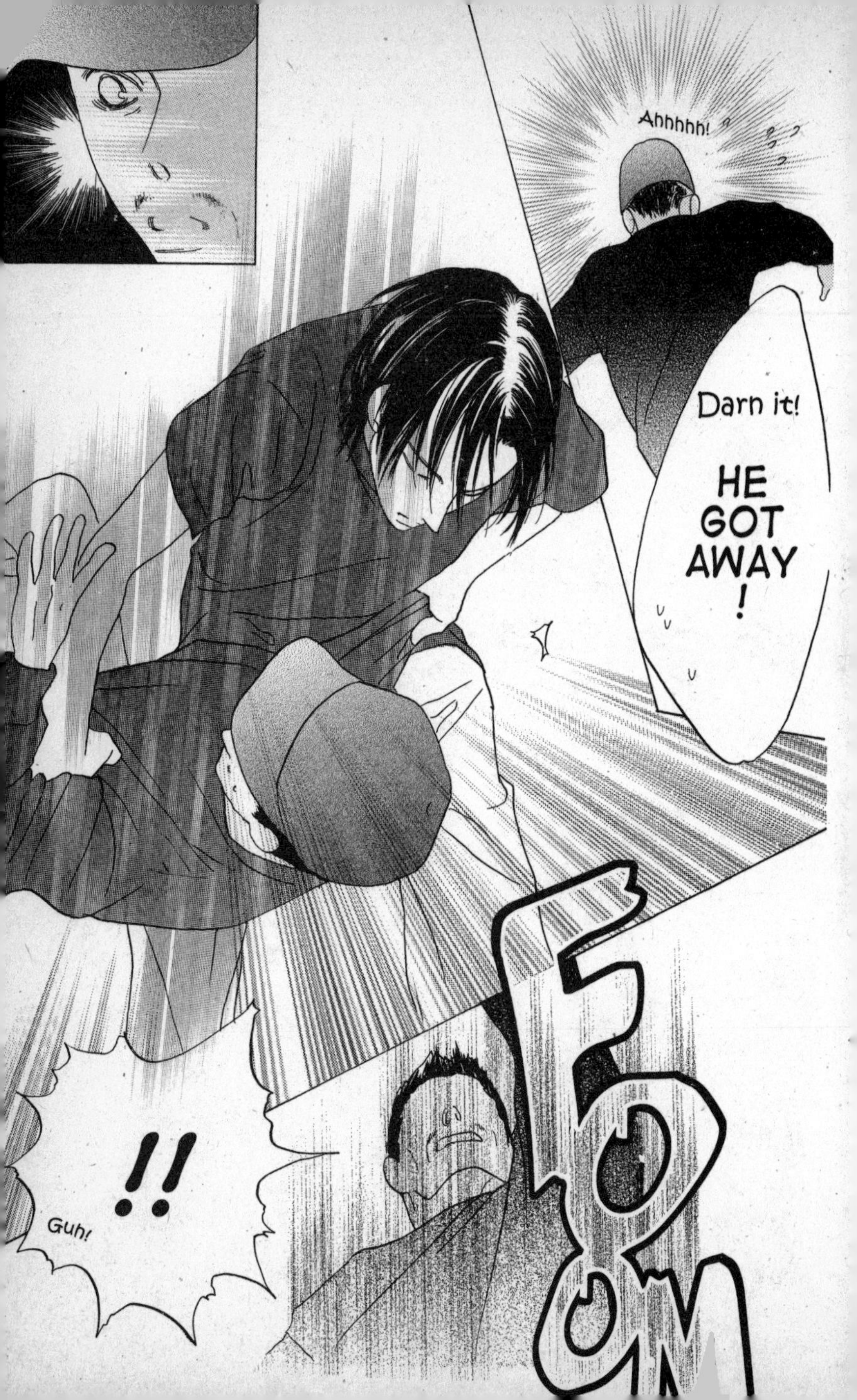
Ahhhhh!
Darn it!
HE GOT AWAY!
!!
Guh!

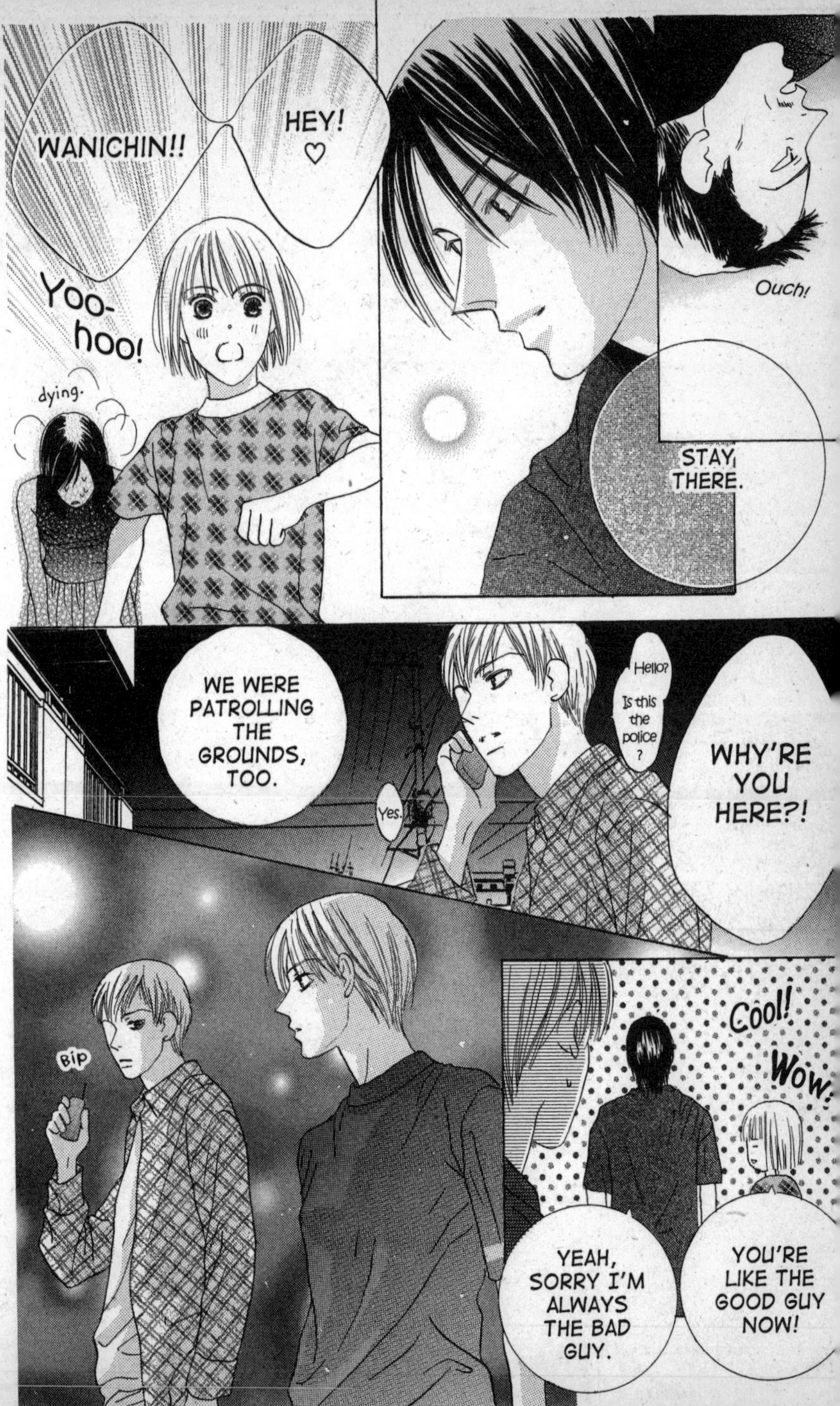
Ouch!
STAY THERE.
HEY! ♡
WANICHIN!!
Yoo-hoo!
dying.
WHY'RE YOU HERE?!
Hello? Is this the police?
Yes.
WE WERE PATROLLING THE GROUNDS, TOO.
Cool!
Wow.
YOU'RE LIKE THE GOOD GUY NOW!
YEAH, SORRY I'M ALWAYS THE BAD GUY.
Bip

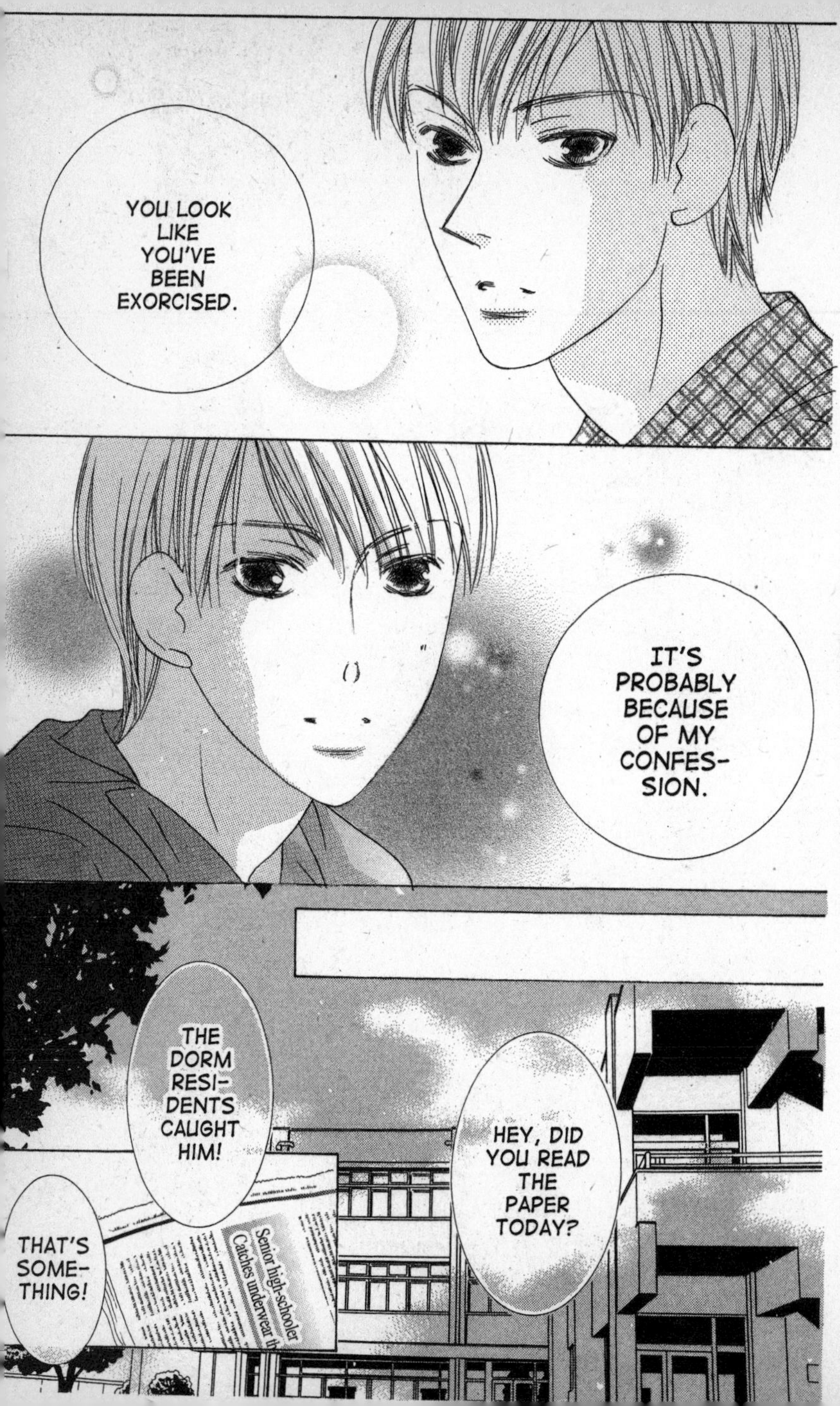
YOU LOOK LIKE YOU'VE BEEN EXORCISED.
IT'S PROBABLY BECAUSE OF MY CONFES-SION.
HEY, DID YOU READ THE PAPER TODAY?
THE DORM RESI-DENTS CAUGHT HIM!
Senior high-schooler
Catches underwear th
THAT'S SOME-THING!

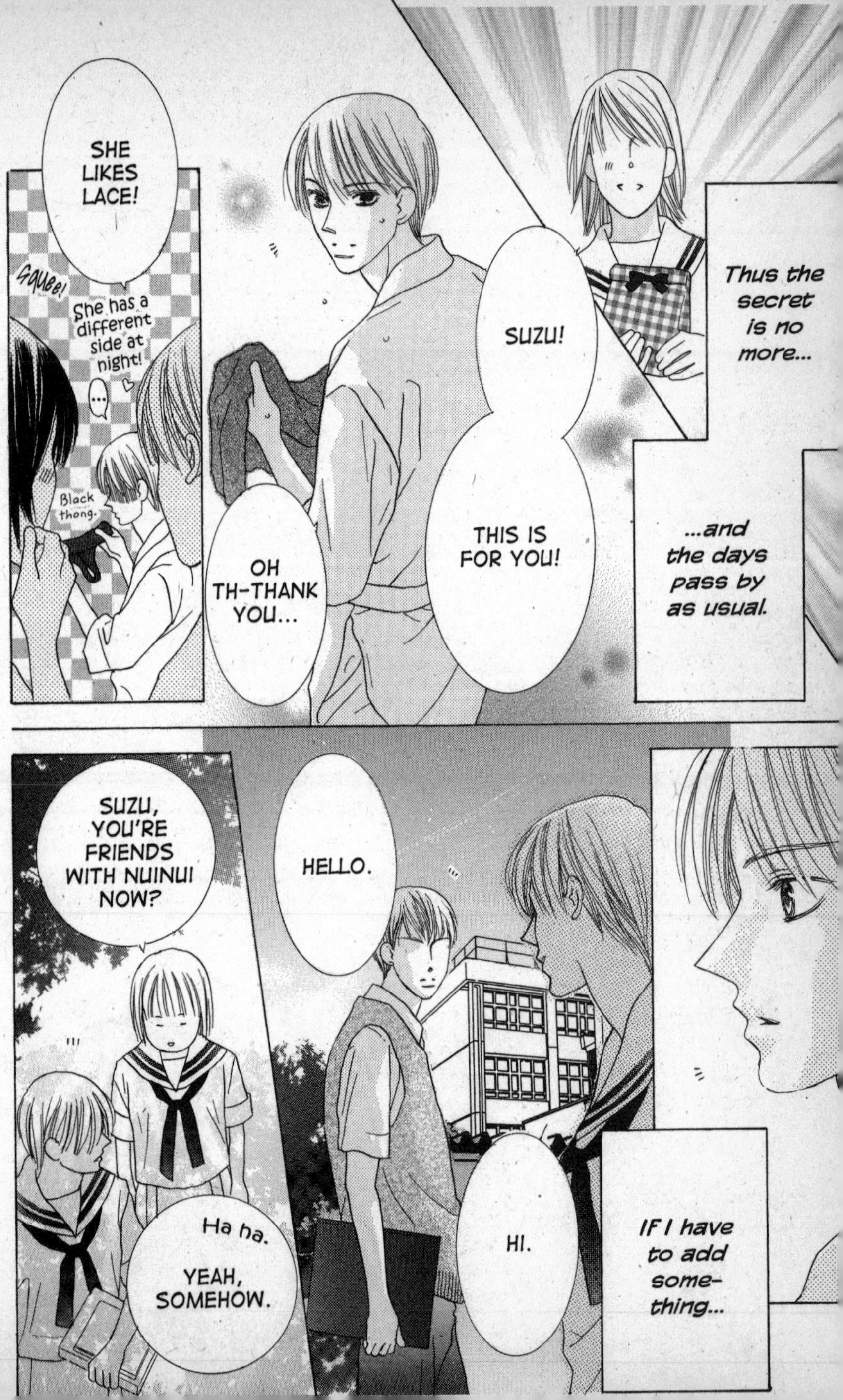
Thus the secret is no more...
SUZU!
THIS IS FOR YOU!
OH TH-THANK YOU...
...and the days pass by as usual.
SHE LIKES LACE!
Squee!
She has a different side at night!
...
Black thong.
IF I have to add some-thing...
HELLO.
HI.
SUZU, YOU'RE FRIENDS WITH NUINUI NOW?
Ha ha.
YEAH, SOMEHOW.

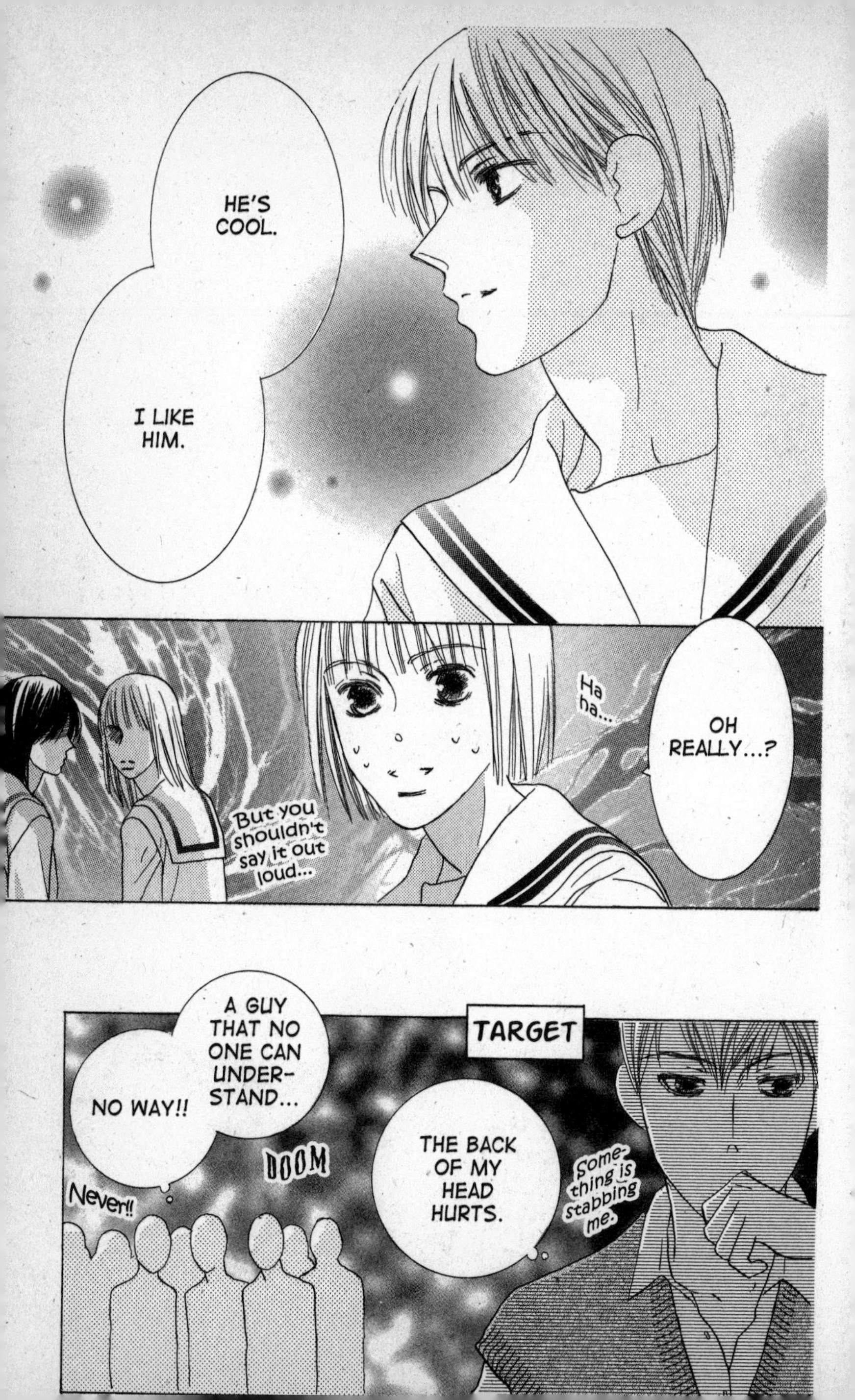
HE'S COOL.
I LIKE HIM.
OH REALLY...?
Ha ha...
But you shouldn't say it out loud...
TARGET
Some-thing is stabbing me.
THE BACK OF MY HEAD HURTS.
A GUY THAT NO ONE CAN UNDER-STAND...
NO WAY!!
DOOM
Never!!

BEAUTY
IS THE
BEAST

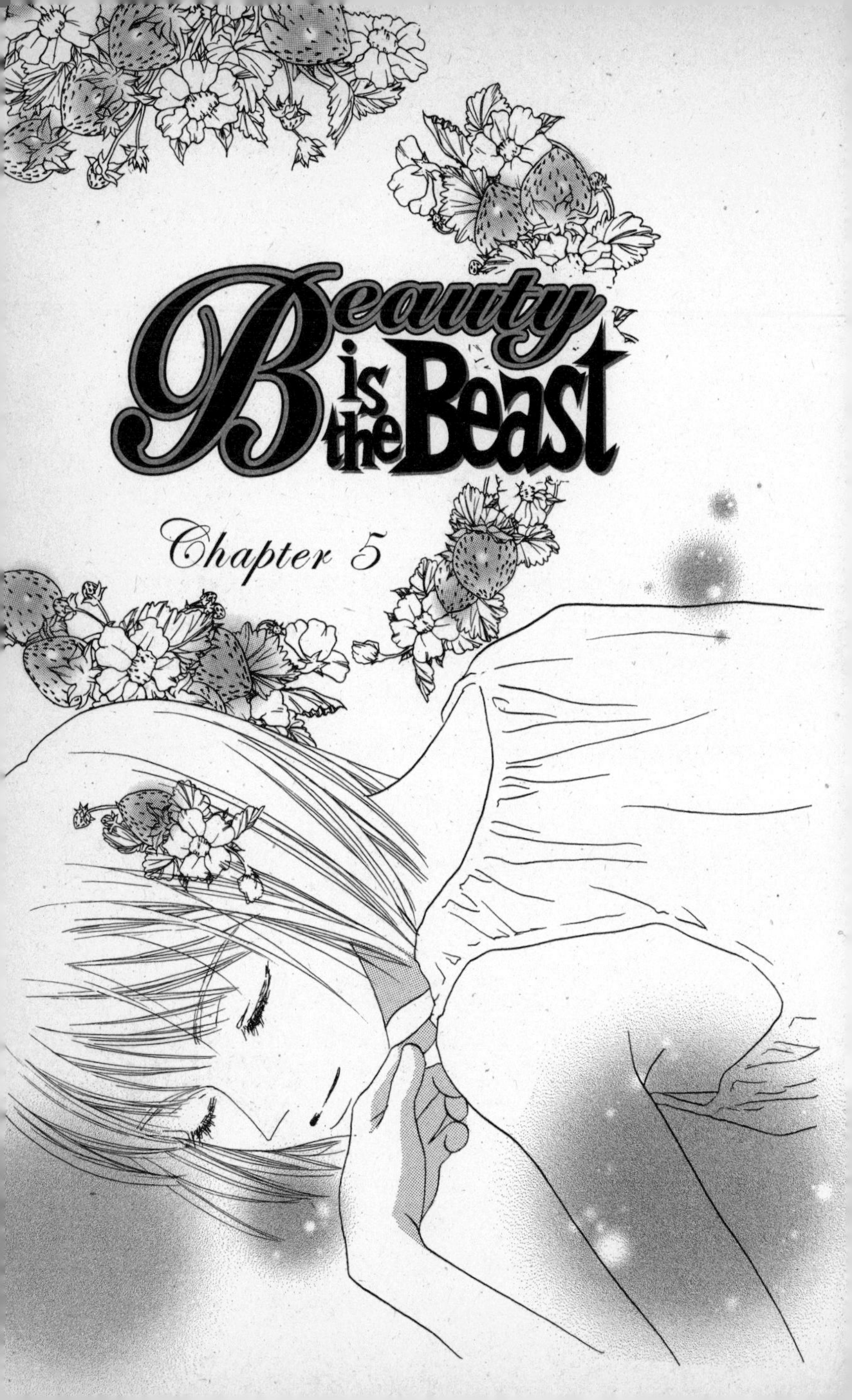
Beauty is the Beast
Chapter 5

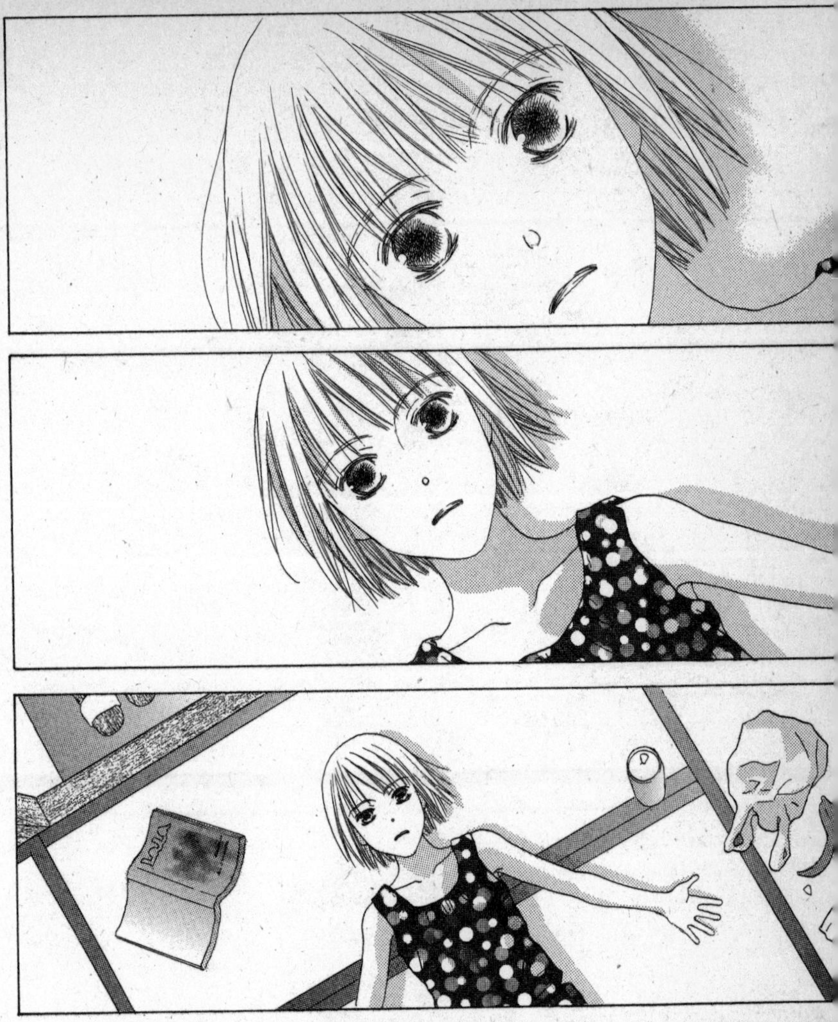

A Must-have for Dorm Life 4: Dotera (Hanten)

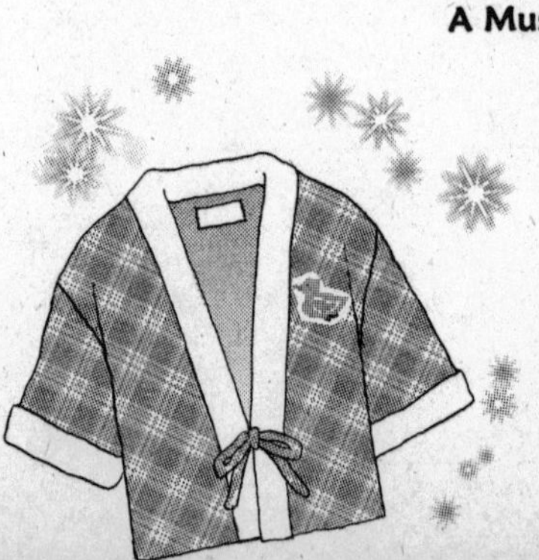

Usually it's quilted, so it's warm. As shown in the illustration, you wear it, and then tie the front.
In the dorm I lived in, everyone wore them, even if it wasn't forced on us.
At first, I didn't understand why, since girls that age were supposed to be really fashion-conscious. Later I understood.
It was out of necessity...it was cold. (Fashion?! As long as it's warm!! That was the reality.)
By the time spring came, it was like a second skin...

**A dotera is like the upper half of a haori, the coat you wear over a kimono. —Ed.*

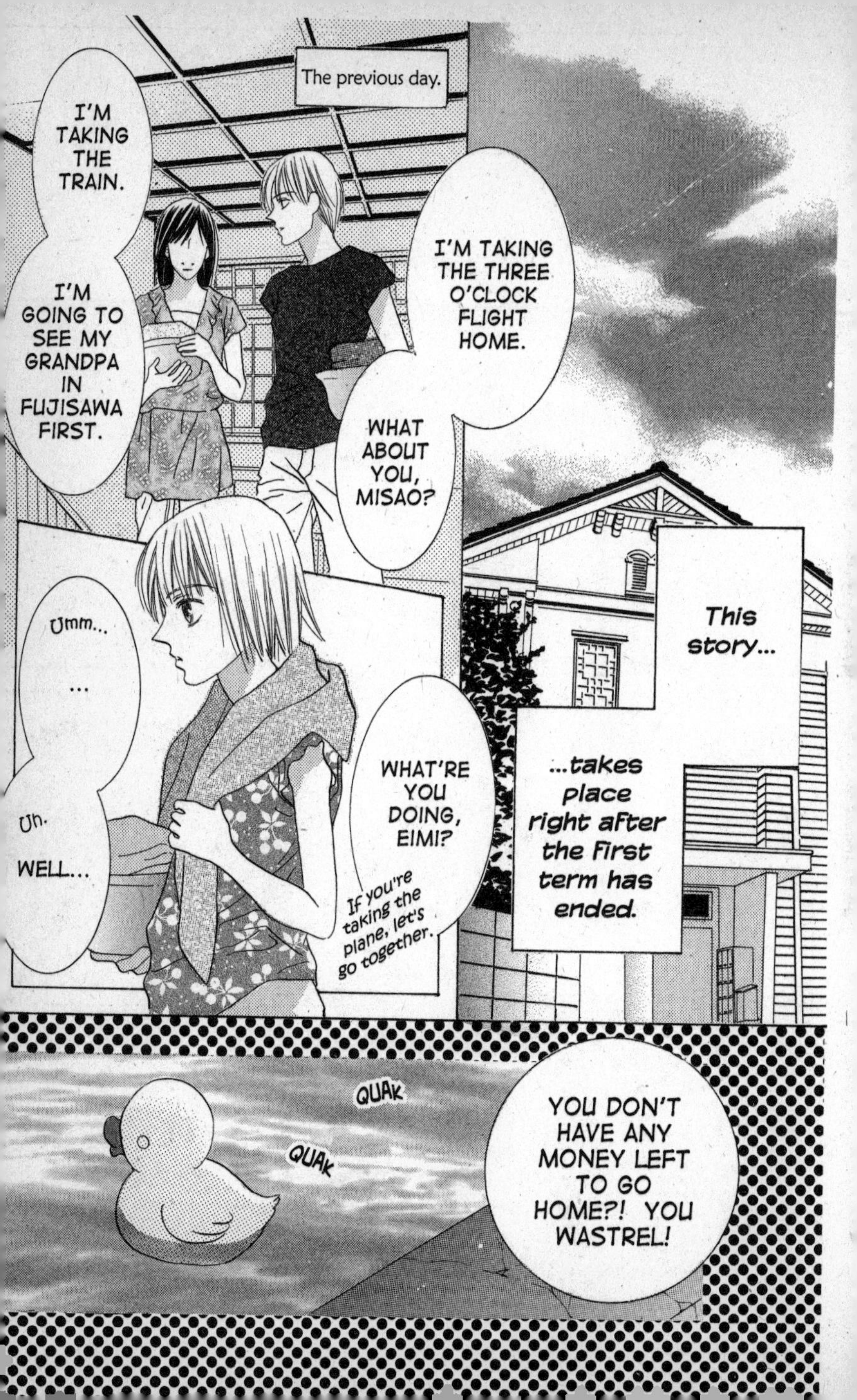

The previous day.
I'M TAKING THE THREE O'CLOCK FLIGHT HOME.
WHAT ABOUT YOU, MISAO?
I'M TAKING THE TRAIN.
I'M GOING TO SEE MY GRANDPA IN FUJISAWA FIRST.
This story...
...takes place right after the first term has ended.
WHAT'RE YOU DOING, EIMI?
If you're taking the plane, let's go together.
Umm...
...
Uh.
WELL...
QUAK
QUAK
YOU DON'T HAVE ANY MONEY LEFT TO GO HOME?! YOU WASTREL!

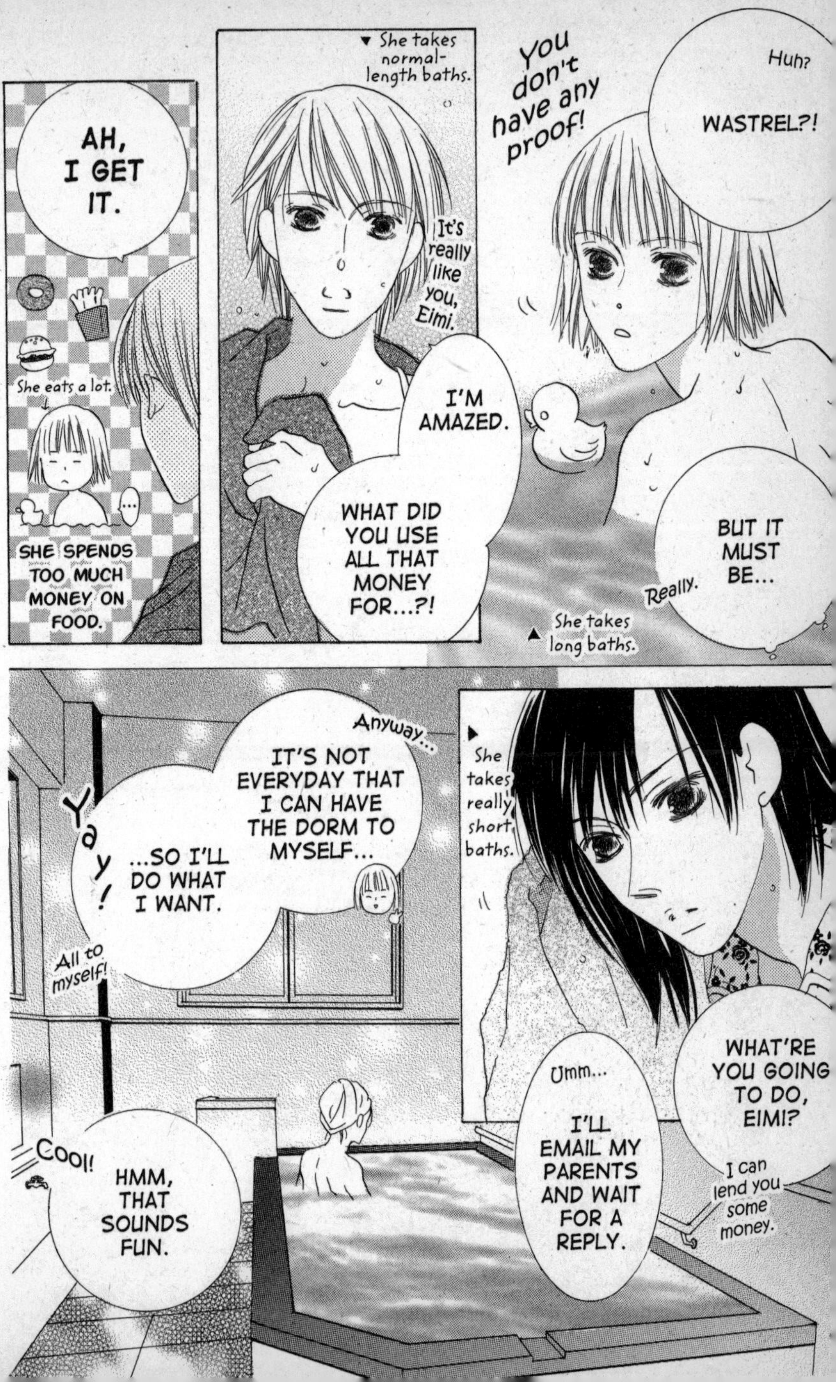

Huh?
WASTREL?!
You don't have any proof!
BUT IT MUST BE...
Really.
She takes long baths.
She takes normal-length baths.
It's really like you, Eimi.
I'M AMAZED.
WHAT DID YOU USE ALL THAT MONEY FOR...?!
AH, I GET IT.
She eats a lot.
...
SHE SPENDS TOO MUCH MONEY ON FOOD.
She takes really short baths.
WHAT'RE YOU GOING TO DO, EIMI?
I can lend you some money.
Umm...
I'LL EMAIL MY PARENTS AND WAIT FOR A REPLY.
Anyway...
IT'S NOT EVERYDAY THAT I CAN HAVE THE DORM TO MYSELF...
...SO I'LL DO WHAT I WANT.
Yay!
All to myself!
HMM, THAT SOUNDS FUN.
Cool!

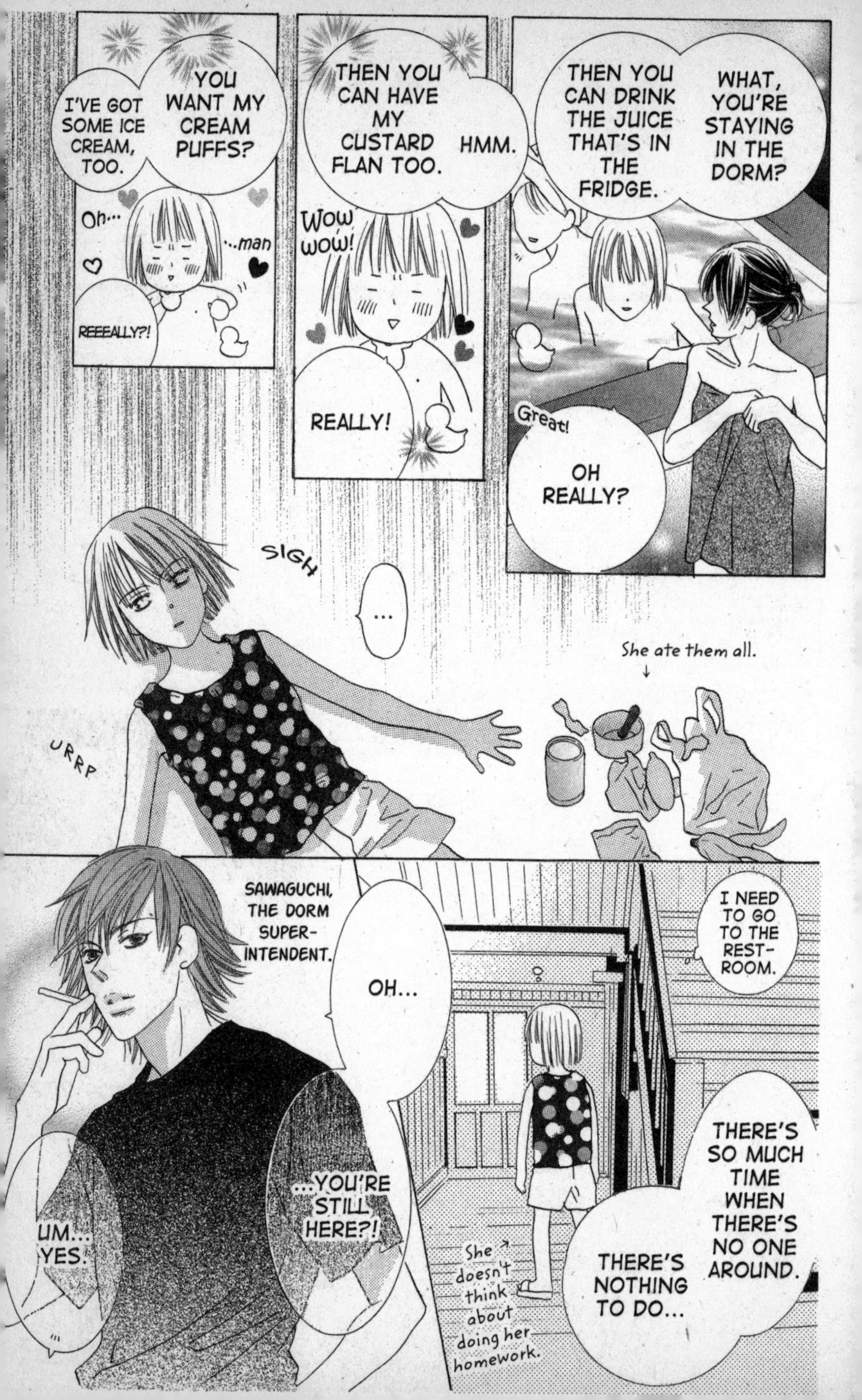
WHAT, YOU'RE STAYING IN THE DORM?
THEN YOU CAN DRINK THE JUICE THAT'S IN THE FRIDGE.
Great!
OH REALLY?
HMM.
THEN YOU CAN HAVE MY CUSTARD FLAN TOO.
Wow wow!
REALLY!
YOU WANT MY CREAM PUFFS?
I'VE GOT SOME ICE CREAM, TOO.
Oh...
...man
REEEALLY?!
She ate them all.
SIGH
...
URRP
THERE'S SO MUCH TIME WHEN THERE'S NO ONE AROUND.
THERE'S NOTHING TO DO...
I NEED TO GO TO THE REST-ROOM.
She doesn't think about doing her homework.
OH...
SAWAGUCHI, THE DORM SUPER-INTENDENT.
...YOU'RE STILL HERE?!
UM... YES.

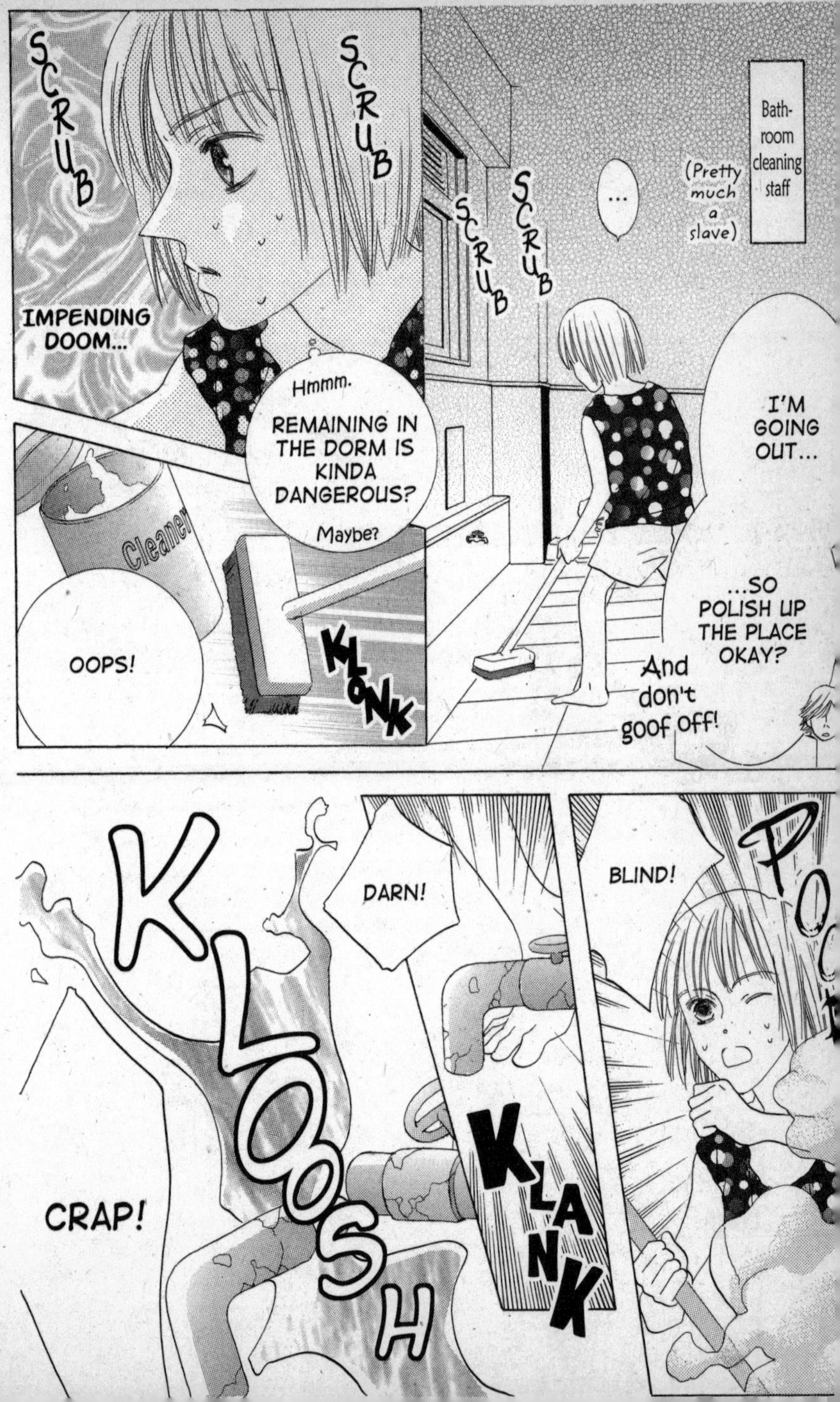
Bath-room cleaning staff
(Pretty much a slave)
...
SCRUB SCRUB
I'M GOING OUT...
...SO POLISH UP THE PLACE OKAY?
And don't goof off!
SCRUB SCRUB
IMPENDING DOOM...
Hmmm.
REMAINING IN THE DORM IS KINDA DANGEROUS?
Maybe?
Cleaner
KLONK
OOPS!
BLIND!
DARN!
KLANK
KLOOSH
CRAP!

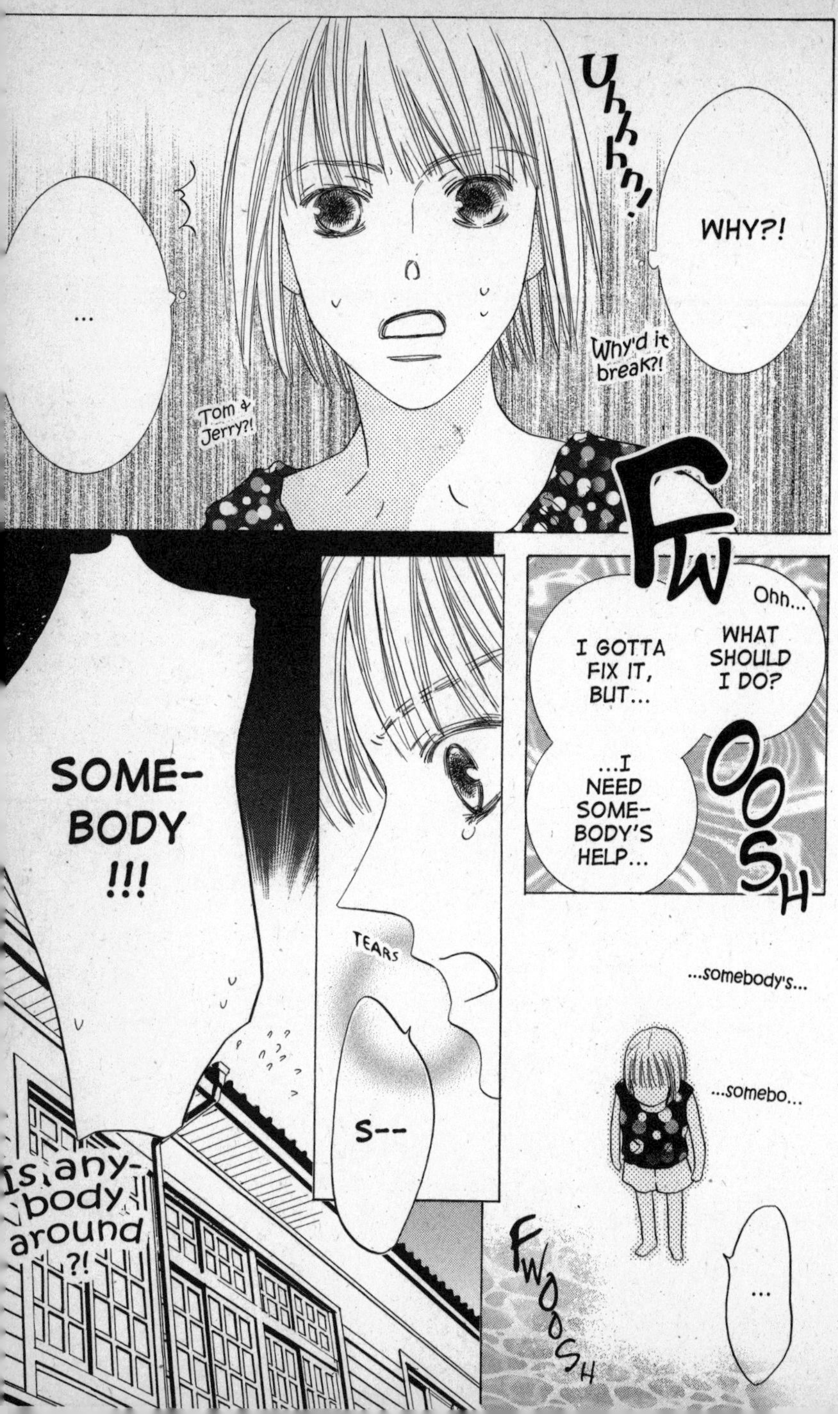
Uhhhhn!
WHY?!
Why'd it break?!
Tom & Jerry?!
...
FWOOOSH
Ohh... WHAT SHOULD I DO?
I GOTTA FIX IT, BUT...
...I NEED SOMEBODY'S HELP...
TEARS
S--
SOME-BODY !!!
Is any-body around ?!
...somebody's...
...somebo...
...
FWOOOSH

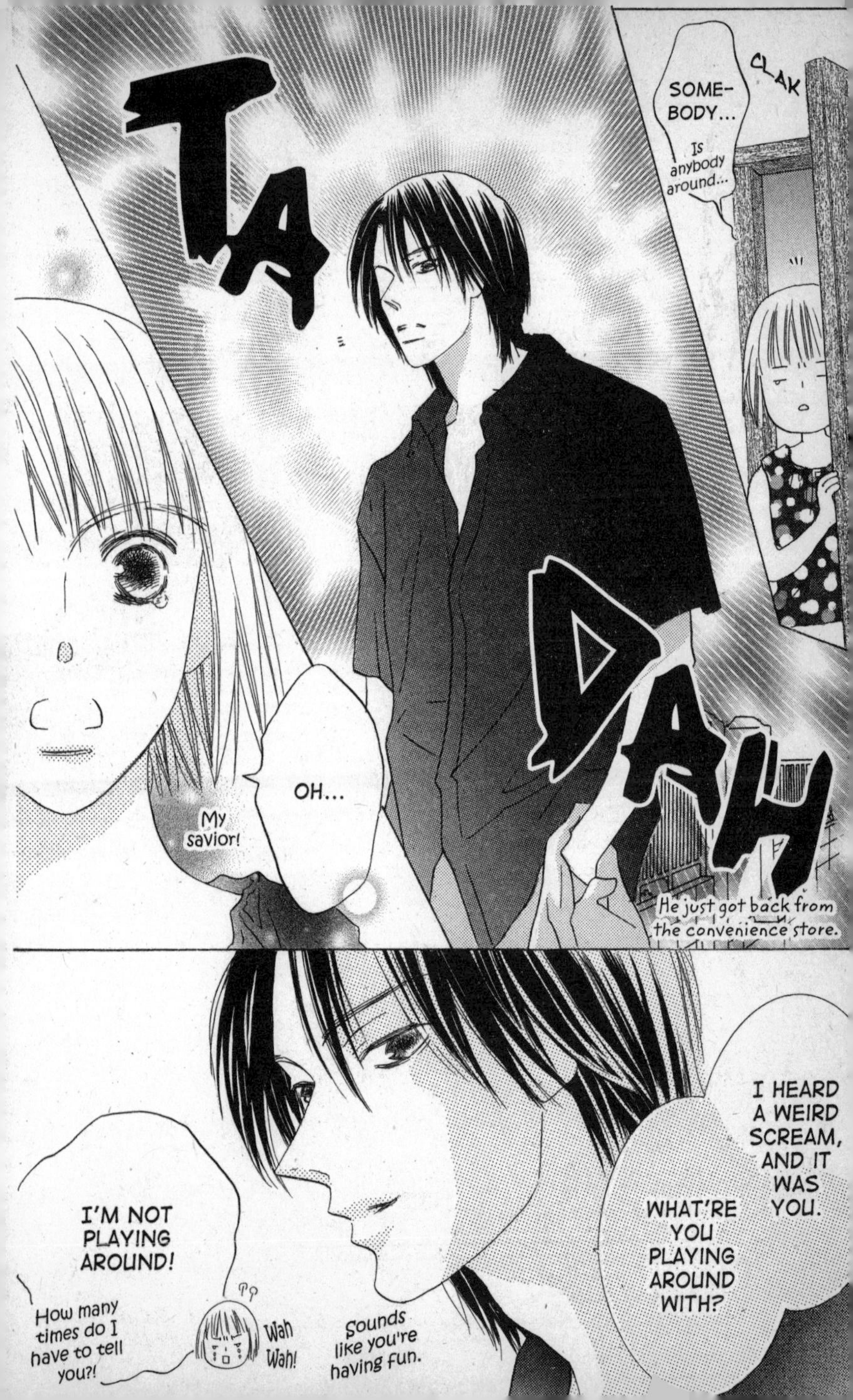
SOME-BODY...
Is anybody around...
CLAK
TA
DAH
He just got back from the convenience store.
OH...
My savior!
I HEARD A WEIRD SCREAM, AND IT WAS YOU.
WHAT'RE YOU PLAYING AROUND WITH?
Sounds like you're having fun.
Wah Wah!
I'M NOT PLAYING AROUND!
How many times do I have to tell you?!

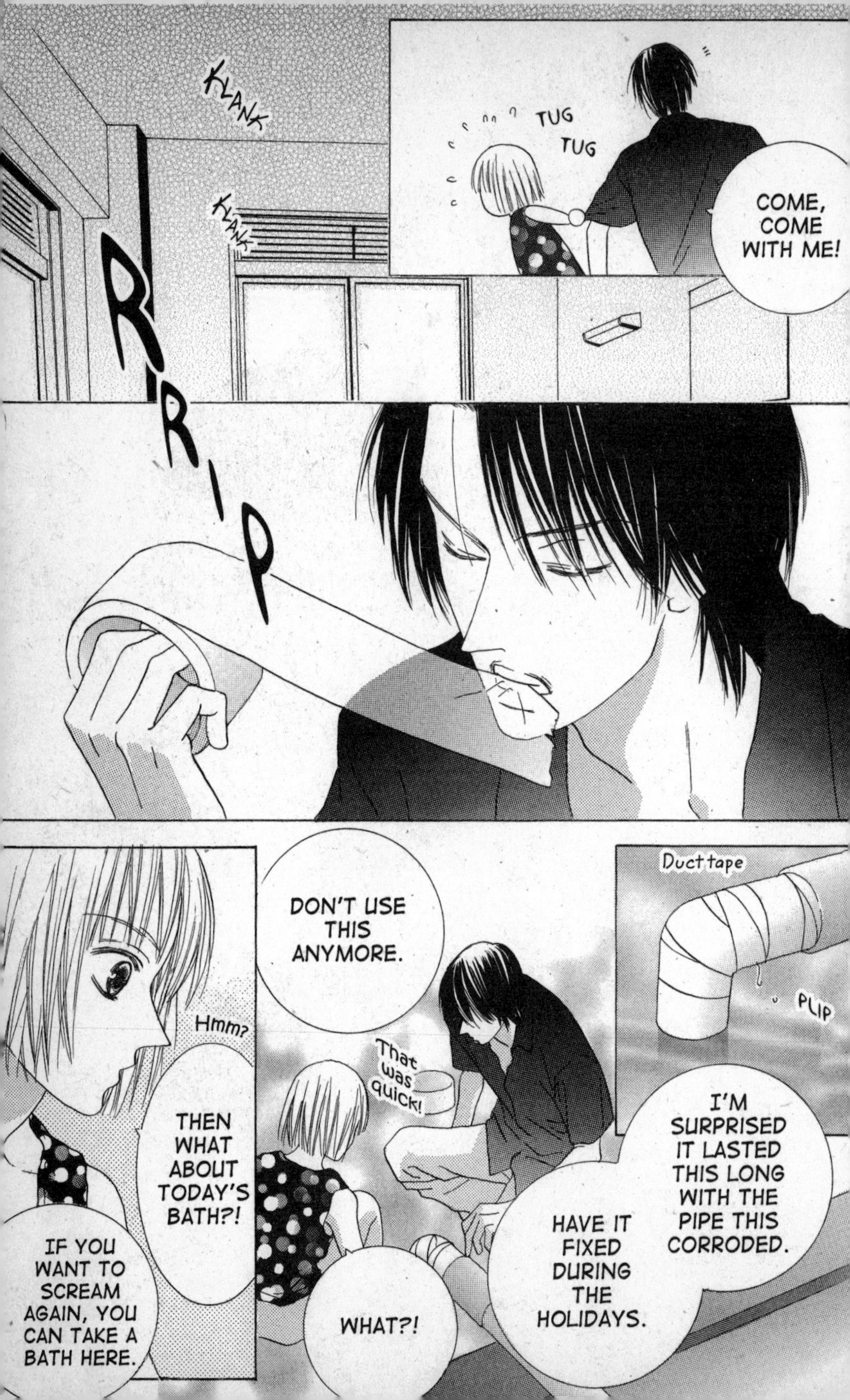
TUG
TUG
COME, COME WITH ME!
KLANK
KLANK
RRIP
Duct tape
PLIP
I'M SURPRISED IT LASTED THIS LONG WITH THE PIPE THIS CORRODED.
HAVE IT FIXED DURING THE HOLIDAYS.
DON'T USE THIS ANYMORE.
That was quick!
WHAT?!
THEN WHAT ABOUT TODAY'S BATH?!
Hmm?
IF YOU WANT TO SCREAM AGAIN, YOU CAN TAKE A BATH HERE.

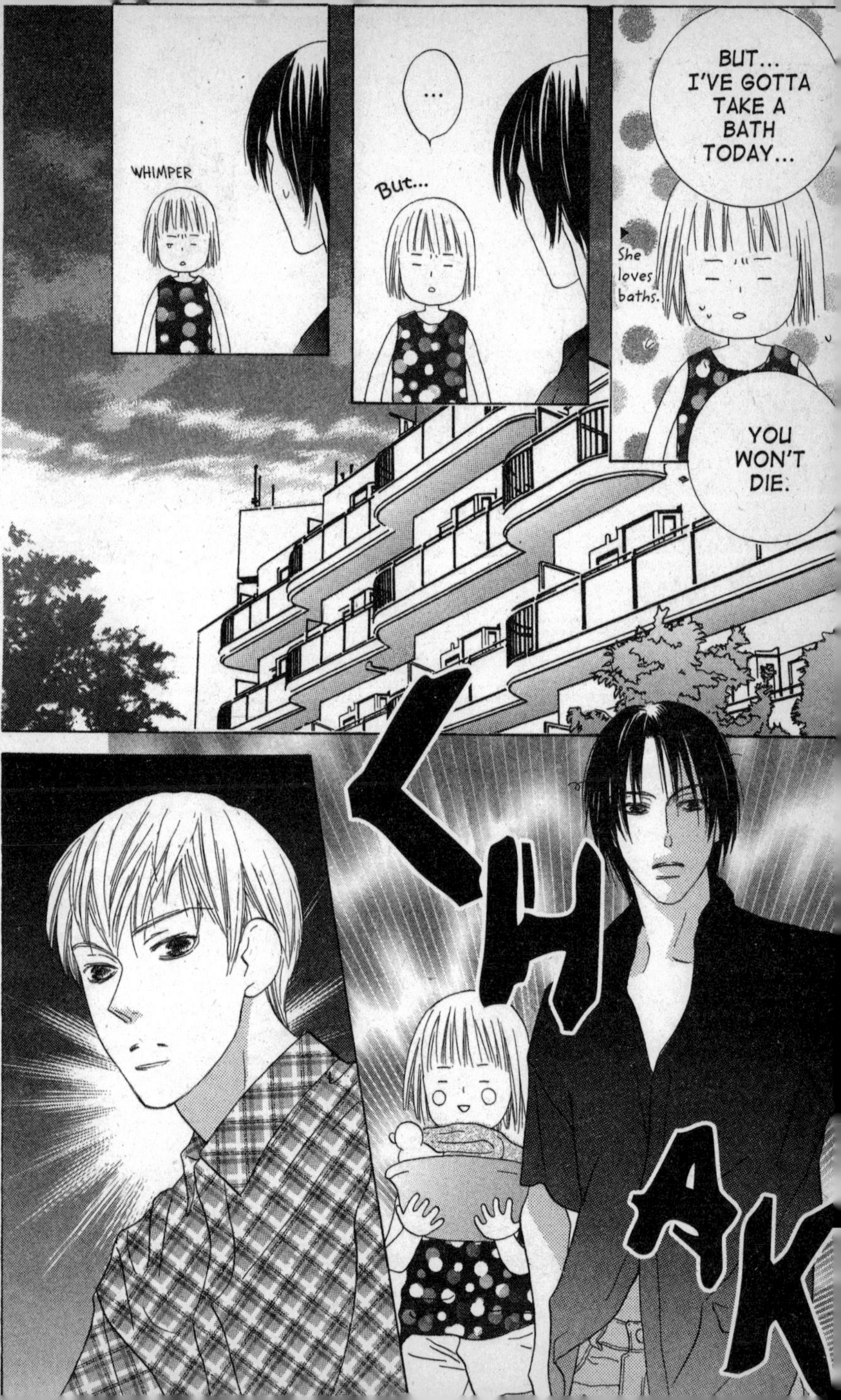
BUT... I'VE GOTTA TAKE A BATH TODAY...
She loves baths.
YOU WON'T DIE.
...
But...
WHIMPER
KHAK

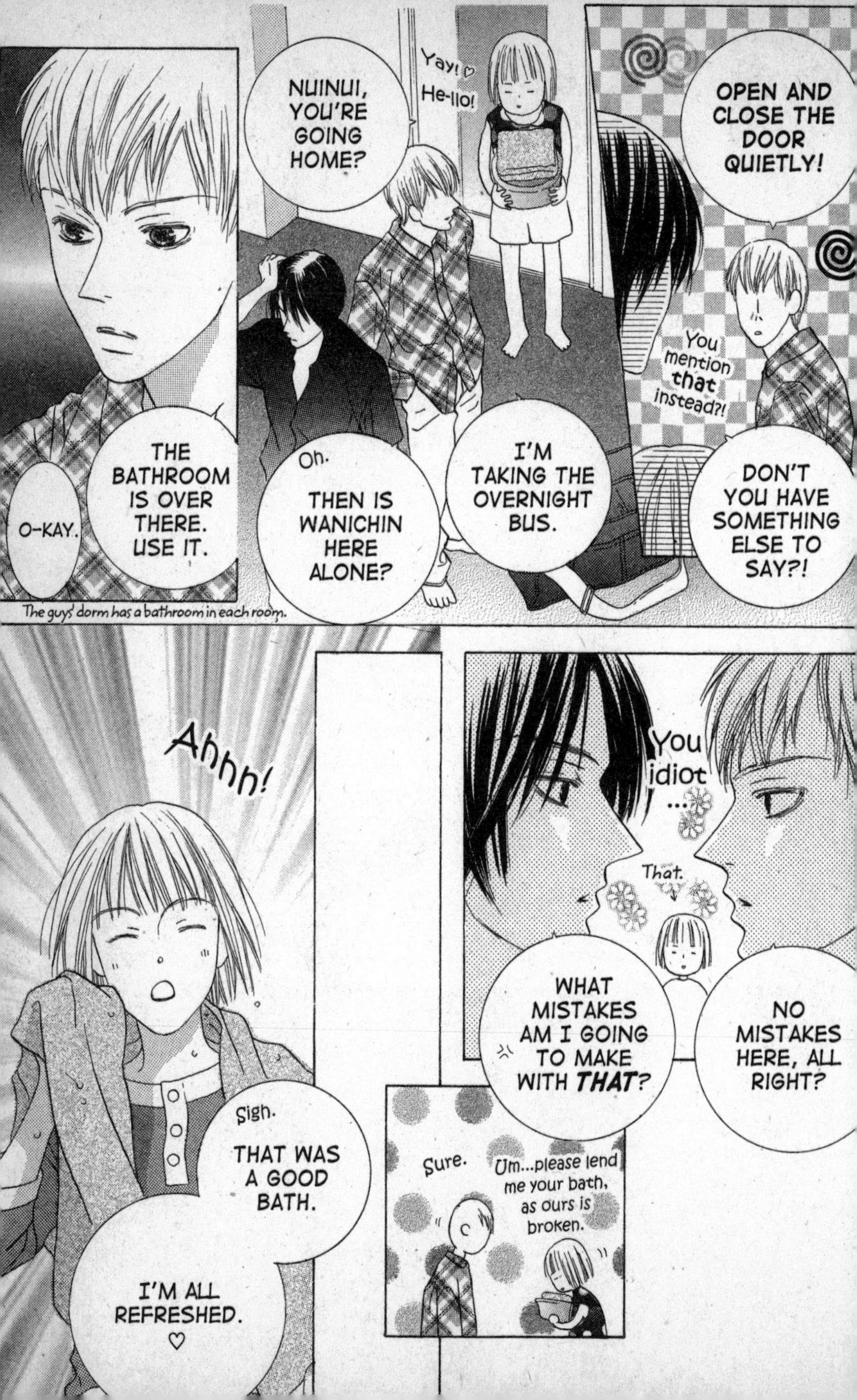
OPEN AND CLOSE THE DOOR QUIETLY!
You mention that instead?!
DON'T YOU HAVE SOMETHING ELSE TO SAY?!
Yay! ♡
He-llo!
NUINUI, YOU'RE GOING HOME?
I'M TAKING THE OVERNIGHT BUS.
Oh.
THEN IS WANICHIN HERE ALONE?
THE BATHROOM IS OVER THERE. USE IT.
O-KAY.
The guys' dorm has a bathroom in each room.
You idiot...
That.
NO MISTAKES HERE, ALL RIGHT?
WHAT MISTAKES AM I GOING TO MAKE WITH THAT?
Um...please lend me your bath, as ours is broken.
Sure.
Ahhh!
Sigh.
THAT WAS A GOOD BATH.
I'M ALL REFRESHED. ♡

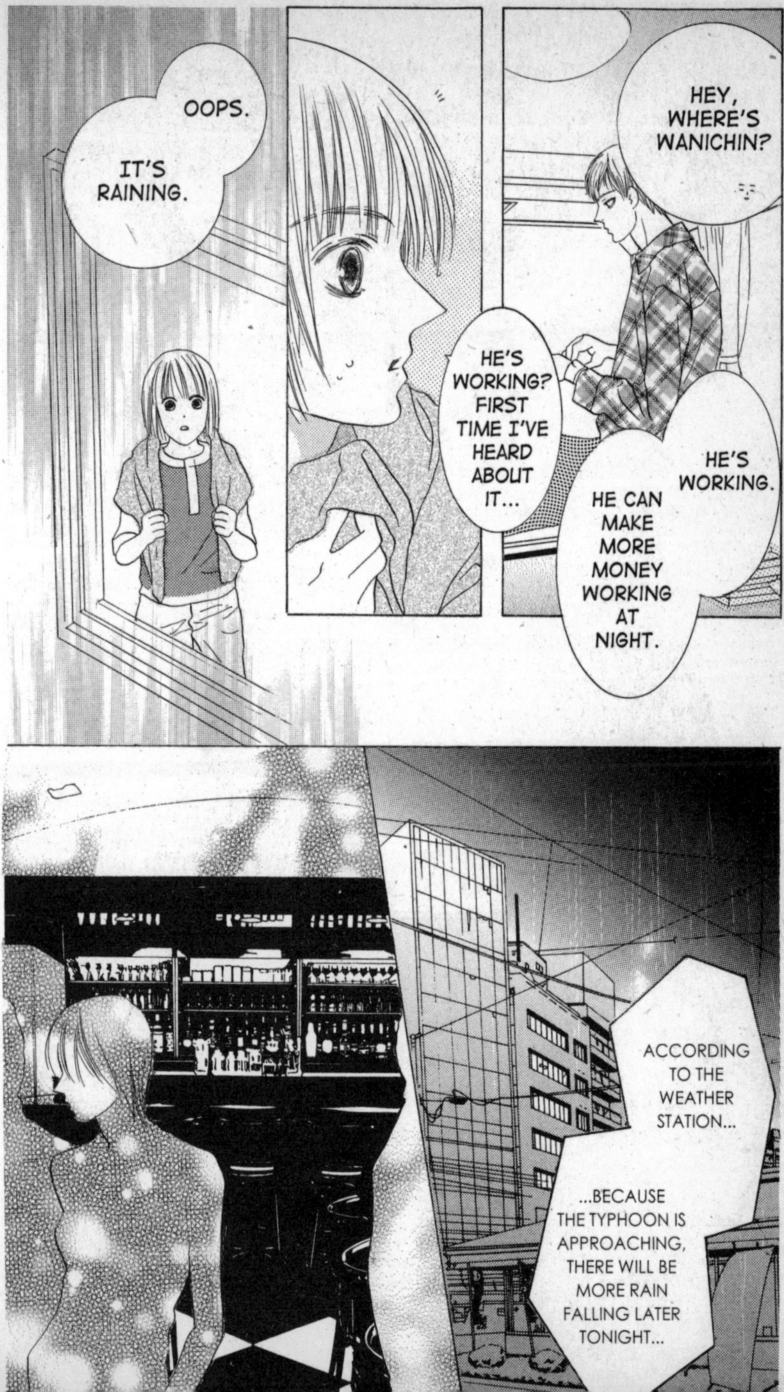
HEY, WHERE'S WANICHIN?
HE'S WORKING.
HE CAN MAKE MORE MONEY WORKING AT NIGHT.
HE'S WORKING? FIRST TIME I'VE HEARD ABOUT IT...
OOPS.
IT'S RAINING.
ACCORDING TO THE WEATHER STATION...
...BECAUSE THE TYPHOON IS APPROACHING, THERE WILL BE MORE RAIN FALLING LATER TONIGHT...

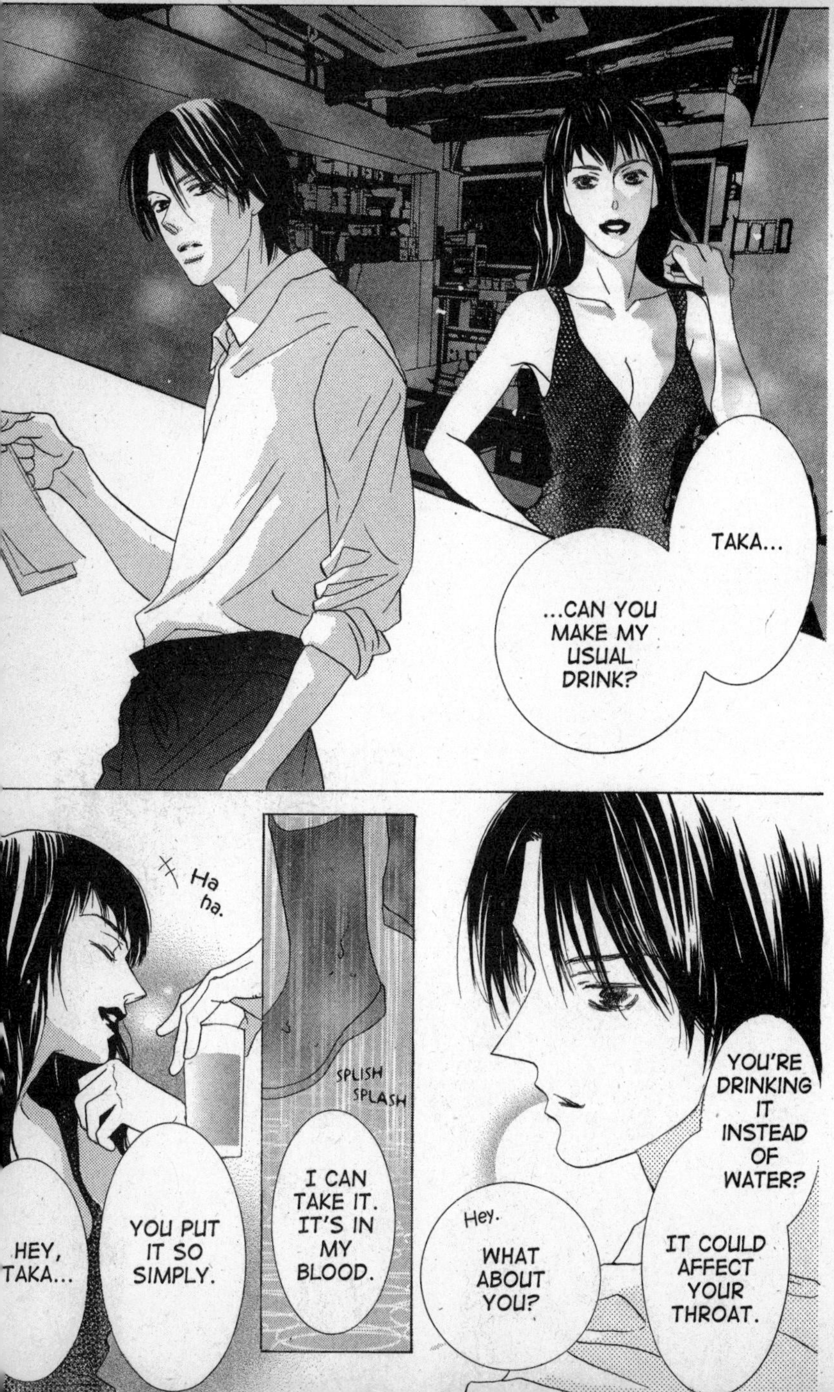
TAKA...
...CAN YOU MAKE MY USUAL DRINK?
YOU'RE DRINKING IT INSTEAD OF WATER?
IT COULD AFFECT YOUR THROAT.
Hey.
WHAT ABOUT YOU?
SPLISH SPLASH
I CAN TAKE IT. IT'S IN MY BLOOD.
Ha ha.
YOU PUT IT SO SIMPLY.
HEY, TAKA...

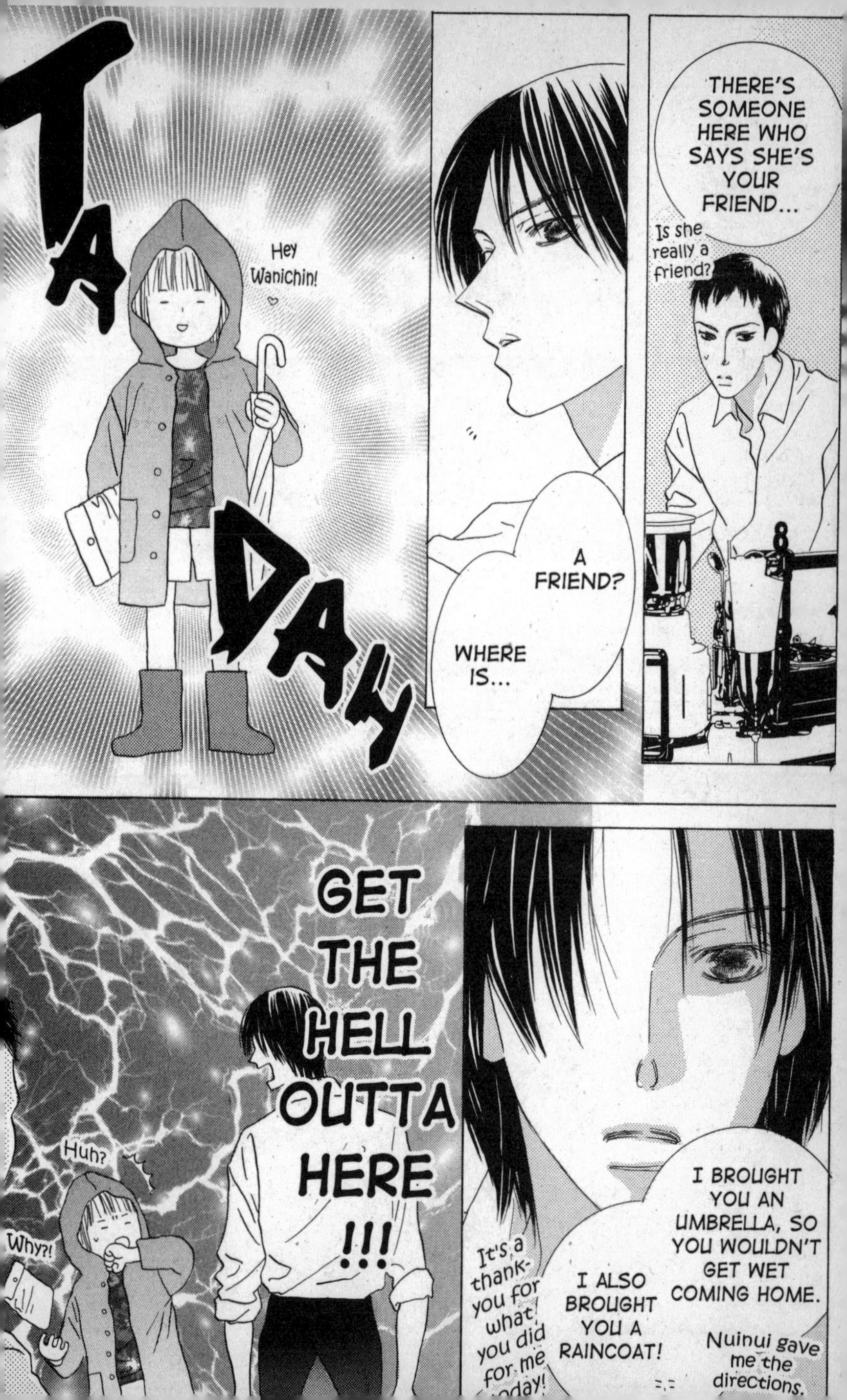

THERE'S SOMEONE HERE WHO SAYS SHE'S YOUR FRIEND...
Is she really a friend?
A FRIEND?
WHERE IS...
TA DAH
Hey Wanichin!
I BROUGHT YOU AN UMBRELLA, SO YOU WOULDN'T GET WET COMING HOME.
Nuinui gave me the directions.
I ALSO BROUGHT YOU A RAINCOAT!
It's a thank-you for what you did for me today!
GET THE HELL OUTTA HERE!!!
Huh?
Why?!

5

I just realized that this is my tenth comic... Wow... (↑ I realize it now!)

When I'm working on the story, I always play some music. There seem to be many mangakas who don't play any music, saying that music interferes with their work. In my case, music seems to take me (pull me) there, so I keep playing music when I'm thinking up a story.

With the series... I think I played... lots of Norah Jones and Jerzee Monet.

They were such cool songs, but the resulting manga has all these fetishes in them. It's a mystery.

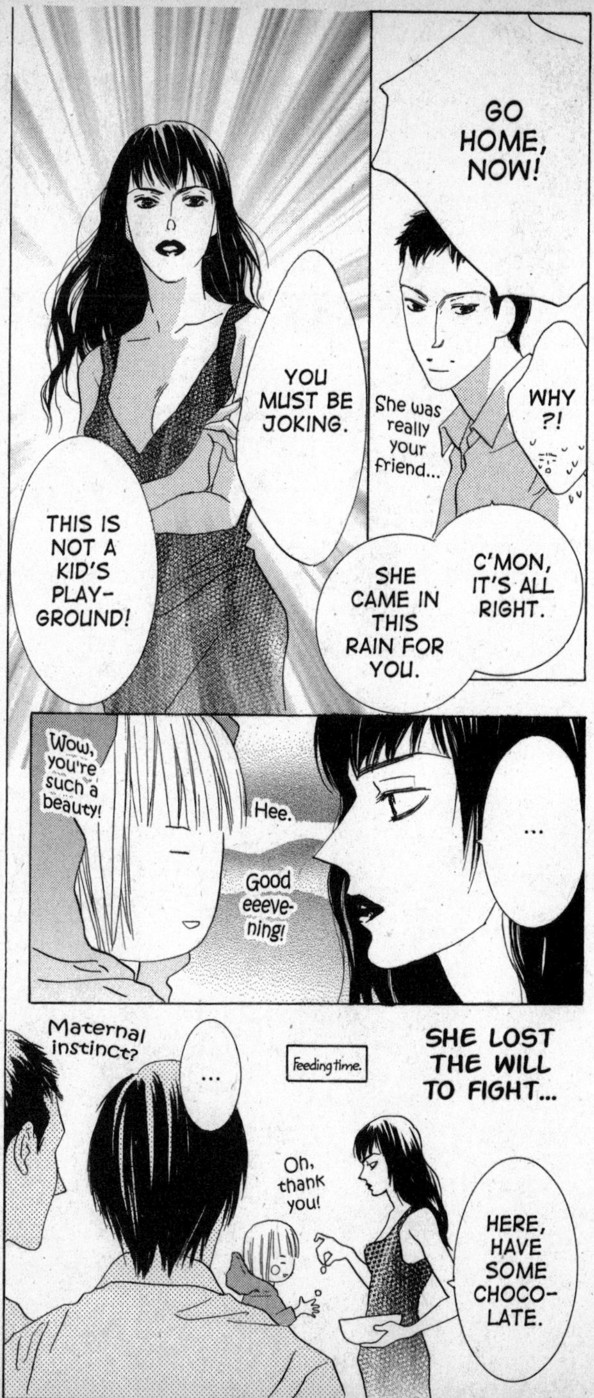
GO HOME, NOW!
WHY?!
She was really your friend...
C'MON, IT'S ALL RIGHT.
SHE CAME IN THIS RAIN FOR YOU.
YOU MUST BE JOKING.
THIS IS NOT A KID'S PLAY-GROUND!
...
Good eeeve-ning!
Hee.
Wow, you're such a beauty!
SHE LOST THE WILL TO FIGHT...
HERE, HAVE SOME CHOCO-LATE.
Oh, thank you!
Feeding time.
...
Maternal instinct?

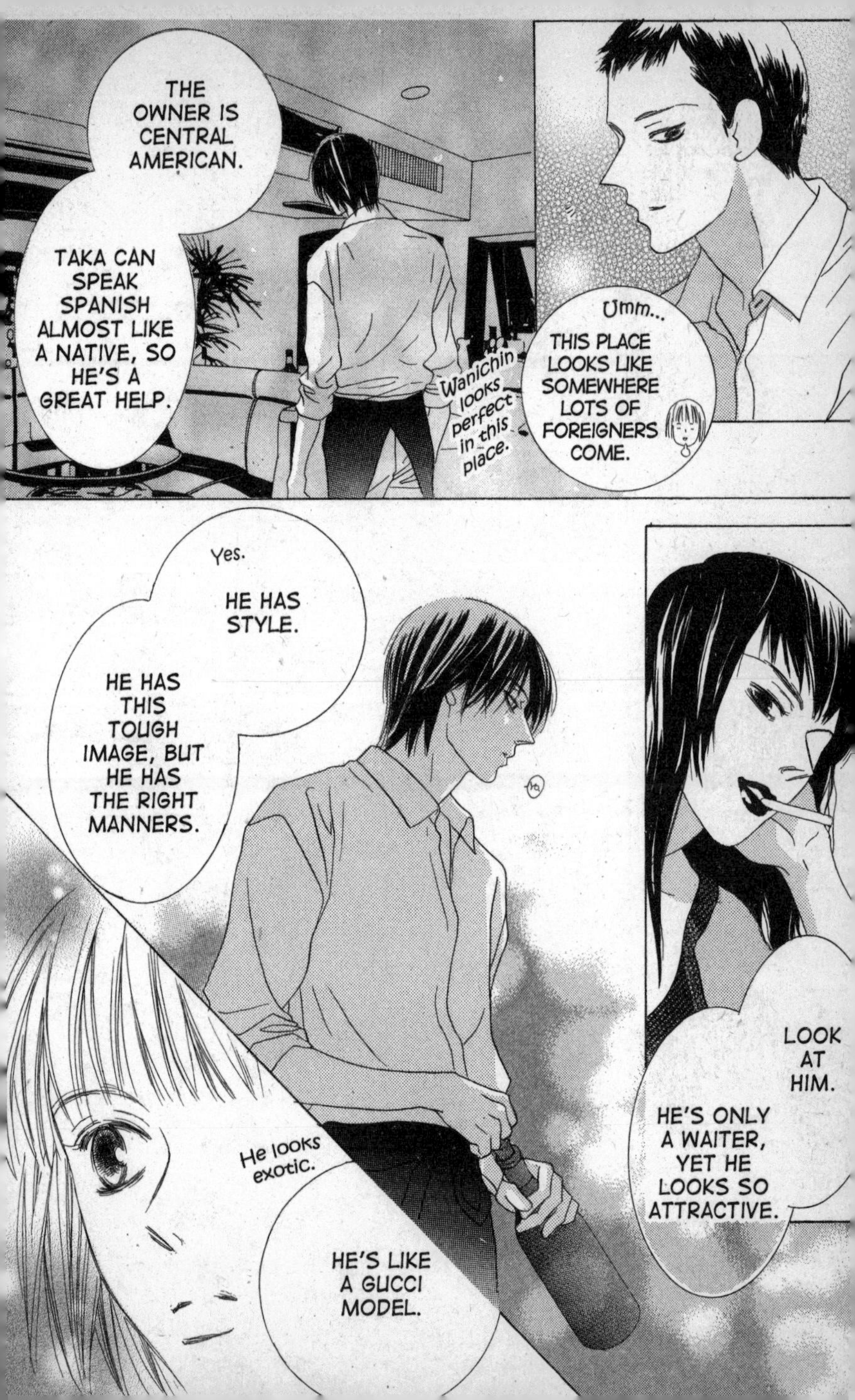
Umm...
THIS PLACE LOOKS LIKE SOMEWHERE LOTS OF FOREIGNERS COME.
Wanichin looks perfect in this place.
THE OWNER IS CENTRAL AMERICAN.
TAKA CAN SPEAK SPANISH ALMOST LIKE A NATIVE, SO HE'S A GREAT HELP.
LOOK AT HIM.
HE'S ONLY A WAITER, YET HE LOOKS SO ATTRACTIVE.
Yes.
HE HAS STYLE.
HE HAS THIS TOUGH IMAGE, BUT HE HAS THE RIGHT MANNERS.
He looks exotic.
HE'S LIKE A GUCCI MODEL.

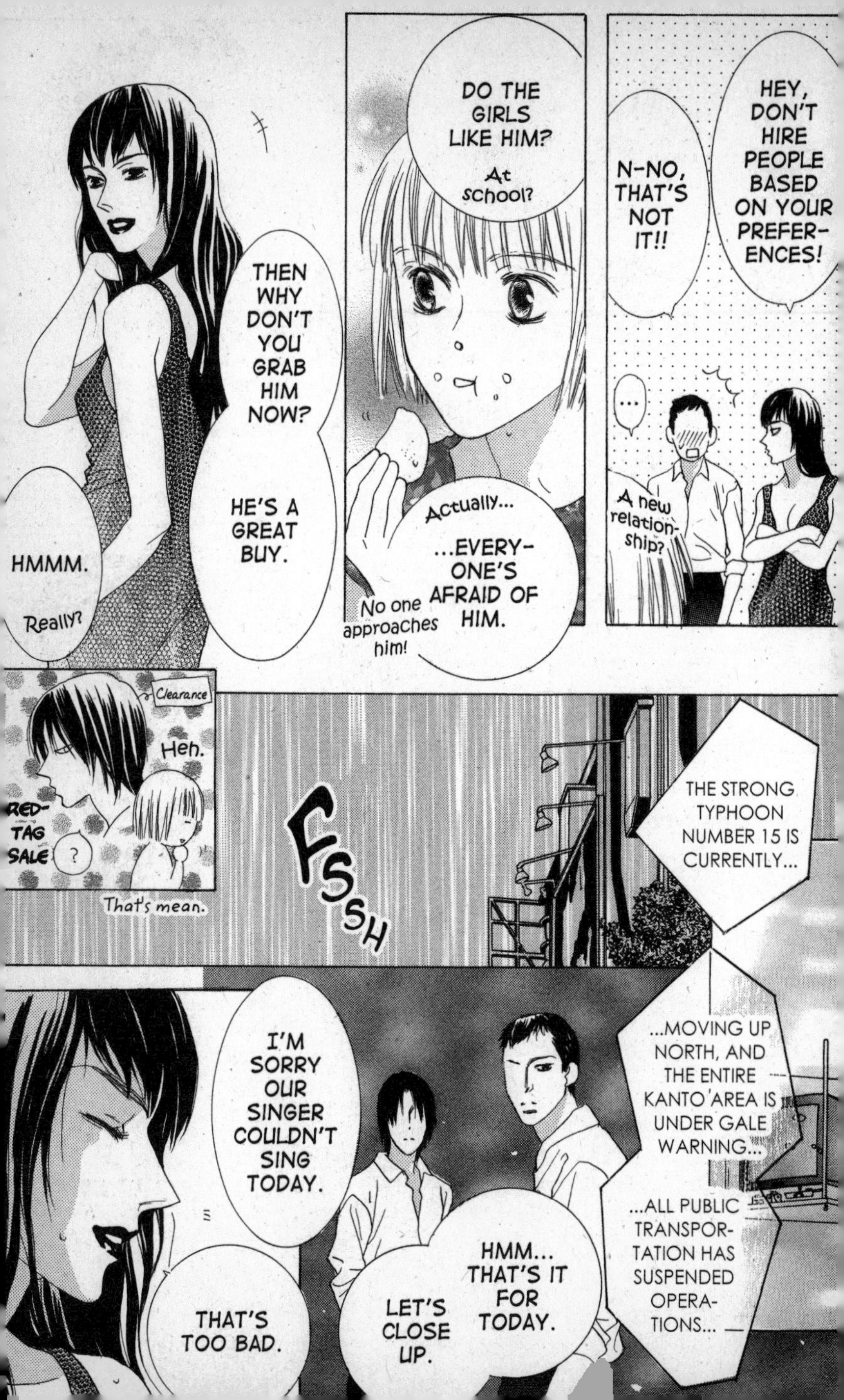
HEY, DON'T HIRE PEOPLE BASED ON YOUR PREFER-ENCES!
N-NO, THAT'S NOT IT!!
...
A new relation-ship?
DO THE GIRLS LIKE HIM?
At school?
Actually...
...EVERY-ONE'S AFRAID OF HIM.
No one approaches him!
THEN WHY DON'T YOU GRAB HIM NOW?
HE'S A GREAT BUY.
HMMM.
Really?
THE STRONG TYPHOON NUMBER 15 IS CURRENTLY...
FSSH
Clearance
Heh.
RED-TAG SALE
?
That's mean.
...MOVING UP NORTH, AND THE ENTIRE KANTO AREA IS UNDER GALE WARNING...
...ALL PUBLIC TRANSPOR-TATION HAS SUSPENDED OPERA-TIONS...
HMM... THAT'S IT FOR TODAY.
LET'S CLOSE UP.
I'M SORRY OUR SINGER COULDN'T SING TODAY.
THAT'S TOO BAD.

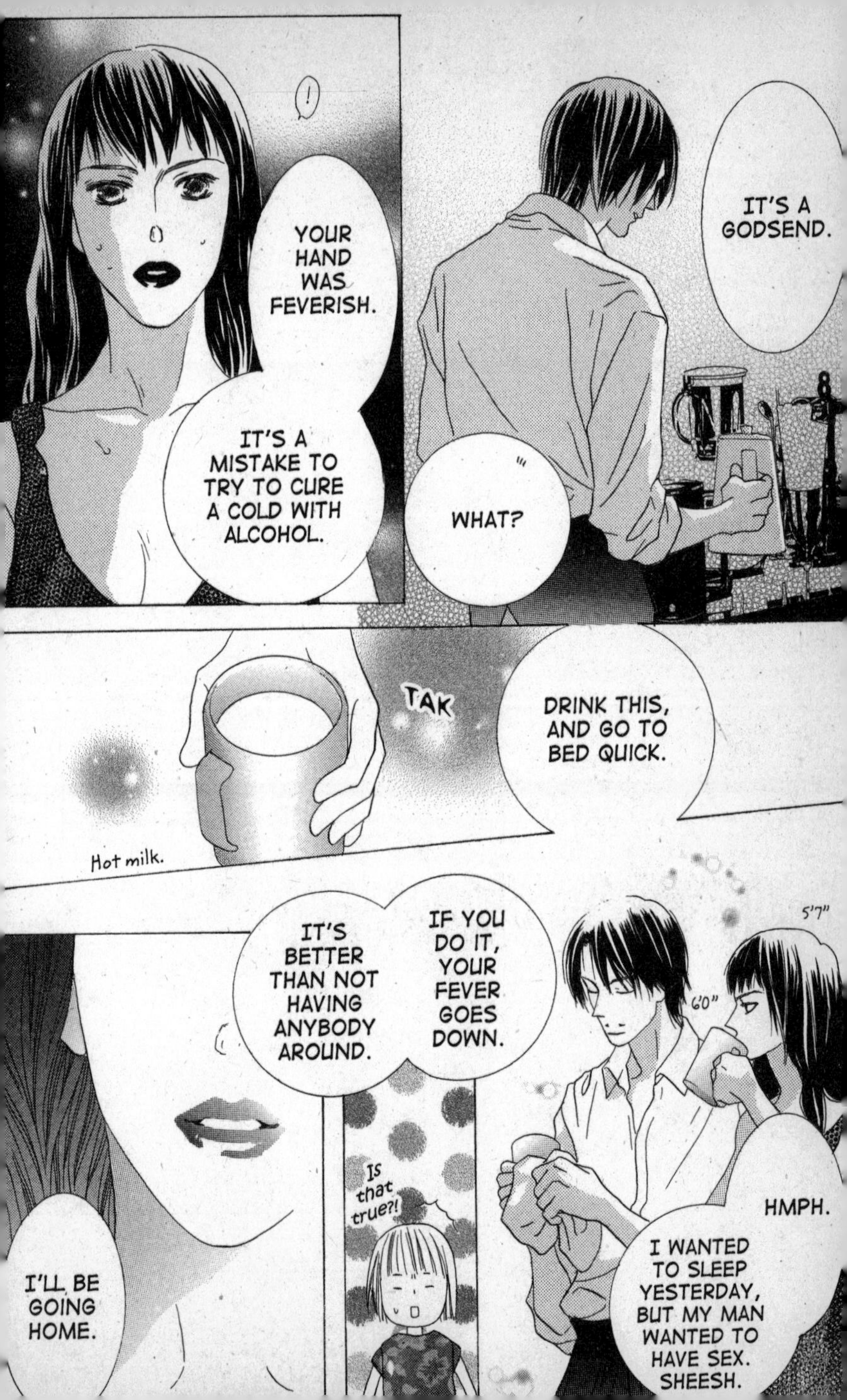

IT'S A GODSEND.
WHAT?
!
YOUR HAND WAS FEVERISH.
IT'S A MISTAKE TO TRY TO CURE A COLD WITH ALCOHOL.
DRINK THIS, AND GO TO BED QUICK.
TAK
Hot milk.
5'7"
6'0"
HMPH.
I WANTED TO SLEEP YESTERDAY, BUT MY MAN WANTED TO HAVE SEX. SHEESH.
IF YOU DO IT, YOUR FEVER GOES DOWN.
Is that true?!
IT'S BETTER THAN NOT HAVING ANYBODY AROUND.
I'LL BE GOING HOME.

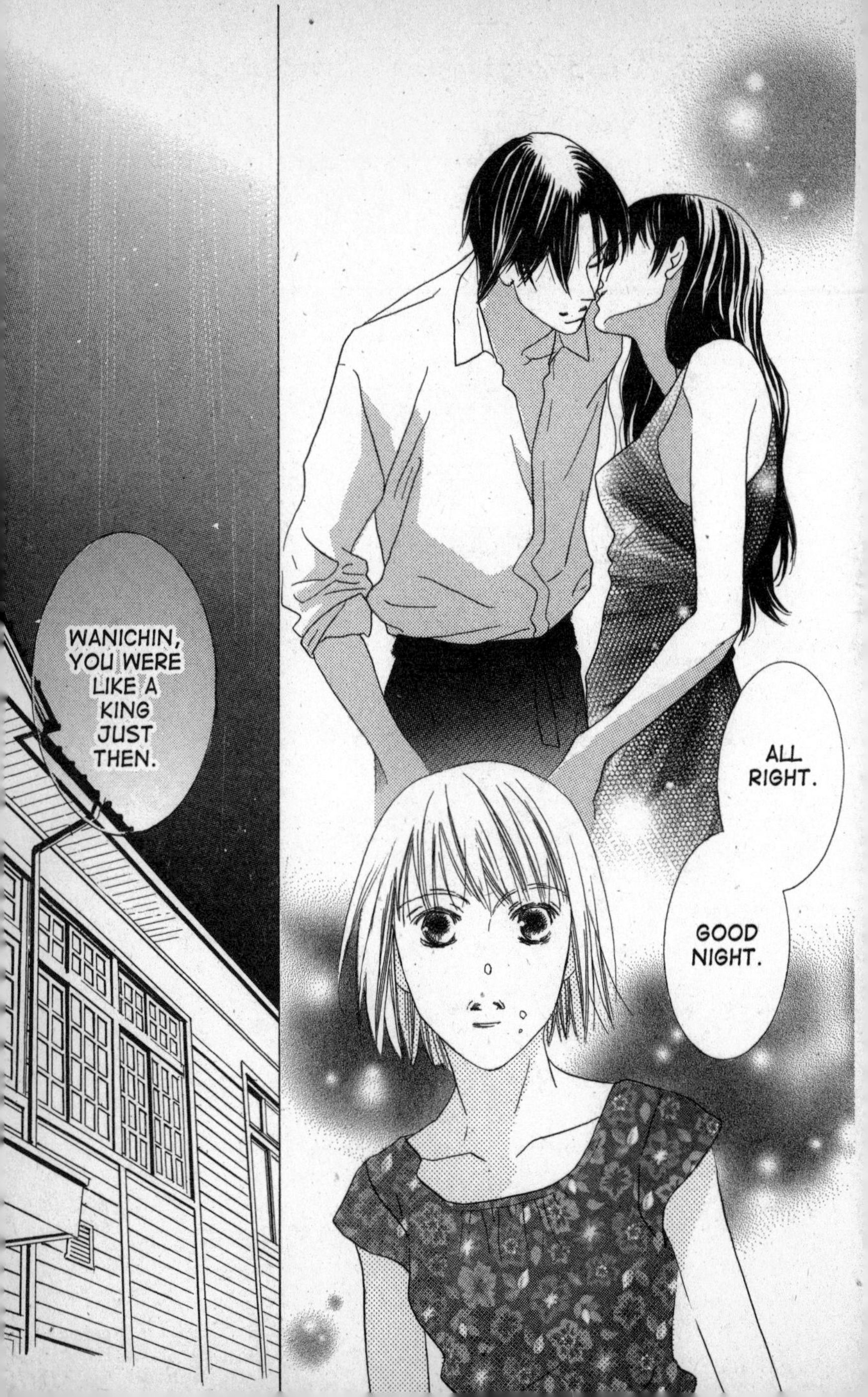
ALL RIGHT.
GOOD NIGHT.
WANICHIN, YOU WERE LIKE A KING JUST THEN.

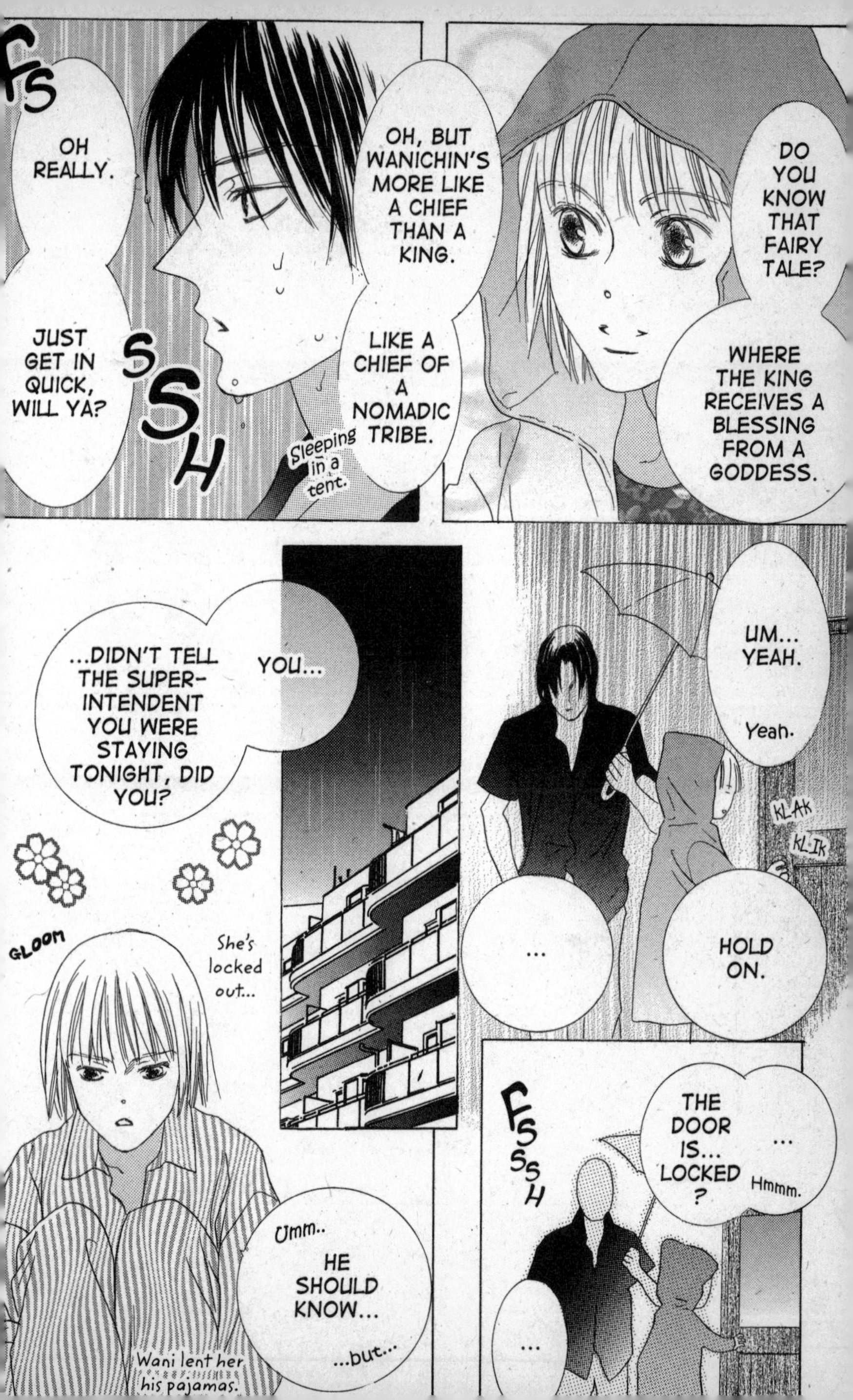
DO YOU KNOW THAT FAIRY TALE?
WHERE THE KING RECEIVES A BLESSING FROM A GODDESS.
OH, BUT WANICHIN'S MORE LIKE A CHIEF THAN A KING.
LIKE A CHIEF OF A NOMADIC TRIBE.
Sleeping in a tent.
FS
OH REALLY.
JUST GET IN QUICK, WILL YA?
SSH
UM... YEAH.
Yeah.
KLAK
KLIK
HOLD ON.
...
FSSH
THE DOOR IS... LOCKED?
...
Hmmm.
...
YOU...
...DIDN'T TELL THE SUPER-INTENDENT YOU WERE STAYING TONIGHT, DID YOU?
GLOOM
She's locked out...
Umm..
HE SHOULD KNOW...
...but...
Wani lent her his pajamas.

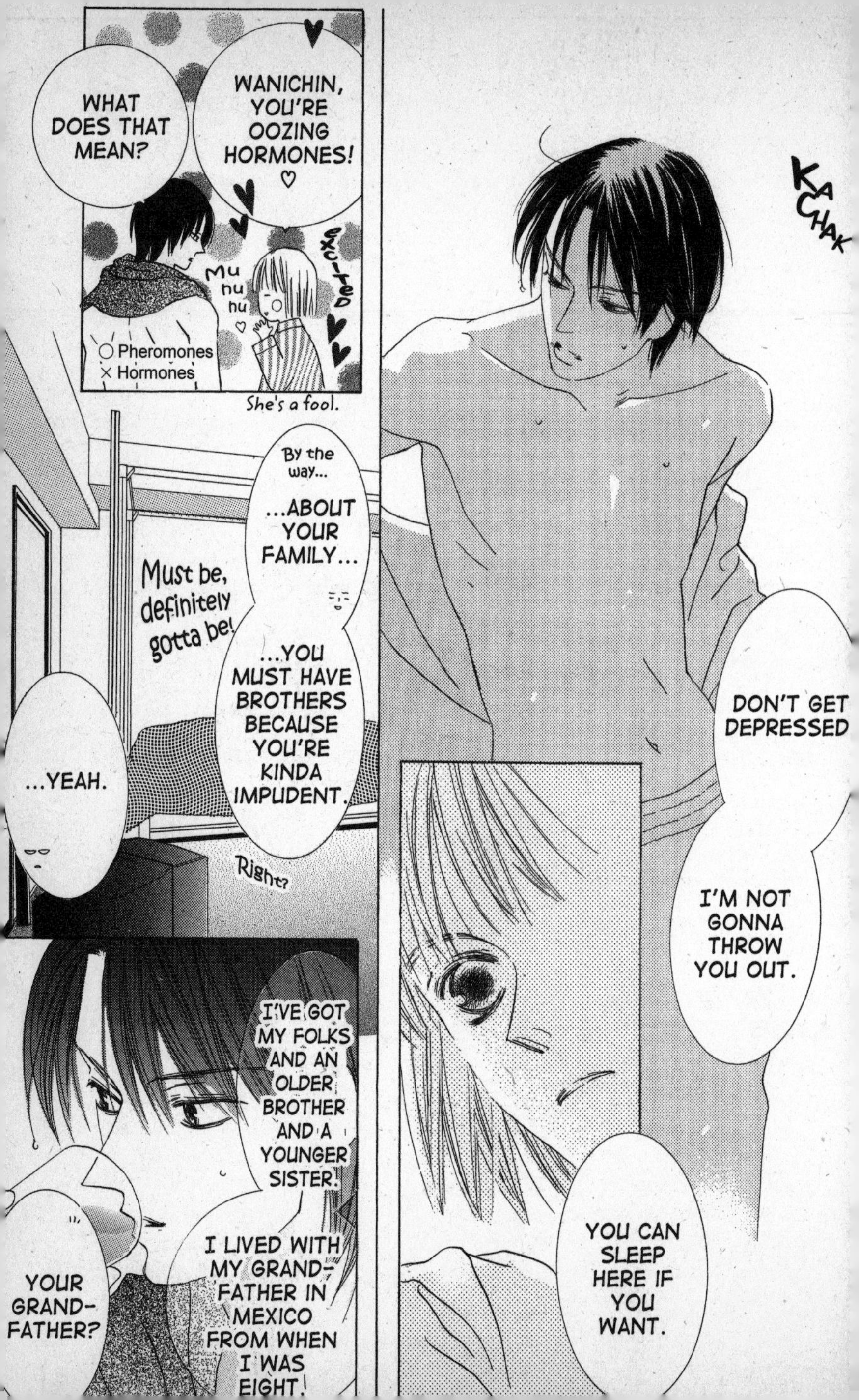
KACHAK
DON'T GET DEPRESSED
I'M NOT GONNA THROW YOU OUT.
YOU CAN SLEEP HERE IF YOU WANT.
WANICHIN, YOU'RE OOZING HORMONES! ♡
WHAT DOES THAT MEAN?
EXCITED
Mu hu hu ♡
○ Pheromones
× Hormones
She's a fool.
By the way...
...ABOUT YOUR FAMILY...
...YOU MUST HAVE BROTHERS BECAUSE YOU'RE KINDA IMPUDENT.
Must be, definitely gotta be!
Right?
...YEAH.
I'VE GOT MY FOLKS AND AN OLDER BROTHER AND A YOUNGER SISTER.
I LIVED WITH MY GRAND-FATHER IN MEXICO FROM WHEN I WAS EIGHT.
YOUR GRAND-FATHER?

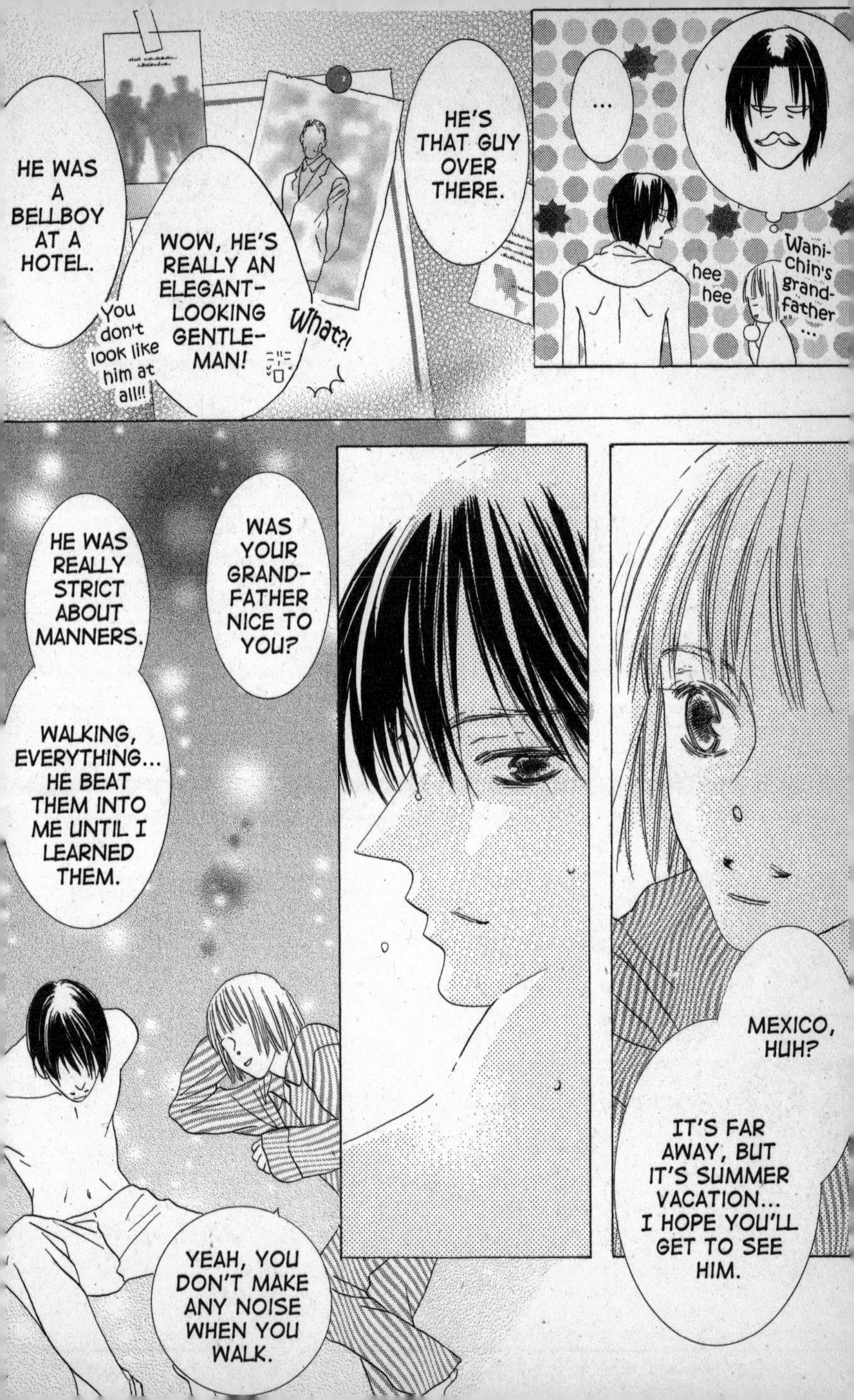
...
Wani-chin's grand-father ...
hee hee
HE'S THAT GUY OVER THERE.
WOW, HE'S REALLY AN ELEGANT-LOOKING GENTLE-MAN!
What?!
HE WAS A BELLBOY AT A HOTEL.
You don't look like him at all!!
MEXICO, HUH?
IT'S FAR AWAY, BUT IT'S SUMMER VACATION... I HOPE YOU'LL GET TO SEE HIM.
WAS YOUR GRAND-FATHER NICE TO YOU?
HE WAS REALLY STRICT ABOUT MANNERS.
WALKING, EVERYTHING... HE BEAT THEM INTO ME UNTIL I LEARNED THEM.
YEAH, YOU DON'T MAKE ANY NOISE WHEN YOU WALK.

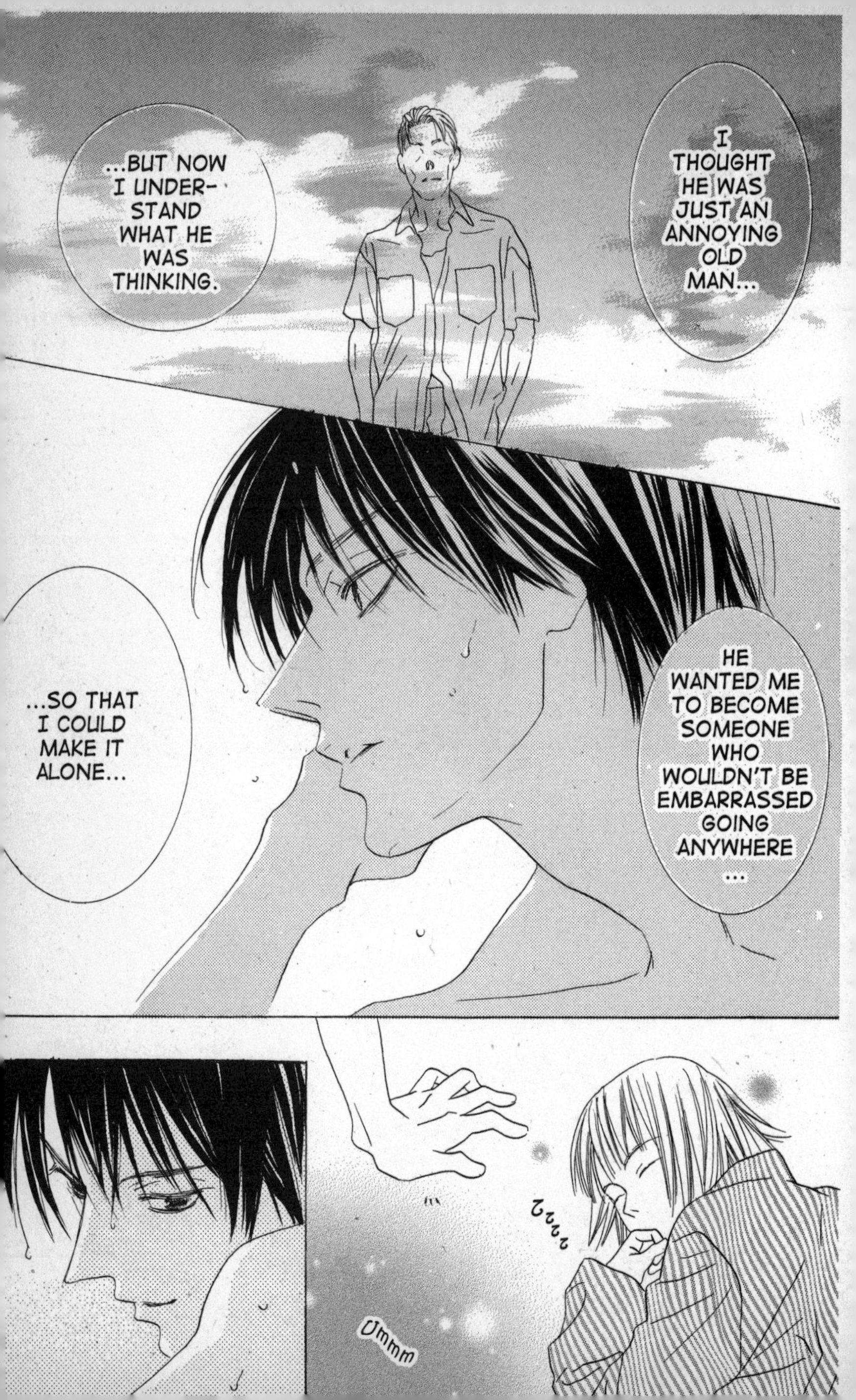
I THOUGHT HE WAS JUST AN ANNOYING OLD MAN...
...BUT NOW I UNDER-STAND WHAT HE WAS THINKING.
HE WANTED ME TO BECOME SOMEONE WHO WOULDN'T BE EMBARRASSED GOING ANYWHERE...
...SO THAT I COULD MAKE IT ALONE...
Ummm

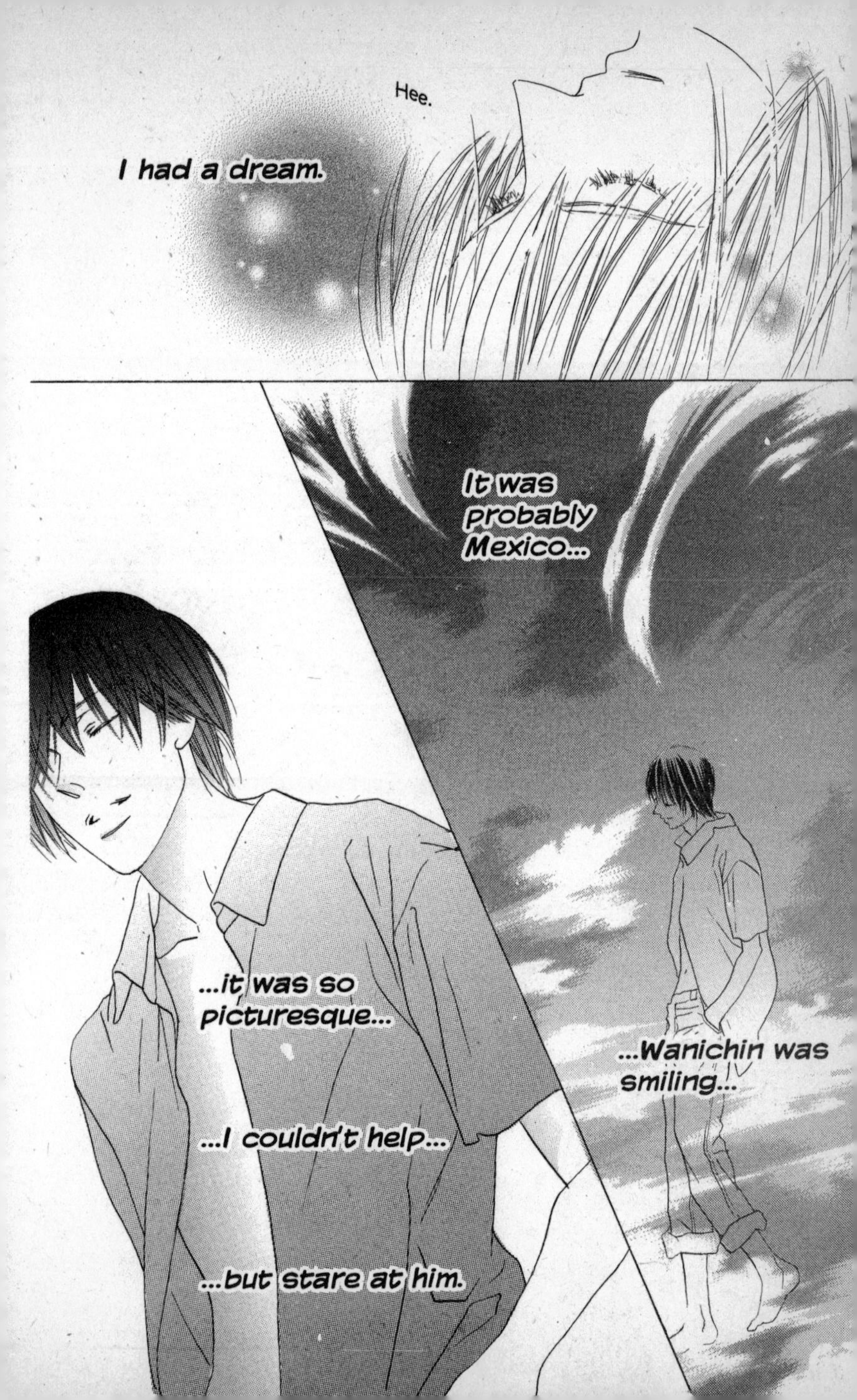
Hee.
I had a dream.
It was probably Mexico...
...Wanichin was smiling...
...it was so picturesque...
...I couldn't help...
...but stare at him.

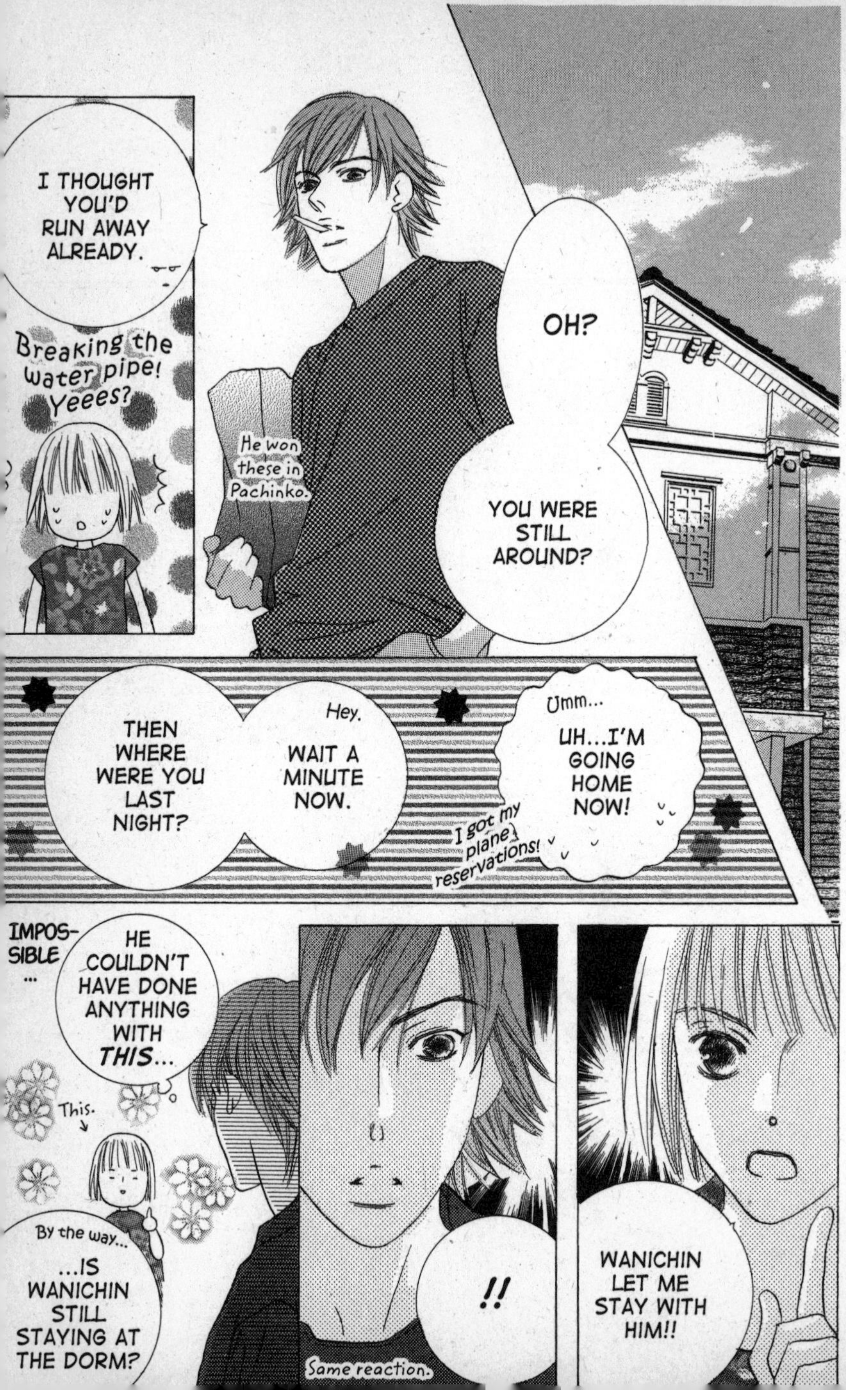
OH?
YOU WERE STILL AROUND?
I THOUGHT YOU'D RUN AWAY ALREADY.
Breaking the water pipe! Yeees?
He won these in Pachinko.
Umm...
UH...I'M GOING HOME NOW!
I got my plane reservations!
Hey.
WAIT A MINUTE NOW.
THEN WHERE WERE YOU LAST NIGHT?
WANICHIN LET ME STAY WITH HIM!!
!!
Same reaction.
IMPOSSIBLE...
HE COULDN'T HAVE DONE ANYTHING WITH THIS...
This.
By the way...
...IS WANICHIN STILL STAYING AT THE DORM?

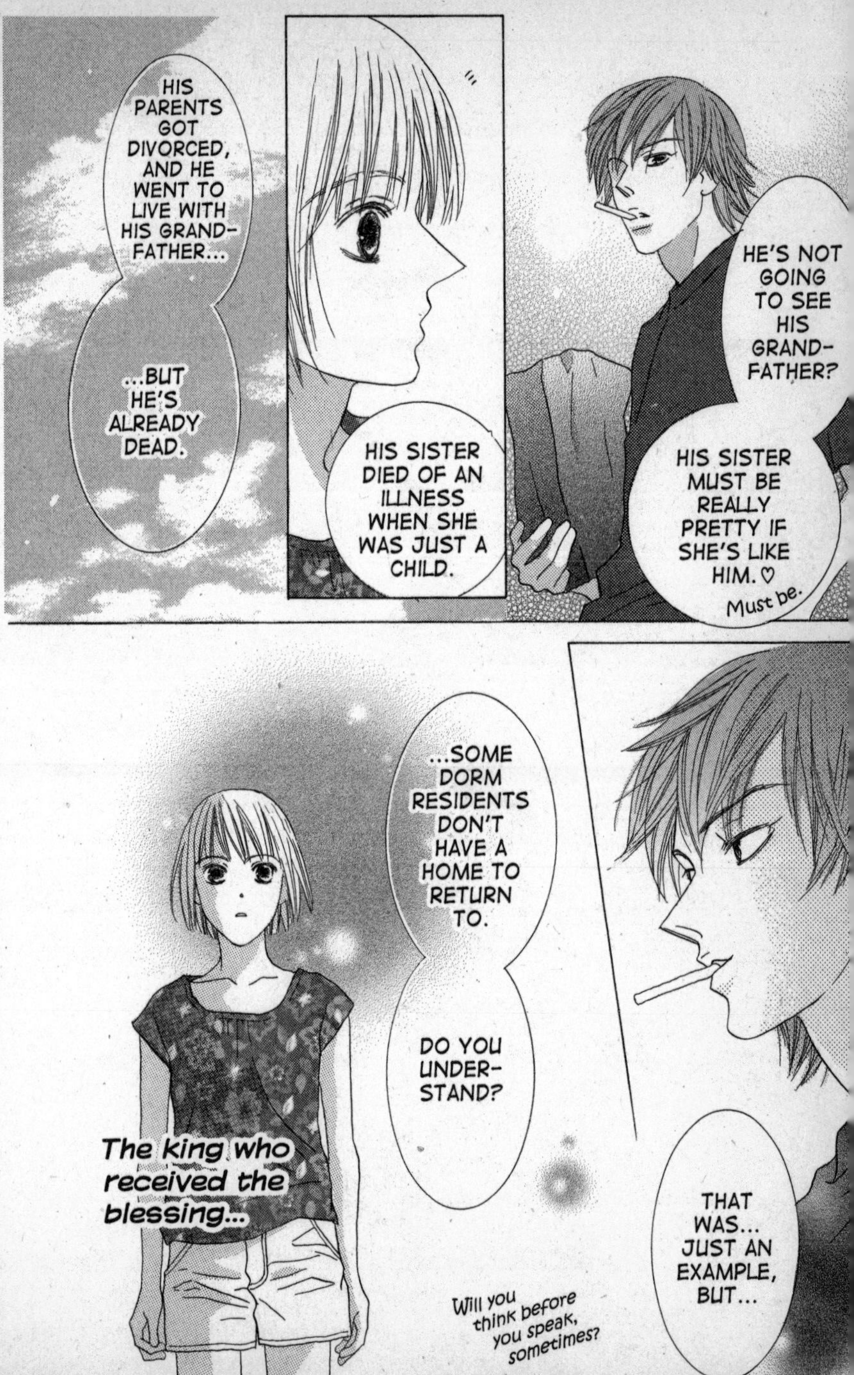
HE'S NOT GOING TO SEE HIS GRANDFATHER?
HIS SISTER MUST BE REALLY PRETTY IF SHE'S LIKE HIM. ♡
Must be.
HIS SISTER DIED OF AN ILLNESS WHEN SHE WAS JUST A CHILD.
HIS PARENTS GOT DIVORCED, AND HE WENT TO LIVE WITH HIS GRANDFATHER...
...BUT HE'S ALREADY DEAD.
THAT WAS... JUST AN EXAMPLE, BUT...
...SOME DORM RESIDENTS DON'T HAVE A HOME TO RETURN TO.
DO YOU UNDERSTAND?
Will you think before you speak, sometimes?
The king who received the blessing...

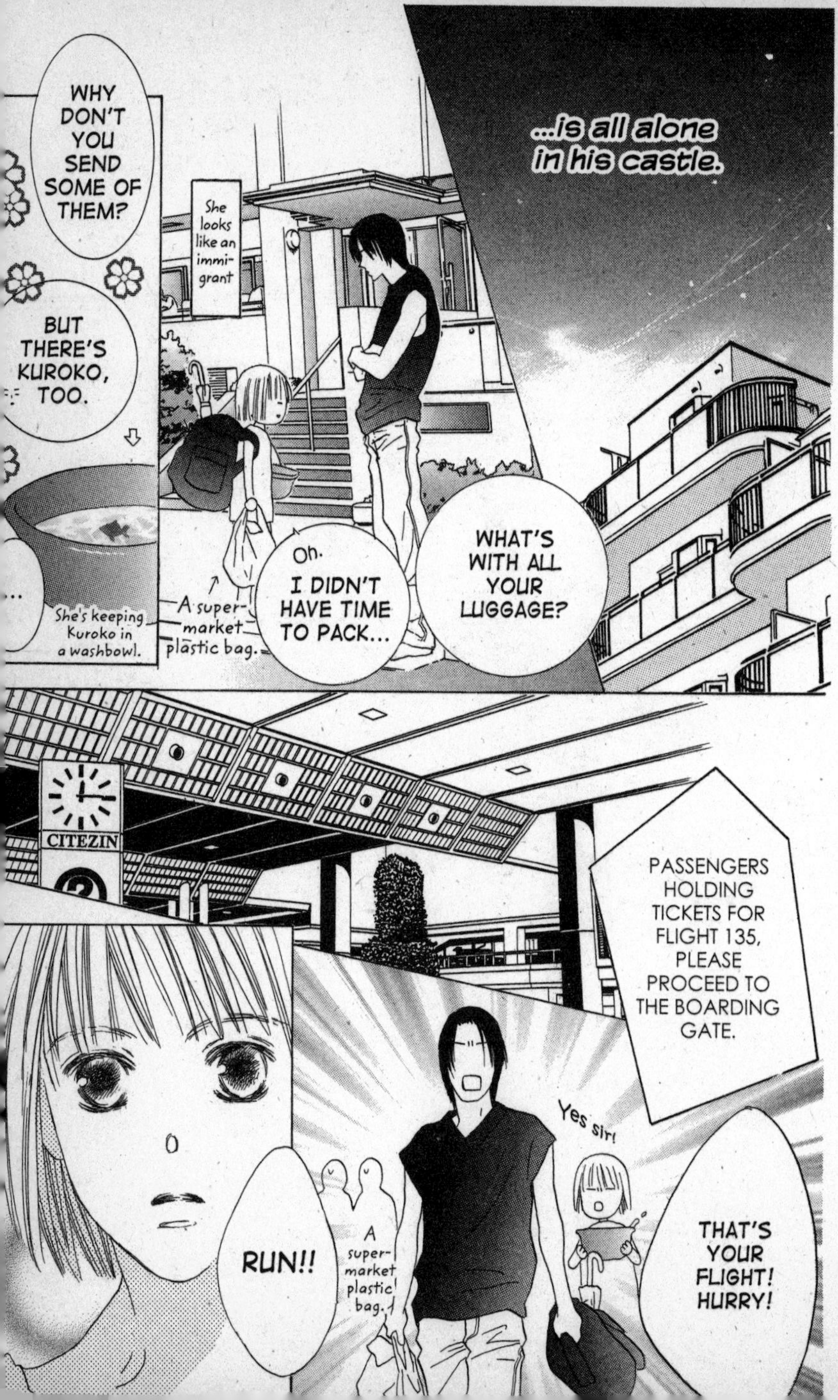
...is all alone in his castle.
WHAT'S WITH ALL YOUR LUGGAGE?
Oh.
I DIDN'T HAVE TIME TO PACK...
She looks like an immigrant
A supermarket plastic bag.
WHY DON'T YOU SEND SOME OF THEM?
BUT THERE'S KUROKO, TOO.
She's keeping Kuroko in a washbowl.
...
CITEZIN
PASSENGERS HOLDING TICKETS FOR FLIGHT 135, PLEASE PROCEED TO THE BOARDING GATE.
THAT'S YOUR FLIGHT! HURRY!
Yes sir!
RUN!!
A supermarket plastic bag.

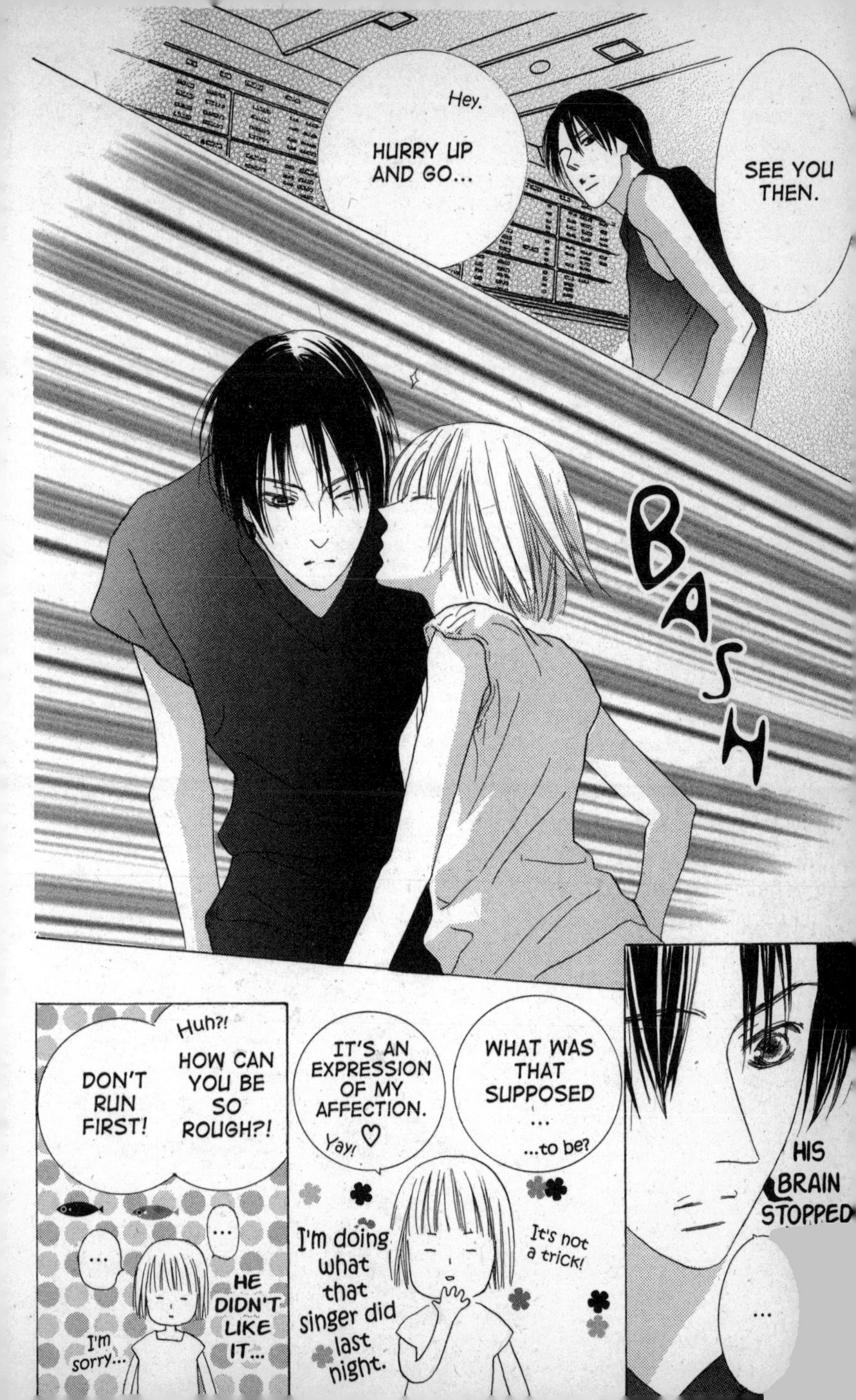
SEE YOU THEN.
Hey.
HURRY UP AND GO...
BASH
HIS BRAIN STOPPED
...
WHAT WAS THAT SUPPOSED ...
...to be?
IT'S AN EXPRESSION OF MY AFFECTION. ♡
Yay!
It's not a trick!
I'm doing what that singer did last night.
Huh?!
HOW CAN YOU BE SO ROUGH?!
DON'T RUN FIRST!
...
...
HE DIDN'T LIKE IT...
I'm sorry...

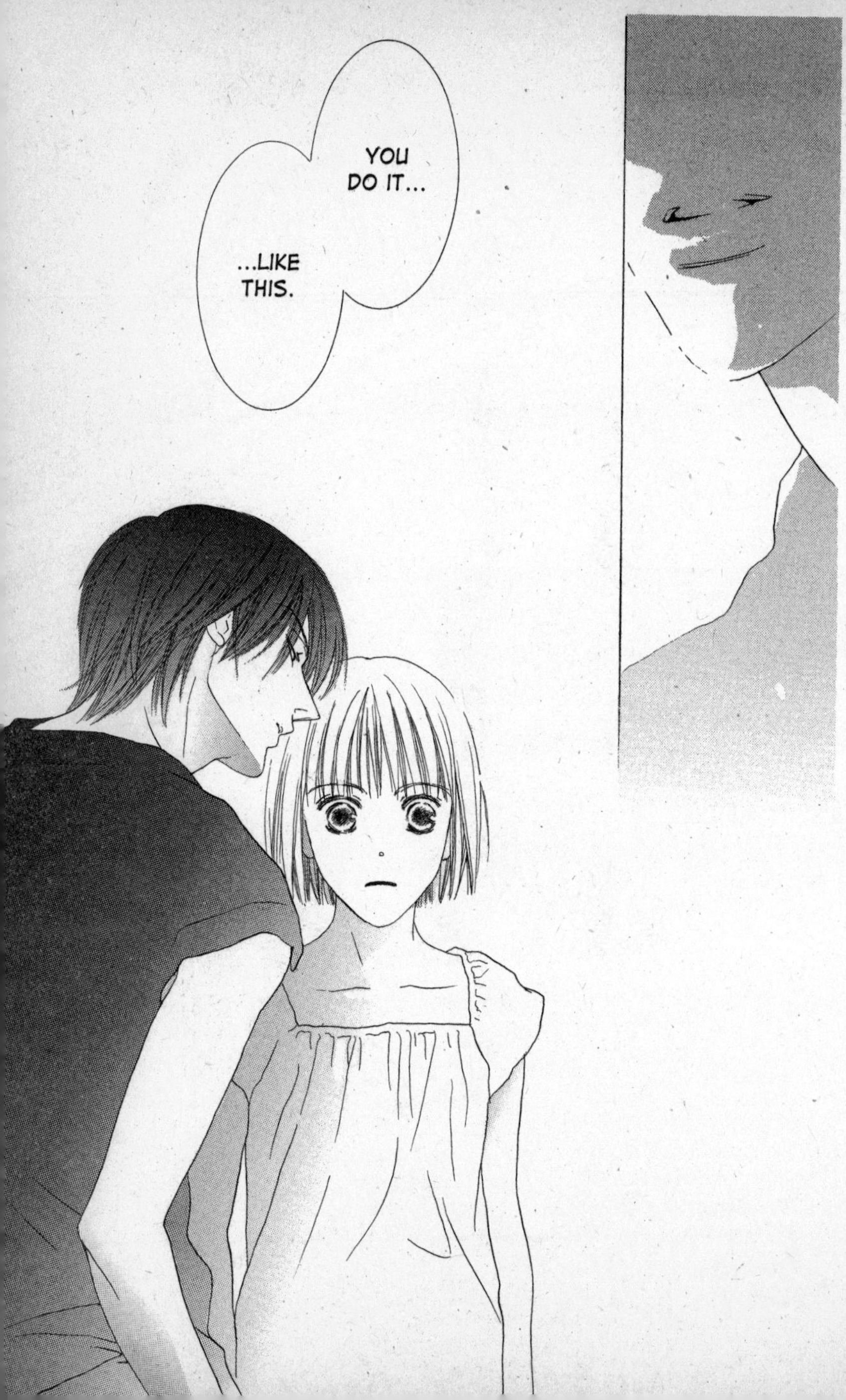
YOU DO IT...
...LIKE THIS.

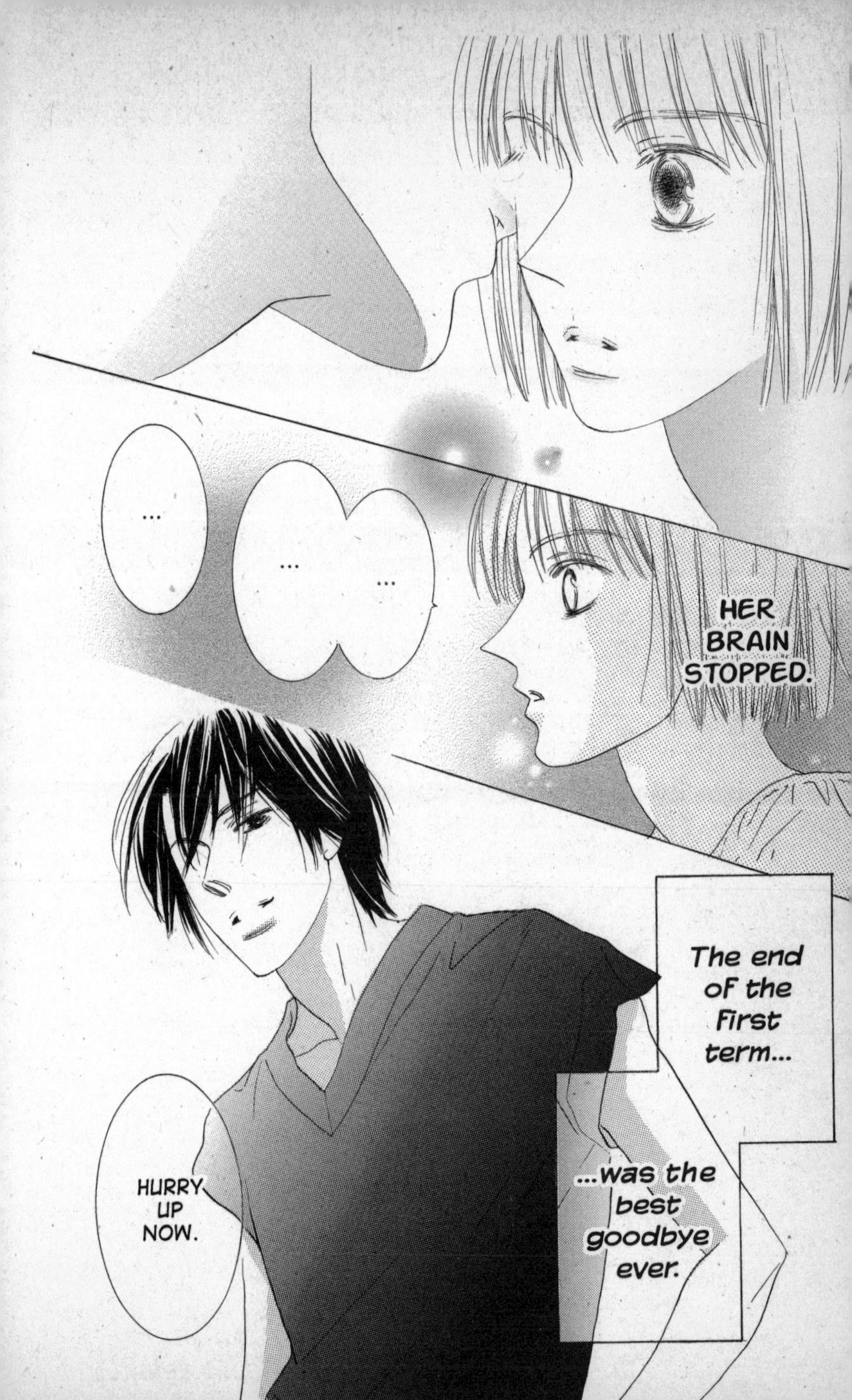
HER BRAIN STOPPED.
...
...
...
The end of the first term...
...was the best goodbye ever.
HURRY UP NOW.

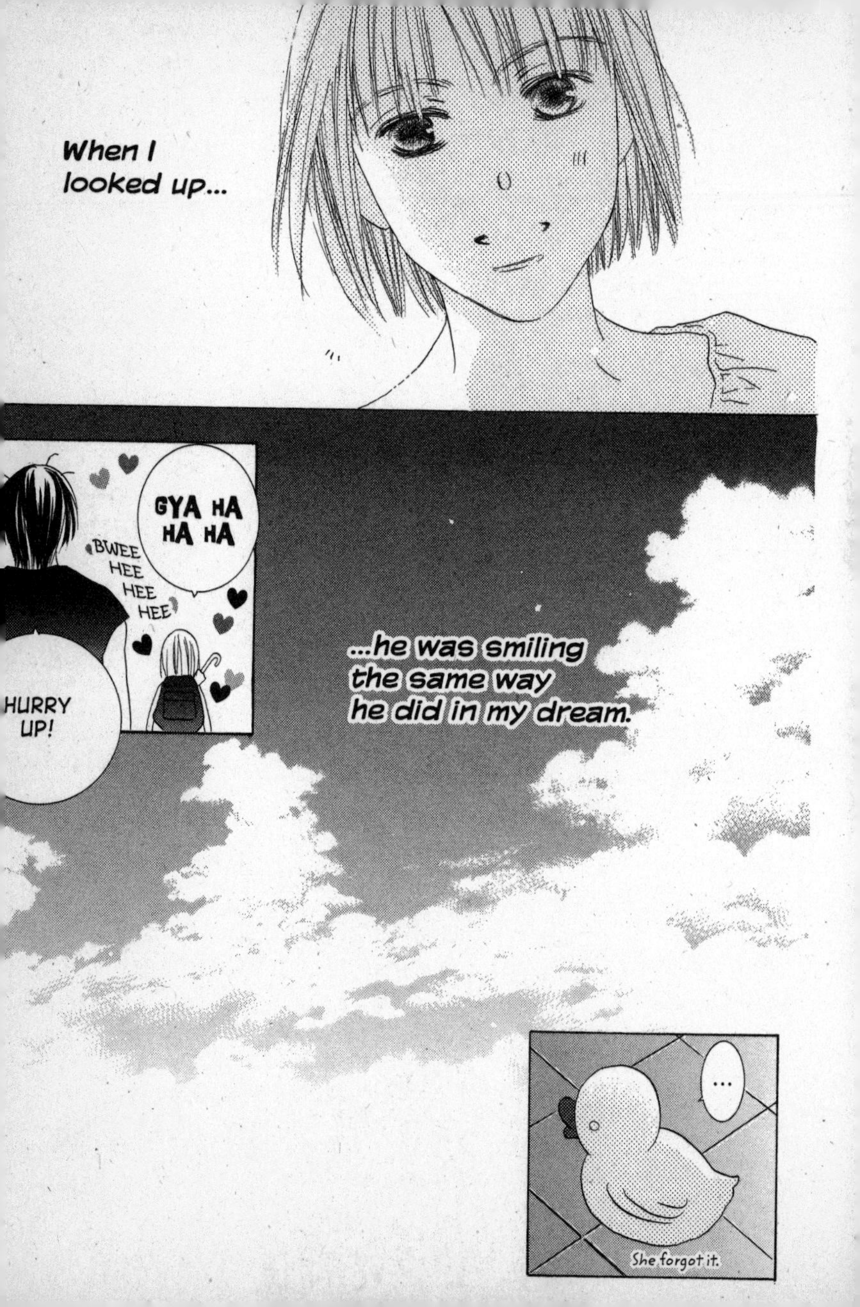
When I looked up...
...he was smiling the same way he did in my dream.
GYA HA HA HA
BWEE HEE HEE HEE
HURRY UP!
...
She forgot it.

BEAUTY
IS THE
BEAST

Dorm Information Pamphlet

Seikei Academy

↓"BEAUTY IS THE BEAST" COLOR AD FOR THE FIRST CHAPTER

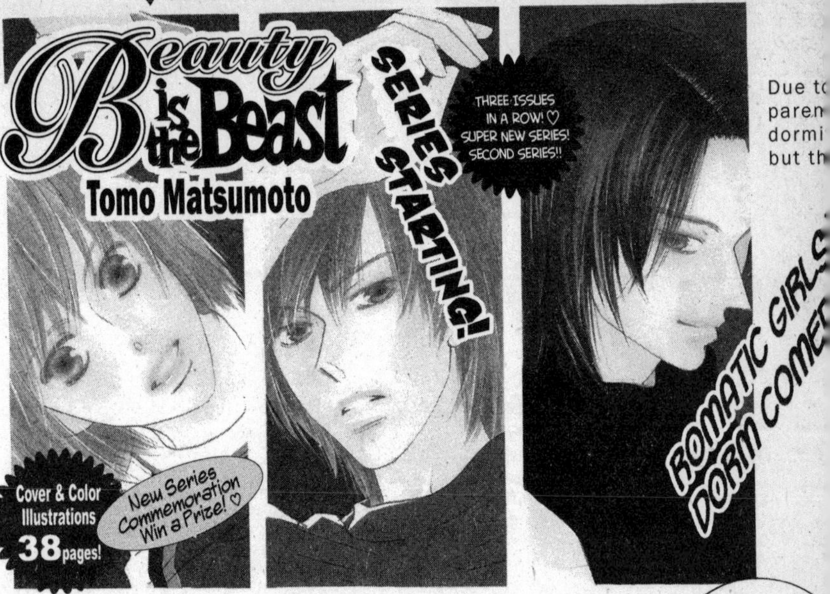
Beauty is the Beast
Tomo Matsumoto
SERIES STARTING!
THREE ISSUES IN A ROW! ♡ SUPER NEW SERIES! SECOND SERIES!!
Cover & Color Illustrations 38 pages!
New Series Commemoration Win a Prize! ♡

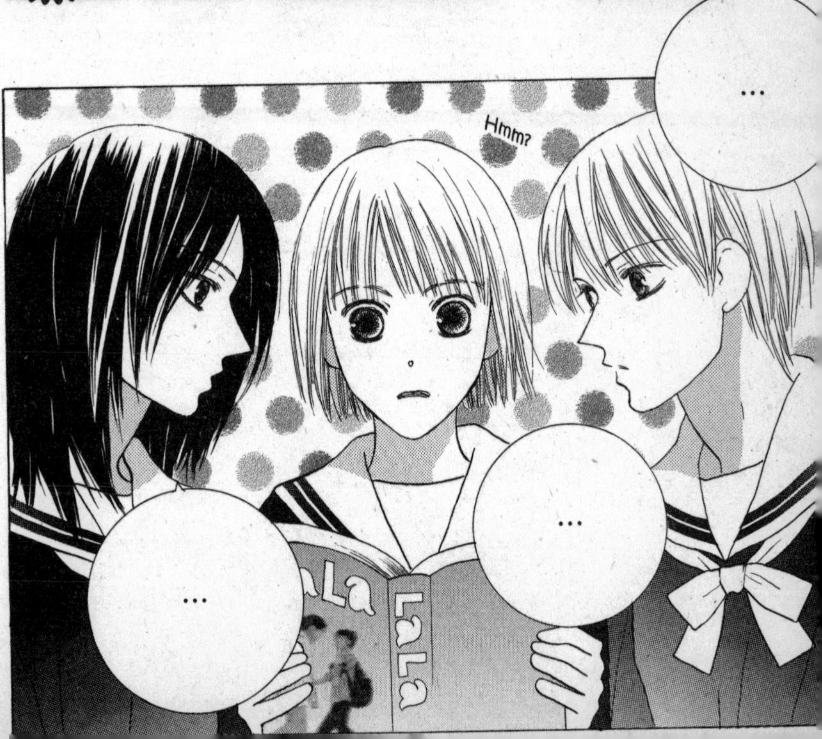
...
Hmm?
...
...
LaLa

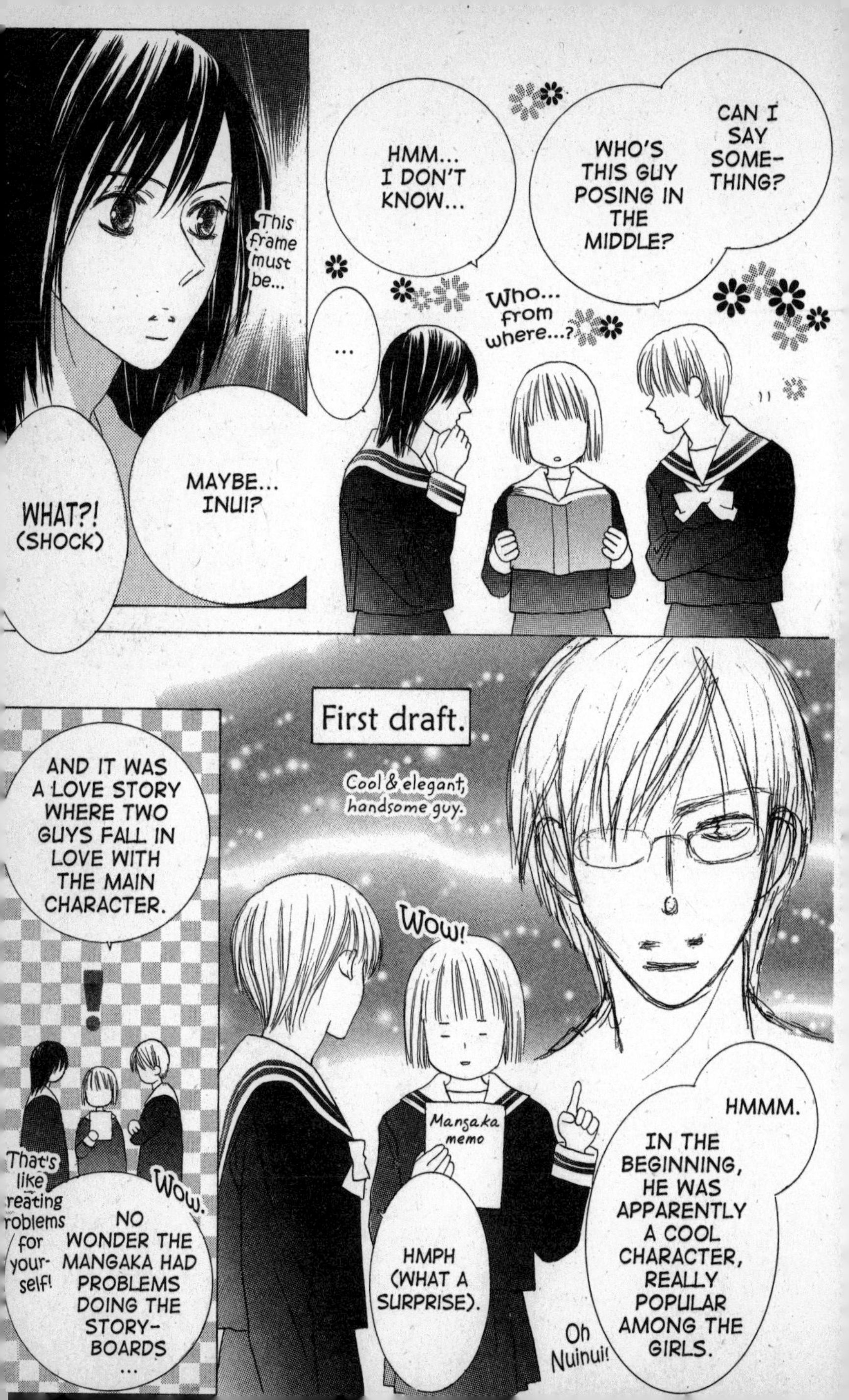
CAN I SAY SOME-THING?
WHO'S THIS GUY POSING IN THE MIDDLE?
HMM... I DON'T KNOW...
Who... from where...?
...
This frame must be...
MAYBE... INUI?
WHAT?! (SHOCK)
First draft.
Cool & elegant, handsome guy.
WOW!
HMMM.
IN THE BEGINNING, HE WAS APPARENTLY A COOL CHARACTER, REALLY POPULAR AMONG THE GIRLS.
Oh Nuinui!
Mangaka memo
HMPH (WHAT A SURPRISE).
AND IT WAS A LOVE STORY WHERE TWO GUYS FALL IN LOVE WITH THE MAIN CHARACTER.
!
Wow.
NO WONDER THE MANGAKA HAD PROBLEMS DOING THE STORY-BOARDS ...
That's like reating roblems for your-self!

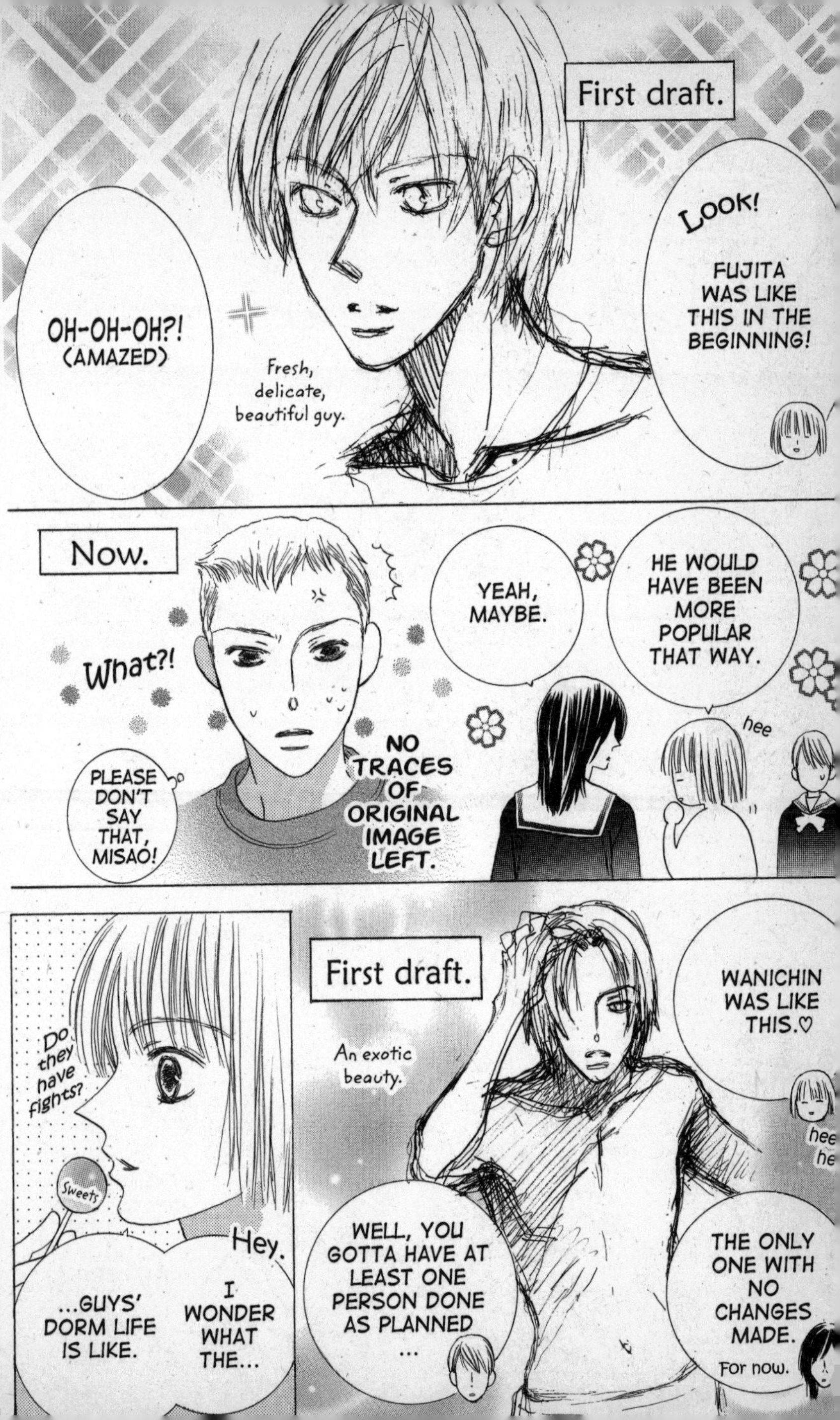
First draft.
LOOK! FUJITA WAS LIKE THIS IN THE BEGINNING!
Fresh, delicate, beautiful guy.
OH-OH-OH?! (AMAZED)
HE WOULD HAVE BEEN MORE POPULAR THAT WAY.
hee
YEAH, MAYBE.
Now.
What?!
NO TRACES OF ORIGINAL IMAGE LEFT.
PLEASE DON'T SAY THAT, MISAO!
WANICHIN WAS LIKE THIS.♡
hee he
First draft.
An exotic beauty.
THE ONLY ONE WITH NO CHANGES MADE.
For now.
WELL, YOU GOTTA HAVE AT LEAST ONE PERSON DONE AS PLANNED ...
Hey.
I WONDER WHAT THE...
...GUYS' DORM LIFE IS LIKE.
Do they have fights?
Sweets

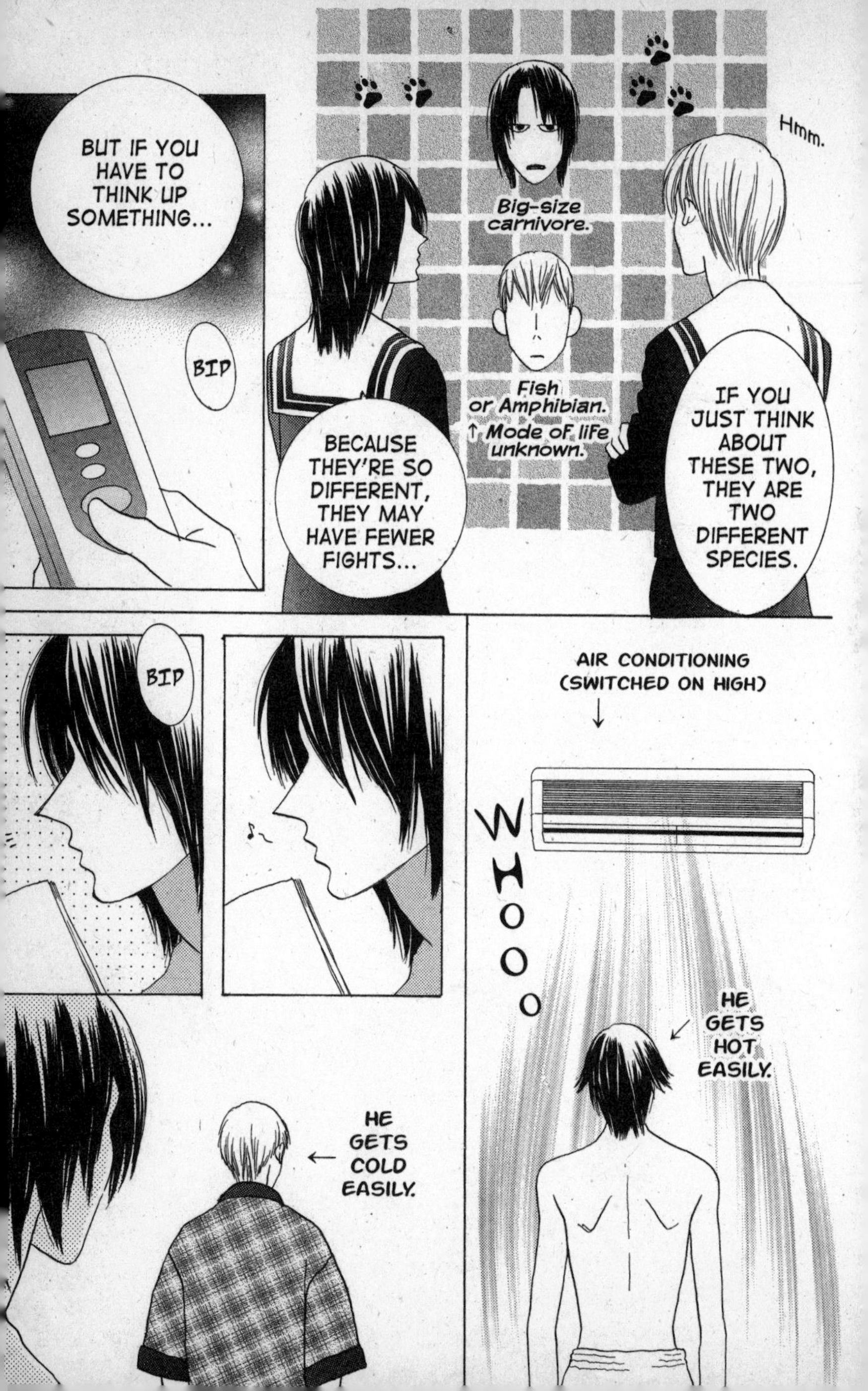
Hmm.
IF YOU JUST THINK ABOUT THESE TWO, THEY ARE TWO DIFFERENT SPECIES.
Big-size carnivore.
Fish or Amphibian.
↑ Mode of life unknown.
BECAUSE THEY'RE SO DIFFERENT, THEY MAY HAVE FEWER FIGHTS...
BUT IF YOU HAVE TO THINK UP SOMETHING...
BIP
AIR CONDITIONING (SWITCHED ON HIGH)
WHOOOO
HE GETS HOT EASILY.
BIP
HE GETS COLD EASILY.

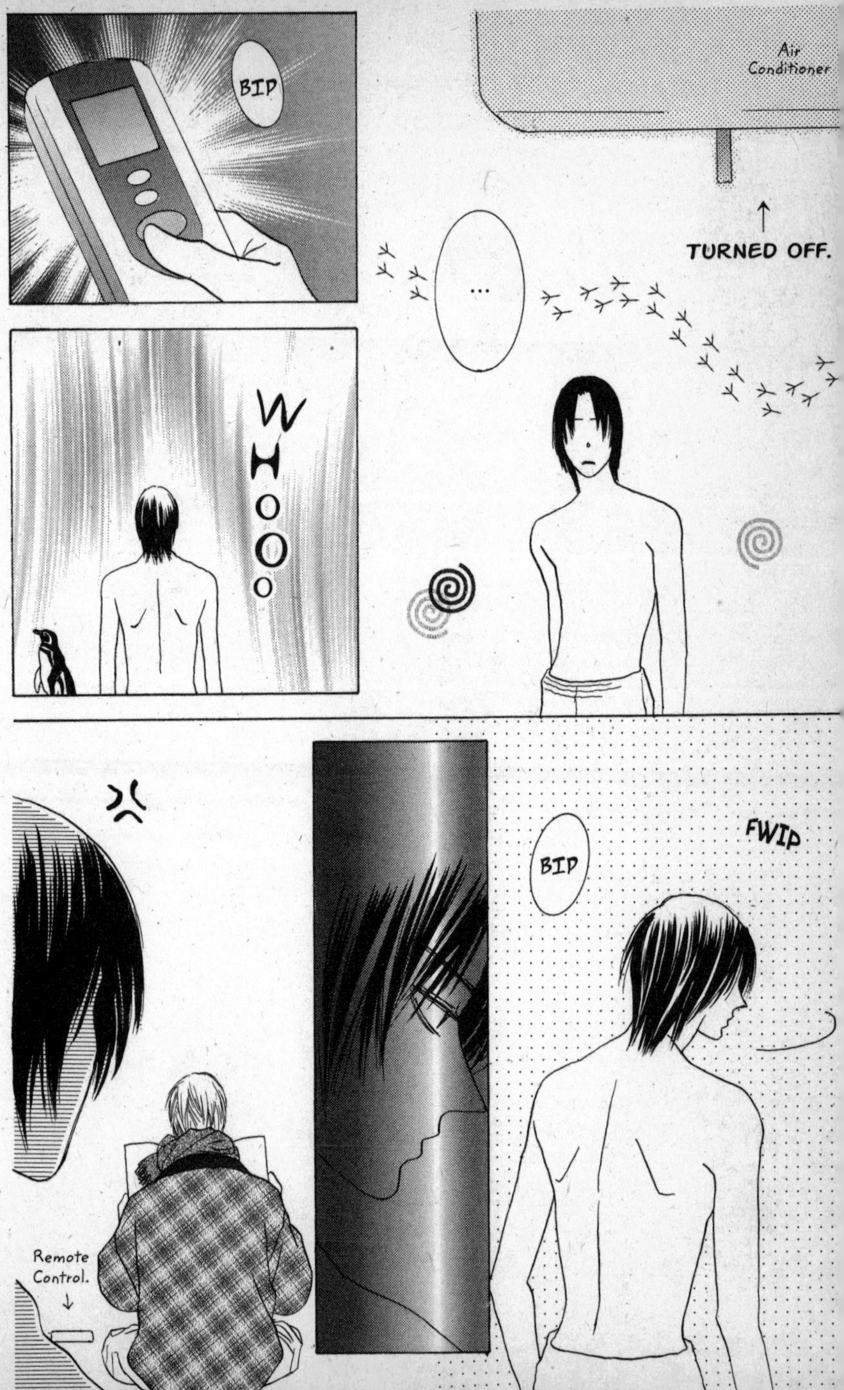
Air Conditioner
TURNED OFF.
...
BIP
WHOOOO
BIP
FWIP
Remote Control.

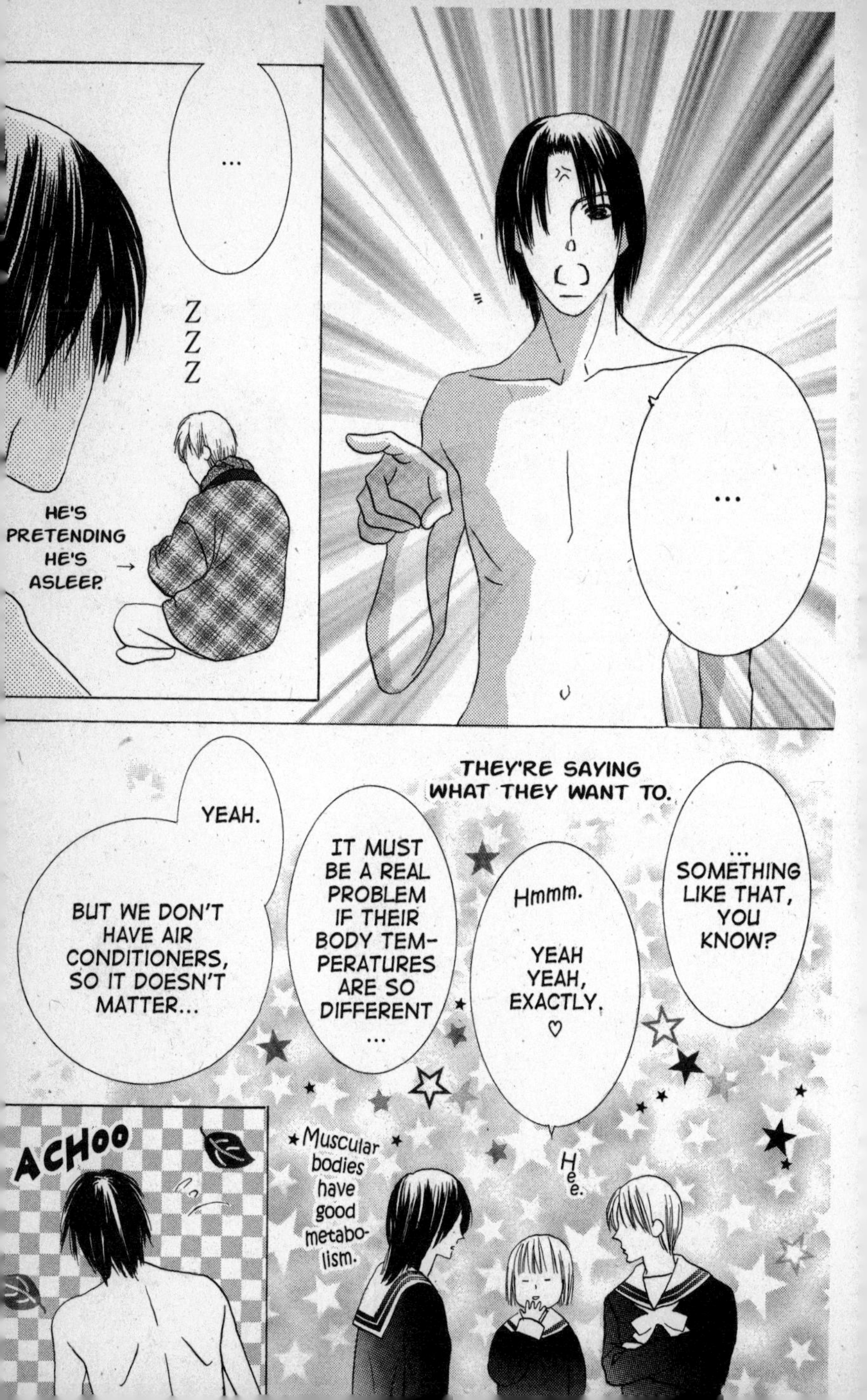
...
...
ZZZ
HE'S PRETENDING HE'S ASLEEP.
THEY'RE SAYING WHAT THEY WANT TO.
... SOMETHING LIKE THAT, YOU KNOW?
Hmmm.
YEAH YEAH, EXACTLY. ♡
IT MUST BE A REAL PROBLEM IF THEIR BODY TEMPERATURES ARE SO DIFFERENT ...
YEAH.
BUT WE DON'T HAVE AIR CONDITIONERS, SO IT DOESN'T MATTER...
Hee.
Muscular bodies have good metabolism.
ACHOO

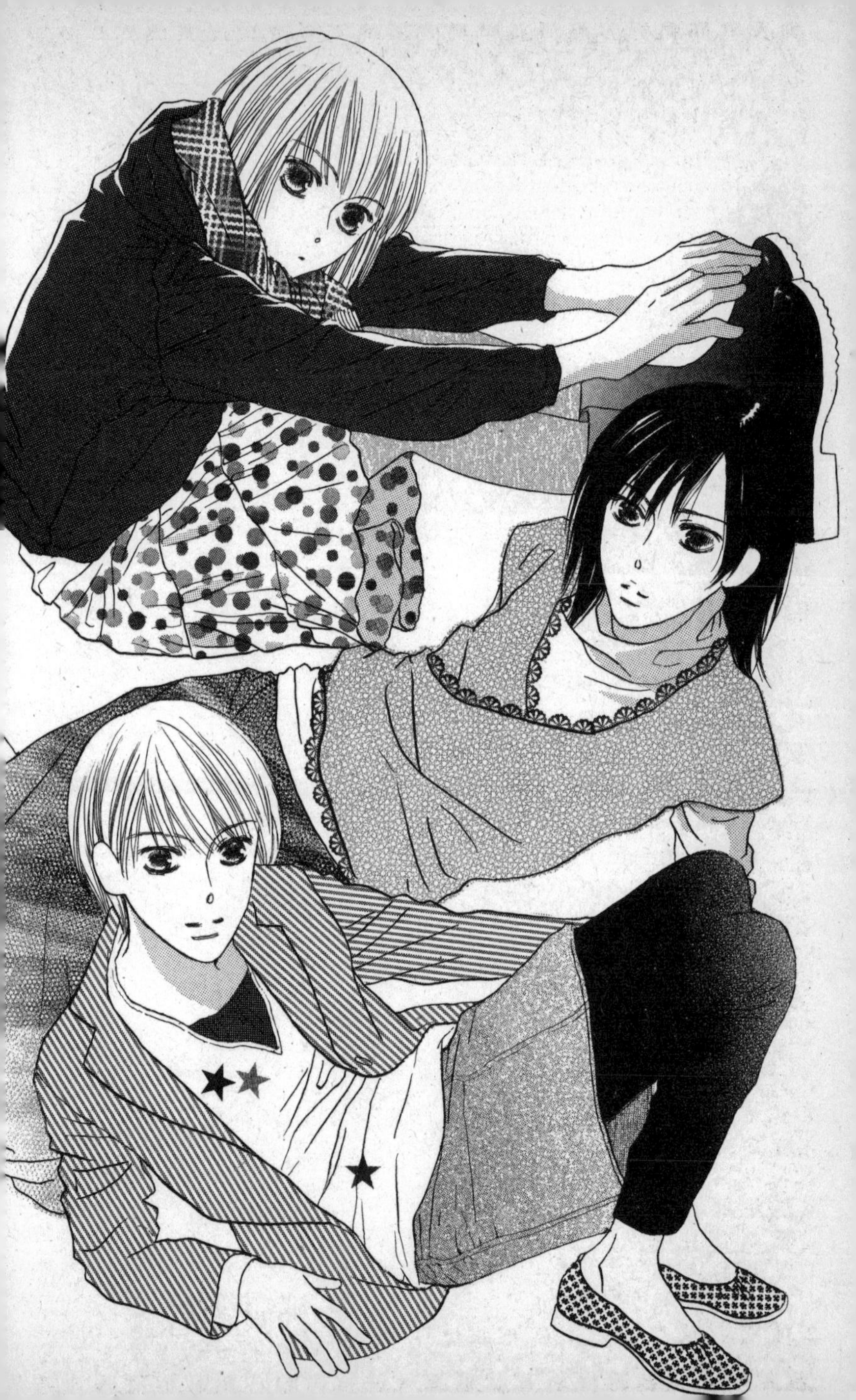

Fashions for Each Character

▶Eimi

Because everybody is weird, I wanted to have someone ordinary, who would neutralize them, but she's getting weirder as I draw..(noooo..!).
She is like an animal, and has this tough ability to live. (←If I have to put it nicely.)
Because her personality can change, she can wear any type of clothes. Cute clothes, and boyish clothes.
I think she'd look perfect in busy-looking, layered clothes, but since she appears often in the manga, it doesn't happen often.

▶Misao

Misao is this mysterious beauty, who you find hard to even approach and talk to.
(But if she's like this inside...)
She mainly wears a young adultish, or a romantic girlish look. This is not so much her preference, but rather, she wears what the sales-people at the stores she shops at recommend.
She's not that particular about her clothes.
Real beauties don't seem to give much thought about having been born beautiful. Since they are that way, they don't seem to be fixated on their beauty.

▶Suzu

She is an androgynous beauty, rather than being boyish. I went to an all-girls high school, and this type was really popular among the girls!
Inside, she's the most girlish of the three.
She mainly wears jeans and sporty clothes.
Although she probably prefers clothes with lots and lots of lace and tulle. (☺)

I talked about all this, but since the manga is mainly about dorm life, I don't have much of a chance to draw them wearing pretty clothes. So no matter what I do, it's not a fashionable manga.
(I am sorry.)

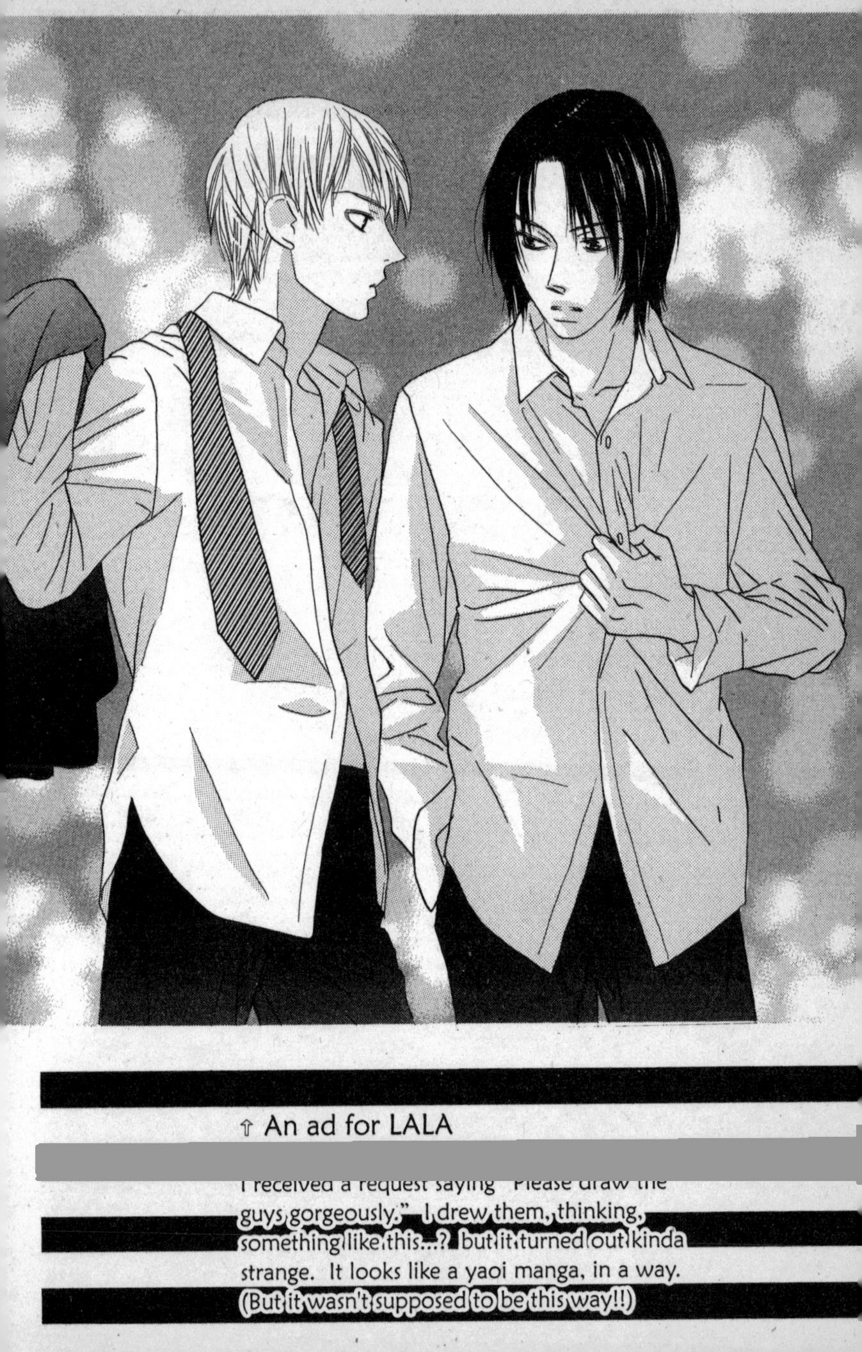

[redacted]

⇧ An ad for LALA

I received a request saying "Please draw the guys gorgeously." I drew them, thinking, something like this...? but it turned out kinda strange. It looks like a yaoi manga, in a way. (But it wasn't supposed to be this way!!)

▶ Wanichin

I wanted to make him a little rough, that's why I had him spend some years in Mexico.

Mexico City, the capital, is notorious for its high crime rate, but there are beautiful and quiet resorts, and the country has an atmosphere that I can't express in just a few words.

Initially, he was a cat-like character, preferring to act alone, but now he is turning into a beast that leads the pack.

Maybe he's the type you get to know better as you draw. (For me, it's very frustrating.)

When we were working one day, my assistant said with a serious face, "Wanichin is this handsome, and he's gonna end up with Eimi?" and I just burst out laughing (☺)

I wonder if he doesn't have much luck with women.

He wears his uniform in a casual, dressed-down fashion.

▶ Nuinui

If Eimi & Co. are weird, he is strange.

As I explained in the extra manga, he was a really cool character in the beginning, but it was difficult trying to figure him out, and I started feeling ill by just looking at his character descriptions, so I changed him.

He's an easy character to move about now, but I draw him, thinking "if there was a strange guy like this, I wouldn't want to have anything to do with him."

He wears his uniform properly. (He buttons up all his uniform buttons.)

But the guys don't appear much in the manga. It's hard to believe this is a co-ed school...

Dorm Entry Form

Thank you for reading this manga!
Nowadays, I receive letters from people who live in dorms, and it's fun reading them.
I'm not the type who can draw my manga easily, so I'm always getting a little down while drawing it daily, but a word in a reader's letter can make it all worthwhile.
Am I too simple a person? Hmmm.

I'd be happy if you'd let me know what you think of this manga. To my readers, to my editor, and to all my staff, thank you so much.

Hope to see you again!

Student Name: *Tomo Matsumoto* (Seal)

Tomo Matsumoto was born on January 8th in Osaka and made the switch from nurse to mangaka with her debut story *Nemuru Hime* (Sleeping Princess) in *Lunatic LaLa* magazine in 1995. Her other works include *Kiss*, a series about piano lessons and love, *23:00*, a book about street dancing, and *Eikaiwa School Wars* (English School Wars), which is currently serialized in *Monthly LaLa* magazine. Ms. Matsumoto loves dancing and taking English lessons.

Beauty Is the Beast
Vol. 1
The Shojo Beat Manga Edition

STORY & ART BY
TOMO MATSUMOTO

English Translation & Adaptation/Tomo Kimura
Touch-Up & Lettering/Inori Fukuda Trant
Graphics & Cover Design/Yukiko Whitley
Editor/Pancha Diaz

Managing Editor/Megan Bates
Director of Production/Noboru Watanabe
Vice President of Publishing/Alvin Lu
Vice President & Editor in Chief/ Yumi Hoashi
Sr. Director of Acquisitions/Rika Inouye
Vice President of Sales & Marketing/Liza Coppola
Publisher/Hyoe Narita

Printed in Canada

Published by VIZ Media, LLC
P.O. Box 77010
San Francisco, CA 94107

Shojo Beat Manga Edition
10 9 8 7 6 5 4 3 2 1
First printing, October 2005

PARENTAL ADVISORY
BEAUTY IS THE BEAST is rated T for Teen and is recommended for ages 13 and up. It contains mature situations.

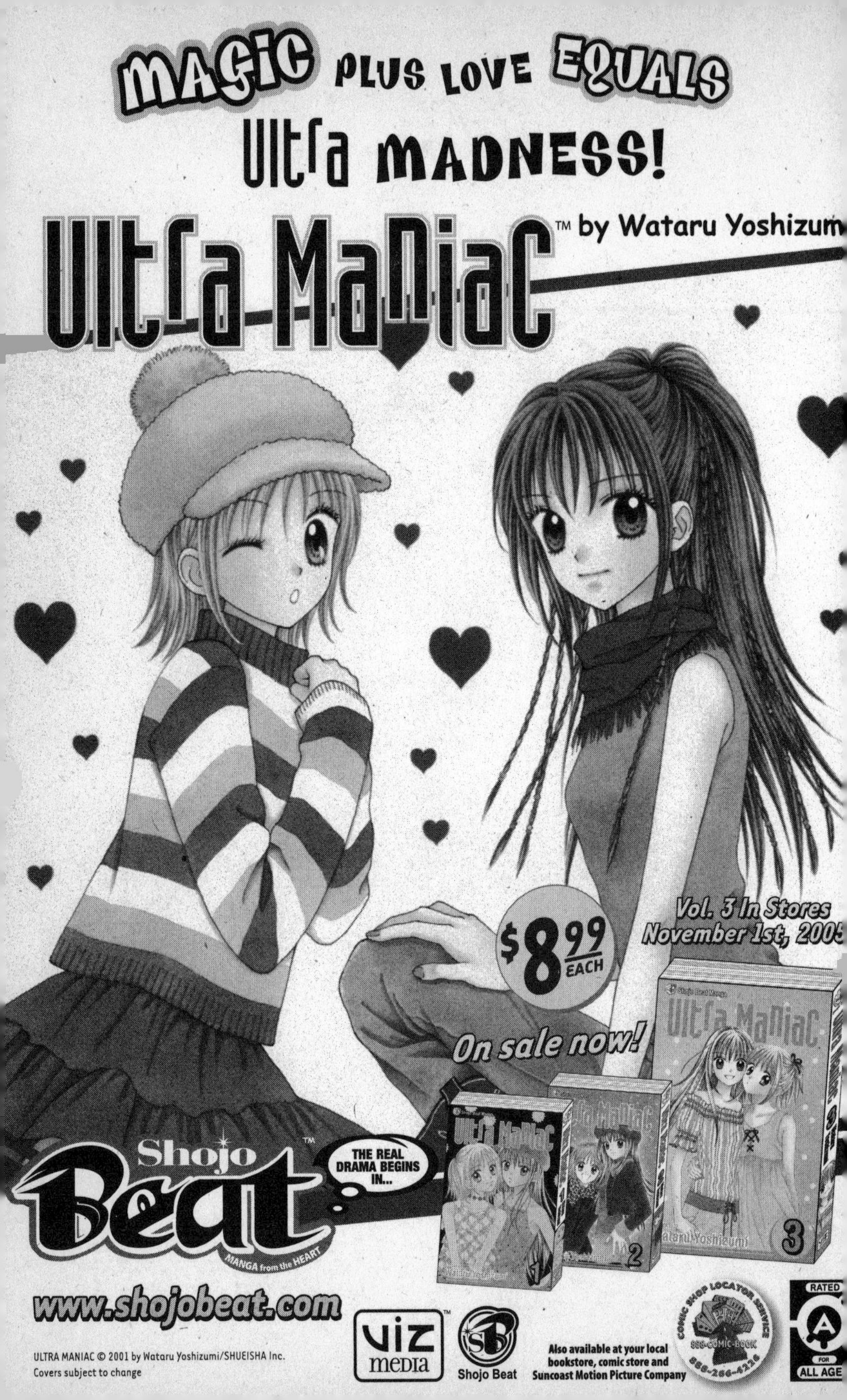
MAGIC PLUS LOVE EQUALS
ULTRA MADNESS!
ULTRA MANIAC™ by Wataru Yoshizumi
$8.99 EACH
Vol. 3 In Stores November 1st, 2005
On sale now!
Shojo Beat™
THE REAL DRAMA BEGINS IN...
MANGA from the HEART
www.shojobeat.com
viz media
Shojo Beat
Also available at your local bookstore, comic store and Suncoast Motion Picture Company
COMIC SHOP LOCATOR SERVICE
888-COMIC-BOOK
888-266-4226
RATED A FOR ALL AGES
ULTRA MANIAC © 2001 by Wataru Yoshizumi/SHUEISHA Inc.
Covers subject to change

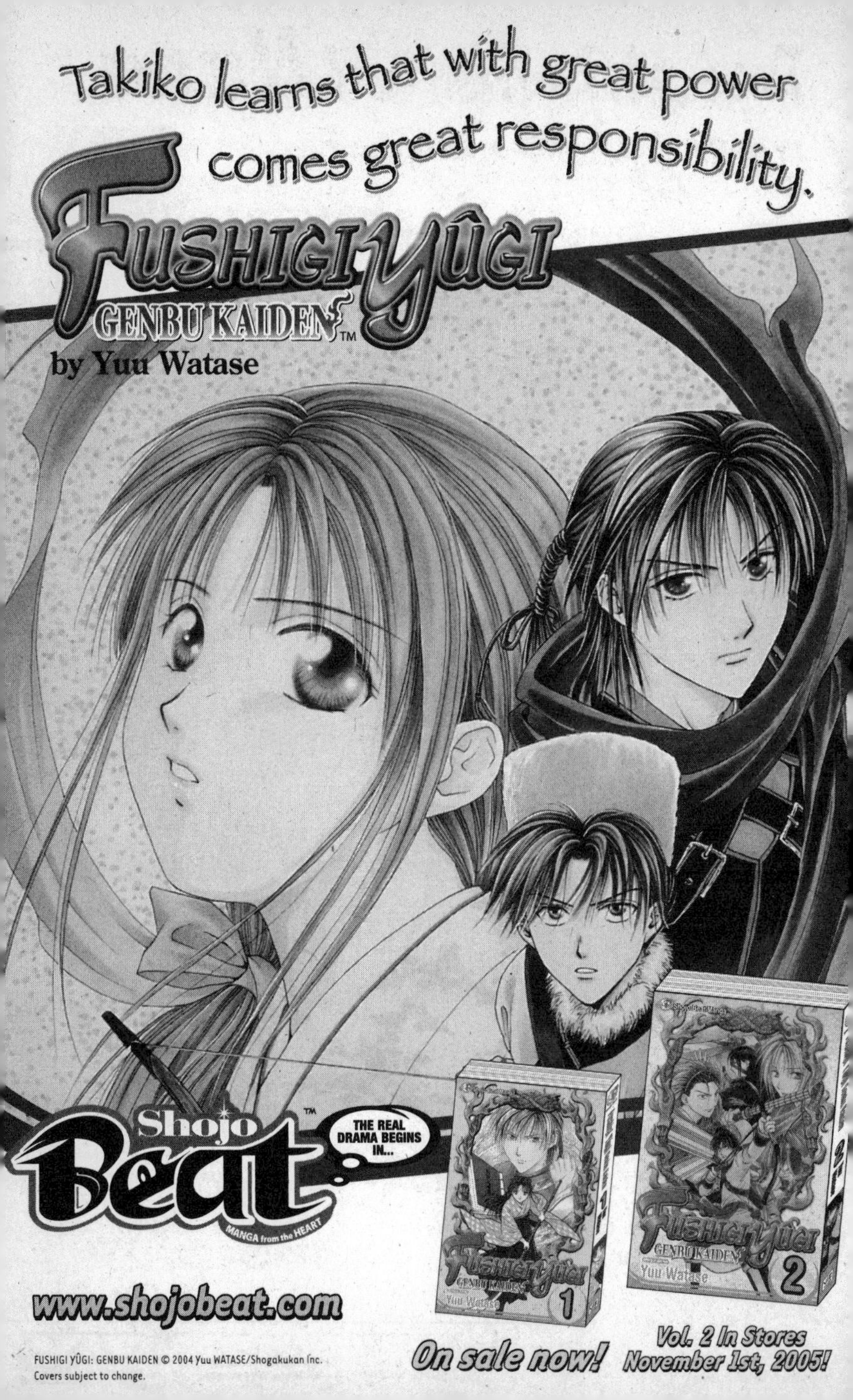
Takiko learns that with great power
comes great responsibility.
FUSHIGI YÛGI
GENBU KAIDEN™
by Yuu Watase
Shojo Beat™
MANGA from the HEART
THE REAL DRAMA BEGINS IN...
www.shojobeat.com
FUSHIGI YÛGI
GENBU KAIDEN
Yuu Watase
1
FUSHIGI YÛGI
GENBU KAIDEN
Yuu Watase
2
On sale now!
Vol. 2 In Stores November 1st, 2005!
FUSHIGI YÛGI: GENBU KAIDEN © 2004 Yuu WATASE/Shogakukan Inc.
Covers subject to change.

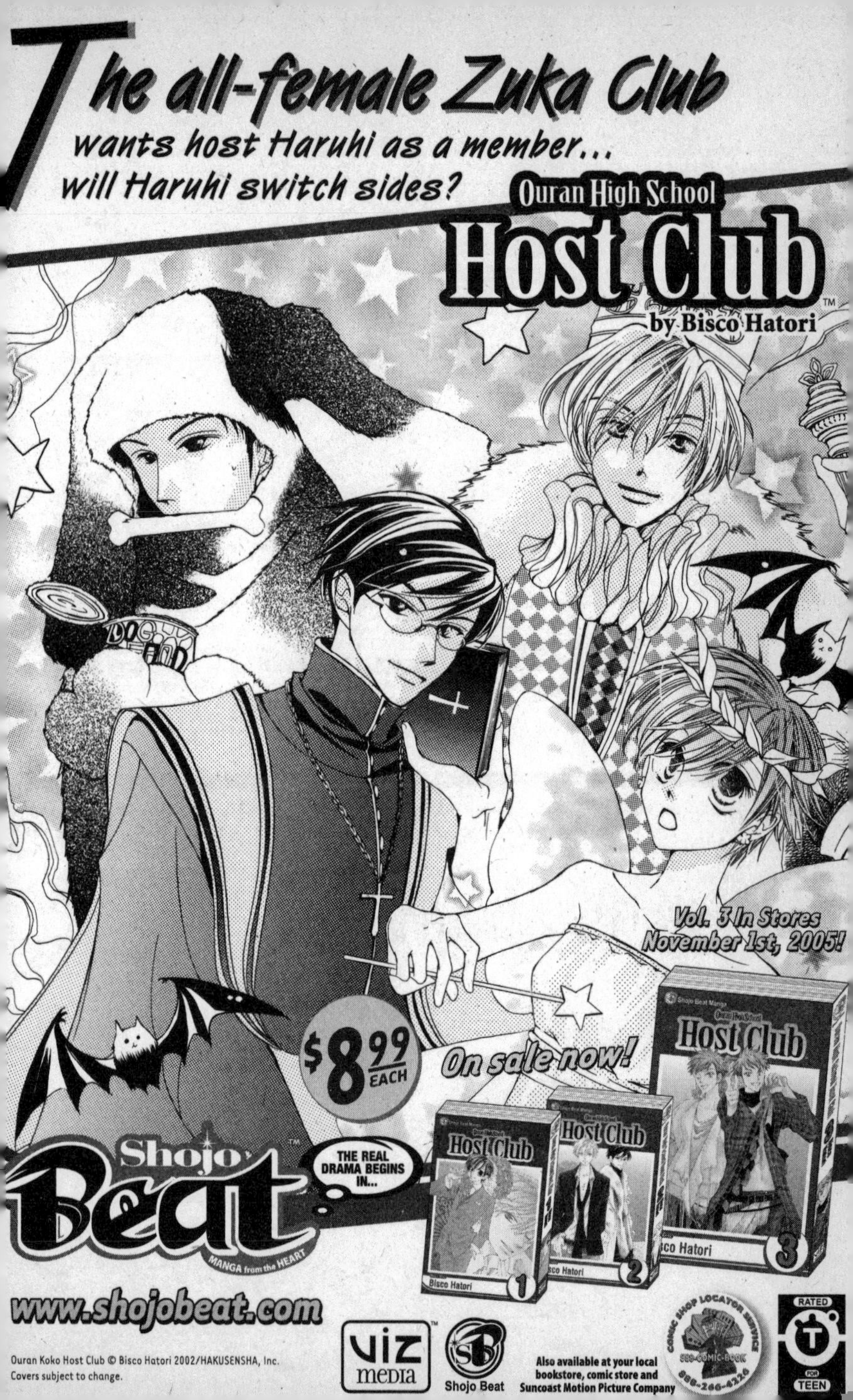

The all-female Zuka Club
wants host Haruhi as a member...
will Haruhi switch sides?
Ouran High School
Host Club
by Bisco Hatori
Vol. 3 In Stores
November 1st, 2005!
$8.99 EACH
On sale now!
Shojo Beat
MANGA from the HEART
THE REAL DRAMA BEGINS IN...
www.shojobeat.com
Ouran Koko Host Club © Bisco Hatori 2002/HAKUSENSHA, Inc.
Covers subject to change.
viz media
Shojo Beat
Also available at your local bookstore, comic store and Suncoast Motion Picture Company
COMIC SHOP LOCATOR SERVICE
888-266-4226
RATED T FOR TEEN